PETERSON'S
#1 IN COLLEGE PREP

TOEFL*
PRACTICE
TESTS

BRUCE ROGERS

Peterson's
Princeton, New Jersey

About Peterson's

Peterson's is the country's largest educational information/communications company, providing the academic, consumer, and professional communities with books, software, and online services in support of lifelong education access and career choice. Well-known references include Peterson's annual guides to private schools, summer programs, colleges and universities, graduate and professional programs, financial aid, international study, adult learning, and career guidance. Peterson's Web site at petersons.com is the only comprehensive—and most heavily traveled—education resource on the Internet. The site carries all of Peterson's fully searchable major databases and includes financial aid sources, test-prep help, job postings, direct inquiry and application features, and specially created Virtual Campuses for every accredited academic institution and summer program in the U.S. and Canada that offers in-depth narratives, announcements, and multimedia features.

Visit Peterson's Education Center on the Internet (World Wide Web) at
www.petersons.com

TOEFL Practice Tests is adapted from *Heinle & Heinle's Complete Guide to TOEFL Test: Practice Tests*, second edition, by Bruce Rogers and published by Heinle & Heinle/ITP.

Library of Congress Cataloging-in-Publication Data

Rogers, Bruce, 1949–
    TOEFL practice tests / Bruce Rogers.
      p.   cm.
    ISBN 0-7689-0015-8 (text and audiocassettes) — ISBN 0-7689-0016-6 (text only).
    1. Test of English as a Foreign language—Study guides. 2. English language—
Textbooks for foreign speakers. 3. English language—Examinations—Study guides.
I. Title.
PE1128.R63447   1997
428′.0076—dc21
                                                                       97-31229
                                                                         CIP

Printed in the United States of America

10 9 8 7 6 5 4 3 2 1

CONTENTS

ACKNOWLEDGMENTS

I would like to thank the following people for reading and commenting on the manuscript for this text during the development process: Gail Stewart, University of Toronto; Ramon Valenzuela, Boston University; Aise Stromsdorfer, St. Louis University; Sydney Kinneman, University of Oregon; Barbara Sihombing, Economics Institute, Boulder, Colorado; and Jim Price, International English Centre, Bangkok.

PREFACE

If you are planning to take TOEFL (*Test of English as a Foreign Language*), you are not alone. Over three quarters of a million people signed up to take the test last year, and the number keeps growing. For almost all nonnative speakers of English who plan to study in either undergraduate or graduate programs at universities or colleges in North America, an acceptable score on the exam is a necessity. Moveover, many schools are raising the minimal TOEFL scores required for admission. However, preparing for this important test can be a difficult, frustrating experience.

One of the best ways to ensure success on TOEFL is to take realistic practice exams. The five tests in this book are accurate and up to date, reflecting the changes in format that ETS instituted in 1995. They are designed to duplicate actual exams in terms of format, content, and level of difficulty. They cover all the types of items that commonly appear on actual exams. All items have been carefully pretested.

This book is designed to supplement Peterson's *TOEFL Success*, which offers an in-depth, point-by-point preparation program for the test. However, the book can also be used by itself.

This book includes the following features:

- A question-and-answer section that supplies the background information you need to understand the format of the test, to register for the exam, and to interpret your scores
- Twelve key strategies that help you maximize your scores on TOEFL
- Four tests in the standard 140-item format (Practice Tests 1, 2, 4, and 5) and one test in the long 210-item format (Practice Test 3)
- Highly realistic test items that look like and "feel like" items on actual tests
- Ten key strategies that help you do your best on the TWE
- Four Practice TWE essay tests
- Scoring guides for the Practice Tests and TWE exams
- Tapescripts for all the Listening Comprehension sections
- Answer keys, including explanatory answers for the Written Expression and Reading Comprehension parts

USING THE TESTS

- In order to complete the Listening Comprehension part of these tests, you will need to purchase the cassette tapes.
- Read over the sections titled "Questions and Answers About TOEFL" and "Twelve Keys to High Scores on TOEFL" before taking the Practice Tests.
- Take each test in its entirety rather than section by section.
- If you need to take an actual TWE, take one of the practice TWEs just before taking Practice Tests 1, 2, 4, and 5.
- Time yourself carefully during Sections 2 and 3. Do not go ahead to the next section even if you finish early. Do not give yourself extra time even if you haven't finished the section.
- Sit at a desk or table, not in an easy chair or on a sofa, and work away from distractions such as a television or a stereo.
- Mark your answers on the answer sheets rather than in the book.
- After completing the test, mark incorrect answers but do not write in the corrections. Instead, go back and answer these questions a second time.
- If you have time, take the entire test over again on another answer sheet. (You may want to make photocopies of the answer sheets in the back of the book before you begin.)
- Use the scoring charts in the back of this book to calculate your scores for each Practice Test.
- Keep track of your scores in the Personal Score Record in the Scoring section of this book.

If you have any comments or questions about this book or the TOEFL test, I'd like to hear from you. Please contact me in care of the publisher:

Peterson's
202 Carnegie Center
P.O. Box 2123
Princeton, New Jersey 08543-2123
Fax: 609-243-9150
World Wide Web:
    http://www.petersons.com/bookstore

Or you can contact me directly on the Internet:

brogers@colorado.edu

And good luck on TOEFL!

WHAT IS COMPUTER-BASED TOEFL?

At the time of this writing (spring 1998), the TOEFL was available throughout the world as a paper-and-pencil test. Starting in July 1998, however, Educational Testing Service (ETS) will introduce the computer-based TOEFL in the United States, Canada, Latin America, Europe, the Middle East, Africa, and selected Asian countries. More countries will be phased in over a three-year period. According to ETS, the computer-based test will completely replace the paper test by 2001. Some parts of the TOEFL will be a linear computerized test, which is scored the same way as a paper test. Other parts of the TOEFL will be a computer-adaptive test (CAT).

WHAT IS A COMPUTER-ADAPTIVE TEST?

A computer-adaptive test (CAT) is—as the title says—adaptive. That means that each time you answer a question the computer adjusts to your responses when determining which question to present next. For example, the first question will be of moderate difficulty. If you answer it correctly, the next question will be more difficult. If you answer it incorrectly, the next question will be easier. The computer will continue presenting questions based on your responses, with the goal of determining your ability level.

It is very important to understand that questions at the beginning of a section affect your score more than those at the end. That's because the early questions are used to determine your general ability level. Once the computer determines your general ability level, it presents questions to identify your specific ability level. As you progress farther into a section, it will be difficult to raise your score very much, even if you answer most items correctly. That's because the later questions affect your score less, as they are used to pinpoint your exact score once the computer has identified your general ability level. Therefore, take as much time as you can afford to answer the early questions correctly. Your score on each section is based on the number of questions you answer correctly, as well as the difficulty level of those questions.

You need only minimal computer skills to take the computer-based TOEFL. You will have plenty of time at the test center to work through a tutorial that allows you to practice such activities as answering questions, using the mouse, using the word processor (which you will need for your essay responses), and accessing the help function.

The computer-based tests will be given at designated universities, bi-national institutes, ETS field offices, and Sylvan Technology Centers all over the world. Once the computer-based test has been phased in, you will no longer have the option of taking the paper-based test. Keep in mind that the computer-based test will be more expensive than the paper-based test. In North America, it will initially cost US$80 and outside of North America, it will cost US$100.

WHAT KINDS OF QUESTIONS WILL BE ON THE COMPUTER-BASED TOEFL?

Like the paper test, the computer-based TOEFL will have three sections:

1. Listening Comprehension (40–60 minutes, 30–50 questions, CAT)

2. Structure and Written Expression (15–20 minutes, 20–25 questions, CAT)

3. Reading Comprehension (70–90 minutes, 44–60 questions, linear)

Some questions will be similar to those on the paper test while others will be very different. The Listening and Reading Comprehension questions will include new question types that are designed specifically for the computer. An essay will also be included that can be handwritten or typed on the computer.

HOW ARE THE COMPUTER-BASED TOEFL SCORES CALCULATED?

The computer-based TOEFL will report separate scores for each of the three test sections. The Listening Comprehension will be scored as a CAT. The Structure and Written Expression section will be scored as a CAT and on the basis of the essay. The Reading Comprehension section will be scored as a linear test. The scores for all three sections will be factored into a scaled total score, just like on the current test.

The range of possible scores on each of the three multiple choice sections is from 0–30. The range for the entire test will be from 0–300. (The range on the paper version is from 200–667).

TEST-TAKING TIPS FOR THE CAT SECTIONS OF THE COMPUTER-BASED TOEFL

- The purpose of TOEFL Success is to help you prepare for all forms of the test. You will increase your chances of scoring high on the TOEFL by being completely familiar with the content and format you will encounter on test day. The strategies and review sections of this book, as well as the practice tests, provide lots of opportunity to review relevant content. Keep in mind the following test-taking tips, most of which are unique to the CAT format.
- Understand the directions for each question type. Learn the directions for each type of question. The directions in this book are very similar to those on the actual test. Understanding the directions for each question type will save you valuable time on the day of the test.

- Focus on answering the questions at the beginning of sections 1 and 2 correctly. Remember that questions at the beginning of a section affect your score more than questions at the end. Be especially careful in choosing answers to questions in the first half of both the quantitative and verbal sections. Once the computer determines your general ability level with these initial questions, you will be unable to dramatically improve your score, even if you answer most of the questions toward the end correctly.
- In sections 1 and 2 be completely sure of each answer before proceeding. With a CAT, you must answer each question as it is presented. You cannot skip a difficult question and return to it later as you can with a paper test. Nor can you review responses to questions that you have already answered. Therefore, you must be confident about your answer before you confirm it and proceed to the next question. If you are completely stumped by a question, eliminate as many answer choices as you can, select the best answer from the remaining choices, and move on.
- Pace yourself. To finish all sections, you will need to work both quickly and accurately to complete each section within the time constraints. You will still receive a score, even if you do not complete all of the questions in a section.

RED ALERT

QUESTIONS AND ANSWERS ABOUT TOEFL

Q: What is TOEFL?

A: TOEFL stands for *Test of English as a Foreign Language*. It is a test designed to measure the English language ability of people who do not speak English as their first language and who plan to study at colleges and universities in North America as either undergraduate or graduate students.

Educational Testing Service (ETS) of Princeton, New Jersey, prepares and administers TOEFL. This organization produces many other standardized tests, such as the Test of English for International Communication (TOEIC), the Scholastic Assessment Test (SAT), the Graduate Management Admission Test (GMAT), and the Graduate Record Examinations (GRE).

Although there are other standardized tests of English, TOEFL is by far the most important in North America. ETS has offered this exam since 1965. Each year, almost 850,000 people take TOEFL at more than 1,250 testing centers all over the world. About 2,500 colleges and universities in the United States and Canada require students from non-English-speaking countries to supply TOEFL scores as part of their application process.

Q: What format does TOEFL follow? How long does it take to complete?

A: All the questions on TOEFL are multiple-choice questions with four answer choices. The test is divided into three sections, each with its own time limit. These sections are always given in the same order.

TOEFL Format		
	Standard Form	**Long Form**
Listening Comprehension	50 items 30 minutes (approx.)	80 items 45 minutes (approx.)
Structure and Written Expression	40 items 25 minutes	60 items 40 minutes
Reading Comprehension	50 items 55 minutes	70 items 80 minutes
Totals	140 items 1 hour, 50 minutes	210 items 2 hours, 45 minutes

The long form of TOEFL is sometimes given in the U.S. and Canada. The exact number of items and time limits vary somewhat from test to test on the long form. Only 140 out of the total number of items are scored. (The rest will appear on future TOEFL tests.) Unfortunately, there is no way to know which items are scored. You may also see some experimental item types on the long form, especially in the Reading Comprehension section.

Because of the time it takes to check identification, show people to their seats, give directions, and pass out and collect exams, you will actually be in the testing room for about 2½ hours for the standard form of the test and about 3 hours for the long form.

Q: How has TOEFL changed?

A: In July 1995, ETS began giving a somewhat different form of TOEFL. In the Listening Comprehension section, the old Part A, called Single Statements, was eliminated. This part was replaced by a greater number of the old Part B, Dialogs (short conversations). This became the new Part A. The old Part C, Extended Conversation and Mini-talks, was divided into two parts. The new Part B consists of Extended Conversations; the new Part C consists of Mini-Talks (short lectures).

RED 1 ALERT

The new Listening Comprehension section lasts about as long as the old one (30 minutes). There are no new types of items.

There were no changes in Part 2, Structure and Written Expression.

In Section 3, Vocabulary and Reading Comprehension became Reading Comprehension. The thirty separate Vocabulary items that formerly began this section were eliminated. Twenty more Reading Comprehension questions were added, including many more vocabulary-in-context items that ask about words in the passages themselves. There are five or six passages, and the passages tend to be longer than before. The new Section 3 takes 10 minutes longer to complete than did the old version. There are no new item types.

There are no changes in the means of calculating scores.

The changes are summarized in the chart below.

Q: What is an Institutional TOEFL?

A: Institutional TOEFL tests are given by English language schools and other institutions. Sometimes they are used for placement in a school's English program or for testing a student's progress. Institutional tests are made up of items that previously appeared on tests administered by ETS.

Because ETS does not supervise these tests, some universities won't accept the results. However, many other universities WILL. You should check with the admissions offices of universities to see what their policy is. You must arrange for the institute where you took the exam to send the scores to the university. Institutional TOEFL tests now follow the same format as official tests.

Old TOEFL Format

Section 1: Listening Comprehension
Part A: Statements
  20 items
Part B: Dialogs
  15 items
Part C: Extended Conversations and Mini-Talks
  4 conversations/talks
  15 items
    ±30 minutes

Section 2: Structure and Written Expression
Structure (Sentence Completion)
  15 items
Written Expression (Error Identification)
  25 items
    25 minutes

Section 3: Vocabulary and Reading Comprehension
Vocabulary
  30 items
Reading Comprehension
  5 passages
  30 items
    45 minutes

New TOEFL Format

Section 1: Listening Comprehension
Part A: Dialogs
  30 items
Part B: Extended Conversations
  2 conversations
  7–8 items
Part C: Mini-Talks
  3 talks
  12–13 items
    ±30 minutes

Section 2: Structure and Written Expression
Structure (Sentence Completion)
  15 items
Written Expression (Error Identification)
  25 items
    25 minutes
  (No changes in Section 2)

Section 3: Reading Comprehension
5–6 passages
50 items (including an increased number of vocabulary-in-context questions)
    55 minutes

Q: What is TWE?

A: TWE (*Test of Written English*) tests your ability to communicate in written English by having you write a short essay on a specified topic. You have 25 minutes to complete your essay. TWE is given before the main part of TOEFL five times a year. There is no additional fee for taking TWE.

The format for TWE has not changed.

Some universities require both TOEFL and TWE scores, but many universities do not require TWE.

Q: How do I register for TOEFL?

A. The first step is to obtain a current copy of the ETS publication *Bulletin of Information for TOEFL and TSE*. In North America, these are usually available at English language centers and at the international student offices or admission offices of universities. You may also request one directly from ETS.

Address:

TOEFL/TSE Services
P.O. Box 6151
Princeton, New Jersey 08541-6151
U.S.A.
Telephone: 609-771-7100
Fax: 609-771-7500
E-mail: toefl@ets.org

If you are going to take TOEFL outside of North America, you will probably need to obtain a *Bulletin* prepared specifically for your country or region. These are available from many U.S. cultural or educational facilities, English language programs, binational centers and libraries, U.S. Information Service offices, and other locations.

The *Bulletin* contains a schedule of tests, a registration form, and an envelope for sending your registration application to ETS. Follow the directions in the *Bulletin* for completing the registration form. Payment for taking TOEFL in the United States must be in the form of a money order (in U.S. dollars) or a check from a U.S. bank. In the past, different fees were charged for tests given on Friday and tests given on Saturday (because it costs more to rent testing sites on Friday), but beginning in the 1997–98 testing year, the fee for taking TOEFL on either day will be the same (U.S.$45).

Q: When should I register for TOEFL?

A: The deadline for applying for TOEFL is approximately one month before the testing date in the United States and Canada, and six weeks before in other countries. To get the location and testing date that you want, apply as early as possible. You might be assigned to an alternate site if your first choice of locations is full.

Q: After I've registered for the test, when will I receive my admission ticket?

A: You should receive it about two weeks before the exam. The admission ticket will tell you exactly when and where to take the test. It's not possible to change the date and location. If you haven't received this form by at least five days before the test date, call ETS at 609-771-7100 and inform them.

When you receive your admission ticket, fill it out according to the directions. Be sure you correctly copy the codes for the institutes that will receive your score. (These codes are listed in the *Bulletin*.)

Keep your admission ticket in a safe place. You'll need it to be admitted to the test center.

Q: What should I bring with me to the exam site?

A: You should bring the following:

- Your passport or other appropriate identification document (the *Bulletin* explains what forms of identification are acceptable)
- Your admission ticket
- A watch
- Several #2 pencils
- Your photo file record, with a recent 2¼ inch by 2½ inch photograph attached (see the *Bulletin*)
- If you take a disclosed test administration and want to receive a copy of the test, you will also need to bring a self-addressed stamped envelope (see Key #4, page 8 for more information).
- Don't bring any reference books, such as dictionaries. You are not permitted to smoke, eat, or drink in the test center.

Q: When will I receive the results of the test?

A: ETS sends scores to you and to the institutions that you request about four weeks after you have taken the test. ETS will not send your scores early or give out scores over the telephone.

Results for Institutional TOEFL tests are available sooner, often in a week or two.

Q: How does ETS calculate these scores?

A: There is a total score and three subscores, one for each section of the test. Each section counts equally toward the total score. To obtain these scores, ETS's computers calculate the number of correct answers in each section. The results are called raw scores. The raw scores are then converted into scaled scores. By means of a statistical process called test equating, a score from one TOEFL test is equivalent to the same score on another TOEFL, even if one of the tests is slightly simpler or more difficult than the other.

The scaled scores from each section are added together, multiplied by 10, and divided by 3 to arrive at a total score, as shown:

	Part 1		Part 2		Part 3	
Scaled Scores	49	+	58	+	55	= 162

$$(162 \times 10) = 1620 \div 3 = 540 \text{ Total Score}$$

Total scores range from a high of 670 to a low of 200, although scores below 320 are rare. (Even if you don't open the test book and fill in the blanks on your answer sheet at random, your score should be about 320.) You must answer at least 25 percent of the questions in all three sections to receive a test score.

Q: Is every item on the test scored?

A: No, there is usually at least one unscored item in each part of the test. This is usually the last item in each part. For example, in Section 2, item 15 (the last item in the Structure part) and item 40 (the last item in the Written Expression part) are usually not scored. However, it is not recommended that you skip these items—ETS could always change its system.

Q: What is a passing score on TOEFL?

A: There isn't any. Each university has its own standards for admission, so you should check the catalogs of universities you are interested in or contact their admission offices. Most undergraduate programs require scores between 500 and 550, and most graduate programs ask for scores between 525 and 600. In recent years, there has been a tendency for universities to raise their minimum TOEFL requirements. Of course, the higher you score, the better your chance of admission.

A chart in the *Bulletin* allows you to compare your TOEFL scores with those of other people who have taken the test in the last year. For example, the chart tells you that if your total score was 540, 60 percent of all test-takers had lower scores than you did.

Q: How are universities informed of my scores?

A: ETS reports your score to three institutions for free. For a charge, ETS will send your scores to additional institutions. There is a form for requesting this service in the *Bulletin*.

Q: If I feel I haven't done well on TOEFL, can I have my scores canceled?

A: Yes, but only for a certain period of time. At the end of the test, you can fill in the Score Cancellation section of the answer sheet. You may also fax ETS at 609-771-7500 within a week of taking a test; write "Attention, TOEFL Score Cancellation" at the top of your fax message. Include your name, test date, number of your testing center, and registration number (from your admission test) and sign the fax.

You can't cancel your scores after you have seen the results, and you can't cancel TOEFL and TWE scores separately.

It is generally NOT a good idea to cancel scores. You may have done better on the test that you thought you did.

Q: Is it possible to improve one's score by cheating?

A: Don't try. Test-takers are seated carefully; it is very difficult for them to see anyone else's answer sheet. Even if a test-taker can see someone else's answers, there are different forms of the same exam. In other words, the items in one person's test book do not appear in the same order as they do in another person's. ETS also runs computer checks to detect patterns of cheating.

It is very difficult to have someone else take the exam for you. You must bring an official identification document with your picture on it. You are also required to bring a photo file record with a recent photo of yourself. ETS copies this photo and sends it with your scores to universities. If the person in the photo is not the same person who enrolls, that person may not be admitted.

The following are also considered cheating:

- Taking notes during the Listening Comprehension section
- Talking to or signaling any other test-takers
- Copying any test material
- Working on one section during the time allotted for another section

- Continuing to work on a section after time is called

Persons who are believed to be cheating will receive a warning for minor acts of cheating. For more serious matters, a person's scores will be canceled.

Q: How many times may I take TOEFL?

A: As often as you want; there is no limit. ETS will only send your most recent scores to institutions. It is not uncommon for people to take the test three, four, or more times before they obtain satisfactory scores.

Q: How can I get more information about TOEFL?

A: You can now contact ETS on the Internet or get updated information about the test from the ETS home page on the World Wide Web at http://www.toefl.org or E-mail at toefl@ets.org

TWELVE KEYS TO HIGH SCORES ON TOEFL

Key #1

Increase your general knowledge of English.

There are two types of knowledge that will lead to high TOEFL scores:

- A knowledge of the tactics used by good test-takers and the ''tricks'' of the test
- A general command of English (which must be built up over a long period of time)

Following a step-by-step TOEFL preparation program, such as that presented in Peterson's *TOEFL Success*, will familiarize you with the tactics you need to raise your scores. The practice tests in this book and in its companion book will help you polish these techniques.

The best way to increase your general knowledge of English is simply to use English as much as possible. You can't learn all that you'll need to do well on the test from any TOEFL preparation program. Other classes in English will be useful and so will opportunities to speak, read, write, or listen to English.

Some people who are preparing for TOEFL think that conversation classes and practice are a waste of time because speaking skills are not tested on the exam. In fact, one of the best ways to get ready for the exam is to speak English whenever you can. Not only will you improve your ability to listen to everyday English, but you'll also learn to think in English. If you are living in an English-speaking country, don't spend all your time with people from your own country. If you are living in your home country, try to arrange opportunities for conversations in English.

You can improve your listening comprehension skills by going to English language lectures and movies. Listening to news and informational broadcasts on the radio is especially useful. Reading books, magazines, and newspapers in English can help you prepare for the Reading Comprehension part of the test.

One of your most important jobs is to systematically improve your vocabulary. Vocabulary building will help you, not just in the Reading Comprehension section, but throughout the exam. You may want to keep a personal vocabulary list. When you come across an unfamiliar word, look it up in a dictionary and write the word and its definition in a notebook. Keep the notebook with you and study it when riding buses, eating lunch, taking coffee breaks, or whenever else you have a free moment.

Key #2

Make the most of your preparation time.

You need to train for TOEFL just as you would train for any important competitive event. The sooner you can start training, the better, but no matter when you begin, you need to get the most out of your preparation time.

Make a time management chart. Draw up an hour-by-hour schedule of your week's activities. Block out those hours when you are busy with classes, work, social activities, and other responsibilities. Then pencil in times for TOEFL preparation. You will remember more of what you study if you schedule a few hours every day or several times weekly than if you schedule all your study time in large blocks on weekends. After following this schedule for a week, make whatever adjustments are necessary. Then, try to keep to this schedule until the week before the testing date. During that last week, reduce your study time and begin to relax.

If possible, reserve a special place where you do nothing but work on TOEFL preparation, separate from where you do your regular homework or other work. This place should be as free of distractions as possible.

A good method of studying for TOEFL is the "30-5-5" method:

- Study for 30 minutes.
- Take a 5-minute break—leave your desk and do something completely different.
- When you return, take 5 minutes to review what you studied before the break and preview what you are going to study next.

Incidentally, it's an excellent idea to meet regularly with a small group of people who are also preparing for TOEFL. Research has shown that this study-group approach to test preparation is very effective.

Key #3

Be in good physical condition when you take the exam.

When you make out your time management schedule, don't forget to leave time for physical activities—sports, aerobics, jogging, bicycling, or whatever else you prefer.

The most important physical concern is that you not become exhausted during your preparation time. If you aren't getting enough sleep, you'll need to reduce your study time or another activity. This is especially important in the last few days before the exam.

Key #4

Choose your test date carefully.

If you need test scores quickly, you should sign up for the earliest test date available. But if it's possible, sign up to take TOEFL on one of the Disclosed Test Administration dates. These dates are marked with an asterisk (*) on the ETS schedule of exams on the cover of the *Bulletin*. They are generally given on Fridays in July and September and on Saturdays in May, August, and October.

There are two advantages to taking tests on these dates:

- You can keep the test book, which can be a valuable tool for study if you take the exam again.

- The tests given on these dates are always standard (140-item) forms. Taking the shorter form of the test is less tiring and stressful than taking the long form.

To receive a copy of the test, you must bring a 6 by 9 inch (15.3 by 22.8 centimeter) envelope that you have addressed to yourself. You'll need enough postage on the envelope for a package weighing 1½ ounces (43 grams). If your mailing address is in the United States, two first-class U.S. postage stamps will be sufficient.

Key #5

Be familiar with the test format and directions.

You should have a clear "map" of the TOEFL test in your mind. Then as you're taking the exam, you'll know exactly where you are and what's coming next. You can familiarize yourself with the basic TOEFL format by looking over the chart on page 1.

The directions for each part of the TOEFL test are always the same; even the same examples are used. If you're familiar with the directions, you won't have to waste time reading them during the test. You can become familiar with these directions by studying the directions for the practice tests in this book.

Key #6

Organize your pre-exam time.

You shouldn't try to "cram" (study intensively) during the last few days before the exam. Last-minute studying can leave you exhausted, and you need to be alert for the test. The night before the exam, don't study at all. Get together the materials you'll need in the morning; then go to a movie, take a long walk, or do something else to take your mind off the test. Go to bed when you usually do.

If the exam is in the morning, have breakfast before you leave. Wear comfortable clothes because you'll be sitting in the same position for a long time. Give yourself plenty of time to get to the test site, keeping in mind traffic, weather, and parking problems. If you have to rush, that will only add to your stress.

Key #7

Use time wisely during the test.

TOEFL would be a far easier test if you could spend an unlimited amount of time working on it. However, there are strict time limits. Doing well on TOEFL means that you must find a balance between speed and accuracy. You don't want to rush through any section, but you do want to finish each section before time is called. The ideal is to finish Sections 2 and 3 with a few minutes remaining so that you can go back to questions that you found difficult. (The timing on Section 1 is controlled by the tape and you can't go back and check your answers after completing this section.)

The questions on TOEFL are not equally difficult. Items can be classified as easy, medium, and difficult.

Approximate Distribution of Items on a Typical TOEFL Test

Easy	30%
Medium	40%
Difficult	30%

Easy items are usually found at the beginning of each part of the test; medium items are usually found in the middle of each part; and difficult items are usually found at the end of each part. You may be tempted to rush through the easy items to save time for the difficult ones at the end of each part. This is not a good strategy. Your goal is to get as many right answers as possible. Therefore, you want to concentrate on the items that give you the best chance of a correct answer—in other words, the easiest ones.

Hint: Remember, you don't get any extra points for answering difficult questions.

Work steadily. Never spend too much time on any one problem. If you are unable to decide on an answer, guess and go on. Answer each question as you come to it, even if you are not sure of the answer. You can mark difficult items on your answer sheet with check marks (as shown in Key #8). Then, if you have time at the end of the section, you can return to these problems. Sometimes when you come back to an item, you will find it easier to choose the right answer. (Be sure to erase all of these check marks before you hand in your answer sheet.)

The most important tool for timing yourself is a watch, preferably one with a "count down" feature that you can set at the beginning of Sections 2 and 3. (Watches with alarms are not permitted.)

Key #8

Know how to mark your answer sheet.

One of the worst surprises you can have during a test is to suddenly discover that the number of the item that you are working on doesn't correspond to the number of the answer you are marking for that item. You have to go back to find where you first got off track then change all the answers after that number. You can avoid this problem by using the test book itself as a marker. Cover all the unanswered items in each column on your answer sheet. Then uncover one item at a time as you advance. Every five items or so, quickly glance at the number of the question that you are working on and the number of the answer to make sure they are the same.

Mark answers by filling in the oval so that the letter cannot be seen. Don't mark answers any other way.

Use a #2 black lead pencil. **Do not** use a pen, a liquid lead pencil, or any other kind of marker.

By the way, you may see either of two types of answer sheets. One has answer choices displayed horizontally, while the other displays them vertically.

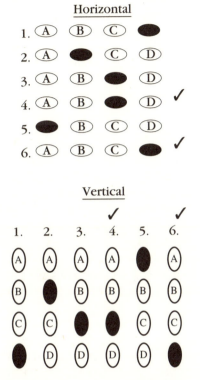

Always be sure you have filled in a circle completely and have filled in only one answer per item. If you have to erase an answer, erase it completely.

Notice the check marks by numbers 4 and 6. The test-taker found these items difficult. He or she guessed at the answers and then used the marks as a reminder to come back to these items if time allowed. These marks should be erased before the end of the test.

Incidentally, if you mark the same answer four times in a row (i.e., choosing answer (A) for questions 1–4), you'll know one of those four answers is wrong. The same correct answer will occur at most three times in a row on TOEFL.

Hint: Don't sharpen your pencils too much before the exam. You can fill in circles more quickly if your pencil is not too sharp.

Key #9

Improve your concentration.

The ability to focus your attention on each item is an important factor in achieving a high score. Two and a half hours or more, after all, is a long time to spend in deep concentration. However, if your concentration is broken, it could cost you points. When an outside concern comes into your mind, just say to yourself, "I'll think about this after the test."

Like any skill, the ability to concentrate can be improved with practice. Work on this while you are taking the practice tests in this book.

Key #10

Use the process of elimination to make the best guess.

Unlike some standardized exams, TOEFL has no penalty for guessing. In other words, incorrect answers aren't subtracted from your total score. Even if you are not sure which answer is correct, you should always, always, always guess. But you want to make an educated guess, not a blind guess. To do so, use the process of elimination.

To understand the process of elimination, it may be helpful to look at the basic structure of a multiple-choice item. On TOEFL, multiple-choice items consist of a **stem** and four **answer choices**. (The stem in the Listening Comprehension section is spoken; in the other two sections, it is written.) One answer choice, called the **key,** is correct. The three incorrect choices are called **distractors** because their function is to distract (take away) your attention from the right answer.

   1. STEM..........................
       (A) distractor
       (B) key
       (C) distractor
       (D) distractor

The three distractors, however, are usually not equally attractive. One is usually "almost correct." This choice is called the **main distractor**. Most people who answer an item incorrectly will choose this answer.

1. STEM.....................
   (A) distractor
   (B) key
   (C) distractor
   (D) main distractor

To see how this works in practice, look at this simple Structure item:

1. Winter wheat _____ planted in the fall.
   (A) because
   (B) is
   (C) which
   (D) has

If you are sure of the answer, you should mark your choice immediately and go on. If not, you should use the process of elimination. In this item, choices (A) and (C) are fairly easy to eliminate. Because this sentence consists of a single clause, connecting words such as *because* and *which* are not needed. It may be a little more difficult to choose between choices (B) and (D) because both form verb phrases. Even if you are unable to decide between these two choices, you have a 50 percent chance of guessing correctly. That's twice as good as the 25 percent chance you would have if you had guessed blindly. (Choice (B) is the key, of course; a passive verb, not a present perfect verb, is required to complete the sentence correctly. Choice (D) is the main distractor.)

What if you eliminate one or two answers but can't decide which of the remaining choices is correct? If you have a "hunch" (an intuitive feeling) that one choice is better than the others, choose it. If not, just pick any remaining answer and go on.

If you have no idea which of the four answers is correct, it's better to use a standard "guess letter" such as (C) than to guess at random.

You should NEVER leave any items unanswered. Even if you don't have time to read an item, you have a 25 percent chance of guessing the key. If you are unable to finish a section, fill in all the unanswered ovals on your answer sheet with your guess letter in the last few seconds before time is called.

Hint: Use the same guess letter all the time so that you can fill in the ovals quickly.

Key #11
Learn to control test anxiety.

A little nervousness before an important test is normal. After all, these tests can have an important effect on your plans for your education and career. If you were going to participate in a big athletic contest or give an important business presentation, you would feel the same way. There is an expression in English that describes this feeling quite well: "butterflies in the stomach." These "butterflies" will mostly disappear once the test starts. And a little nervousness can actually help by making you more alert and focused. However, too much nervousness can slow you down and cause you to make mistakes.

You may become anxious during the test because it seems very hard and you feel like you are making many mistakes. Try not to panic. The test seems hard because it *is* hard. You can miss quite a few items and still get a high score.

One way to avoid stress on test day is to give yourself plenty of time to get to the test center. If you have to rush, you'll be even more nervous during the exam.

If you begin to feel extremely anxious during the test, try taking a short break—a "10-second vacation." Close your eyes and put down your pencil. Take a few deep breaths, shake out your hands, roll your head on your neck, relax—then go back to work.

Of course, you can't take a break during the Listening Comprehension section when the items are being read. However, if you're familiar with the directions, you can relax during the times when the directions are being read.

A positive, confident attitude toward the exam can help you overcome anxiety. Think of TOEFL not as a test of your knowledge or of you as a person but as an intellectual challenge, a series of puzzles to be solved.

Key #12

Learn from taking practice tests and official TOEFL exams.

One of the most important steps in preparing for TOEFL is taking realistic, complete practice tests. There are five tests in this book and three in its companion volume, *TOEFL Success*.

In addition, you may take the official TOEFL test several times. Each time you take a test, either a practice test or a real one, you should learn from it. Right after the exam, write down your reactions: Which section seemed difficult? Did you have problems finishing any sections? When you look at your results, is the score for one section significantly lower or higher than the scores for the other two sections? You can use this information to help you focus your studies for the next time you take the test.

Hint: Whenever you take a practice test, pretend that you are taking an actual TOEFL exam. Whenever you take an actual exam, pretend you are taking a practice test.

Practice Test 1

Section 1

This section tests your ability to comprehend spoken English. It is divided into three parts, each with its own directions. During actual exams, you are *not* permitted to turn the page during the reading of the directions or to take notes at any time.

PART A

Directions: Each item in this part consists of a brief conversation involving two speakers. Following each conversation, a third voice will ask a question. You will hear the conversations and questions only once, and they will *not* be written out.

   When you have heard each conversation and question, read the four answer choices and select the *one*—(A), (B), (C), or (D)—that best answers the question based on what is directly stated or on what can be inferred. Then fill in the space on your answer sheet that matches the letter of the answer that you have selected.

Here is an example.

You will hear:

You will read:

   (A) Open the window.
   (B) Move the chair.
   (C) Leave the room.
   (D) Take a seat.

   From the conversation you find out that the woman thinks the man should put the chair over by the window. The best answer to the question, "What does the woman think the man should do?" is (B), "Move the chair." You should fill in (B) on your answer sheet.

Sample Answer

 Ⓐ ● Ⓒ Ⓓ

WAIT

15

1. (A) This is the first time she's seen the piano.
   (B) The photographs have not been developed.
   (C) The photographs are on the piano.
   (D) The man should photograph the piano.

2. (A) Because he was so hungry, he rushed off to eat.
   (B) He found some good buys at the store.
   (C) Everybody was angry at him for leaving.
   (D) He was too mad to say anything when he left.

3. (A) She's trying to find a good chair.
   (B) She doesn't know where the chair is now.
   (C) She thinks the chair is actually comfortable.
   (D) She's never sat in that chair before.

4. (A) The gardens are on the opposite side of the park.
   (B) The roses in this park are not the best.
   (C) The rose gardens are located on the west side.
   (D) The roses grow outside the park, not inside it.

5. (A) He doesn't know where she lives.
   (B) He believes she's going to leave tonight.
   (C) He doesn't know where she's going.
   (D) He didn't hear what she said.

6. (A) He has finished cleaning the drain.
   (B) He feels that he has wasted two days.
   (C) He will start his experiment in two days.
   (D) He thinks his experiment was a success.

7. (A) She is riding her brother's bicycle now.
   (B) She fixed the bike for her brother.
   (C) Her bicycle can't be repaired.
   (D) Her brother did the repair work.

8. (A) A half hour.
   (B) An hour.
   (C) Ninety minutes.
   (D) Two hours.

9. (A) She doesn't take her car to campus anymore.
   (B) She doesn't have a long way to drive.
   (C) She doesn't need to go to campus tomorrow.
   (D) She doesn't have a car anymore.

10. (A) Swimming is as tiring as dancing.
    (B) She's taking a dancing course.
    (C) Dancing provides good exercise too.
    (D) She'd rather swim than dance.

11. (A) The rain has just begun.
    (B) It's not raining as hard now.
    (C) It only rained a little bit.
    (D) It's raining too hard to go out.

12. (A) Robert deserves her thanks for his help.
    (B) Robert didn't help much with the project.
    (C) She finished her project before Robert finished his.
    (D) She and Robert hadn't finished planning their project yet.

13. (A) He makes his students work very hard.
    (B) He refused to let the man take his class.
    (C) He stayed home today because he was tired.
    (D) He won't be teaching next semester.

14. (A) Send flowers to someone.
    (B) Deliver a package to the hospital.
    (C) Arrange some flowers.
    (D) Talk to a doctor.

15. (A) Get a new watch.
    (B) Run around the block.
    (C) Shop for jewelry.
    (D) Have his watch repaired.

16. (A) How long he'll be in Montreal.
    (B) How he plans to travel to Montreal.
    (C) What form of transportation he'll use there.
    (D) What other cities he's planning to visit.

17. (A) He thinks the woman wants to relax.
    (B) He has plans for the rest of the weekend.
    (C) He believes the woman should be more patient.
    (D) He wants to go to a small, quiet restaurant.

18. (A) She doesn't talk very much.
    (B) She'd like to become a better skater.
    (C) She skates a lot these days.
    (D) She doesn't really like skating.

19. (A) He can get his money refunded.
    (B) The sweater fits him perfectly.
    (C) The sweater isn't available in a larger size.
    (D) He can't get a refund without a receipt.

20. (A) She has never heard of the Fisherman's Grotto.
    (B) She has stopped going to that restaurant.
    (C) She enjoys eating at the Fisherman's Grotto.
    (D) She never goes to the beach anymore.

21. (A) Play the guitar while she sings.
    (B) Sing a song with him.
    (C) Write the music for her song.
    (D) Go with her to the guitar concert.

22. (A) He should rest before he cleans the kitchen.
    (B) All of his apartment needs to be cleaned.
    (C) Only the kitchen needs to be cleaned up.
    (D) He should wait until this afternoon to begin.

23. (A) He doesn't know much about acting.
    (B) The acting seemed professional to him.
    (C) Acting is a very difficult profession.
    (D) He didn't think they were actors.

24. (A) Paintbrushes.
    (B) Some soap.
    (C) A can of paint.
    (D) Some milk.

25. (A) The bananas have all been eaten.
    (B) He didn't buy any bananas.
    (C) Those are not the right bananas.
    (D) The bananas aren't ready to eat yet.

26. (A) Some of the students thought the test was fair.
    (B) There are only a few students in the class.
    (C) Everyone thinks that Professor Murray is unfair.
    (D) Most students thought that the test was too long.

27. (A) He wrote a book about great restaurants.
    (B) He always makes reservations for dinner.
    (C) He always finds good places to eat.
    (D) He read a book while he was eating dinner.

28. (A) Stay out of the garden.
    (B) Protect himself from the sun.
    (C) Buy another hat.
    (D) Get some new gardening tools.

29. (A) No one looked out of the windows.
    (B) Only one window had been locked.
    (C) All the windows were locked.
    (D) Some of the windows were broken.

30. (A) He's very friendly.
    (B) He goes out a lot.
    (C) He's out of town now.
    (D) He's quitting his job.

PART B

Directions: This part of the test consists of extended conversations between two speakers. After each of these conversations there are a number of questions. You will hear each conversation and question only once, and the questions are *not* written out.

When you have heard the questions, read the four answer choices and select the *one*—(A), (B), (C), or (D)—that best answers the question based on what is directly stated or on what can be inferred. Then fill in the space on your answer sheet that matches the letter of the answer that you have selected.

Don't forget: During actual exams, taking notes or writing in your test book is *not* permitted.

31. (A) She didn't know about the painting exhibit.
    (B) She wasn't very familiar with the name ''Reynolds Hall.''
    (C) She didn't realize the man was speaking to her.
    (D) She wasn't sure where the Art Building was.

32. (A) The main library.
    (B) A painting.
    (C) A service road.
    (D) A metal sculpture.

33. (A) She's a graduate student.
    (B) She works at the library.
    (C) She's waiting for the man.
    (D) She teaches art.

34. (A) Annoyed.
    (B) Apologetic.
    (C) Surprised.
    (D) Cooperative.

35. (A) The possibility of life on other planets.
    (B) Einstein's concept of the speed of light.
    (C) Revolutionary new designs for spaceships.
    (D) The distance from Earth to the closest star.

36. (A) Only a few days.
    (B) Several months.
    (C) Four or five years.
    (D) Hundreds of years.

37. (A) A new means of propelling space-ships.
    (B) A deeper understanding of Einstein's theories.
    (C) Another method for measuring the speed of light.
    (D) A new material from which to build spaceships.

38. (A) As unlikely in the near future.
    (B) As strongly inadvisable.
    (C) As impossible at any time.
    (D) As probably unnecessary.

PART C

Directions: This part of the test consists of several talks each given by a single speaker. After each of these talks, there are a number of questions. You will hear each talk and question only once, and the questions are *not* written out.

When you have heard each question, read the four answer choices and select the *one*—(A), (B), (C), or (D)—that best answers the question based on what is directly stated or on what can be inferred. Then fill in the space on your answer sheet that matches the letter of the answer that you have selected.

Here is an example.

You will hear:

Now here is a sample question.

You will hear:

You will read:

(A) Philosophy.
(B) Meteorology.
(C) Astronomy.
(D) Photography.

The lecture concerns a lunar eclipse, a topic that would typically be discussed in an astronomy class. The choice that best answers the question "In what course is this lecture probably being given?" is (C), "Astronomy." You should fill in (C) on your answer sheet.

Sample Answer

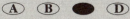

Here is another sample question.

You will hear:

You will read:

(A) The Earth's shadow moves across the Moon.
(B) Clouds block the view of the Moon.
(C) The Moon moves between the Earth and the Sun.
(D) The Sun can be observed without special equipment.

From the lecture, you learn that a lunar eclipse occurs when the Earth moves between the Sun and the Moon and the shadow of the Earth passes across the Moon. The choice that best answers the question "According to the speaker, which of the following occurs during a lunar eclipse?" is (A), "The Earth's shadow moves across the Moon." Don't forget: During actual exams, taking notes or writing in your test book is *not* permitted.

Sample Answer

39. (A) Journalism students.
    (B) Reporters.
    (C) Editorial writers.
    (D) Teachers.

40. (A) The International Desk.
    (B) The Circulation Department.
    (C) The Production Department.
    (D) The City Desk.

41. (A) Distributing the newspaper through-
        out the city.
    (B) Reporting local news.
    (C) Printing the newspaper.
    (D) Gathering news from international
        sources.

42. (A) The background of the professors.
    (B) Costs.
    (C) Social events.
    (D) The academic program.

43. (A) Archaeology.
    (B) History.
    (C) Architecture.
    (D) Language.

44. (A) The Eastern Mediterranean program.
    (B) The Southeast Asian program.
    (C) The North American program.
    (D) The Western Mediterranean program.

45. (A) They are exactly like classes at Hunt
        University.
    (B) They take up all of the participants'
        time.
    (C) They can earn students credit at their
        universities.
    (D) They are completely optional.

46. (A) Instructors in the program.
    (B) Students from the professor's class at
        Hunt University.
    (C) Representatives of "Semester Afloat."
    (D) Former participants in the program.

47. (A) Better types of skates.
    (B) Improved conditions on ice tracks.
    (C) Changes in skating techniques.
    (D) New world records.

48. (A) They all had equal opportunities of
        winning.
    (B) They couldn't compete in the Winter
        Olympics.
    (C) They all wore the same kinds of
        skates.
    (D) They had to skate on outdoor tracks.

49. (A) It chips easily.
    (B) It becomes covered with frost.
    (C) It becomes too soft.
    (D) It provides too much resistance.

50. (A) Speed skating will become more
        popular.
    (B) Speed skaters will skate faster than
        ever before.
    (C) Speed skating events will return to
        outside tracks.
    (D) New rules for speed skating will be
        needed.

THIS IS THE END OF SECTION 1, LISTENING COMPREHENSION.

STOP WORK ON SECTION 1.

Section 2

This section tests your ability to recognize grammar and usage suitable for standard written English. This section is divided into two parts, each with its own directions.

STRUCTURE

Directions: Items in this part are incomplete sentences. Following each of these sentences, there are four words or phrases. You should select the *one* word or phrase—(A), (B), (C), or (D)—that best completes the sentence. Then fill in the space on your answer sheet that matches the letter of the answer that you have selected.

Example I

Pepsin _____ an enzyme used in digestion.

(A) that
(B) is
(C) of
(D) being

This sentence should properly read "Pepsin is an enzyme used in digestion." You should fill in (B) on your answer sheet.

Sample Answer
Ⓐ ● Ⓒ Ⓓ

Example II

_____ large natural lakes are found in the state of South Carolina.

(A) There are no
(B) Not the
(C) It is not
(D) No

This sentence should properly read "No large natural lakes are found in the state of South Carolina." You should fill in (D) on your answer sheet. As soon as you understand the directions, begin work on this part.

Sample Answer
Ⓐ Ⓑ Ⓒ ●

WAIT

23

1. _____ dancer Isadora Duncan played a major role in the revolution in dance that took place in the early twentieth century.
   (A) Because the
   (B) The
   (C) She was a
   (D) Being a

2. Water pressure _____ cracks open small rocks but also breaks great slabs of stone from the faces of cliffs.
   (A) either
   (B) not only
   (C) and so
   (D) moreover

3. _____ types of guitars: acoustic and electric.
   (A) Basically, there are two
   (B) Two of the basic
   (C) Basically, two
   (D) They are two basic

4. Both longitude and latitude _____ in degrees, minutes, and seconds.
   (A) measuring
   (B) measured
   (C) are measured
   (D) being measured

5. New words are constantly being invented _____ new objects and concepts.
   (A) to describe
   (B) a description of
   (C) they describe
   (D) describe

6. Modern saw blades are coated with a special _____ plastic.
   (A) reduction of friction
   (B) reduced-friction
   (C) friction is reduced
   (D) friction-reducing

7. Bricks baked in a kiln are much harder _____ that are dried in the sun.
   (A) those
   (B) than do those
   (C) than those
   (D) ones

8. Exactly _____ humans domesticated animals is not known.
   (A) how
   (B) by means of
   (C) if
   (D) by which

9. Jerome Kern's most famous work is *Showboat,* _____, most enduring musical comedies.
   (A) it is one of the finest
   (B) of the finest one
   (C) the finest one
   (D) one of the finest

10. _____ snowfield on a mountain slope reaches a depth of about 100 feet, it begins to move slowly forward under its own weight.
    (A) Whenever a
    (B) A
    (C) That a
    (D) Should a

11. Most comets have two kinds of tails, one made up of dust, _____ made up of electrically charged particles called plasma.
    (A) one another
    (B) the other
    (C) other ones
    (D) each other

12. By 1820, there were over sixty steamboats on the Mississippi River, _____ were quite luxurious.
    (A) many of them
    (B) which many
    (C) many of which
    (D) many that

13. _____ in 1772, Maryland's state capitol is still in use and is one of the most attractive public buildings in the United States.
    (A) It was built
    (B) Built
    (C) To build it
    (D) Building

14. Four miles off the southeastern coast of Massachusetts _____, a popular summer resort.

  (A) lies the island of Martha's Vineyard
  (B) the island of Martha's Vineyard lies there
  (C) does lie the island of Martha's Vineyard
  (D) where the island of Martha's Vineyard lies

15. Copperplate, a highly ornate form of handwriting, is _____ longer in common use.

  (A) not
  (B) none
  (C) never
  (D) no

WRITTEN EXPRESSION

Directions: The items in this part have four underlined words or phrases. You must identify the *one* underlined expression—(A), (B), (C), or (D)—that must be changed for the sentence to be correct. Then fill in the space on your answer sheet that matches the letter of the answer that you have selected.

Example I

Lenses may to have either concave or convex shapes.
      A   B C   D

    This sentence should read "Lenses may have either concave or convex shapes." You should therefore select answer (A).

Sample Answer

● Ⓑ Ⓒ Ⓓ

Example II

When painting a fresco, an artist is applied paint directly to the damp plaster of a wall.
A   B   C   D

    This sentence should read "When painting a fresco, an artist applies paint directly to the wet plaster of a wall." You should therefore select answer (B). As soon as you understand the directions, begin work on this part.

Sample Answer

Ⓐ ● Ⓒ Ⓓ

WAIT

25

16. In an essay writing in 1779, Judith Sargeant
    ___A___ ___B___
    Murray promoted the cause of
                     ___C___
    women's education.
    ___D___

17. A metallic object that is in contact with a
                       ___A___   ___B___
    magnet becomes a magnet themselves.
           ___C___   ___D___

18. The change from summer to winter occurs
                 ___A___   ___B___
    very abrupt in the tundra regions of North
         ___C___   ___D___
    America.

19. In outer space, spacecraft can be maneu-
    ___A___   ___B___
    vered by means small steering rockets.
          ___C___   ___D___

20. Echoes occur when sound waves strike a
                 ___A___   ___B___
    smooth surface and bounces backwards.
    ___C___   ___D___

21. A good carpentry must possess a wide
           ___A___   ___B___
    variety of skills.
    ___C___ ___D___

22. Grover Cleveland was the only American
                          ___A___
    president which served two nonconsecutive
              ___B___ ___C___
    terms.
    ___D___

23. The American soprano Mary Gardner,

    who had one of the greatest operatic voices
    ___A___   ___B___
    of her era, retired at the height of the
                             ___C___   ___D___
    career.

24. On nights when is the sky clear and the air
                    ___A___
    calm, the Earth's surface rapidly radiates
    ___B___   ___C___
    heat into the atmosphere.
         ___D___

25. Dreams are commonly made up of both
                  ___A___   ___B___
    visual or verbal images.
    ___C___   ___D___

26. The trap-door spider makes a hole in the
                          ___A___
    ground, lines it with silk, and closing it
                  ___B___   ___C___
    with a hinged door.
          ___D___

27. Sleepiness is one symptom of hypothermia,
    ___A___   ___B___
    the extreme lost of body heat.
        ___C___ ___D___

28. The flute is the only woodwind instrument
    ___A___   ___B___
    that is not done of wood.
               ___C___ ___D___

29. F. Scott Fitzgerald's novel *The Great Gatsby*

    is about the pursuit of wealthy, status, and
    ___A___   ___B___   ___C___
    love in the 1920s.
    ___D___

30. Whenever there are red, orange, or brown
    ___A___   ___B___
    coloring in sandstone, iron ore is probably
                                      ___C___
    present.
    ___D___

31. Feathers keep birds warm and dry also
                        ___A___   ___B___
    enable them to fly.
    ___C___ ___D___

32. Some species of penicillin mold are used to
    ___A___   ___B___
    ripe cheeses.
    ___C___ ___D___

33. In about 1920, experimental psychologists
    ___A___   ___B___
    have devoted more research to learning
                                 ___C___
    than to any other topic.
         ___D___

34. Natural asphalt lakes are find in many parts
                      ___A___ ___B___ ___C___
    of the world.
    ___D___

35. All living creatures pass on inherited traits
        ___A___   ___B___
    from one generation to other.
    ___C___   ___D___

36. Many of the events that led up to the
                   ___A___   ___B___
    American Revolution took placed in
                         ___C___   ___D___
    Massachusetts.

37. Mass production is the <u>manufacture</u> of
                                    A
<u>machineries</u> and other articles in <u>standard</u>
    B   C
sizes and large <u>numbers</u>.
                    D

38. <u>Not much</u> people <u>realize</u> that apples
         A   B
have been <u>cultivated</u> for <u>over</u> 3,000 years.
              C   D

39. The <u>destructive</u> force of <u>running</u> water
              A   B
depends <u>entirely almost</u> on the velocity
                C
of <u>its flow</u>.
        D

40. The eastern bluebird <u>is considered</u> the
                                  A
<u>most attractive</u> bird <u>native of</u> North America
        B   C
<u>by many</u> bird-watchers.
    D

THIS IS THE END OF SECTION 2.

IF YOU FINISH BEFORE THE TIME LIMIT, CHECK YOUR WORK
ON SECTION 2 ONLY.

DO NOT READ OR WORK ON ANY OTHER SECTION OF THE TEST.

Section 3

This section of the test measures your ability to comprehend written materials.

Directions: This section contains several passages, each followed by a number of questions. Read the passages and, for each question, choose the *one* best answer—(A), (B), (C), or (D)—based on what is stated in the passage or on what can be inferred. Then fill in the space on your answer sheet that matches the letter of the answer that you have selected.

Read the Following Passage

Line   Like mammals, birds claim their own territories. A bird's territory may be small or large. Some birds claim only their nest and the area right around it, while others claim far larger territories that include their feeding areas. Gulls, penguins, and other waterfowl nest in huge colonies, but even in the biggest colonies, each male and his mate have small territories of their own
5   immediately around their nests.

   Male birds defend their territory chiefly against other males of the same species. In some cases, a warning call or threatening pose may be all the defense needed, but in other cases, intruders may refuse to leave peacefully.

Example I

What is the main topic of this passage?

(A) Birds that live in colonies
(B) Birds' mating habits
(C) The behavior of birds
(D) Territoriality in birds

The passage mainly concerns the territories of birds. You should fill in (D) on your answer sheet.

Sample Answer

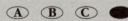

Example II

According to the passage, male birds defend their territory primarily against

(A) Female birds
(B) Birds of other species
(C) Males of their own species
(D) Mammals

The passage states that "Male birds defend their territory chiefly against other males of the same species." You should fill in (C) on your answer sheet. As soon as you understand the directions, begin work on this section.

Sample Answer

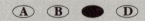

WAIT

QUESTIONS 1–10

Line Just as optical fibers have transformed communication, they are also revolutionizing medicine. These
ultra-thin, flexible fibers have opened a window into the living tissues of the body. By inserting
optical fibers through natural openings or small incisions and threading them along the body's
established pathways, physicians can look into the lungs, intestines, heart, and other areas that were
5   formerly inaccessible to them.

      The basic fiber-optics system is called a fiberscope, which consists of two bundles of fibers.
One, the illuminating bundle, carries light to the tissues. It is coupled to a high-intensity light source.
Light enters the cores of the high-purity silicon glass and travels along the fibers. A lens at the end of
the bundle collects the light and focuses it into the other bundle, the imaging bundle. Each fiber in
10   the bundle transmits only a tiny fraction of the total image. The reconstructed image can be viewed
through an eyepiece or displayed on a television screen. During the last five years, improved methods
of fabricating optical fibers have led to a reduction in fiberscope diameter and an increase in the
number of fibers, which in turn has increased resolution.

      Optical fibers can also be used to deliver laser light. By use of laser beams, physicians can
15   perform surgery inside the body, sometimes eliminating the need for invasive procedures in which
healthy tissue must be cut through to reach the site of disease. Many of these procedures do not
require anesthesia and can be performed in a physician's office. These techniques have reduced the
risk and the cost of medical care.

1. What is the main subject of the passage?

   (A) A revolution in communication
   (B) The invention of optical fibers
   (C) New surgical techniques
   (D) The role of optical fibers in medicine

2. In line 2, the author uses the expression *have opened a window* to indicate that the use of optical fibers

   (A) has enabled scientists to make amazing discoveries
   (B) sometimes requires a surgical incision
   (C) allows doctors to see inside the body without major surgery
   (D) has been unknown to the general public until quite recently

3. Which of the following is closest in meaning to the word *formerly* in line 5?

   (A) Previously
   (B) Completely
   (C) Usually
   (D) Theoretically

4. The word *them* in line 5 refers to

   (A) optical fibers
   (B) pathways
   (C) other areas of the body
   (D) physicians

5. According to the passage, what is the purpose of the illuminating bundle in a fiberscope?

   (A) To carry light into the body
   (B) To collect and focus light
   (C) To reconstruct images
   (D) To perform surgery inside the body

6. Which of the following is closest in meaning to the word *cores* in line 8?

   (A) Tips
   (B) Centers
   (C) Clusters
   (D) Lines

7. According to the passage, how do the fiberscopes used today differ from those used five years ago?

   (A) They use brighter lights.
   (B) They are longer.
   (C) They contain more fibers.
   (D) They are larger in diameter.

8. The word *resolution* in line 13 is closest in meaning to which of the following?

   (A) Strength
   (B) Sharpness
   (C) Inconvenience
   (D) Efficiency

9. Which of the following is NOT mentioned by the author as one of the advantages of laser surgery techniques?

   (A) They can be performed in a physician's office.
   (B) They are safer than conventional surgery.
   (C) They can often be performed without anesthesia.
   (D) They are relatively easy to teach to physicians.

10. Where in the passage does the author provide a basic description of a fiberscope?

   (A) Lines 1–2
   (B) Line 6
   (C) Lines 10–11
   (D) Line 14

QUESTIONS 11–18

Line   Alice Walker has written books of poetry and short stories, a biography, and several novels. She is probably best known for her novel *The Color Purple*, published in 1982. The book vividly narrates the richness and complexity of black people—especially black women—in Georgia in the 1920s and 1930s. Although the novel came under bitter attack by certain critics and readers, it was applauded

5   by others and won both the American Book Award and the Pulitzer Prize for fiction. It became a bestseller, selling over 4 million copies, and it was made into a successful film by noted director Steven Spielberg. The novel reveals the horror, drudgery, and joy of black life in rural Georgia. It gets much of its special flavor from its use of the words, rhythm, and grammar of black English and from its epistolary style. Telling a story through letters was a narrative structure commonly used by

10   eighteenth-century novelists, but it is not often used in contemporary fiction. Unlike most epistolary novels, which have the effect of distancing the reader from the events described by the letter writer, *The Color Purple* uses the letter form to draw the reader into absolute intimacy with the poor, uneducated, but wonderfully observant Celie, the main character of the novel. So the reader applauds when Celie, like William Faulkner's character Dilsey, does not simply survive, but prevails.

11. What is the passage mainly about?
    (A) A film by Steven Spielberg
    (B) The life of Alice Walker
    (C) Characters in the novels of William Faulkner
    (D) A book by Alice Walker and reactions to it

12. According to the passage, *The Color Purple* is a book of
    (A) poetry
    (B) criticism
    (C) fiction
    (D) biography

13. The word *vividly* in line 2 is closest in meaning to
    (A) intellectually
    (B) graphically
    (C) surprisingly
    (D) temporarily

14. Which of the following is closest in meaning to the word *drudgery* in line 7?
    (A) Hard work
    (B) Culture
    (C) Uniqueness
    (D) Long history

15. The author mentions eighteenth-century novelists (line 10) because
    (A) their books, like *The Color Purple*, made use of the epistolary style
    (B) *The Color Purple* is based on episodes in their books
    (C) their novels have a sense of absolute intimacy
    (D) their books, like those of Alice Walker, were attacked by critics but enjoyed by readers

16. Why does the author mention Dilsey in line 14?
    (A) He is a main character in *The Color Purple*.
    (B) He is similar to Celie in one way.
    (C) He is the person on whom Celie was based.
    (D) He wrote a book somewhat similar to *The Color Purple*.

17. The word *prevails* in line 14 is closest in meaning to
    (A) changes
    (B) resists
    (C) triumphs
    (D) impresses

18. The attitude of the author toward *The Color Purple* is best described as one of
    (A) admiration
    (B) alarm
    (C) indifference
    (D) anger

QUESTIONS 19–30

Line   Many flowering plants woo insect pollinators and gently direct them to their most fertile blossoms by changing the color of individual flowers from day to day. Through color cues, the plant signals to the insect that it would be better off visiting one flower on its bush than another. The particular hue tells the pollinator that the flower is full of far more pollen than are neighboring blooms. That nectar-rich
5   flower also happens to be fertile and ready to disperse its pollen or to receive pollen the insect has picked up from another flower. Plants do not have to spend precious resources maintaining reservoirs of nectar in all their flowers. Thus, the color-coded communication system benefits both plant and insect.

    For example, on the lantana plant, a flower starts out on the first day as yellow, when it is rich
10   with pollen and nectar. Influenced by an as-yet-unidentified environmental signal, the flower changes color by triggering the production of the pigment anthromyacin. It turns orange on the second day and red on the third. By the third day, it has no pollen to offer insects and is no longer fertile. On any given lantana bush, only 10 to 15 percent of the blossoms are likely to be yellow and fertile. But in tests measuring the responsiveness of butterflies, it was discovered that the insects visited the
15   yellow flowers at least 100 times more than would be expected from haphazard visitation. Experiments with paper flowers and painted flowers demonstrated that the butterflies were responding to color cues rather than, say, the scent of the nectar.

    In other types of plants, blossoms change from white to red, others from yellow to red, and so on. These color changes have been observed in some 74 families of plants.

19. The first paragraph of the passage implies that insects benefit from the color-coded communication system because

   (A) the colors hide them from predators
   (B) they can gather pollen efficiently
   (C) the bright colors attract fertile females
   (D) other insect species cannot understand the code

20. The word *woo* in line 1 is closest in meaning to

   (A) frighten
   (B) trap
   (C) deceive
   (D) attract

21. The word *it* in line 3 refers to

   (A) a plant
   (B) an insect
   (C) a signal
   (D) a blossom

22. The word *hue* in line 3 is closest in meaning to

   (A) smell
   (B) texture
   (C) color
   (D) shape

23. The word *Thus* in line 7 is closest in meaning to which of the following?

   (A) However
   (B) Therefore
   (C) Probably
   (D) Generally

24. Which of the following describes the sequence of color changes that lantana blossoms undergo?

   (A) Red to yellow to white
   (B) White to red
   (C) Yellow to orange to red
   (D) Red to purple

25. The word *triggering* in line 11 is closest in meaning to

   (A) maintaining
   (B) renewing
   (C) limiting
   (D) activating

26. The passage implies that insects would be most attracted to lantana blossoms

   (A) on the first day that they bloom
   (B) when they turn orange
   (C) on the third day that they bloom
   (D) after they produce anthromyacin

27. According to the passage, what is the purpose of the experiments involving paper flowers and painted flowers?

    (A) To strengthen the idea that butterflies are attracted by the smell of flowers
    (B) To prove that flowers do not always need pollen to reproduce
    (C) To demonstrate how insects change color depending on the type of flowers they visit
    (D) To support the idea that insects respond to the changing color of flowers

28. The word *haphazard* in line 15 is closest in meaning to which of the following?

    (A) Dangerous
    (B) Random
    (C) Fortunate
    (D) Expected

29. What is known from the passage about the *other types of plants* mentioned in line 18?

    (A) They follow various sequences of color changes.
    (B) They use scent and other methods of attracting pollinators.
    (C) They have not been studied as thoroughly as the lantana.
    (D) They have exactly the same pigments as the lantana.

30. According to the passage, in approximately how many families of plants has the color-changing phenomenon described in the passage been observed?

    (A) 10
    (B) 15
    (C) 74
    (D) 100

QUESTIONS 31–39

Line   The 1960s, however, saw a rising dissatisfaction with the Modernist movement, especially in North
America where its failings were exposed in two influential books, Jane Jacobs' *The Death and Life of
Great American Cities* in 1961 and Robert Venturi's *Complexity and Contradiction in Architecture*
in 1966. Jacobs highlighted the destruction of the richness of American cities by massive, impersonal
5   buildings. Venturi implied that Modernist structures were without meaning because they lacked the
complexity and intimacy of historical buildings.

    This dissatisfaction was translated into action in 1972 with the demolition of several fourteen-
story Modernist apartment blocks that only twenty years before had won architectural prizes. Similar
housing developments were destroyed elsewhere in North America in the following decades, but it
10   was in St. Louis that the post-Modernist era began.

    Post-Modernist architects have little in common in terms of style or theory. They are united
mainly in their opposition to the Modernist style. Robert Venturi's designs show wit, humanity, and
historical reference. These tendencies can be seen in his bold design for the Tucker House (1975) in
Katonah, New York, and the Brant-Johnson House (1975) in Vail, Colorado, which owes something
15   to the Italian Renaissance. Similar characteristics are apparent in the work of Venturi's disciple
Michael Graves. Graves' Portland Public Service Building (1982) in Portland, Oregon, and his Humana
Tower (1986) in Louisville, Kentucky, have the bulk of skyscrapers but incorporate historical
souvenirs such as colonnades, belvederes, keystones, and decorative sculpture.

    Other post-Modernists rejected the playfulness of Venturi and his group. They chose a more
20   historically faithful classical style, as in Greenberg and Blateau's reception rooms at the U.S. Department of State in Washington, D.C. (1984–86). The most complete instance of historical accuracy is
the J. Paul Getty Museum in Malibu, California (1970–75), designed by Langdon and Wilson. They
relied on archaeological advice to achieve the authentic quality of a Roman villa.

31. With which of the following topics did the paragraph preceding the passage probably deal?

(A) The Modernist movement
(B) Architecture outside North America
(C) A history of post-modernism
(D) Books of the 1950s

32. Which of the following is closest in meaning to the word *highlighted* in line 4?

(A) Celebrated
(B) Denied
(C) Emphasized
(D) Exaggerated

33. The word *they* in line 5 refers to

(A) historical buildings
(B) Venturi and Jacobs
(C) North American cities
(D) Modernist structures

34. According to the passage, what do the two books mentioned in the first paragraph have in common?

(A) They were both written by the same author.
(B) They both lack complexity.
(C) They are both critical of Modernism.
(D) They both outline post-Modernist theory.

35. According to the author, which event signalled the beginning of post-Modernism?

(A) The publication of a book
(B) The building of a housing development
(C) The awarding of a prize
(D) The destruction of some buildings

36. The author mentions that a house designed by Robert Venturi in a style influenced by the Italian Renaissance was built in

(A) Katonah, New York
(B) Vail, Colorado
(C) Portland, Oregon
(D) Louisville, Kentucky

37. Which of the following is closest in meaning to *disciple* in line 15?

(A) Adviser

(B) Follower

(C) Critic

(D) Partner

38. What does the author imply about the Portland Public Service Building and the Humana Building?

(A) They are popular places for tourists to visit and to buy souvenirs.

(B) They have great historical significance.

(C) They feature elements not generally seen in modern buildings.

(D) They are much smaller than most skyscrapers.

39. The J. Paul Getty Museum is given as an example of

(A) a massive, impersonal Modernist building

(B) a faithful reproduction of classical architecture

(C) a typical Malibu structure

(D) playful architecture

Section 2

This section tests your ability to recognize grammar and usage suitable for standard written English. It is divided into two parts, each with its own directions.

STRUCTURE

Directions: Items in this part are incomplete sentences. Following each of these sentences, there are four words or phrases. You should select the *one* word or phrase—(A), (B), (C), or (D)—that best completes the sentence. Then fill in the space on your answer sheet that matches the letter of the answer that you have selected.

Example I

Pepsin _____ an enzyme used in digestion.

(A) that
(B) is
(C) of
(D) being

This sentence should properly read "Pepsin is an enzyme used in digestion." You should fill in (B) on your answer sheet.

Sample Answer

Ⓐ ● Ⓒ Ⓓ

Example II

_____ large natural lakes are found in the state of South Carolina.

(A) There are no
(B) Not the
(C) It is not
(D) No

This sentence should properly read "No large natural lakes are found in the state of South Carolina." You should fill in (D) on your answer sheet. As soon as you understand the directions, begin work on this part.

Sample Answer

Ⓐ Ⓑ Ⓒ ●

WAIT

73

1. Extensive forests, _____, abundant wildlife, and beautiful waterfalls are among the attractions of Glacier National Park.
   - (A) it has spectacular mountain scenery
   - (B) the mountain scenery is spectacular
   - (C) spectacular mountain scenery
   - (D) and the spectacular scenery of the mountains

2. A network of railroads to unite the continent and encourage Western settlement _____ before the Civil War by Asa Whitney.
   - (A) when proposed
   - (B) a proposal
   - (C) was proposed
   - (D) to propose

3. The chief advantage of using satellites to predict weather _____ can survey vast regions of the Earth at one time.
   - (A) they
   - (B) is that they
   - (C) is that
   - (D) that they

4. The small, _____ farms of New England were not appropriate for the Midwest.
   - (A) self-support
   - (B) they supported themselves
   - (C) self-supporting
   - (D) supporting themselves

5. _____ art appreciation is an individual matter, no work of art is ever perceived by two persons in exactly the same way.
   - (A) Since
   - (B) According to
   - (C) Because of
   - (D) Perhaps

6. _____ a black singer and actor, first came to the public's attention for his role in Eugene O'Neill's play *The Emperor Jones*.
   - (A) Paul Robeson was
   - (B) Because Paul Robeson
   - (C) It was Paul Robeson, as
   - (D) Paul Robeson,

7. Dragonflies remain stationary in the air while _____ their prey to come near.
   - (A) waited for
   - (B) they wait
   - (C) waiting for
   - (D) to wait

8. Fiction writer Zona Gale wrote about the small Wisconsin town _____ she grew up, showing both its positive and negative qualities.
   - (A) in which
   - (B) which in
   - (C) which
   - (D) in where

9. A collectible coin _____ in mint condition when it looks as it did when it was made.
   - (A) to be is said
   - (B) said is to be
   - (C) is to be said
   - (D) is said to be

10. Dust storms most often occur in areas where the ground has little vegetation to protect _____ of the wind.
    - (A) from the effects
    - (B) it the effects
    - (C) it from the effects
    - (D) the effects from it

11. _____ of their size and weight, grizzly bears are remarkably nimble animals.
    - (A) Animals
    - (B) For animals
    - (C) As animals
    - (D) To be animals

12. _____ most fruits, cherries must ripen on the vine.
    - (A) Unlikely
    - (B) Different
    - (C) Dislike
    - (D) Unlike

13. _____ who made Thanksgiving an official holiday in the United States.
    - (A) Abraham Lincoln
    - (B) He was Abraham Lincoln
    - (C) Abraham Lincoln was
    - (D) It was Abraham Lincoln

14. The higher _____ octane number of gasoline, the less knocking occurs in the engine as the fuel is burned.
    - (A) some
    - (B) the
    - (C) is
    - (D) than

15. Historian Barbara Tuchman was the first woman _____ president of the Academy of Arts and Sciences.

    (A) whose election as
    (B) to elect
    (C) was elected
    (D) to be elected

16. Although drama is a form of literature, _____ from the other types in the way it is presented.

    (A) it differs
    (B) is different
    (C) despite the difference
    (D) but it is different

17. Not only _____ the most populous city in the United States in 1890, but it had also become the most congested.

    (A) was New York City
    (B) that New York City was
    (C) New York City was
    (D) has New York City

18. In 1989, President George Bush appointed Carla A. Hills _____ a special trade representative.

    (A) to
    (B) as
    (C) like
    (D) be

19. Iguanas are different from most other lizards _____ they are not carnivores.

    (A) in spite of
    (B) even
    (C) so that
    (D) in that

20. _____ are considered humorous is mainly due to his characters' use of slang.

    (A) Damon Runyan's stories
    (B) Damon Runyan's stories, which
    (C) That Damon Runyan's stories
    (D) Because Damon Runyan's stories

21. The spores of ferns are almost microscopic and are far simpler than _____ in structure.

    (A) that of seeds
    (B) so are seeds
    (C) seeds do
    (D) seeds

22. Good pencil erasers are soft enough not _____ paper but hard enough so that they crumble gradually when used.

    (A) by damaging
    (B) so that they damage
    (C) to damage
    (D) damaging

23. _____ the outer rings of a gyroscope are turned or twisted, the gyroscope itself continues to spin in exactly the same position.

    (A) However
    (B) Somehow
    (C) Otherwise
    (D) No matter

WRITTEN EXPRESSION

Directions: The items in this part have four underlined words or phrases. You must identify the *one* underlined expression—(A), (B), (C), or (D)—that must be changed for the sentence to be correct. Then fill in the space on your answer sheet that matches the letter of the answer that you have selected.

Example I

Lenses may to have either concave or convex shapes.
      A   B   C   D

This sentence should read "Lenses may have either concave or convex shapes." You should therefore select answer (A).

Sample Answer

Example II

When painting a fresco, an artist is applied paint directly to the damp plaster of a wall.
     A   B   C   D

This sentence should read "When painting a fresco, an artist applies paint directly to the wet plaster of a wall." You should therefore select answer (B). As soon as you understand the directions, begin work on this part.

Sample Answer

WAIT

24. Alike the United States, Canada conducts a
    A   B
    complete census of its population every ten
    C   D
    years.

25. Natural resources provide the raw material
    A
    are needed to produce finished goods.
    B   C   D

26. Because they are so secretive, blind snakes
    A
    are seldom seen, and its habits are not
    B   C
    well known.
    D

27. The main rotor and tail rotor of a helicopter
    A
    make the same job as the wings, propellers,
    B   C   D
    and rudder of an airplane.

28. X rays are too powerful that they can
    A
    penetrate most solids as easily as light
    B   C
    passes through glass.
    D

29. Machines that use hydraulic pressure
    A
    including elevators, dentist chairs, and
    B   C
    automobile brakes.
    D

30. The Franklin stove, which became common
    A   B
    in the 1780s, burned wood more efficiency
    C
    than an open fireplace.
    D

31. The coastline of Maine is marked by
    A   B
    thousand of islands and inlets.
    C   D

32. Metals can be beaten into thin sheets,
    A   B
    melted and poured into molds, or drawing
    C   D
    into fine wire.

33. Stone Mountain, a huge dome of granite
    A
    near the city of Atlanta, is 1,686 feet height
    B   C
    and measures 7 miles around at its base.
    D

34. Since ancient times, some people wore
    A   B
    amulets, objects that are supposed to give
    C
    the wearer magical powers.
    D

35. Dance notation is a means of recording the
    A   B
    movements of dances by using of special
    C   D
    symbols.

36. Approximately the third of Alaska's
    A
    land area lies north of the Arctic Circle.
    B   C   D

37. No cactus has flowers most beautiful or
    A   B
    fragrant than those of the night-blooming
    C   D
    cereus.

38. The poet Amy Lowell sometimes wrote
    A   B
    literary criticism and biographical.
    C   D

39. Each of the chemical elements have its own
    A   B   C   D
    standard symbol.

40. A balloon rises because of the hot air or gas
    A   B
    inside the balloon is lighter than the air
    C
    outside.
    D

41. Just three years <u>afterwards</u> Martha Graham's
                            A
<u>first</u> dance lesson, <u>she</u> starred <u>in the</u> ballet
  B   C   D
Xochitl.

42. The <u>delicate</u> color of rose quartz is <u>due the</u>
        A   B
<u>presence</u> of manganese in <u>the mineral.</u>
  C   D

43. <u>Most</u> large <u>corporations</u> have personnel
    A
departments <u>responsible to</u> hiring and <u>firing</u>
              B   C
workers and for keeping <u>employee</u> records.
                     D

44. Costume jewelry <u>is made of</u> plastic, wood,
                   A
or <u>inexpensive</u> metal, and <u>they</u> may
   B   C
<u>be set</u> with semiprecious or imitation
  D
stones.

45. The <u>medicine</u> of prehistoric peoples
      A
probably <u>consisted of</u> a mixture of
        B
<u>scientific practices</u>, superstitions, and
       C
religious <u>believes.</u>
       D

46. The <u>sculptors</u> of Louise Nevelson <u>typically</u>
       A   B
consisted of complex <u>arrangements</u> of
                  C
large black wooden boxes.
        D

47. <u>Engineering</u> is a profession <u>who</u> puts
    A   B
<u>scientific</u> knowledge <u>to</u> practical use.
  C   D

48. Fire blight, <u>a common</u> disease of <u>apples</u> and
          A   B
pear trees, can sometimes <u>be controlled</u>
                    C
<u>with</u> an antibiotic spray.
  D

49. Radio stations <u>at which</u> broadcast
            A
<u>only news</u> first <u>appeared</u> <u>in the</u> 1970s.
  B   C   D

50. Newspaper <u>editor</u> James G. Bennett
        A
believed that the journalist's task was

<u>not merely</u> <u>to inform</u> readers but to startle
 B   C
them <u>as well as.</u>
    D

51. In the tundra regions of North America,
   A
the change from summer <u>to winter</u> occurs
   B   C
very <u>sudden.</u>
    D

52. Natural bridges of stone are formed <u>the</u>
             A   B
action of water or <u>wind-driven</u> sand.
        C   D

53. In *Babbitt* and <u>other novels</u>, Sinclair Lewis
             A
presented <u>critical</u> portraits of middle-class
       B
Americans <u>who thought</u> of <u>them</u> as model
        C   D
citizens.

54. Quite <u>logically</u>, <u>nearly all</u> early roads
     A   B
followed <u>course</u> of <u>river valleys.</u>
      C   D

55. The plants of the desert are so

<u>spaced widely</u> <u>because of</u> a scarcity of
  A   B
water that there is <u>little or no</u> competition
                 C
for water <u>among them.</u>
       D

56. Drowsiness is one <u>symptom</u> of hypother-
              A
mia, <u>the extreme</u> <u>lost</u> of <u>body heat.</u>
    B   C   D

57. A globe <u>presents</u> a picture of <u>the Earth</u> with
      A   B
<u>practically</u> <u>not</u> distortions.
  C   D

58. It is about 125 years for the cedar tree to
      A   B
reach its full height.
       C   D

59. Compared to those of animals, the fossil
        A   B
record for plants is quite sketchy.
            C   D

60. Life that we know it is based on the
           A   B   C
element carbon.
   D

THIS IS THE END OF SECTION 2.

IF YOU FINISH BEFORE THE TIME LIMIT, CHECK YOUR WORK ON SECTION 2 ONLY.

DO NOT READ OR WORK ON ANY OTHER SECTION OF THE TEST.

Section 3

READING COMPREHENSION
TIME—80 MINUTES

This section of the test measures your ability to comprehend written materials.

Directions: This section contains several passages, each followed by a number of questions. Read the passages and, for each question, choose the *one* best answer—(A), (B), (C), or (D)—based on what is stated in the passage or on what can be inferred from the passage. Then fill in the space on your answer sheet that matches the letter of the answer that you have selected.

Read the Following Passage

Line   Like mammals, birds claim their own territories. A bird's territory may be small or large. Some birds claim only their nest and the area right around it, while others claim far larger territories that include their feeding areas. Gulls, penguins, and other waterfowl nest in huge colonies, but even in the biggest colonies, each male and his mate have small territories of their own
5   immediately around their nests.
       Male birds defend their territory chiefly against other males of the same species. In some cases, a warning call or threatening pose may be all the defense needed, but in other cases, intruders may refuse to leave peacefully.

Example I

What is the main topic of this passage?

(A) Birds that live in colonies
(B) Birds' mating habits
(C) The behavior of birds
(D) Territoriality in birds

The passage mainly concerns the territories of birds. You should fill in (D) on your answer sheet.

Sample Answer

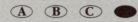

Example II

According to the passage, male birds defend their territory primarily against

(A) Female birds
(B) Birds of other species
(C) Males of their own species
(D) Mammals

The passage states that "Male birds defend their territory chiefly against other males of the same species." You should fill in (C) on your answer sheet. As soon as you understand the directions, begin work on this section.

Sample Answer

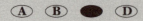

QUESTIONS 1–11

Line Lighthouses are towers with strong lights that help mariners plot their position, inform them that land is near, and warn them of dangerous rocks and reefs. They are placed at prominent points on the coast and on islands, reefs, and sandbars.

Every lighthouse has a distinctive pattern of light known as its characteristic. There are five
5 basic characteristics: fixed, flashing, occulting, group flashing, and group occulting. A fixed signal is a steady beam. A flashing signal has periods of darkness longer than periods of light, while an occulting signal's periods of light are longer. A group-flashing light gives off two or more flashes at regular intervals, and a group-occulting signal consists of a fixed light with two or more periods of darkness at regular intervals. Some lighthouses use lights of different colors as well, and today, most light-
10 houses are also equipped with radio beacons. The three types of apparatus used to produce the signals are the catoptric, in which metal is used to reflect the light; the dioptric, in which glass is used; and the catadioptric, in which both glass and metal are used.

In the daytime, lighthouses can usually be identified by their structure alone. The most typical structure is a tower tapering at the top, but some, such as the Bastion Lighthouse on the Saint
15 Lawrence River, are shaped like pyramids, and others, such as the Race Rock Light, look like wooden houses sitting on high platforms. Still others, such as the American Shoal Lighthouse off the Florida Coast, are skeletal towers of steel. Where lighthouses might be confused in daylight, they can be distinguished by day-marker patterns—designs of checks and stripes painted in vivid colors on lighthouse walls.

20 In the past, the job of lighthouse keeper was lonely and difficult, if somewhat romantic. Lighthouse keepers put in hours of tedious work maintaining the lights. Today, lighthouses are almost entirely automated with humans supplying only occasional maintenance. Because of improvements in navigational technology, the importance of lighthouses has diminished. There are only about 340 functioning lighthouses in existence in the United States today, compared to about 1,500 in 1900,
25 and there are only about 1,400 functioning lighthouses outside the United States. Some decommissioned lighthouses have been preserved as historical monuments.

1. Which of the following is NOT mentioned in the passage as one of the functions of lighthouses?

(A) To help sailors determine their location
(B) To warn of danger from rocks and reefs
(C) To notify sailors that bad weather is approaching
(D) To indicate that land is near

2. The word *their* in line 1 refers to

(A) mariners'
(B) lighthouses'
(C) dangers'
(D) lights'

3. The word *prominent* in line 2 is closest in meaning to

(A) dangerous
(B) conspicuous
(C) picturesque
(D) famous

4. In the context of this passage, the author uses the term *characteristic* (line 4) to refer to a

(A) period of darkness
(B) person who operates a lighthouse
(C) pattern painted on a lighthouse
(D) distinctive light signal

5. According to the passage, what kind of signal has long periods of light that are regularly broken by two or more periods of darkness?

(A) Group occulting
(B) Flashing
(C) Occulting
(D) Group flashing

6. According to the passage, a catoptric apparatus is one that uses

(A) lights of various colors
(B) metal
(C) glass
(D) a radio beacon

7. For which of the following does the author NOT provide a specific example in the third paragraph?

   (A) A lighthouse shaped like a pyramid
   (B) A lighthouse made of steel
   (C) A lighthouse with day-marker patterns
   (D) A lighthouse that resembles a house on a platform

8. The word *tapering* in line 14 is closest in meaning to which of the following?

   (A) Narrowing
   (B) Soaring
   (C) Opening
   (D) Rotating

9. It can be concluded from the passage that lighthouses with day-marker patterns would most likely be found in areas where

   (A) the weather is frequently bad
   (B) the structures themselves cannot be easily seen by passing mariners
   (C) there are not many lighthouses
   (D) there are a number of lighthouses with similar structures

10. The author implies that, compared to those of the past, contemporary lighthouses

    (A) employ more powerful lights
    (B) require less maintenance
    (C) are more difficult to operate
    (D) are more romantic

11. There is information in the fourth paragraph to support which of these statements?

    (A) There are more lighthouses in the United States now than there were in 1900.
    (B) There are more lighthouses in the United States today than in any other single country.
    (C) There are more functioning lighthouses in the United States today than there are lighthouses preserved as historical monuments.
    (D) There were more lighthouses in the United States in 1900 than there are elsewhere in the world today.

QUESTIONS 12–23

Line   Although both Luther Burbank and George Washington Carver drastically changed American agriculture and were close friends besides, their methods of working could hardly have been more dissimilar. Burbank's formal education ended with high school, but he was inspired by the works of Charles Darwin. In 1872, on his farm near Lunenberg, Massachusetts, he produced his first "plant cre-

5   ation"—a superior potato developed from the Early Rose variety. It still bears his name. After moving to Santa Rosa, California, in 1875, Burbank created a stream of creations, earning the nickname "the plant wizard." He developed new varieties of fruits, vegetables, flowers, and other plants, many of which are still economically important. He began his work some thirty years before the rediscovery of Gregor Mendel's work on heredity, and while he did not participate in the developing science of

10   plant genetics, his work opened the country's eyes to the productive possibilities of plant breeding. However, the value of his contributions was diminished by his methods. He relied on his keen memory and powers of observation and kept records only for his own use. He thus thwarted attempts by other scientists to study his achievements.

     Carver, on the other hand, was a careful researcher who took thorough notes. Born a slave, he

15   attended high school in Kansas, Simpson College in Iowa, and Iowa State College, which awarded him a master's degree. When the eminent black educator Booker T. Washington offered him a position at Tuskegee Institute in Alabama, he accepted. While Burbank concentrated on developing new plants, Carver found new uses for existing ones. He produced hundreds of synthetic products made from the soybean, the sweet potato, and especially the peanut, helping to free Southern agriculture from the tyranny of cotton.

12. What is the author's main purpose in writing the passage?

(A) To compare the products created by two agricultural scientists

(B) To demonstrate how Carver and Burbank influenced American agriculture

(C) To contrast the careers and methods of two scientists

(D) To explain how Charles Darwin inspired both Carver and Burbank

13. The word *drastically* in line 1 is closest in meaning to

(A) dramatically

(B) initially

(C) unintentionally

(D) potentially

14. According to the passage, which of the following best describes the relationship between Burbank and Carver?

(A) They were competitors.

(B) Carver was one of Burbank's teachers.

(C) Burbank invited Carver to work with him.

(D) They were personal friends.

15. It can be inferred that Burbank's first "plant creation" is known as the

(A) Early Rose potato

(B) Burbank potato

(C) Lunenberg potato

(D) Wizard potato

16. The word *his* in line 10 refers to

(A) George Washington Carver's

(B) Gregor Mendel's

(C) Luther Burbank's

(D) Charles Darwin's

17. Which of the following is closest in meaning to the word *thwarted* in line 12?

(A) Restored

(B) Predated

(C) Nurtured

(D) Defeated

18. The word *thorough* in line 14 is closest in meaning to

(A) complete

(B) general

(C) puzzling

(D) precise

19. The author implies that a significant difference between the techniques of Burbank and those of Carver is that

    (A) while Carver kept careful research records, Burbank did not
    (B) Carver popularized his achievements, but those of Burbank were relatively unknown
    (C) unlike Burbank, Carver concentrated mainly on developing new varieties of plants
    (D) Burbank bred both plants and animals, but Carver worked only with plants

20. According to the passage, what school awarded Carver a master's degree?

    (A) Simpson College
    (B) Iowa State College
    (C) Tuskegee Institute
    (D) The University of Alabama

21. Carver developed new uses for all of the following crops EXCEPT

    (A) cotton
    (B) soybeans
    (C) peanuts
    (D) sweet potatoes

22. The word *tyranny* in line 20 is closest in meaning to

    (A) history
    (B) dependence
    (C) control
    (D) unreliability

23. At what point in the passage does the author focus on Burbank's weaknesses as a researcher?

    (A) Lines 3–4
    (B) Lines 5–7
    (C) Line 11
    (D) Lines 16–17

QUESTIONS 24–36

Line Visitors to Prince Edward Island, Canada, delight in the "unspoiled" scenery—the well-kept farms and peaceful hamlets of the island's central core and the rougher terrain of the east and west. In reality, the Island ecosystems are almost entirely artificial.

5   Islanders have been tampering with the natural environment since the eighteenth century and long ago broke down the Island's natural forest cover to exploit its timber and clear land for agriculture. By 1900, 80 percent of the forest had been cut down and much of what remained had been destroyed by disease. Since then, however, some farmland has been abandoned and has returned to forest through the invasion of opportunist species, notably spruce. Few examples of the original climax forest, which consisted mostly of broadleaved trees such as maple, birch, and oak, survive

10   today.

       Apart from a few stands of native forest, the only authentic habitats on Prince Edward Island are its sand dunes and salt marshes. The dunes are formed from sand washed ashore by waves and then dried and blown by the wind to the land beyond the beach. The sand is prevented from spreading farther by marram grass, a tall, long-rooted species that grows with the dunes and keeps them

15   remarkably stable. Marram grass acts as a windbreak and allows other plants such as beach pea and bayberry to take hold. On dunes where marram grass is broken down—for instance, where it is trampled—the dunes may spread inland and inundate agricultural lands or silt up fishing harbors. The white dunes of the north coast are the most impressive. There are also white dunes on the east and west coasts. Only in the south are there red dunes, created when the soft sandstone cliffs crumble

20   into the sea and subsequently wash ashore as red sand. The dunes were once used as cattle pasture but were abandoned as the early settlers moved inland.

       Salt marshes are the second remaining authentic habitat. These bogs are the result of the flooding of low coastal areas during unusually high tides. In the intervals between tides, a marsh area remains and plants take root, notably cord grass, the "marsh hay" used by the early settlers as winter

25   forage for their livestock. Like the dunes, though, the marshes were soon dismissed as wasteland and escaped development.

24. On what aspect of Prince Edward Island does the author focus?

(A) Its tourist industry
(B) Its beaches
(C) Its natural habitats
(D) Its agriculture

25. Why does the author use quotation marks around the word *unspoiled* in line 1?

(A) He is quoting from another author.
(B) The scenery is not as attractive as it once was.
(C) The scenery looks unspoiled but is not.
(D) He disagrees with the ideas in this paragraph.

26. The word *hamlets* in line 2 in closest in meaning to

(A) villages
(B) forests
(C) rivers
(D) pastures

27. The phrase *tampering with* in line 4 is closest in meaning to

(A) preserving
(B) interfering with
(C) remembering
(D) dealing with

28. What can be inferred about Prince Edward Island's forests?

(A) Only a few small stands of trees still exist.
(B) They are more extensive than they were in 1900.
(C) They are virtually the same as they were in the eighteenth century.
(D) About 80 percent of the island is covered by them.

29. Which of the following type of tree is most common in the forests of Prince Edward Island today?

(A) Oak
(B) Birch
(C) Spruce
(D) Maple

30. What does the author say about beach pea and bayberry?

 (A) They have become commercially important plants.
 (B) They grow on dunes after marram grass is established.
 (C) They were once an important food crop for early settlers.
 (D) They are spreading across the Island, destroying important crops.

31. According to the passage, what effect does the destruction of marram grass have?

 (A) It permits the sand dunes to cover farmland.
 (B) It creates better conditions for fishing.
 (C) It allows seawater to flood agricultural land.
 (D) It lets the sand wash into the sea.

32. The word *trampled* in line 17 is closest in meaning to

 (A) ripped up
 (B) flooded
 (C) stepped on
 (D) burned

33. Which of the following words in paragraph 4 is given as a synonym for the word *marshes* (line 22)?

 (A) Tides
 (B) Plants
 (C) Bogs
 (D) Settlers

34. According to the passage, in which part of Prince Edward Island are red sand dunes found?

 (A) The north
 (B) The east
 (C) The south
 (D) The west

35. What conclusion can be drawn from the passage about both the sand dunes and salt marshes of Prince Edward Island?

 (A) They have never been used.
 (B) They were once used but have long since been abandoned.
 (C) They have been used continuously since the island was first settled.
 (D) They were long unused but have recently been exploited.

36. In which of these paragraphs does the author discuss the destruction of an ecosystem?

 (A) The first
 (B) The second
 (C) The third
 (D) The fourth

QUESTIONS 37–44

Line   Lichens may grow on the bark of a tree in a steaming tropical rain forest, on the bricks of big-city buildings on rocks in hot springs, on wind-swept mountain tops, and in the driest desserts. In the Arctic, they provide the principal food for caribou, and they are one of the few plants that grow in Antarctica. They are pioneers, appearing in barren rocky areas and starting the formation of soil in
5   which mosses, then ferns, and then other plants can take root.

Lichens are a partnership of two plants—fungi and algae. The lichen body is made up of a network of fungal strands. In the upper layers of these grow groups of algae. The two organisms live together to the benefit of both, a relationship known as symbiosis. The fungi provide support, absorb water, and shelter the tender algae from direct sunlight. The algae carry on photosynthesis and
10   provide the fungi with food. The algae can live independently and are recognizable as a species that grows alone. The fungi, on the other hand, cannot live apart from their partners. They can be placed in known classes of fungi but are unlike any species that live independently.

So definite are the form, color, and characteristics of these double organisms that for hundreds of years, they were classified as one. More than 15,000 "species" were named. If these organisms are
15   classified as separate species, it is difficult to fit them into the existing system of classification. But if they are classified separately, these species of fungi seem rather strange. Lichens are a splendid example of the difficulties faced by taxonomists in classifying species.

37. What does the author imply about lichens in the first paragraph?

(A)   They require a lot of moisture to live.
(B)   They primarily live in cold places.
(C)   They can live anywhere except around people.
(D)   They have adapted to a wide variety of environments.

38. Why does the author call lichens *pioneers* (line 4)?

(A)   Because they developed so early in the history of the planet
(B)   Because of their primitive structure
(C)   Because they prepare soil for other plants
(D)   Because they were the first plants to live in Antarctica

39. The word *barren* in line 4 is closest in meaning to

(A)   lifeless
(B)   frigid
(C)   jagged
(D)   uncovered

40. Which of the following is an example of symbiosis as it is described in the second paragraph?

(A)   Certain types of tall grass conceal tigers because of the tigers' striped markings.
(B)   Fish called remoras attach themselves to sharks and eat the scraps of the sharks' meals.
(C)   Mistletoe, a type of shrub, grows on trees and harms them by extracting water and nutrients.
(D)   Protozoa in the intestines of termites digest the cellulose that the termites eat, and their waste products nourish the termites.

41. Which of the following can be inferred about the effect of direct sunlight on lichens?

(A)   It damages the algae.
(B)   It helps the fungi absorb water.
(C)   It is required for the algae to carry on photosynthesis.
(D)   It destroys the fungi.

42. Why does the author say that "these species of fungi seem rather strange" (line 16)?

(A)   They are larger than typical fungi.
(B)   Unlike other fungi, they can produce their own food.
(C)   They exist only as partners of algae.
(D)   They do not fit into any known class of fungi.

43. Which of the following best expresses the main idea of the second paragraph?

(A) Because of their characteristics as double organisms, it is difficult to classify lichens.

(B) Over 15,000 varieties of lichens have been identified.

(C) Double organisms should always be classified as separate species.

(D) Taxonomists always find it difficult to classify new species of plants.

44. The word *splendid* in line 16 is closest in meaning to

(A) unique

(B) improbable

(C) excellent

(D) famous

QUESTIONS 45–53

Line Fifty-five delegates representing all thirteen states except Rhode Island attended the Constitutional Convention in Philadelphia from May to September 1787. The delegates had been instructed by the Continental Congress to revise the old Articles of Confederation, but most believed that a stronger central government was needed. There were differences, however, about what structure the govern-

5   ment should take and how much influence large states should have.

Virginia was by far the most populous state, with twice as many people as New York, four times as many as New Jersey, and ten times as many as Delaware. The leader of the Virginia delegation, James Madison, had already drawn up a plan for government, which became known as the Large State Plan. Its essence was that congressional representation would be based on population. It

10 provided for two or more national executives. The smaller states feared that under this plan, a few large states would lord over the rest. New Jersey countered with the Small State Plan. It provided for equal representation for all states in a national legislature and for a single national executive. Angry debate, heightened by a stifling heat wave, led to deadlock.

A cooling of tempers seemed to come with lower temperatures. The delegates hammered out

15 an agreement known as the Great Compromise—actually a bundle of shrewd compromises. They decided that Congress would consist of two houses. The larger states were granted representation based on population in the lower house, the House of Representatives. The smaller states were given equal representation in the upper house, the Senate, in which each state would have two senators regardless of population. It was also agreed that there would be a single executive, the president.

20 This critical compromise broke the logjam, and from then on, success seemed within reach.

45. What is the main topic of this passage?

(A) James Madison's plan to create a stable structure for the government of the United States

(B) A disagreement at the Constitutional Convention and a subsequent compromise

(C) The differences in population and relative power between the original states

(D) The most important points of the Small State Plan

46. According to the passage, how many states were represented at the Constitutional Convention?

(A) Twelve
(B) Thirteen
(C) Fourteen
(D) Fifty-five

47. It can be inferred from the passage that the Articles of Confederation

(A) were supported by a majority of the delegates at the Convention

(B) were revised and presented as the Large State Plan

(C) allowed small states to dominate large ones

(D) provided for only a weak central government

48. According to the passage, in 1787 which of the following states had the FEWEST people?

(A) Virginia
(B) Delaware
(C) New York
(D) New Jersey

49. In line 10, the phrase *this plan* refers to

(A) the Small State Plan
(B) a plan suggested by the national legislature
(C) the Large State Plan
(D) a compromise plan

50. According to the passage, the weather had what effect on the Constitutional Convention?

(A) Hot weather intensified the debate while cooler weather brought compromise.

(B) Bad weather prevented some of the delegates from reaching Philadelphia.

(C) Delegates hurried to achieve an agreement before winter arrived.

(D) Cold temperatures made Independence Hall an uncomfortable place to work.

51. The word *shrewd* in line 15 is closest in meaning to

(A) practical

(B) unfair

(C) important

(D) clever

52. Which of the following is NOT given in the passage as one of the provisions of the Great Compromise?

(A) There would be only one national executive.

(B) The president would be elected by popular vote.

(C) Each state would have two senators.

(D) Congress would be divided into two bodies.

53. The author uses the phrase *broke the logjam* (line 20) to indicate that

(A) the government was nearly bankrupt

(B) some major problems had been solved

(C) the Convention came to a sudden end

(D) the situation had become desperate

QUESTIONS 54–60

Line   Wood has long been a popular building material in North America because it has generally been
plentiful and cheap. Swedish settlers in Delaware built log cabins as early as the 1630s. In New
England, British colonists built wooden "saltbox houses." Most of the wooden homes of Colonial
times could be built with simple tools and minimal skills.

5   In the early nineteenth century, the standard wooden house was built with beams set into
heavy posts and held together with wooden pegs. This method of construction was time consuming
and required highly skilled workers with special tools. The balloon-frame house, invented in 1833 in
Chicago by a carpenter from Hartford, Connecticut, used a framework of lightweight lumber, mostly
2 × 4 and 2 × 6 inches. This type of house could be assembled by any careful worker who could saw
10   in a straight line and drive a nail.
           This revolution in building was made possible by improved sawmills that could quickly cut
boards to standard sizes and the lower cost of lumber that resulted. There were also new machines
that could produce huge quantities of inexpensive nails. Skeptics predicted that a strong wind would
send such houses flying through the air like balloons and, at first "balloon frame" was a term of
15   derision. But the light frames proved practical, and wooden houses have been basically built this way
ever since.

54. What is the main purpose of this passage?

(A) To trace the influence of Swedish and
British settlers on American styles of
building
(B) To stress the importance of wood as a
building material
(C) To compare methods of constructing
wooden houses in various parts of the
country
(D) To describe a revolutionary technique
for constructing wooden houses

55. According to the passage, where did the
inventor of the balloon-frame house
originally come from?

(A) Connecticut
(B) Chicago
(C) Sweden
(D) Delaware

56. Which of the following questions about the
balloon-frame house is NOT answered in
the passage?

(A) Where was it invented?
(B) What was its inventor's name?
(C) What size was most of the lumber
used in its framework?
(D) In what year was it invented?

57. The author implies that which of the
following types of houses required the most
skill to produce?

(A) The log cabins built by Swedish
settlers
(B) Saltbox houses
(C) Standard wooden houses of the early
nineteenth century
(D) Balloon-frame houses

58. All of the following are factors in the
development of the balloon-frame house
EXCEPT

(A) the invention of sophisticated tools
(B) the production of cheap nails
(C) improvements in sawmills
(D) the falling price of lumber

59. According to the passage, why was the
term *balloon frame* (line 7) applied to
certain houses?

(A) They could be moved from place to
place.
(B) They could be easily expanded.
(C) They had rounded frames that slightly
resembled balloons.
(D) They were made of lightweight
materials.

60. The word *derision* in line 15 is closest in
meaning to

(A) affection
(B) ignorance
(C) ridicule
(D) regret

QUESTIONS 61–70

Line   Rachel Carson was born in 1907 in Springsdale, Pennsylvania. She studied biology in college and zoology at Johns Hopkins University, where she received her master's degree in 1933. In 1936, she was hired by the U.S. Fish and Wildlife Service, where she worked most of her life.

5   Carson's first book, *Under the Sea Wind,* was published in 1941. It received excellent reviews, but sales were poor until it was reissued in 1952. In that year, she published *The Sea Around Us,* which provided a fascinating look beneath the ocean's surface, emphasizing human history as well as geology and marine biology. Her imagery and language had a poetic quality. Carson consulted no less than 1,000 printed sources. She had voluminous correspondence and frequent discussions with experts in the field. However, she always realized the limitations of her nontechnical readers.

10   In 1962, Carson published *Silent Spring,* a book that sparked considerable controversy. It proved how much harm was done by the uncontrolled, reckless use of insecticides. She detailed how they poison the food supply of animals, kill birds and fish, and contaminate human food. At the time, spokesmen for the chemical industry mounted personal attacks against Carson and issued propaganda to indicate that her findings were flawed. However, her work was vindicated by a 1963 report of the

15   President's Science Advisory Committee.

61. The passage mainly discusses Rachel Carson's work

(A) as a researcher
(B) at college
(C) at the U.S. Fish and Wildlife Service
(D) as a writer

62. According to the passage, what did Carson primarily study at Johns Hopkins University?

(A) Oceanography
(B) History
(C) Literature
(D) Zoology

63. When she published her first book, Carson was closest to the age of

(A) 26
(B) 29
(C) 34
(D) 45

64. It can be inferred from the passage that in 1952, Carson's book *Under the Sea Wind*

(A) was outdated
(B) became more popular than her other books
(C) was praised by critics
(D) sold many copies

65. Which of the following was NOT mentioned in the passage as a source of information for *The Sea Around Us*?

(A) Printed matter
(B) Talks with experts
(C) A research expedition
(D) Letters from scientists

66. Which of the following words or phrases is LEAST accurate in describing *The Sea Around Us*?

(A) Highly technical
(B) Poetic
(C) Fascinating
(D) Well researched

67. The word *reckless* in line 11 is closest in meaning to

(A) unnecessary
(B) limited
(C) continuous
(D) irresponsible

68. According to the passage, *Silent Spring* is primarily

(A) an attack on the use of chemical preservatives in food
(B) a discussion of the hazards insects pose to the food supply
(C) a warning about the dangers of misusing insecticides
(D) an illustration of the benefits of the chemical industry

69. Which of the following is closest in meaning to the word *flawed* in line 14?

(A) Faulty
(B) Deceptive
(C) Logical
(D) Offensive

70. Why does the author of the passage mention the report of the President's Science Advisory Committee (line 15)?

(A) To provide an example of government propaganda
(B) To support Carson's ideas
(C) To indicate a growing government concern with the environment
(D) To validate the chemical industry's claims

THIS IS THE END OF SECTION 3.

IF YOU FINISH BEFORE THE TIME LIMIT, CHECK YOUR WORK ON SECTION 3 ONLY.

DO NOT READ OR WORK ON ANY OTHER SECTION OF THE TEST.

Practice Test 4

Section 1

This section tests your ability to comprehend spoken English. It is divided into three parts, each with its own directions. During actual exams, you are not permitted to turn the page during the reading of the directions or to take notes at any time.

PART A

Directions: Each item in this part consists of a brief conversation involving two speakers. Following each conversation, a third voice will ask a question. You will hear the conversations and questions only once, and they will *not* be written out.

When you have heard each conversation and question, read the four answer choices and select the *one*—(A), (B), (C), or (D)—that best answers the question based on what is directly stated or on what can be inferred. Then fill in the space on your answer sheet that matches the letter of the answer that you have selected.

Here is an example.

You will hear:

You will read:
  (A) Open the window.
  (B) Move the chair.
  (C) Leave the room.
  (D) Take a seat.

From the conversation you find out that the woman thinks the man should put the chair over by the window. The best answer to the question "What does the woman think the man should do?" is (B), "Move the chair." You should fill in (B) on your answer sheet.

Sample Answer

 Ⓐ ● Ⓒ Ⓓ

 WAIT

97

1. (A) He wants to know how Donna feels.
   (B) Maybe Donna can organize the slide show.
   (C) He wants to know what present Donna got.
   (D) Donna has already seen the show.

2. (A) Make some tea.
   (B) Wash out a cup.
   (C) Get the key.
   (D) Clean the spoon.

3. (A) He hasn't been alone lately.
   (B) He hasn't been here recently.
   (C) He has been acting strangely.
   (D) He has to be reminded several times.

4. (A) She will do anything but play golf.
   (B) She seldom wants to do anything.
   (C) She never plays, but she'd like to.
   (D) She is an enthusiastic golfer.

5. (A) It's too hot to eat.
   (B) There's not enough of it.
   (C) He doesn't like the way it tastes.
   (D) He thinks it's too cool.

6. (A) The merchandise is in storage.
   (B) That store sells fine housewares.
   (C) No one knows where the store is.
   (D) The goods are upstairs somewhere.

7. (A) She finds reading poetry rewarding.
   (B) She made some beautiful pottery.
   (C) She wrote some award-winning poems.
   (D) She is now writing for a newspaper.

8. (A) They were free.
   (B) He's going to give them away.
   (C) They were inexpensive.
   (D) He has to return them soon

9. (A) He repaired her guitar.
   (B) He sold her a new guitar.
   (C) He has a better guitar now.
   (D) He's a good guitarist.

10. (A) He isn't going out today.
    (B) The wind is dying down.
    (C) He thinks today is Wednesday.
    (D) The wind is strong today.

11. (A) His picture appears on the book.
    (B) His photographs are in the box.
    (C) He autographed the new book.
    (D) His new book is very interesting.

12. (A) He didn't understand the manual.
    (B) The electricity has gone off.
    (C) He couldn't find the manual.
    (D) The printer is out of order.

13. (A) She's not home now.
    (B) He's not sure if she's there.
    (C) She's talking on another phone.
    (D) He can see her.

14. (A) Forget about the concert.
    (B) Spend some time practicing.
    (C) Find a new place to live.
    (D) Go to another concert.

15. (A) He didn't like mathematics.
    (B) He'll be a great mathematician someday.
    (C) He's no longer studying mathematics.
    (D) He was failing mathematics.

16. (A) Anger.
    (B) Surprise.
    (C) Confusion.
    (D) Happiness.

17. (A) She couldn't get dinner reservations.
    (B) She didn't need reservations for dinner.
    (C) She was the last person to arrive at the restaurant.
    (D) She had made reservations for dinner a long time ago.

18. (A) Go to a lecture.
    (B) Call her sister.
    (C) Attend a planning meeting.
    (D) Go bowling.

19. (A) Where he went to buy the camcorder.
    (B) How much a good used camcorder costs.
    (C) What condition the camcorder is in.
    (D) How many days he's had his camcorder.

20. (A) She should wear her old glasses.
    (B) Her headaches will soon disappear.
    (C) She ought to take off her glasses.
    (D) Her glasses look a little like his.

21. (A) He paid it today for the first time.
    (B) He pays it after it's due.
    (C) He pays it on the last day of the month.
    (D) He's planning to pay it tomorrow.

22. (A) She'll be home on time.
    (B) She was late for work.
    (C) She's working overtime.
    (D) She missed work again.

23. (A) The man must wait before taking it.
    (B) The second half is even more difficult.
    (C) The man should take only the first half.
    (D) It's not as hard as the man thinks.

24. (A) She only read it two times.
    (B) She doesn't understand it.
    (C) She likes it very much.
    (D) She has dozens of copies.

25. (A) Make an important discovery.
    (B) Perform an experiment with penicillin.
    (C) Study something other than biology.
    (D) Discover a substitute for penicillin.

26. (A) A lot of people attended.
    (B) The debate involved only a few issues.
    (C) Many people changed their plans.
    (D) The debate lasted a long time.

27. (A) Order a meal.
    (B) Write a check.
    (C) Look for the waiter.
    (D) Get the waiter's atttention.

28. (A) She will probably win.
    (B) She hasn't improved her game recently.
    (C) No one ever sees her on the court.
    (D) She doesn't think she can win.

29. (A) They couldn't finish cleaning in time.
    (B) They helped her clean the apartment.
    (C) They didn't have much cleaning to do.
    (D) They had to work and couldn't clean.

30. (A) After class today.
    (B) After today's meeting.
    (C) Before class on Friday.
    (D) After class on Friday.

PART B

Directions: This part of the test consists of extended conversations between two speakers. After each of these conversations there are a number of questions. You will hear each conversation and question only once, and the questions are *not* written out.

When you have heard each questions, read the four answer choices and select the *one*—(A), (B), (C), or (D)—that best answers the question based on what is directly stated or on what can be inferred. Then fill in the space on your answer sheet that matches the letter of the answer that you have selected.

Don't forget: During actual exams, taking notes or writing in your test book is *not* permitted.

31. (A) A multiple-choice exam.
(B) A chemistry exam.
(C) An essay exam.
(D) A geology exam.

32. (A) Its relative hardness.
(B) Its true color.
(C) Its chemical composition.
(D) Its relative purity.

33. (A) They are never effective.
(B) They are simple to perform.
(C) They are not always conclusive.
(D) They are usually undependable.

34. (A) Flight attendant.
(B) Rental-car agent.
(C) Hotel manager.
(D) Travel agent.

35. (A) Miami.
(B) Minneapolis.
(C) Key West.
(D) Chicago.

36. (A) A hotel room.
(B) A flight to Chicago.
(C) A rental car.
(D) A flight to Miami.

37. (A) Make reservations for his flight sooner.
(B) Spend his vacation somewhere else.
(C) Read a travel book.
(D) Stay at a different hotel.

PART C

Directions: This part of the test consists of several talks, each given by a single speaker. After each of these talks there are a number of questions. You will hear each talk and question only once, and the questions are *not* written out.

When you have heard each question, read the four answer choices and select the *one*—(A), (B), (C), or (D)—that best answers the question based on what is directly stated or on what can be inferred. Then fill in the space on your answer sheet that matches to the letter of the answer that you have selected. HEARHere is an example.

You will hear:

Now here is a sample question.

You will hear:

You will read:

(A) Philosophy.
(B) Meteorology.
(C) Astronomy.
(D) Photography.

The lecture concerns a lunar eclipse, a topic that would typically be discussed in an astronomy class. The choice that best answers the question "In what course is this lecture probably being given?" is (C), "Astronomy." You should fill in (C) on your answer sheet.

Sample Answer

Here is another sample question.

You will hear:

You will read:

(A) The Earth's shadow moves across the Moon.
(B) Clouds block the view of the Moon.
(C) The Moon moves between the Earth and the Sun.
(D) The Sun can be observed without special equipment.

From the lecture, you learn that a lunar eclipse occurs when the Earth moves between the Sun and the Moon and the shadow of the Earth passes across the Moon. The choice that best answers the question "According to the speaker, which of the following occurs during a lunar eclipse?" is (A), "The Earth's shadow moves across the Moon." Don't forget: During actual exams, taking notes or writing in your test book is *not* permitted.

Sample Answer

38. (A) In the home of an art collector.
(B) In a restaurant.
(C) In a museum.
(D) In a private art gallery.

39. (A) Not all of it is folk art.
(B) Most of it was made for this event.
(C) All of it was created for display.
(D) Some of it has been in previous exhibits.

40. (A) It is still brightly colored.
(B) It was used to advertise a restaurant.
(C) It is less than a hundred years old.
(D) It once hung in front of a bootmaker's shop.

41. (A) Unpopular.
(B) Charming.
(C) Complex.
(D) Disturbing.

42. (A) There are no signatures on the signs.
(B) The plaques haven't been put on the wall yet.
(C) The signatures are too faded to read.
(D) The sign painters needed to conceal their identities.

43. (A) To present an award.
(B) To say goodbye to Professor Callaghan.
(C) To explain computer models.
(D) To welcome a new college president.

44. (A) An administrator.
(B) A faculty member.
(C) A chancellor of the college.
(D) A graduate student.

45. (A) Computer science.
(B) History.
(C) Economics.
(D) Physics.

46. (A) Two years.
(B) Four years.
(C) Six years.
(D) Eight years.

47. (A) He greatly influenced Emily Dickinson.
(B) His poetry was similar to Emily Dickinson's.
(C) He and Emily Dickinson were very influential poets.
(D) He and Emily Dickinson became good friends.

48. (A) For her unusual habits.
(B) For her success as a poet.
(C) For her personal wealth.
(D) For her eventful life.

49. (A) Their titles.
(B) Their great length.
(C) Their range of subject matter.
(D) Their economy.

50. (A) None.
(B) About 10.
(C) Around 50.
(D) Over 1,700.

THIS IS THE END OF SECTION 1, LISTENING COMPREHENSION.

STOP WORK ON SECTION 1.

Section 2

This section tests your ability to recognize grammar and usage suitable for standard written English. This section is divided into two parts, each with its own directions.

STRUCTURE

Directions: Items in this part are incomplete sentences. Following each of these sentences, there are four words or phrases. You should select the *one* word or phrase—(A), (B), (C), or (D)—that best completes the sentence. Then fill in the space on your answer sheet that matches the letter of the answer that you have selected.

Example I

Pepsin _____ an enzyme used in digestion.

(A) that
(B) is
(C) of
(D) being

This sentence should properly read "Pepsin is an enzyme used in digestion." You should fill in (B) on your answer sheet.

Sample Answer

Ⓐ ● Ⓒ Ⓓ

Example II

_____ large natural lakes are found in the state of South Carolina.

(A) There are no
(B) Not the
(C) It is not
(D) No

This sentence should properly read "No large natural lakes are found in the state of South Carolina." You should fill in (D) on your answer sheet. As soon as you understand the directions, begin work on this part.

Sample Answer

Ⓐ Ⓑ Ⓒ ●

WAIT

1. _____ a blend of the actual note sounded and related tones called overtones.

    (A) Musical tones consist of every
    (B) All musical tones consisting of
    (C) It consists of all musical tones
    (D) Every musical tone consists of

2. _____, all animals need oxygen, water, food, and the proper range of temperatures.

    (A) To survive
    (B) Their survival
    (C) Surviving
    (D) They survive

3. Billie Holiday's rough _____ emotional voice made her stand out as a jazz singer.

    (A) so
    (B) but
    (C) nor
    (D) still

4. The Breed Test, _____ method of counting bacteria in fresh milk, was developed by R. S. Breed in Geneva, New York, in 1925.

    (A) which, as a
    (B) is a
    (C) it is a
    (D) a

5. _____ a liquid changes to a solid, heat is given off.

    (A) That
    (B) Sometimes
    (C) Whenever
    (D) From

6. Completed in 1756, Nassau Hall is the oldest building now _____ on the campus of Princeton University.

    (A) standing
    (B) it stands
    (C) has stood
    (D) stood

7. The one person most responsible for making New York City a center of furniture design in the early nineteenth century _____ cabinetmaker Duncan Phyfe.

    (A) was the hardworking
    (B) through his hard work
    (C) he was hardworking
    (D) by working hard, the

8. Candles _____ from beeswax burn with a very clean flame.

    (A) are made
    (B) making
    (C) which make
    (D) made

9. Hydroponics is the cultivation of plants _____ soil.

    (A) not having
    (B) without
    (C) a lack of
    (D) do not have

10. _____ a language family is a group of languages with a common origin and similar vocabulary, grammar, and sound systems.

    (A) What linguists call
    (B) It is called by linguists
    (C) Linguists call it
    (D) What do linguists call

11. In the eighteenth century the town of Bennington, Vermont, was famous for _____ pottery.

    (A) it made
    (B) its
    (C) the making
    (D) where its

12. _____ bacterial infection is present in the body, the bone marrow produces more white blood cells than usual.

    (A) A
    (B) That a
    (C) If a
    (D) During a

13. Anyone who has ever pulled weeds from a garden _____ roots firmly anchor plants to the soil.

    (A) is well aware that
    (B) well aware
    (C) is well aware of
    (D) well aware that

14. So thick and rich _____ of Illinois that early settlers there were unable to force a plow through it.

    (A) as the soil
    (B) the soil was
    (C) was the soil
    (D) the soil

15. _____ because of the complexity of his writing, Henry James never became a popular author, but his works are admired by critics and other writers.

    (A) It may be
    (B) Perhaps
    (C) Besides
    (D) Why is it

WRITTEN EXPRESSION

Directions: The items in this part have four underlined words or phrases. You must identify the *one* underlined expression—(A), (B), (C), or (D)—that must be changed for the sentence to be correct. Then fill in the space on your answer sheet that matches the letter of the answer that you have selected.

Example I

Lenses may to have either concave or convex shapes.
        A   B   C   D

This sentence should read "Lenses may have either concave or convex shapes." You should therefore select answer (A).

Sample Answer

Example II

When painting a fresco, an artist is applied paint directly to the damp plaster of a wall.
A   B   C   D

This sentence should read "When painting a fresco, an artist applies paint directly to the wet plaster of a wall." You should therefore select answer (B). As soon as you understand the directions, begin work on this part.

Sample Answer

WAIT

107

16. A rattlesnake has a spot <u>between</u> <u>one's</u> eyes
                               A   B
that is <u>sensitive to</u> <u>heat</u>.
         C   D

17. <u>Improvements</u> in people's health are
      A
due <u>in part</u> to advances <u>in</u> medical care and
      B   C
better <u>sanitary</u>.
      D

18. <u>In</u> 1792, a corporation <u>constructed</u> a
  A   B
<u>60-miles</u> toll road <u>from</u> Philadelphia to
  C   D
Lancaster, Pennsylvania.

19. Insects <u>appeared</u> <u>on</u> earth <u>before long</u> the
           A   B   C
<u>earliest mammals</u>.
     D

20. <u>All of Agnes Repplier's writings</u>, <u>even those</u>
  A   B
on <u>the most serious</u> subjects, show her
       C
sense of <u>humorous</u>.
         D

21. Fungi are <u>the most important</u> decomposers
                A
of <u>forest soil</u> <u>just like</u> bacteria are <u>the chief</u>
    B   C   D
decomposers of grassland soil.

22. Halifax Harbor in Nova Scotia is one <u>of</u>
                         A
<u>the most safe</u> <u>harbors</u> <u>in the world</u>.
    B   C   D

23. Ballpoint pens <u>require</u> a tiny,
             A
<u>perfectly</u> <u>round</u> ball for <u>its</u> tips.
  B   C   D

24. <u>Since the 1930s</u>, <u>the archaeology</u> has
  A   B
become a <u>precise</u> science with strict
         C
<u>rules</u> and procedures.
  D

25. Interstate Highway 80 is <u>so</u> an <u>important</u>
                  A   B
road that <u>it is</u> sometimes <u>referred to as</u>
       C   D
"America's Main Street."

26. John Jay, a <u>diplomat</u> and statesman, first
           A
<u>entered</u> <u>public</u> <u>live</u> in 1773.
  B   C   D

27. Mount Hood in Oregon is <u>a</u> center for
                    A
<u>alpine</u> sports such as <u>skiing</u>, climbing, and
  B   C
<u>hikes</u>.
  D

28. The chameleon's <u>able</u> to change color to
              A
match <u>its</u> surroundings is <u>shared</u> by quite
     B   C
<u>a few</u> lizards.
  D

29. Florence Sabin is <u>recognized</u> not only <u>for</u>
             A   B
her theoretical research in <u>anatomy</u> and
                C
physiology <u>and</u> for her work in public
       D
health.

30. The <u>top layer</u> of the ocean stores <u>as much</u>
     A   B
heat as <u>does</u> all the gases in the
       C
<u>atmosphere</u>.
  D

31. <u>Almost</u> lemons <u>grown</u> in the United States
  A   B
come <u>from</u> <u>farms</u> in Florida and California.
     C   D

32. <u>Hair</u> is made of the same basic material
  A
<u>as both</u> the nails, claws, and <u>hooves of</u>
  B   C
mammals <u>are made of</u>.
      D

33. Not until geologists <u>began</u> to study <u>exposed</u>
              A   B
rocks in ravines and <u>on</u> mountainsides
               C
<u>they did</u> discover many of the earth's
  D
secrets.

34. The water of the Gulf Stream may be
as much as 20 <u>percentage</u> warmer <u>than</u> the
  A   B   C
<u>surrounding</u> water.
  D

35. Mathematics have taken centuries
                    A
to develop the methods that we now use in
   B   C   D
arithmetic.

36. One of the most beautiful botanical gardens
                A   B
in the United States is the wildly and lovely
                        C
Magnolia Gardens near Charleston, South
              D
Carolina.

37. Benthic organisms are those that live on or
                     A   B
in a bottom of a body of water.
    C   D

38. It has been known since the eighteenth
   A   B
century that the adrenal glands are essential
        C
of life.
 D

39. The making of leather goods from animal
      A   B
skins is one of the soonest accomplish-
 C   D
ments of humankind.

40. Married customs differ greatly from society
    A   B   C
to society.
 D

THIS IS THE END OF SECTION 2.

IF YOU FINISH BEFORE THE TIME LIMIT, CHECK YOUR WORK ON SECTION 2 ONLY.

DO NOT READ OR WORK ON ANY OTHER SECTION OF THE TEST.

Section 3

READING COMPREHENSION
TIME—55 MINUTES

This section of the test measures your ability to comprehend written materials.

Directions: This section contains several passages, each followed by a number of questions. Read the passages and, for each question, choose the *one* best answer—(A), (B), (C), or (D)—based on what is stated in the passage or on what can be inferred from the passage. Then fill in the space on your answer sheet that matches the letter of the answer that you have selected.

Read the Following Passage

Line   Like mammals, birds claim their own territories. A bird's territory may be small or large. Some birds claim only their nest and the area right around it, while others claim far larger territories that include their feeding areas. Gulls, penguins, and other waterfowl nest in huge colonies, but even in the biggest colonies, each male and his mate have small territories of their own
5   immediately around their nests.

Male birds defend their territory chiefly against other males of the same species. In some cases, a warning call or threatening pose may be all the defense needed, but in other cases, intruders may refuse to leave peacefully.

Example I

What is the main topic of this passage?

(A) Birds that live in colonies
(B) Birds' mating habits
(C) The behavior of birds
(D) Territoriality in birds

The passage mainly concerns the territories of birds. You should fill in (D) on your answer sheet.

Sample Answer

Example II

According to the passage, male birds defend their territory primarily against

(A) Female birds
(B) Birds of other species
(C) Males of their own species
(D) Mammals

The passage states that "Male birds defend their territory chiefly against other males of the same species." You should fill in (C) on your answer sheet. As soon as you understand the directions, begin work on this section.

Sample Answer

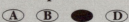

QUESTIONS 1–10

Line   Cooperation is the common endeavor of two or more people to perform a task or reach a jointly
        cherished goal. Like competition and conflict, there are different forms of cooperation, based on
        group organization and attitudes.

            In the first form, known as primary cooperation, group and individual fuse. The group contains
5   nearly all of each individual's life. The rewards of the group's work are shared with each member.
        There is an interlocking identity of individual, group, and task performed. Means and goals become
        one, for cooperation itself is valued.

            While primary cooperation is most often characteristic of preliterate societies, secondary
        cooperation is characteristic of many modern societies. In secondary cooperation, individuals devote
10   only part of their lives to the group. Cooperation itself is not a value. Most members of the group
        feel loyalty, but the welfare of the group is not the first consideration. Members perform tasks so that
        they can *separately* enjoy the fruits of their cooperation in the form of salary, prestige, or power.
        Business offices and professional athletic teams are examples of secondary cooperation.

            In the third type, called tertiary cooperation or accommodation, latent conflict underlies the
15   shared work. The attitudes of the cooperating parties are purely opportunistic; the organization is
        loose and fragile. Accommodation involves common means to achieve antagonistic goals; it breaks
        down when the common means cease to aid each party in reaching its goals. This is not, strictly
        speaking, cooperation at all, and hence the somewhat contradictory term *antagonistic cooperation* is
        sometimes used for this relationship.

1. What is the author's main purpose in the first paragraph of the passage?

   (A) To explain how cooperation differs from competition and conflict
   (B) To show the importance of group organization and attitudes
   (C) To offer a brief definition of cooperation
   (D) To urge readers to cooperate more often

2. The word *cherished* in line 2 is closest in meaning to

   (A) prized
   (B) agreed on
   (C) defined
   (D) set up

3. The word *fuse* in line 4 is closest in meaning to

   (A) react
   (B) unite
   (C) evolve
   (D) explore

4. Which of the following statements about primary cooperation is supported by information in the passage?

   (A) It was confined to prehistoric times.
   (B) It is usually the first stage of cooperation achieved by a group of individuals attempting to cooperate.
   (C) It is an ideal that can never be achieved.
   (D) It is most commonly seen among people who have not yet developed reading and writing skills.

5. According to the passage, why do people join groups that practice secondary cooperation?

   (A) To experience the satisfaction of cooperation
   (B) To get rewards for themselves
   (C) To associate with people who have similar backgrounds
   (D) To defeat a common enemy

6. Which of the following is an example of the third form of cooperation as it is defined in the fourth paragraph?

   (A) Students form a study group so that all of them can improve their grades.
   (B) A new business attempts to take customers away from an established company.
   (C) Two rival political parties temporarily work together to defeat a third party.
   (D) Members of a farming community share work and the food that they grow.

7. Which of the following is NOT given as a name for the third type of cooperation?

   (A) Tertiary cooperation
   (B) Accommodation
   (C) Latent conflict
   (D) Antagonistic cooperation

8. The word *fragile* in line 16 is closest in meaning to

   (A) inefficient
   (B) easily broken
   (C) poorly planned
   (D) involuntary

9. As used throughout the passage, the term *common* is closest in meaning to which of the following?

   (A) Ordinary
   (B) Shared
   (C) Vulgar
   (D) Popular

10. Which of the following best describes the overall organization of the passage?

   (A) The author describes a concept by analyzing its three forms.
   (B) The author compares and contrasts two types of human relations.
   (C) The author presents the points of view of three experts on the same topic.
   (D) The author provides a number of concrete examples and then draws a conclusion.

QUESTIONS 11–22

Line The first scientific attempt at coaxing moisture from a cloud was in 1946, when scientist Vincent
Schaefer dropped 3 pounds of dry ice from an airplane into a cloud and, to his delight, produced
snow. The success of the experiment was modest, but it spawned optimism among farmers and
ranchers around the country. It seemed to them that science had finally triumphed over weather.

5   Unfortunately, it didn't work out that way. Although there were many cloud-seeding operations
during the late 1940s and the 1950s, no one could say whether they had any effect on precipitation.
Cloud seeding, or weather modification as it came to be called, was clearly more complicated than
had been thought. It was not until the early 1970s that enough experiments had been done to
understand the processes involved. What these studies indicated was that only certain types of clouds
10   are amenable to seeding. One of the most responsive is the winter orographic cloud, formed when
air currents encounter a mountain slope and rise. If the temperature in such a cloud is right, seeding
can increase snow yield by 10 to 20 percent.

There are two major methods of weather modification. In one method, silver iodide is burned
in propane-fired ground generators. The smoke rises into the clouds where the tiny silver-iodide
15   particles act as nuclei for the formation of ice crystals. The alternate system uses airplanes to deliver
dry-ice pellets. Dry ice does not provide ice-forming nuclei. Instead, it lowers the temperature near
the water droplets in the clouds so that they freeze instantly—a process called spontaneous nucleation. Seeding from aircraft is more efficient but also more expensive.

About 75 percent of all weather modification in the United States takes place in the Western
20   states. With the population of the West growing rapidly, few regions of the world require more
water. About 85 percent of the waters in the rivers of the West comes from melted snow. As one
expert put it, the water problems of the future may make the energy problems of the 70s seem like
child's play to solve. That's why the U.S. Bureau of Reclamation, along with state governments,
municipal water districts, and private interests such as ski areas and agricultural cooperatives, is
25   putting increased effort into cloud-seeding efforts. Without consistent and heavy snowfalls in the
Rockies and Sierras, the West would literally dry up. The most intensive efforts to produce precipitation was during the West's disastrous snow drought of 1976–77. It is impossible to judge the
efficiency of weather modification based on one crash program, but most experts think that such
hurry-up programs are not very effective.

11. What is the main subject of the passage?
   (A) The scientific contributions of Vincent Schaefer
   (B) Developments in methods of increasing precipitation
   (C) The process by which snow crystals form
   (D) The effects of cloud seeding

12. The word *spawned* in line 3 is closest in meaning to
   (A) intensified
   (B) reduced
   (C) preceded
   (D) created

13. After the cloud-seeding operations of the late 1940s and the 1950s, the farmers and ranchers mentioned in the first paragraph probably felt
   (A) triumphant
   (B) modest
   (C) disappointed
   (D) optimistic

14. Which of the following can be inferred from the passage about the term *weather modification*?
   (A) It is not as old as the term *cloud seeding*.
   (B) It has been in use since at least 1946.
   (C) It refers to only one type of cloud seeding.
   (D) It was first used by Vincent Schaefer.

15. According to the passage, winter orographic clouds are formed

(A) on relatively warm winter days
(B) over large bodies of water
(C) during intense snow storms
(D) when air currents rise over mountains

16. To which of the following does the word
they in line 17 refer?

(A) Water droplets
(B) Clouds
(C) Ice-forming nuclei
(D) Airplanes

17. When clouds are seeded from the ground,
what actually causes ice crystals to form?

(A) Propane
(B) Silver-iodide smoke
(C) Dry-ice pellets
(D) Nuclear radiation

18. Clouds would most likely be seeded from
airplanes when

(A) it is important to save money
(B) the process of spontaneous nucleation
cannot be employed
(C) the production of precipitation must
be efficient
(D) temperatures are lower than usual

19. About what percentage of the western
United States' water supply comes from
run-off from melted snow?

(A) 10 percent
(B) 20 percent
(C) 75 percent
(D) 85 percent

20. What does the author imply about the
energy problems of the 1970s?

(A) They were caused by a lack of water.
(B) They took attention away from water
problems.
(C) They may not be as critical as water
problems will be in the future.
(D) They were thought to be minor at the
time but turned out to be serious.

21. The author mentions agricultural cooperatives (line 24) as an example of

(A) state government agencies
(B) private interests
(C) organizations that compete with ski
areas for water
(D) municipal water districts

22. It can be inferred from the passage that the
weather-modification project of 1976–77
was

(A) put together quickly
(B) a complete failure
(C) not necessary
(D) easy to evaluate

QUESTIONS 23–30

Line   The biological community changes again as one moves from the city to the suburbs. Around all cities is a biome called the "suburban forest." The trees of this forest are species that are favored by man, and most of them have been deliberately planted. Mammals such as rabbits, skunks, and opossums have moved in from the surrounding countryside. Raccoons have become experts at opening garbage
5   cans, and in some places even deer wander suburban thoroughfares. Several species of squirrel get along nicely in suburbia, but usually only one species is predominant in any given suburb—fox squirrels in one place, red squirrels in another, gray squirrels in a third—for reasons that are little understood. The diversity of birds in the suburbs is great, and in the South, lizards thrive in gardens and even houses. Of course, insects are always present.

10   There is an odd biological sameness in these suburban communities. True, the palms of Los Angeles are missing from the suburbs of Boston, and there are species of insects in Miami not found in Seattle. But over wide stretches of the United States, ecological conditions in suburban biomes vary much less than do those of natural biomes. And unlike the natural biomes, the urban and suburban communities exist in spite of, not because of, the climate.

23. If there was a preceding paragraph to this passage it would most likely be concerned with which of the following topics?
- (A) The migration from cities to suburbs
- (B) The biological community in urban areas
- (C) The mammals of the American countryside
- (D) The history of American suburbs

24. The author implies that the mammals of the "suburban forest" differ from most species of trees there in which of the following ways?
- (A) They were not deliberately introduced.
- (B) They are considered undesirable by humans.
- (C) They are represented by a greater number of species.
- (D) They have not fully adapted to suburban conditions.

25. The word *thoroughfares* in line 5 is closest in meaning to
- (A) neighborhoods
- (B) lawns
- (C) open spaces
- (D) streets

26. Which of the following conclusions about squirrels is supported by information in the passage?
- (A) The competition among the three species is intense.
- (B) Fox squirrels are more common than gray or red squirrels.
- (C) Two species of squirrels seldom inhabit the same suburb.
- (D) The reasons why squirrels do well in the suburbs are unknown.

27. The word *thrive* in line 8 is closest in meaning to
- (A) remain
- (B) flourish
- (C) reproduce
- (D) survive

28. The word *odd* in line 10 is closest in meaning to
- (A) unusual
- (B) appropriate
- (C) unforgettable
- (D) expected

29. Which of the following best expresses the main idea of the second paragraph of the passage?

    (A) Biological communities in East Coast suburbs differ greatly from those on the West Coast.
    (B) The suburban forest occupies an increasingly large segment of the American landscape.
    (C) Suburbs in the United States have remarkably similar biological communities.
    (D) Natural biomes have been studied more than suburban biomes.

30. What does the author imply about the effect of climate on the suburban biome?

    (A) It is more noticeable than the effect of climate on the urban biome.
    (B) It is not as important as it once was.
    (C) It depends on the location of the biome.
    (D) It is not as dramatic as the effect of climate on natural biomes.

QUESTIONS 31–39

Line   Deep within the Earth there seethes a vast cauldron called Hot Dry Rock, or HDR, that observers
believe could make the United States and other nations practically energy independent. HDR is a
virtually limitless source of energy that generates neither pollution nor dangerous wastes.

5   The concept, now being tested at the Los Alamos National Laboratory in New Mexico, is quite
simple, at least in theory. Two adjacent wells are punched several miles into the Earth to reach this
subterranean furnace. Water is pumped down one well to collect inside the Hot Dry Rock, creating a
pressurized reservoir of superheated liquid. This is then drawn through the other well to the surface,
and there the water's accumulated load of heat energy is transferred to a volatile liquid that, in turn,
drives an electric power-producing turbine.

10   David Duchane, HDR program manager at Los Alamos, believes that an economically competitive, 1-megawatt plant of this type will be up and running in around two decades. A small prototype
station will be built in half that time. But Duchane dreams an even grander dream. "We could build
an HDR plant near the seacoast," he says. "Could you imagine pumping seawater down to where it
heats up well above its boiling point? Then you bring it to the surface to make electrical energy, and
15   you turn some into vapor to get as much pure water as you need."

31. What is the main idea of the passage?

(A)   Despite certain advantages, there are many drawbacks involved in the use of Hot Dry Rock.

(B)   Hot Dry Rock is a potentially important energy source.

(C)   By drilling deep wells in the ground, researchers at Los Alamos discovered Hot Dry Rock.

(D)   Hot Dry Rock power plants are more useful if they are built near the seacoast.

32. Which of the following terms is NOT used in the passage to refer to Hot Dry Rock?

(A)   A vast cauldron (line 1)

(B)   A virtually limitless source of power (line 3)

(C)   Subterranean furnace (line 6)

(D)   A pressurized reservoir (line 7)

33. The word *adjacent* in line 5 is closest in meaning to

(A)   up-and-down

(B)   deep

(C)   advanced

(D)   side-by-side

34. The second paragraph of the passage implies that the concept of utilizing Hot Dry Rock as an energy source

(A)   might be difficult to put into practice

(B)   is hard for nonscientists to understand

(C)   is theoretically possible but technologically impractical

(D)   may involve unknown dangers

35. The word *there* in line 8 refers to

(A)   a place deep inside the Earth

(B)   a place near the seacoast

(C)   Los Alamos National Laboratory

(D)   the surface of the Earth

36. The power-producing turbine in the Hot Dry Rock power plant described in the second paragraph is actually driven by

(A)   electricity

(B)   volatile liquid

(C)   superheated water

(D)   Hot Dry Rock

37. According to David Duchane, how long will it probably take to build a small prototype Hot Dry Rock power station?

(A)   Two years

(B)   Four years

(C)   Ten years

(D)   Twenty years

38. What is the *grander dream*, mentioned in line 12?

(A) The opportunity for the United States to become energy independent

(B) The chance to generate power without increasing pollution

(C) The possibility of obtaining pure water from seawater while generating electricity

(D) The hope that scientists can continue their research on Hot Dry Rock

39. The word *some* in line 15 refers to

(A) seawater

(B) electrical energy

(C) water vapor

(D) pure water

QUESTIONS 40–50

Line The brilliant light, crystalline air, and spectacular surroundings have long drawn people to the tiny
New Mexican town of Taos. Today, the homes of some of those who have settled there during Taos'
300-year history have been restored and are open to the public. Along with the churches and art
galleries, these residences make up a part of the unique cultural heritage of Taos.

5   Representing the Spanish Colonial era is the meticulously restored hacienda of Don Antonio
Severino Martinez. He moved his family to Taos in 1804 and transformed a simple cabin into a huge,
imposing fortress. Its twenty-one rooms and two courtyards now house a living museum where
visitors can watch potters and weavers at work. The American territorial era is represented by two
houses: the home of the explorer and scout Kit Carson, located off Taos Square, and that of Charles

10   Bent, a trader who later became governor of the New Mexico territory. Carson's house was built in
1843, Bent's three years later.
           In the twentieth century, Taos, like its bigger sister Santa Fe to the south, blossomed into a
center for artists and artisans. One of the first artists to move there was Ernest Blumenschein, who is
known for his illustrations, including those for the works of Jack London and other bestselling

15   authors. In 1898, while on a Denver-to-Mexico City sketching tour, Blumenschein's wagon broke
down near Taos. He walked into town carrying his broken wheel, looked around, and decided to
stay. His rambling, twelve-room house is furnished as it was when he lived there. Not far from the
Blumenschein house is the home of another artist, Russian-born painter Nicolai Fechin, who moved
to Taos in the 1920s. He carved and decorated the furniture, windows, gates, and fireplaces himself,

20   transforming the interior of his adobe house into that of a traditional country house in his homeland.
A few miles north of town is the Millicent Rogers Museum, the residence of a designer and collector
who came to Taos in 1947. An adobe castle, it contains a treasure trove of Native American and
Hispanic jewelry, pots, rugs, and other artifacts.

40. The passage mainly discusses which aspect of Taos?

(A) Its famous families
(B) Events from its 300-year history
(C) Its different architectural styles
(D) Its historic houses

41. The word *meticulously* in line 5 is closest in meaning to

(A) tastefully
(B) privately
(C) carefully
(D) expensively

42. The word *imposing* in line 7 is closest in meaning to

(A) striking
(B) complex
(C) threatening
(D) antiquated

43. According to the passage, the home of Don Antonio Severino Martinez is now

(A) a fortress
(B) an art gallery
(C) a museum
(D) a simple cabin

44. According to the passage, what were Charles Bent's two occupations?

(A) Merchant and politician
(B) Artist and artisan
(C) Explorer and scout
(D) Potter and weaver

45. Charles Bent's house was probably built in

(A) 1804
(B) 1840
(C) 1843
(D) 1846

46. The town of Santa Fe is probably referred to as Taos's "bigger sister" (line 12) because it

(A) is older
(B) has a larger population
(C) is more famous
(D) has more artists

47. The word *works* in line 14 is used in the context of this passage to mean

(A) books
(B) factories
(C) designs
(D) paintings

48. According to the passage, what was Ernest Blumenschein's original destination when he went on a sketching tour in 1898?

(A) Denver
(B) Santa Fe
(C) Mexico City
(D) Taos

49. The author implies that the interior of Nicolai Fechin house is decorated in what style?

(A) Spanish colonial
(B) American territorial
(C) Native American
(D) Traditional Russian

50. Which of the following people is NOT mentioned as a resident of Taos?

(A) Nicolai Fechin
(B) Jack London
(C) Ernest Blumenschein
(D) Millicent Rogers

THIS IS THE END OF SECTION 3.

IF YOU FINISH BEFORE THE TIME LIMIT, CHECK YOUR WORK ON SECTION 3 ONLY.

DO NOT READ OR WORK ON ANY OTHER SECTION OF THE TEST.

PRACTICE TEST 5

Section 1

This section tests your ability to comprehend spoken English. It is divided into three parts, each with its own directions. During actual exams, you are *not* permitted to turn the page during the reading of the directions or to take notes at any time.

PART A

Directions: Each item in this part consists of a brief conversation involving two speakers. Following each conversation, a third voice will ask a question. You will hear the conversations and questions only once, and they will *not* be written out.

When you have heard each conversation and question, read the four answer choices and select the *one*—(A), (B), (C), or (D)—that best answers the question based on what is directly stated or on what can be inferred. Then fill in the space on your answer sheet that matches the letter of the answer that you have selected.

Here is an example.

You will hear:

You will read:

  (A) Open the window.
  (B) Move the chair.
  (C) Leave the room.
  (D) Take a seat.

From the conversation you find out that the woman thinks the man should put the chair over by the window. The best answer to the question "What does the woman think the man should do?" is (B), "Move the chair." You should fill in (B) on your answer sheet. Don't forget: During actual exams, taking notes or writing in your test book is *not* permitted.

Sample Answer

(A) ● (C) (D)

WAIT

1. (A) He picked these strawberries himself.
    (B) He chose the freshest strawberries.
    (C) The strawberries were displayed outside Bailey's market.
    (D) The market had just sold the last strawberries.

2. (A) He's the worst lecturer they've ever heard.
    (B) He gave one of his standard lectures.
    (C) His article was the worst they've ever read.
    (D) His lectures are generally better.

3. (A) Ate breakfast quickly.
    (B) Came late to an appointment.
    (C) Skipped breakfast.
    (D) Waited in line.

4. (A) What kind it is.
    (B) Where he bought it.
    (C) How much it cost.
    (D) What color it is.

5. (A) She'd like to watch it, but she hasn't.
    (B) She didn't find it enjoyable.
    (C) She tried to understand it, but she couldn't.
    (D) She doesn't know when it comes on.

6. (A) Go skiing some other day.
    (B) Take their lunch with them.
    (C) Buy sandwiches at the ski lodge.
    (D) Eat at an expensive restaurant.

7. (A) Botany.
    (B) Mathematics.
    (C) Acting.
    (D) Astronomy.

8. (A) She wrote them herself.
    (B) She thinks they're sentimental.
    (C) She sings them with feeling.
    (D) She knows them from memory.

9. (A) Take a taxi.
    (B) Stay at another hotel.
    (C) Ask the driver for directions.
    (D) Walk to the hotel.

10. (A) Windows.
    (B) Dishes.
    (C) Eyeglasses.
    (D) Automobiles.

11. (A) That Dean Metzger will have a reception.
    (B) That the reception will be held tonight.
    (C) That the reception will be at seven.
    (D) That Dean Metzger's reception has been canceled.

12. (A) He's not very good at math.
    (B) He's taking two advanced classes.
    (C) He doesn't remember seeing the woman in class.
    (D) He found the class too easy.

13. (A) He never seems to have any plans.
    (B) She was disappointed with his planning.
    (C) She enjoyed the event that he planned.
    (D) He will do all the planning in the future.

14. (A) He had an accident because of his nervousness.
    (B) He seemed very jumpy last night.
    (C) He was upset because he'd almost had an accident.
    (D) He was nervous about acting in the play last night.

15. (A) Professor Dixon asked his students to wait outside.
    (B) The weather isn't very good today.
    (C) Professor Dixon's class is meeting outside today.
    (D) The class was suddenly canceled.

16. (A) He's changed his mind.
    (B) He's taking statistics a second time.
    (C) He considered it briefly.
    (D) He finally decided to take economics.

17. (A) He hasn't seen many operas.
    (B) Tickets for the opera don't cost much.
    (C) He didn't attend the opera yesterday.
    (D) The opera wasn't as good as others.

18. (A) Listen to music.
    (B) Address a letter.
    (C) Get his hair cut.
    (D) Send a package.

19. (A) He and his roommate are alike.
    (B) He is a helpful person.
    (C) He always comes late to dinner.
    (D) His roommate likes him a lot.

20.
(A) It was sad.
(B) It was believable.
(C) It was boring.
(D) It was funny.

21.
(A) In room 301.
(B) Next door to room 301.
(C) On another floor.
(D) In another building.

22.
(A) He didn't think she would attend.
(B) She was the last person to come into the meeting.
(C) She didn't think the meeting would last long.
(D) He thought she would be late.

23.
(A) Who Marie is.
(B) Where the newspaper is.
(C) What picture was in the paper.
(D) Why Marie's picture appeared.

24.
(A) She knew the traffic would be heavy.
(B) She was sure that the flight would be late.
(C) She told the man to leave earlier.
(D) She just returned from Boston herself.

25.
(A) He's sorry it's going out of business.
(B) He doesn't know when it's open.
(C) It has moved to another location.
(D) It's not a very good restaurant.

26.
(A) He wanted a large hamburger.
(B) He ordered a small drink, not a large one.
(C) He didn't call the waiter.
(D) He thinks the drink looks small.

27.
(A) Do some work in the yard.
(B) Play softball.
(C) Go to a bookstore.
(D) Buy some wood.

28.
(A) She didn't need to practice.
(B) She was feeling much better.
(C) She didn't belong to the choir anymore.
(D) She was too sick to go out.

29.
(A) She has no information about it.
(B) There was an announcement about it on the radio.
(C) Someone told her about it.
(D) She read about it somewhere.

30.
(A) He will stay at the Sherman Hotel.
(B) The Buckley House is preferable.
(C) A decision must be made soon.
(D) He doesn't have to attend the conference.

PART B

31. (A) Go to a meeting of the fencing club.
(B) Watch a fencing match.
(C) Review for an exam.
(D) Attend a physical education class.

32. (A) Speed.
(B) Concentration.
(C) Strength.
(D) Agility.

33. (A) Both are fast-moving sports.
(B) Both depend on good tactics.
(C) Both provide a lot of exercise.
(D) Both require a lot of training.

34. (A) Required textbooks.
(B) Used books.
(C) Books on a "suggested readings" list.
(D) Children's books.

35. (A) At the beginning.
(B) After three weeks.
(C) Around the middle.
(D) Near the end.

36. (A) $40.
(B) $80.
(C) $120.
(D) $160.

37. (A) If a student has written a note in it.
(B) If it was purchased at another store.
(C) If a professor decides to use another text.
(D) If it is more than a year old.

PART C

Directions: This part of the test consists of several talks, each given by a single speaker. After each of these talks there are a number of questions. You will hear each talk and question only once, and the questions are *not* written out.

When you have heard the question, read the four answer choices and select the one—(A), (B), (C), or (D)—that best answers the question based on what is directly stated or on what can be inferred. Then fill in the space on your answer sheet that matches the letter of the answer that you have selected.

Here is an example.

You will hear:

Now here is a sample question.

You will hear:

You will read:

(A) Philosophy.
(B) Meteorology.
(C) Astronomy.
(D) Photography.

The lecture concerns a lunar eclipse, a topic that would typically be discussed in an astronomy class. The choice that best answers the question "In what course is this lecture probably being given?" is (C), "Astronomy." You should fill in (C) on your answer sheet.

Sample Answer

Here is another sample question.

You will hear:

You will read:

(A) The Earth's shadow moves across the Moon.
(B) Clouds block the view of the Moon.
(C) The Moon moves between the Earth and the Sun.
(D) The Sun can be observed without special equipment.

From the lecture, you learn that a lunar eclipse occurs when the Earth moves between the Sun and the Moon and the shadow of the Earth passes across the Moon. The choice that best answers the question "According to the speaker, which of the following occurs during a lunar eclipse?" is (A), "The Earth's shadow moves across the Moon." Don't forget: During actual exams, taking notes or writing in your test book is *not* permitted.

Sample Answer

WAIT

38. (A) A professor.
    (B) An architecture student.
    (C) A professional architect.
    (D) An interior designer.

39. (A) Auto tires.
    (B) A solar-powered generator.
    (C) Straw and mud.
    (D) A water pump.

40. (A) Visited an Earthship.
    (B) Interviewed the inventor.
    (C) Built an Earthship himself.
    (D) Read books about Earthships.

41. (A) A room in an Earthship.
    (B) A large Earthship.
    (C) A group of Earthships.
    (D) A small Earthship.

42. (A) A photograph.
    (B) An architectural design.
    (C) An architectural model.
    (D) A book of plans.

43. (A) Once.
    (B) Twice.
    (C) Three times.
    (D) Four times.

44. (A) The heaviest kite.
    (B) The kite with the most unusual shape.
    (C) The kite that flies the highest.
    (D) The funniest kite.

45. (A) Only engineering students.
    (B) Only young children.
    (C) Any Central State University student.
    (D) Anyone who wants to enter.

46. (A) Saturday at the commons.
    (B) Saturday on top of the Engineering Tower.
    (C) Sunday at the commons.
    (D) Sunday at the stadium.

47. (A) Potluck dinners.
    (B) A Native American ceremony.
    (C) Marriage customs.
    (D) The economy of the Pacific Northwest.

48. (A) Only the Kwakiutl tribe.
    (B) All Native American tribes.
    (C) Only tribes in British Columbia.
    (D) All the tribes in the Pacific Northwest.

49. (A) To receive valuable gifts.
    (B) To celebrate his birthday.
    (C) To improve his social position.
    (D) To taste different dishes.

50. (A) They cost the host so much money.
    (B) The guests had to have potlatches in turn.
    (C) The guests brought money and valuables.
    (D) The host's children had to have similar ceremonies.

THIS IS THE END OF SECTION 1.

STOP WORK ON SECTION 1.

DO NOT READ OR WORK ON ANY OTHER SECTION OF THE TEST.

Section 2

This section tests your ability to recognize grammar and usage suitable for standard written English. It is divided into two parts, each with its own directions.

STRUCTURE

Directions: Items in this part are incomplete sentences. Following each of these sentences, there are four words or phrases. You should select the *one* word or phrase—(A), (B), (C), or (D)—that best completes the sentence. Then fill in the space on your answer sheet that matches the letter of the answer that you have selected.

Example I

Pepsin _____ an enzyme used in digestion.

(A) that
(B) is
(C) of
(D) being

This sentence should properly read "Pepsin is an enzyme used in digestion." You should fill in (B) on your answer sheet.

Sample Answer

Ⓐ ● Ⓒ Ⓓ

Example II

_____ large natural lakes are found in the state of South Carolina.

(A) There are no
(B) Not the
(C) It is not
(D) No

This sentence should properly read "No large natural lakes are found in the state of South Carolina." You should fill in (D) on your answer sheet. As soon as you understand the directions, begin work on this part.

Sample Answer

Ⓐ Ⓑ Ⓒ ●

WAIT

130

1. Indian summer is a period of mild weather _____ during the autumn.

   (A) occurs
   (B) occurring
   (C) it occurs
   (D) is occurring

2. Bacteria may be round, _____, or spiral.

   (A) rod shapes
   (B) in the shape of rods
   (C) like a rod's shape
   (D) rod-shaped

3. _____ of his childhood home in Hannibal, Missouri, provided Mark Twain with the inspiration for two of his most popular novels.

   (A) Remembering
   (B) Memories
   (C) It was the memories
   (D) He remembered

4. Most of the spices and many of the herbs _____ today originate from plants native to tropical regions.

   (A) using
   (B) use of
   (C) in use
   (D) are used

5. _____ many improvements made to highways during the nineteenth century, but Americans continued to depend on water routes for transportation.

   (A) Despite the
   (B) There were
   (C) However
   (D) Though there were

6. There are believed _____ over 300 species of trees in El Yunque rain forest in Puerto Rico.

   (A) to be
   (B) being
   (C) they are
   (D) there are

7. First performed in 1976, _____.

   (A) William Lane wrote the one-character play *The Belle of Amherst* about the life of Emily Dickinson
   (B) the life of Emily Dickinson was the subject of the one-character play *The Belle of Amherst* by William Lane
   (C) William Lane's one-character play *The Belle of Amherst* was about the life of Emily Dickinson
   (D) there was only one character in William Lane's play *The Belle of Amherst* about the life of Emily Dickinson

8. Minnesota's thousands of lakes _____ over 4,000 square miles.

   (A) that cover
   (B) covering
   (C) are covered
   (D) cover

9. Mushrooms have no vascular tissue, they reproduce by means of spores, and they _____ chlorophyll.

   (A) lack
   (B) no
   (C) without
   (D) not have

10. _____ get older, the games they play become increasingly complex.

    (A) Children
    (B) Children, when they
    (C) As children
    (D) For children to

11. _____ is the ancestor of most types of domestic ducks is well documented.

    (A) That the mallard
    (B) The mallard
    (C) Because the mallard
    (D) The mallard which

12. Rarely _____ last longer than an hour.

    (A) do tornados
    (B) tornados
    (C) tordados that
    (D) tornados do

131

13. Adobe bricks tend to crumble if _____ to excessive moisture or cold.

(A) they expose
(B) exposed
(C) are exposed
(D) to be exposed

14. _____ play *Alison's House*, the author Susan Glaspell won a Pulitzer Prize in 1931.

(A) Her
(B) By her
(C) It was her
(D) For her

15. _____ type of insects that pollinate plants.

(A) Not only are the bees
(B) Bees are not the only
(C) Not the only bees are
(D) Bees are not only the

WRITTEN EXPRESSION

Directions: The items in this part have four underlined words or phrases. You must identify the *one* underlined expression—(A), (B), (C), or (D)—that must be changed for the sentence to be correct. Then fill in the space on your answer sheet that matches the letter of the answer that you have selected.

Example I

Lenses may to have either concave or convex shapes.
        A   B C   D

This sentence should read "Lenses may have either concave or convex shapes." You should therefore select answer (A).

Sample Answer

● Ⓑ   Ⓒ   Ⓓ

Example II

When painting a fresco, an artist is applied paint directly to the damp plaster of a wall.
    A   B   C   D

This sentence should read "When painting a fresco, an artist applies paint directly to the wet plaster of a wall." You should therefore select answer (B). As soon as you understand the directions, begin work on this part.

Sample Answer

Ⓐ ●   Ⓒ   Ⓓ

WAIT

133

16. Machines <u>used to</u> harvest tree crops,
           A
<u>such as</u> cherries and almonds, can be
  B
classified <u>both</u> as shakers or <u>as</u> pickup
       C   D
machines.

17. An extended family consists <u>not only</u> of
                      A
parents and <u>children</u> but also <u>of others</u>
         B   C
relatives, such as grandparents and

  <u>unmarried</u> aunts and uncles.
     D

18. Draft horses <u>are</u> the <u>tallest</u>, most <u>powerful</u>,
          A   B   C
and <u>heavy</u> group of horses.
    D

19. The <u>sculptor</u> John Rogers produced many
      A
<u>replica</u> of <u>his</u> <u>bronze</u> statues.
  B   C   D

20. <u>Archaeological</u> sites are sometimes revealed
    A
<u>when</u> the <u>construction</u> of roads
  B   C
<u>and buildings.</u>
    D

21. <u>Acting teacher</u> Stella Adler <u>played</u> a
    A   B
<u>pivotal role</u> in the <u>develop</u> of the Method
    C   D
School of acting.

22. Medical students must <u>learning</u> both the
               A
theory <u>and</u> the <u>practice</u> of <u>medicine</u>.
      B   C   D

23. The first <u>recorded</u> use of natural gas <u>to light</u>
        A   B
street lamps <u>it was</u> in <u>the</u> town of Freder-
        C   D
ick, New York, in 1825.

24. Quinine, cinnamon, and other <u>useful</u>
                    A
substances <u>are</u> all derived <u>of the</u>
      B   C
<u>bark of trees.</u>
    D

25. Although the social sciences <u>different</u> a
                    A
<u>great deal</u> from <u>one another</u>, they share a
    B   C
common interest in human <u>relationships</u>.
                  D

26. Admiral Grace Hopper <u>created</u> the
               A
<u>computer</u> language COBOL, which is used
  B
<u>primary</u> for scientific <u>purposes</u>.
  C   D

27. Unlike competitive <u>running</u>, race walkers
           A
must <u>always</u> keep some portion of <u>their</u> feet
    B   C
<u>in contact with</u> the ground.
    D

28. Henry David Thoreau's book *Walden: A Life*

  in the Woods is a <u>record</u> of <u>his</u> <u>simply</u>
            A   B   C
existence <u>in a cabin</u> on Walden Pond.
       D

29. A promissory note is a <u>written agreement</u>
                  A
<u>to pay</u> a certain sum of money <u>at</u> some
  B   C
<u>time future.</u>
  D

30. Mario Pei helped <u>provide</u> the world <u>with</u> a
          A   B
popular <u>understand</u> of <u>linguistics</u>.
    C   D

31. <u>Even though</u> they are among <u>the smallest</u>
  A   B
carnivores, weasels will attack animals <u>that</u>
                       C
are <u>double</u> their size.
    D

32. Wilson Alwyn Bentley was a Vermont

  <u>farmer</u> who <u>took</u> over 6,000 <u>close-up</u>
  A   B   C
photographs of snowflakes during <u>the</u>
                    D
lifetime.

33. New York City <u>surpassed</u> the other Atlantic
          A
seaports in <u>partly</u> because it <u>developed</u> the
       B   C
best transportation links <u>with</u> the interior of
                D
the country.

34. All of mammals, dolphins are undoubtedly
     A   B
among the friendliest to humans.
 C   D

35. Harmonize, melody, and rhythm are
     A   B
important elements in most forms of music.
                   C   D

36. When babies are around fifteen months old,
     A
they can pick up objects and put
  B   C
themselves into small containers.
      D

37. Loblolly pines, chiefly found in the South-
              A
eastern United States, has strong wood used
                    B
as lumber and for paper pulp.
  C   D

38. All root vegetables grow underground, and
     A   B
not all vegetables that grow underground
                         C
are roots.
   D

39. Tiny pygmy shrews breathe ten
              A
times as fast as humans beings.
  B   C   D

40. Before diamonds can be used as jewels,
     A   B
they must be cut and polish.
    C   D

THIS IS THE END OF SECTION 2.

IF YOU FINISH BEFORE THE TIME LIMIT, CHECK YOUR WORK ON SECTION 2 ONLY.

DO NOT READ OR WORK ON ANY OTHER SECTION OF THE TEST.

Section 3

This section of the test measures your ability to comprehend written materials.

Directions: This section contains several passages, each followed by a number of questions. Read the passages and, for each question, choose the *one* best answer—(A), (B), (C), or (D)—based on what is stated in the passage or on what can be inferred from the passage. Then fill in the space on your answer sheet that matches the letter of the answer that you have selected.

Read the Following Passage

Line
Like mammals, birds claim their own territories. A bird's territory may be small or large. Some birds claim only their nest and the area right around it, while others claim far larger territories that include their feeding areas. Gulls, penguins, and other waterfowl nest in huge colonies, but even in the biggest colonies, each male and his mate have small territories of their own
5   immediately around their nests.

Male birds defend their territory chiefly against other males of the same species. In some cases, a warning call or threatening pose may be all the defense needed, but in other cases, intruders may refuse to leave peacefully.

Example I

What is the main topic of this passage?

(A) Birds that live in colonies
(B) Birds' mating habits
(C) The behavior of birds
(D) Territoriality in birds

The passage mainly concerns the territories of birds. You should fill in (D) on your answer sheet.

Sample Answer

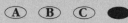

Example II

According to the passage, male birds defend their territory primarily against

(A) Female birds
(B) Birds of other species
(C) Males of their own species
(D) Mammals

The passage states that "Male birds defend their territory chiefly against other males of the same species." You should fill in (C) on your answer sheet. As soon as you understand the directions, begin work on this section.

Sample Answer

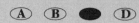

WAIT

QUESTIONS 1–12

Line Galaxies are not evenly distributed throughout the universe. A few are found alone, but almost all are
grouped in formations termed *galactic clusters*. These formations should not be confused with stellar
clusters, globular clusters of stars that exist within a galaxy. The size of galactic clusters varies
enormously, with some clusters containing only a dozen or so members and others containing as
5 many as 10,000. Moreover, galactic clusters themselves are part of larger clusters of clusters, termed
superclusters. It is surmised that even clusters of superclusters are possible.
   Our galaxy, the Milky Way, is part of a galactic cluster called the Local Group, which has
twenty members and is typical in terms of the types of galaxies it contains. There are three large
spiral galaxies: Andromeda, the largest galaxy in the group; the Milky Way, the second-largest galaxy;
10 and the Triangulum Spiral, the third largest. There are also four medium-sized spiral galaxies, including the Large Cloud of Magellan and the Small Cloud of Magellan. There are four regular elliptical
galaxies; the remainder are dwarf ellipticals. Other than our own galaxy, only Andromeda and the
Clouds of Magellan can be seen with the naked eye, and the Clouds are visible only from the
Southern Hemisphere.
15   In the vicinity of the Local Group are several clusters, each containing around twelve members.
The nearest cluster rich in members is the Virgo Cluster, which contains thousands of galaxies of all
types. Like most large clusters, it emits X rays. The Local Group, the small neighboring clusters, and
the Virgo Cluster form part of a much larger cluster of clusters—the Local Supercluster.
   The existence of galactic clusters presented a riddle to scientists for many years—the "missing
20 mass" problem. Clusters are presumably held together by the gravity generated by their members.
However, measurements showed that the galaxies did not have enough mass to explain their
apparent stability. Why didn't these clusters disintegrate? It is now thought that galaxies contain great
amounts of "dark matter," which cannot be directly observed but which generates gravitational pull.
This matter includes gas, dust, burnt-out stars, and even black holes.

1. Which of the following does the passage
   mainly discuss?
   (A) Clusters and superclusters of galaxies
   (B) An astronomical problem that has
       never been solved
   (C) A recent development in astronomy
   (D) The incredible distance between
       galaxies

2. The word *evenly* in line 1 is closest in
   meaning to
   (A) uniformly
   (B) predictably
   (C) relatively
   (D) paradoxically

3. What conclusion can be made about
   galaxies that are not found in clusters?
   (A) They have never been observed.
   (B) They are larger than other galaxies.
   (C) They are not actually galaxies but
       parts of galaxies.
   (D) They are outnumbered by galaxies
       that do occur in clusters.

4. The word *globular* in line 3 is closest in
   meaning to
   (A) immense
   (B) spherical
   (C) dense
   (D) brilliant

5. The author would probably characterize the
   existence of clusters of superclusters as
   (A) impossible
   (B) surprising
   (C) theoretical
   (D) certain

6. According to the passage, in what way is
   the Local Group typical of galactic clusters?
   (A) In its size
   (B) In the number of galaxies it contains
   (C) In its shape
   (D) In the types of galaxies that make it
       up

7. In the Local Group, which of the following
   types of galaxies are most numerous?
   (A) Large spirals
   (B) Medium-sized spirals
   (C) Regular ellipticals
   (D) Dwarf ellipticals

8. All of the following are visible from somewhere on Earth without a telescope EXCEPT

   (A) the Clouds of Magellan
   (B) Andromeda
   (C) the Triangulum Spiral
   (D) the Milky Way

9. According to the passage, the Local Group and the Virgo Cluster have which of the following in common?

   (A) Both are rich in galaxies.
   (B) Both emit X rays.
   (C) Both are part of the same supercluster.
   (D) Both are small clusters.

10. The word *riddle* in line 19 is closest in meaning to

    (A) tool
    (B) puzzle
    (C) theory
    (D) clue

11. Which of the following is NOT true about the ''dark matter'' mentioned in line 23?

    (A) It is impossible to observe directly.
    (B) It may include black holes.
    (C) It helps explain the ''missing mass'' problem.
    (D) It is found in the space between galaxies.

12. As used throughout the passage, the word *members* refers to

    (A) stars
    (B) galaxies
    (C) scientists
    (D) clusters

QUESTIONS 13–24

Line The Roman alphabet took thousands of years to develop, from the picture writing of the ancient
Egyptians through modifications by Phoenicians, Greeks, Romans, and others. Yet in just a dozen
years, one man, Sequoyah, invented an alphabet for the Cherokee people. Born in eastern Tennessee,
Sequoyah was a hunter and a silversmith in his youth, as well as an able interpreter who knew
5 Spanish, French, and English.

Sequoyah wanted his people to have the secret of the "talking leaves," as he called the books
of white people, and so he set out to design a written form of Cherokee. His chief aim was to record
his people's ancient tribal customs. He began by designing pictographs for every word in the
Cherokee vocabulary. Reputedly his wife, angry at him for his neglect of garden and house, burned
10 his notes, and he had to start over. This time, having concluded that picture-writing was cumbersome, he made symbols for the sounds of the Cherokee language. Eventually he refined his system to
eighty-five characters, which he borrowed from the Roman, Greek, and Hebrew alphabets. He
presented this system to the Cherokee General Council in 1821, and it was wholeheartedly approved.
The response was phenomenal. Cherokees who had struggled for months to learn English lettering in
15 school picked up the new system in days. Several books were printed in Cherokee, and in 1828, a
newspaper, the *Cherokee Phoenix*, was first published in the new alphabet. Sequoyah was acclaimed
by his people.

In his later life, Sequoyah dedicated himself to the general advancement of his people. He went
to Washington, D.C., as a representative of the Western tribes. He helped settle bitter differences
20 among Cherokee after their forced movement by the federal government to the Oklahoma territory in
the 1830s. He died in Mexico in 1843 while searching for groups of lost Cherokee. A statue of
Sequoyah represents Oklahoma in the Statuary Hall in the Capitol building in Washington, D.C.
However, he is probably chiefly remembered today because sequoias, the giant redwood trees of
California, are named for him.

13. The passage is mainly concerned with

(A) the development of the Roman alphabet
(B) the accomplishments of Sequoyah
(C) the pictographic system of writing
(D) Sequoyah's experiences in Mexico

14. According to the passage, how long did it take to develop the Cherokee alphabet?

(A) Twelve years
(B) Twenty years
(C) Eighty-five years
(D) Thousands of years

15. There is NO indication in the passage that, as a young man, Sequoyah

(A) served as an interpreter
(B) made things from silver
(C) served as a representative in Washington
(D) hunted game

16. According to the passage, Sequoyah used the phrase *talking leaves* (line 6) to refer to

(A) redwood trees
(B) books
(C) symbols for sounds
(D) newspapers

17. What was Sequoyah's main purpose in designing a Cherokee alphabet?

(A) To record Cherokee customs
(B) To write books in Cherokee
(C) To write about his own life
(D) To publish a newspaper

18. The word *cumbersome* in line 10 is closest in meaning to

(A) awkward
(B) radical
(C) simplistic
(D) unfamiliar

19. In the final version of the Cherokee alphabet system, each of the characters represents a

(A) word
(B) picture
(C) sound
(D) thought

20. All of the following were mentioned in the passage as alphabet systems that Sequoyah borrowed from EXCEPT

(A) Egyptian
(B) Roman
(C) Hebrew
(D) Greek

21. The word *wholeheartedly* in line 13 is closest in meaning to

(A) unanimously
(B) enthusiastically
(C) immediately
(D) ultimately

22. According to the passage, a memorial statue of Sequoyah is located in

(A) Oklahoma
(B) Mexico
(C) Tennessee
(D) Washington, D.C.

23. Why does the author mention the giant redwood trees of California in the passage?

(A) Sequoyah took his name from those trees.
(B) The trees inspired Sequoyah to write a book.
(C) Sequoyah was born in the vicinity of the redwood forest.
(D) The trees were named in Sequoyah's honor.

24. The author begins to describe the Cherokees' reaction to the invention of a written language in

(A) lines 2–3
(B) lines 7–8
(C) lines 14–17
(D) lines 18–19

QUESTIONS 25–32

Line For a long time, amphibians were confused with reptiles. Like reptiles, they have three-chambered hearts and are cold-blooded. Some amphibians, such as salamanders, are even shaped like lizards. However, unlike reptiles, amphibians never have claws on their toes or scales on their bodies. Furthermore, the eggs of amphibians lack shells, so they must be laid in water or moist places.

5   Amphibians were the first creatures to spend sizable amounts of their lives on land. The larvae of most amphibians, such as frog tadpoles, are born with gills and live in water. However, their gills disappear as they develop lungs. Most retain the ability to breathe through the moist surface of their skin. This comes in handy when they hibernate in the bottom mud of lakes and ponds during the coldest months. They take in the small amount of oxygen they need through their skin. Some

10 amphibians undergo what is known as a ''double metamorphosis,'' changing not only from gill breathers to lung breathers but also from vegetarians to insectivores.

    Although the amphibian class is rather small in number of species, it shows great diversity. There are three major types. The caecilians of the tropics are long, legless, burrowing creatures. Caudate amphibians, such as newts and salamanders, mostly have long tails and stubby legs. Salien-

15 tians, which include both frogs and toads, are tailless as adults and have powerful hind legs. Toads differ from frogs primarily in that they have dry, warty skin.

25. The author's main purpose in writing the passage is to

(A) define and describe amphibians
(B) contrast different types of amphibians
(C) trace the development of amphibians from larvae to adults
(D) explain how amphibians differ from other creatures

26. According to the passage, which of the following is NOT a characteristic of amphibians?

(A) They have three-chambered hearts.
(B) They lay eggs without shells.
(C) They have claws on their toes.
(D) They are cold-blooded.

27. As used in line 3, the term *scales* is closest to which of the following in meaning?

(A) Devices used to measure weight
(B) Plates covering the bodies of certain animals
(C) Sounds made by various animals
(D) Proportions between different sets of dimensions

28. According to the passage, the term *double metamorphosis* (line 10) refers to the fact that amphibians

(A) first breathe through their gills, then through their lungs, then through their skin
(B) change both the shape of their bodies and the way in which they lay eggs

(C) first live in the water, then on land, then in mud in the bottom of ponds and lakes
(D) change both their methods of breathing and their feeding habits

29. It can be inferred from the passage that amphibians' ability to breathe through their skin is especially useful during the

(A) summer
(B) fall
(C) winter
(D) spring

30. All of the following are identified in the passage as amphibians EXCEPT

(A) newts
(B) salamanders
(C) caecilians
(D) lizards

31. The word *stubby* in line 14 is closest in meaning to

(A) long and thin
(B) undeveloped
(C) thick and short
(D) powerful

32. In line 16, the word *they* refers to

(A) toads
(B) tails
(C) adults
(D) frogs

QUESTIONS 33–44

Line The first animated film, *Humorous Phases of Funny Faces*, was made in 1906 by newspaper
illustrator James Blackton. He filmed faces that were drawn on a blackboard in progressive stages. In
New York City, Winsor McCay exhibited his most famous films, *Little Nemo* (1910) and *Gertie the
Dinosaur* (1914). His films featured fluid motion and characters with individual personalities. For the
5 first time, characters drawn of lines seemed to live on the screen. In 1914, John R. Bray streamlined
the animation process, using assembly-line techniques to turn out cartoons.

By 1915, film studios began producing cartoon series. The Pat Sullivan studio produced the
series featuring Felix the Cat. He became one of the most beloved characters of the silent-film era.
The Max Fleischer studio produced series starring Ko-Ko the Clown and, later, Betty Boop and
10 Popeye.

The first cartoon with sound was *Steamboat Willie* (1928), which introduced Mickey Mouse.
This film was produced by Walt Disney, the most famous of American animators. His early success
enabled Disney to train his animators in anatomy, acting, drawing, and motion studies. The results of
this are apparent in *Snow White and the Seven Dwarfs* (1937), the first full-length animated feature.
15 It became an instant success, and still remains popular. Other important Disney films followed.

Warner Brothers' studio challenged Disney for leadership in the field with cartoons starring
Bugs Bunny, Daffy Duck, and other characters. These films were faster-paced and featured slapstick
humor. In the 1950s, a group of animators splintered off from Disney and formed United Production
of America, which rejected Disney's realism and employed a bold, modernistic approach.
20 In the 1950s, children's cartoons began to be broadcast on Saturday morning television and,
later, in prime time. Among the most successful were those made by William Hanna and Joseph
Barbera, such as those featuring Yogi Bear and the Flintstones.

The full-length animated film became popular again in the 1980s and '90s. Producer Steven
Spielberg released his first animated film, *An American Tail* (1986), and Disney began a series of
25 remarkable annual hits with *The Little Mermaid* (1989). *Who Framed Roger Rabbit?* (1988), a joint
production of Spielberg and Disney, blurred the lines between live action and animation. Animation
returned to prime-time television with the Fox Network's *The Simpsons*. Animators had experimented with computer animation as early as the 1950s, but *Toy Story* (1995) was the first full-length
film to be entirely computer animated. These developments promise to bring about the most exciting
30 era in animation since its heyday.

33. What does the passage mainly discuss?

(A) the history of animated film
(B) the life of Walt Disney
(C) the development of one animated cartoon
(D) the use of computers in animation

34. It can be inferred from the passage that the characters in *Little Nemo* and *Gertie the Dinosaur*

(A) were first drawn on a blackboard
(B) were part of a cartoon series
(C) seemed to have their own personalities
(D) did not look as lifelike as Blackton's characters

35. The word *streamlined* in line 5 is closest in meaning to

(A) simplified
(B) revolutionized
(C) bypassed
(D) invented

36. The word *he* in line 8 refers to

(A) Pat Sullivan
(B) Felix the Cat
(C) Max Fleischer
(D) Ko Ko the Clown

37. What can be inferred from the passage about animated films produced before 1928?

(A) They were not very popular.
(B) They were longer than later movies.
(C) They were not drawn by hand.
(D) They were silent films.

38. According to the passage, the film *Snow White and the Seven Dwarfs*

(A) showed the benefits of training the Disney animators

(B) was the first movie produced by Walt Disney

(C) was the last movie Disney made before his death

(D) did not become successful until many years later

39. The phrase *splintered off from* in line 18 is closest in meaning to

(A) competed with

(B) broke away from

(C) merged with

(D) released from

40. The author does NOT specifically mention characters produced by

(A) Walt Disney

(B) Hanna and Barbera

(C) United Productions of America

(D) Warner Brothers

41. The phrase *blurred the lines* in line 26 is closest in meaning to

(A) eliminated the distinctions

(B) obscured the issues

(C) answered the questions

(D) emphasized the problems

42. The first experiments with computer animation took place during the

(A) 1950s

(B) 1960s

(C) 1980s

(D) 1990s

43. Which of the following is closest in meaning to the word *heyday* in line 30?

(A) Beginning

(B) Decline

(C) Prime

(D) Rebirth

44. Where in the passage does the author first mention animation on television?

(A) Line 7

(B) Line 11

(C) Lines 20–21

(D) Lines 26–27

Questions 45–50

Line Fog is a cloud in contact with or just above the surface of land or sea. It can be a major environmental hazard. Fog on highways can cause chain-reaction accidents involving dozens of cars. Delays and shutdowns at airports can cause economic losses to airlines and inconvenience to thousands of travelers. Fog at sea has always been a danger to navigation. Today, with supertankers carrying vast
5 quantities of oil, fog increases the possibility of catastrophic oil spills.

The most common type of fog, radiation fog, forms at night, when moist air near the ground loses warmth through radiation on a clear night. This type of fog often occurs in valleys, such as California's San Joaquin Valley. Another common type, advection fog, results from the movement of warm, wet air over cold ground. The air loses temperature to the ground and condensation sets in.
10 This type of fog often occurs along the California coast and the shores of the Great Lakes. Advection fog also forms when air associated with a warm ocean current blows across the surface of a cold current. The thick fogs of the Grand Banks off Newfoundland, Canada, are largely of this origin, because here the Labrador Current comes in contact with the warm Gulf Stream.

Two other types of fog are somewhat more unusual. Frontal fog occurs when two fronts of
15 different temperatures meet, and rain from the warm front falls into the colder one, saturating the air. Steam fog appears when cold air picks up moisture by moving over warmer water.

45. The first paragraph focuses on which aspect of fog?

(A) its dangers
(B) its composition
(C) its beauty
(D) its causes

46. The word *catastrophic* in line 5 is closest in meaning to

(A) accidental
(B) inevitable
(C) unexpected
(D) disastrous

47. According to the article, fog that occurs along the California coast is generally

(A) radiation fog
(B) advection fog
(C) frontal fog
(D) steam fog

48. It can be inferred from the passage that the Labrador Current is

(A) cold
(B) weak
(C) polluted
(D) warm

49. The author organizes the discussion of the different types of fog according to

(A) their geographic locations
(B) their relative density
(C) the types of problems they cause
(D) their relative frequency

50. The author of the passage is probably an expert in the field of

(A) physics
(B) economics
(C) transportation
(D) meteorology

THIS IS THE END OF SECTION 3.

IF YOU FINISH BEFORE THE TIME LIMIT, CHECK YOUR WORK ON SECTION 3 ONLY.

DO NOT READ OR WORK ON ANY OTHER SECTION OF THE TEST.

Test of Written English (TWE)

INTRODUCTION

The TWE is given before the other three sections of TOEFL. It is currently given five times a year: in February, May, August, September, and October. There is no additional fee required to take the TWE.

TWE differs from the rest of TOEFL in that it is **productive**. Instead of choosing one of four answer choices, you must write your own short essay. TWE consists of a single essay topic; there is no choice as to what to write about. You have 30 minutes in which to write an essay based on the topic. A typical TWE answer is about 200 to 300 words long and is divided into four or five paragraphs.

The most common type of TWE topic asks you to write a contrast/opinion essay. In this type of essay, you must contrast two points of view, then defend one of those positions. Another type of essay asks you to select some development, invention, or phenomenon and explain its importance. Essay topics that ask you to interpret the information given in a graph or chart are no longer given.

Important: Don't take TWE if you don't need to! Many universities that require TOEFL scores do NOT require TWE scores. There is no way to cancel your TWE score without canceling your TOEFL score, and a low TWE score may have a negative effect on your application *even though you were not required to take the test.* If you are certain that you won't need a TWE score, sign up for a test administration when TWE is not given. If you must sign up for a test when TWE is given, you may fill in your name and registration number, then sit quitely for the next half hour. You will then receive a "score" of NR, indicating that you did not respond. University admission officers will then ignore your TWE results.

RED ALERT

Key #1

Budget your time carefully.

You have only a half hour in which to complete your work. You should use your time more or less as shown below:

Reading and thinking about the topic	2–3 minutes
Planning and taking notes	2–3 minutes
Writing the essay	approximately 20 minutes
Checking the essay	3–5 minutes

As with all parts of the TOEFL, be familiar with the directions for TWE so that you don't have to waste time reading them.

Key #2

Read the question carefully.

You must write on the topic exactly as it is given, so be sure that you understand it. If you write about another topic, you won't receive a score at all. If you don't completely address the topic, you will receive a lower score.

Key #3

Brainstorm!

Before you begin to write, spend a minute or two ''brainstorming.'' Think about the topic and the best way to approach it. Remember: there is no ''correct'' answer for the TWE questions. You can choose to support any position as long as you can adequately support your choice. Jot down any ideas you have while you're brainstorming.

Key #4

Plan your essay before you write.

You don't have to write out a formal outline with Roman numerals, capital letters, and so on. However, you *should* make some notes. By following your notes, you can organize your essay *before* you write, leaving you free to concentrate on the task of writing.

When making notes, don't worry about writing complete, grammatical sentences; use abbreviations if possible. The point of taking notes is to simply get your ideas down on paper as quickly as possible.

Key #5

Be sure your handwriting is as clear and legible as possible.

Handwriting that is hard to read may unconsciously prejudice the readers who are grading your essay. Be sure your handwriting is not too small or too large.

Key #6

Follow a clear, logical organization.

All TWE essays should consist of three basic parts: an **introductory paragraph**, a **body** that consists of two or three paragraphs, and a **concluding paragraph**. You need to include all of these elements in your essay. The introduction states the main idea of the essay in one sentence called the **thesis statement** and may provide some background about that idea. The body develops the main idea brought up in the introduction. Specific examples are given to make the thesis statement seem stronger and believable to the reader. The conclusion evaluates and summarizes the material that is in the body. It provides the reader with a sense of closure—the feeling that the essay is really finished, not that the writer simply ran out of time.

The exact plan of organization you use depends on the type of topic you are given. The following patterns could be used for the two main types of topics commonly given. Of course, these are not the only patterns that could be used in writing TWE essays, but they are effective plans for organizing your ideas.

TOPIC TYPE A: CONTRAST/OPINION

Introduction: Paragraph 1:   Present the two sides of the issue; give a brief amount of background information.

Body: Paragraph 2:   Discuss the negative side of the issue; give examples.

Paragraph 3:   Discuss the positive side of the issue; give examples.

Conclusion: Paragraph 4:   Express your own opinion about the issue; give specific reasons for your decision.

TOPIC TYPE B: EXPLAIN THE IMPORTANCE OF A DEVELOPMENT, INVENTION, OR PHENOMENON

Introduction: Paragraph 1:   Explain what development you have chosen to write about and why.

Body: Paragraph 2:   Discuss one aspect of why this development is important; give examples.

Paragraph 3:   Discuss another aspect of why this development is important; give examples.

Conclusion: Paragraph 4:   Summarize the points made in paragraphs 2 and 3.

Key #7

Use concrete examples and specific reasons.

Whenever you make a general statement, you should support it with specific examples. Don't just say, "Computers are important to modern business." Give specific examples of how computers can benefit businesses. If you state an opinion, give reasons. Don't just say, "I believe television is harmful to children." Explain exactly why you think television hurts children.

Key #8

Use signal words to indicate transitions.

Signal words can be used to join paragraph to paragraph and sentence to sentence. These words make your essay clearer and easier to follow. Some of these expressions and their meanings are given below.

Expressions Used to List Points, Examples, or Reasons

First example or reason
> First . . .
> The first example is . . .
> The first reason it . . .

Additional examples or reasons
> Second, . . . (Third, Fourth)
> A second (third, fourth) example is that . . .
> Another example is . . .
> Another reason is . . .
> In addition, . . .
> Furthermore, . . .
> Moreover, . . .

Final examples or reasons
> Finally, . . .

To give individual examples
> For example, . . .
> For instance, . . .
> To give a specific example, . . .
> X is an example of Y.

To show contrast
> However, . . .
> On the other hand, . . .
> Nevertheless, . . .

To show a conclusion
> Therefore, . . .
> Consequently, . . .

To show similarity
> Likewise, . . .
> Similarly, . . .

To begin a concluding paragraph
> In conclusion, . . .
> In summary, . . .

Examples of the Use of Signal Words

I agree with the idea of stricter gun control for a number of reasons. *First*, statistics show that guns are not very effective in preventing crime. *Second*, accidents involving guns occur frequently. *Finally*, guns can be stolen and later used in crimes.

I believe that a good salary is an important consideration when looking for a career. *However,* the nature of the work is more important to me. *Thus*, I would not accept a job that I did not find rewarding.

For me, the reasons for living in an urban area are stronger than the reasons for living in a rural community. *Therefore*, I agree with those people who believe it is an advantage to live in a big city.

Key #9

Use a variety of sentence types.

Good writing in English consists of a more or less equal balance between short, simple sentences consisting of only one clause and longer sentences containing two or more clauses. Therefore, make an effort to use sentences of various lengths.

You should also vary sentence structures. Begin some sentences with prepositional phrases or subordinate clauses.

Examples of various sentence types

Instead of . . .

I agree with this idea for several reasons.

Try . . .

For several reasons, I agree with this idea.

Instead of . . .

I support Idea A even though Idea B has some positive attributes.

Try . . .

Even though Idea B has some positive attributes, I support Idea A.

Key #10

Check your essay for errors.

Allow a few minutes to proofread the essay. However, don't make any major changes at this time. Don't cross out long sections or try to add a lot of new material. Look for obvious errors in punctuation, spelling, and capitalization as well as common grammatical mistakes: subject-verb agreement, wrong tense, incorrect use of plurals, incorrect word forms, and so on. If you have ever taken a writing class in English, look at the corrections the teacher made on your papers to see what types of mistakes you commonly make, and look for these.

FOUR PRACTICE TWE TESTS

The following exams are similar to actual TWE tests. Time yourself carefully while taking these practice tests. You can use the scoring chart on p. 168 to estimate your score. If you are taking an English course, you may want to ask your English teacher to score your test and to make recommendations for improving your essay.

PRACTICE TWE—30 MINUTES

1. When you are ready, turn the page and carefully read the essay prompt.

2. Before you begin writing, think about the prompt. You will probably want to make some notes to organize your thoughts. Use only the space marked NOTES to write notes or an outline.

3. Write on only one topic. If you do not write on the topic given, you will not receive a score.

4. Your essay should be clear and precise. Support your ideas with facts. The quality of your writing is more important than the quantity, but you will probably want to write more than one paragraph.

5. Begin your essay on the first line of the essay page. Use the next page if you need to. Write as neatly as possible. Don't write in large letters. Don't skip lines or leave large margins.

6. Check your essay after you have finished. Give yourself enough time to read over your essay and make minor revisions before the end of the exam.

7. After 30 minutes, stop writing and put your pencil down.

PRACTICE TWE 1

Some people believe that it is more advantageous to study at a small college or university. Others take the opposite view, that a large college or university offers better educational opportunities. Discuss these two positions. Tell which one you agree with, and explain your decision.

NOTES

Use this space for essay notes only. Write the final version of your essay on the next two pages.

_____

_____

_____

_____

_____

_____

_____

_____

_____

_____

_____

_____

_____

_____

_____

_____

_____

_____

_____

_____

_____

Name: _____

Write your essay here.

_____

_____

_____

_____

_____

_____

_____

_____

_____

_____

_____

_____

_____

_____

_____

_____

_____

_____

_____

_____

_____

_____

_____

_____

_____

PRACTICE TWE 2

One reason that a job is desirable is a good salary. Choose one other factor that you think is important in choosing a job. Give specific reasons for your choice.

NOTES

Use this space for essay notes only. Write the final version of your essay on the next two pages.

_____

_____

_____

_____

_____

_____

_____

_____

_____

_____

_____

_____

_____

_____

_____

_____

_____

_____

_____

_____

Name: _____

Write your essay here.

_____

_____

_____

_____

_____

_____

_____

_____

_____

_____

_____

_____

_____

_____

_____

_____

_____

_____

_____

_____

_____

_____

_____

_____

PRACTICE TWE 3

The use of modern technology has had significant effects on many fields. For example, the use of modern communication devices and computers has practically revolutionized the banking industry. Select another industry, profession, or field of study that has been influenced by modern technology. Give specific examples of the effects technology has had on that field.

NOTES

Use this space for essay notes only. Write the final version of your essay on the next two pages.

_____

_____

_____

_____

_____

_____

_____

_____

_____

_____

_____

_____

_____

_____

_____

_____

_____

_____

_____

_____

_____

Name: _____

Write your essay here.

_____

_____

_____

_____

_____

_____

_____

_____

_____

_____

_____

_____

_____

_____

_____

_____

_____

_____

_____

_____

_____

_____

_____

_____

_____

_____

PRACTICE TWE 4

Some people believe that all schoolchildren of a certain age should be educated together. Others take the position that children should be separated into groups, depending on their skills and abilities. Discuss both positions. Tell which one you agree with, and explain why.

NOTES

Use this space for essay notes only. Write the final version of your essay on the next two pages.

_____

_____

_____

_____

_____

_____

_____

_____

_____

_____

_____

_____

_____

_____

_____

_____

_____

_____

_____

_____

Name: _____

Write your essay here.

_____

_____

_____

_____

_____

_____

_____

_____

_____

_____

_____

_____

_____

_____

_____

_____

_____

_____

_____

_____

_____

_____

_____

SCORING THE PRACTICE TESTS

The level of difficulty varies slightly from one TOEFL test to another. ETS uses a statistical process called "test equating" to adjust each set of scores. The chart given below can be used only to determine a range of scores. ETS, of course, reports your score as a single number, not as a range.

After completing each test, obtain a raw score for each of the three sections by counting the number of correct answers in the three sections. Then look at the score conversion chart to determine the range of scaled scores for each section. Add the three low scores from the range of scores for each section, then the three high scores. Multiply both totals by 10 and divide by 3. Your "actual" TOEFL score will lie somewhere in that range of numbers.

For example, suppose that you had 32 correct answers in Listening Comprehension, 29 in Structure and Written Expression, and 37 in Reading Comprehension:

	Raw Score (number correct)	Range of Scaled Scores (from conversion chart)
Section 1	32	49-50
Section 2	29	50-52
Section 3	37	53-54

49 + 50 + 53 = 152
50 + 52 + 54 = 156

152 × 10 = 1,520 ÷ 3 = 507
156 × 10 = 1,560 ÷ 3 = 520

Your score on the practice test would be between 507 and 520.

SCORE CONVERSION CHART I
PRACTICE TESTS 1, 2, 4, AND 5

SECTION 1 RAW SCORES	RANGE OF SCALED SCORES	SECTION 2 RAW SCORES	RANGE OF SCALED SCORES	SECTION 3 RAW SCORES	RANGE OF SCALED SCORES
48-50	65-68	39-40	64-68	48-50	65-67
45-47	57-64	36-38	60-64	45-47	57-64
42-44	55-57	34-35	57-59	42-44	56-57
39-41	54-55	31-33	53-56	39-41	55-56
36-38	52-54	29-30	50-52	36-38	53-54
33-35	50-52	27-28	49-50	33-35	51-52
30-32	49-50	24-26	48-49	30-32	50-51
27-29	47-48	21-23	46-48	27-29	48-49
24-26	45-47	18-20	43-45	24-26	46-47
21-23	44-45	15-17	39-42	21-23	44-45
18-20	42-44	12-14	36-38	18-20	42-44
15-17	39-41	9-11	32-35	15-17	39-41
12-14	36-38	6-8	28-32	12-14	36-38
9-11	33-36	3-5	24-27	9-11	33-36
6-8	29-32	0-2	20-23	6-8	29-32
3-5	25-28			3-5	25-28
0-2	23-24			0-2	21-24

SCORE CONVERSION CHART II
PRACTICE TEST 3 (LONG FORM)

SECTION 1		SECTION 2		SECTION 3	
RAW SCORES	**RANGE OF SCALED SCORES**	**RAW SCORES**	**RANGE OF SCALED SCORES**	**RAW SCORES**	**RANGE OF SCALED SCORES**
77–80	64–68	58–60	64–68	72–75	65–67
72–76	59–63	54–57	59–63	69–70	61–64
68–71	57–58	50–53	56–58	65–68	58–60
63–67	54–56	45–49	53–55	61–64	56–57
59–62	52–53	41–44	50–52	57–60	54–55
54–58	50–51	36–40	48–49	53–56	53–54
50–53	49–50	32–35	45–47	50–52	51–52
45–49	47–48	27–31	43–44	46–49	49–50
41–44	46–47	23–26	40–42	42–45	47–48
36–40	44–45	18–22	36–39	40–42	45–46
32–35	42–43	14–17	31–35	36–40	43–45
27–31	40–41	9–13	26–30	32–35	40–42
23–26	37–39	5–8	23–25	27–31	38–39
18–22	33–36	0–4	20–22	23–26	35–37
14–17	31–35			18–22	33–34
9–13	26–30			14–17	31–32
5–8	24–25			9–13	27–30
0–4	22–23			5–8	23–26
				0–4	20–22

PERSONAL SCORE RECORD

Practice Test 1			
Section 1 Range of Scores	Section 2 Range of Scores	Section 3 Range of Scores	Total Range of Scores

Practice Test 2			
Section 1 Range of Scores	Section 2 Range of Scores	Section 3 Range of Scores	Total Range of Scores

Practice Test 3			
Section 1 Range of Scores	Section 2 Range of Scores	Section 3 Range of Scores	Total Range of Scores

Practice Test 4			
Section 1 Range of Scores	Section 2 Range of Scores	Section 3 Range of Scores	Total Range of Scores

Practice Test 5			
Section 1 Range of Scores	Section 2 Range of Scores	Section 3 Range of Scores	Total Range of Scores

SCORING THE PRACTICE TWE TESTS

ETS uses a scoring system similar to the one given below to score TWEs. You can use this chart to estimate your TWE score when you take the TWE Practice Tests. If you are taking an English course, you may want to ask your teacher to "score" the exam for you, and to make recommendations for improving your essay.

Score   **Explanation of Score**

6 Strongly indicates the ability to write a well-organized, well-developed, and logical essay. Specific examples and details support the main ideas. All the elements of the essay are unified and cohesive. A variety of sentence structures are used successfully, and sophisticated vocabulary is employed. Grammatical errors are infrequent but a few minor mistakes may occur.

5 Indicates the ability to write an organized, developed, and logical essay. The main ideas are adequately supported by examples and details. Sentence structure may be less varied than that of a level 6 essay, and vocabulary less sophisticated. Some grammatical errors will appear.

4 Indicates a moderate ability to write an acceptable essay. Although main ideas may be adequately supported, weaknesses in organization and development will be apparent. Sentence structure and vocabulary may lack sophistication or be used inappropriately. Grammatical errors may be frequent.

3 Indicates some minimal ability in writing an acceptable essay, but involves serious weaknesses in organization and development. Significant sentence structure and vocabulary problems occur, and there are frequent grammatical errors that sometimes make the writer's ideas difficult to comprehend.

2 Indicates the inability to write an acceptable essay. Organization and development are weak or nonexistent. Lacks unity and cohesion. Few if any specific details may be given in support of the writer's ideas. If details are given, they may seem inappropriate. Significant and frequent errors in grammar occur throughout the essay. The writer may not have fully understood the essay topic.

1 Strongly indicates the inability to write an acceptable essay. No apparent development or organization. Sentences may be brief and fragmentary and unrelated to one another. Significant grammatical errors occur throughout the essay and make it difficult to understand any of the author's ideas. The writer may have completely misunderstood the essay topic.

OFF Did not write on the topic assigned.

NR Did not write the essay.

The average TWE score is between 3.5 and 4.0. TWE is scored separately from the rest of the test and has no effect on your overall TOEFL score.

PERSONAL SCORE RECORD: PRACTICE TWEs

Practice TWE 1 _____

Practice TWE 2 _____

Practice TWE 3 _____

Practice TWE 4 _____

Practice Tests

ANSWER KEYS AND TAPESCRIPTS

Practice Test 1

SECTION 1: LISTENING COMPREHENSION

Answer Key

1. C	11. B	21. A	31. B	41. B
2. D	12. B	22. B	32. D	42. D
3. C	13. D	23. B	33. A	43. C
4. A	14. A	24. C	34. D	44. A
5. B	15. D	25. D	35. B	45. C
6. B	16. C	26. A	36. C	46. D
7. D	17. A	27. C	37. A	47. B
8. C	18. D	28. B	38. A	48. D
9. A	19. D	29. C	39. A	49. C
10. C	20. C	30. A	40. B	50. B

PART A

TAPESCRIPT*

1. M1: I can't find those photographs I just had developed.
   F1: I think I saw them on the piano.
   M2: What does the woman mean?

2. F2: Fred sure was angry.
   M1: I'll say. He left without saying goodbye to anyone.
   M2: What does the man say about Fred?

3. M1: What an uncomfortable-looking chair.
   F1: Well, it may look that way—but just try it out!
   M2: What does the woman imply?

4. M1: So, where are the rose gardens? Didn't you say they were here on the west side of the park?
   F2: No, no—I said they were on the *east* side.
   M2: What does the woman mean?

5. F2: George, is Linda leaving tonight?
   M1: I *think* that's what she said.
   M2: What does George say about Linda?

6. M1: Two weeks' work—down the drain!
   F1: On, no—your experiment wasn't successful?
   M2: What is learned about the man from this conversation?

7. F1: I see Carrie's riding her bike again. Did she fix it herself?
   M1: I think she got her brother to do it.
   M2: What does the man believe about Carrie?

---

* Note: M1 = first male voice   M2 = second male voice   F1 = first female voice   F2 = second female voice

8. M1: Did the band play for about 2 hours?
F1: No. This time, the concert was over in an hour and a half.
M2: How long did the concert last?

9. F2: Maybe you could get a ride to campus with Peggy tomorrow.
M1: Oh, Peggy no longer drives to class.
M2: What does the man say about Peggy?

10. M1: Swimming is good exercise.
F1: Of course. And so is dancing.
M2: What does the woman mean?

11. M1: I need to go out. Is it still raining?
F1: Yes, but it's starting to let up a little.
M2: What does the woman mean?

12. M1: Then you and Robert finished your project on time?
F2: Yes—no thanks to Robert!
M2: What does the woman imply?

13. F2: I just heard that Professor Hendrix is retiring at the end of the semester.
F1: Too bad—I was hoping to take his chemistry course next semester.
M2: What is learned about Professor Hendrix from this conversation?

14. M1: I'd like some flowers delivered to Hillcrest Hospital.
F1: Certainly. If you step over here, I'll show you some arrangements.
M2: What is the man going to do?

15. M1: My watch isn't running.
F2: Why not have the jeweler around the corner fix it?
M2: What does the woman suggest the man do?

16. M1: Just think—in another couple of days, I'll be in Montreal.
F1: How will you get around once you get there?
M2: What does the woman ask the man?

17. F1: I'm exhausted. I can't wait for the weekend to get here.
M1: Need a little rest, do you?
M2: What does the man mean?

18. F2: Diane is always saying she loves to go ice-skating.
M1: Yes, but when's the last time you actually saw her out on the ice?
M2: What does the man imply about Diane?

19. M1: I'd like to return this sweater because it's too small. I don't have the receipt with me, though.
F2: You could exchange the sweater for another size. But if you don't have the receipt, I won't be able to give you your money back.
M2: What does the woman tell the man?

20. M1: Have you ever eaten at the Fisherman's Grotto?
F1: Have I? I never go to the beach without stopping there.
M2: What does the woman mean?

21. M1: Brenda, will you play that song you wrote?
F1: Only if you accompany me on the guitar.
M2: What does Brenda want the man to do?

22. M1: I'm planning to clean up the kitchen this afternoon.
F2: Shouldn't you clean the rest of your apartment while you're at it?
M2: What does the woman tell the man?

23. F2: That was a great play, wasn't it?

M1: Yeah, the cast was wonderful. I could hardly believe they weren't professional actors.

M2: What does the man mean?

24. F1: There are only a few drops left in the can. I guess we'll have to buy some in the morning.

M1: Well, we can finish up this job tomorrow. Let's just wash out our brushes for now.

M2: What will they probably buy in the morning.

25. F1: Jim, can I have one of those bananas you bought?

M1: Sorry—they're still not ripe enough.

M2: What does Jim mean?

26. F2: The students in Professor Murray's class think that the test he gave was unfair.

F1: A few of them do, anyway.

M2: What can be inferred from this conversation?

27. M1: John sure knows some good places to eat, doesn't he?

F2: Yeah, when it comes to finding great restaurants, John wrote the book.

M2: What does the woman say about John?

28. M1: Look at my face! I got sunburned again yesterday.

F2: Maybe next time you'll remember to wear your hat when you're working in the garden.

M2: What does the woman think the man should do?

29. F1: Were any of the windows unlocked?

M1: Not one of them.

M2: What does the man mean?

30. F2: Harry, what's your new roommate like?

M1: Well, for one thing, he's very outgoing.

M2: What does Harry say about his roommate?

PART B

Questions 31 to 34: Listen to a conversation on a college campus.

M1: Excuse me, I'm trying to find my way to Reynolds Hall.

F1: Reynolds Hall? I don't think I know where that is.

M1: I'm looking for an exhibit of graduate student paintings. The campus newspaper said it was in Reynolds Hall.

F1: Oh, now I know where you mean. Everyone on campus just calls that the Art Building.

M1: So how do I get there?

F1: Go straight ahead until you come to the main library. You'll see a walkway leading off to the left. Go that way, and then past the Chemistry Building . . .

M1: Let's see . . . to the library, take the walkway to the right . . .

F1: No, to the left.

M1: To the left, and past the Chemistry Building . . .

F1: That's right, and then you'll cross a little service road. Walk just a little bit farther and there's the Art Building. You can't miss it because there's a big abstract metal sculpture right in front of it.

M1: I think I've got it.

F1: I hope you enjoy the exhibit. Usually the graduate student exhibits are very interesting, and I've heard this one is especially good.

M1: Actually, the main reason I'm going is that my sister has a couple of paintings in the show. I wanted to take a look at them.

31. M2: Why was the woman at first confused when the man asked her for directions?

32. M2: According to the woman, what is directly in front of the Art Building?

33. M2: What can be inferred from the conversation about the man's sister?

34. M2: What is the woman's attitude toward the man?

Questions 35 to 38: Listen to a conversation in an astronomy class.

M1: Professor Carmichael, I'd like to ask a question. You just said that, according to Einstein, nothing can go faster than the speed of light. Is that right?

F2: Yes, Ted, that's what Einstein said, and most scientists agree with him.

M1: Then does that mean that we could never build spaceships to go to other stars?

F2: Well, let's think about it. Do you remember how far it is to the nearest star?

M1: Umm . . . I think you said a few days ago that it's about four light years.

F2: About that. And how fast does light travel?

M1: Around 186,000 miles per second.

F2: Yes, and a light-year is the distance light travels in a YEAR! Imagine that! A light-year is the equivalent of almost 6 trillion miles.

M1: But what if we built a ship that could go ALMOST as fast as light. Then we could get to the closest star in four or five years.

F2: That's true in theory. Unfortunately, there are no spaceships that can even approach the speed of light. Even if we built ships that are MUCH faster than the rockets we have today, it would probably take hundreds or thousands of years to get to the closest stars. How could you carry enough fuel to last that long? We'd need a completely different method of powering spaceships.

M1: So you're saying that you don't think people will ever be able to travel to the stars?

F2: Well, I don't want to say never, Ted. Who knows what kinds of scientific breakthroughs there will be? But I think for the foreseeable future, there will only be starships in science fiction movies and books.

35. M2: What had Professor Carmichael been talking about when Ted asked her a question?

36. M2: If a ship could travel almost as fast as light, how long would it take to get to the closest star?

37. M2: According to Professor Carmichael, what must be developed before ships can travel to the closest stars?

38. M2: How does Professor Carmichael characterize travel to other stars?

PART C

Questions 39 to 41: Listen to a talk given at a newspaper office.

F2: Good afternoon, ladies and gentlemen, and welcome to the *Daily Gazette* Building. As I'm sure you're aware from your journalism classes, large newspapers are divided into a number of areas, all of them important to the success of the overall operation. We'll be visiting three important departments today. We'll begin our tour with a visit to the Circulation Department, which is responsible for distributing the paper all over the city. Then we'll move to the Editorial Department. In that department, there's the City Desk, which is responsible for gathering and reporting local news. The National Desk and the International Desk are there, too, and various feature desks. Since you're probably most interested in that part of our operation, we'll be spending most of our time there, and you'll have a chance to chat with some of our reporters. Finally, we'll visit the Production Department, where the newspaper is printed. Please step this way.

39. M2: Whom is the speaker addressing?

40. M2: Where will the people listening to this talk go first?

41. M2: According to the speaker, what type of work is done at the City Desk?

Questions 42 to 46: Listen to part of a talk about a special student program.

M1: Good evening. For you who don't know me, I'm Professor Mackenzie of the School of Architecture here at Hunt University. I've been involved with "Semester Afloat" for some years now, so I've been asked to give this introductory talk about the program. So, what is "Semester Afloat"? It's an educational program that is held aboard an ocean-going ship, the *S. S. Apollo.* There are three programs you can sign up for—one in the eastern Mediterranean, one in the western Mediterranean, and one in Southeast Asia. You'll have the opportunity to see some unforgettable sights. There are many social activities, and you'll make lasting friendships during the semester you spend on the ship, but tonight I want to talk mainly about the academic program. The *S. S. Apollo* is a floating university. The faculty is recruited from the top universities in North America. There's an excellent library aboard. You'll study the history, language, art, and architecture of the countries that you visit. I, myself, have taught courses in historical architecture during two eastern Mediterranean programs, and I can tell you, those classes are unlike any classes you can take here at Hunt or anywhere else. For example, last semester I gave a lecture about Greek temple design one morning, and that afternoon, I took my class out to see several Greek temples for themselves. Oh, and of course, for all the classes you take, you'll receive academic credit at almost any university in the United States. Now, I have a lot more information about this program for you, but before I go on, I want to introduce two students who took part in "Semester Afloat" last semester, and you can ask them any questions you like.

42. M2: What aspect of the "Semester Afloat" program does Professor Mackenzie's talk focus on?

43. M2: What did Professor Mackenzie teach during the "Semester Afloat" programs?

44. M2: With which of these "Semester Afloat" programs was Professor Mackenzie associated?

45. M2: What does Professor Mackenzie say about "Semester Afloat" classes?"

46. M2: Whom will Professor Mackenzie introduce to the audience next?

Questions 47 to 50: Listen to a talk about olympic speedskating.

F1: Speed skating has been a Winter Olympic event for many years, but in recent years, conditions on the ice tracks used by speed skaters have gotten better. Until the most recent Winter Olympics, speed-skating events were held outdoors. Conditions on outdoor ice tracks vary from hour to hour, depending on the weather. On indoor tracks, conditions can be controlled, giving all skaters an equal opportunity to skate at the top of their form. On indoor tracks, a constant temperature of 20° Fahrenheit can be maintained. This is important because if the ice is too cold, it forms frost, slowing down the skaters, and it chips easily. If the temperature is too high, the ice begins to melt. Also, ice tracks today are made with extremely pure water. Minerals in water make ice soft, and soft ice doesn't provide enough resistance for skates. Recent improvements in making and maintaining ice will almost certainly lead to new world records in speed skating in the near future.

47. M2: What aspect of speed skating does the speaker primarily discuss?

48. M2: What does the speaker imply about speed skaters who competed before the most recent Winter Olympics?

49. M2: According to the speaker, what happens to ice that contains too many minerals?

50. M2: What prediction does the speaker make about the near future?

SECTION 2: STRUCTURE AND WRITTEN EXPRESSION

Answer Key

1. B	11. B	21. A	31. B
2. B	12. C	22. B	32. C
3. A	13. B	23. D	33. A
4. C	14. A	24. A	34. B
5. A	15. D	25. C	35. D
6. D	16. B	26. C	36. C
7. C	17. D	27. D	37. B
8. A	18. C	28. C	38. A
9. D	19. C	29. C	39. C
10. A	20. D	30. B	40. C

EXPLANATION: WRITTEN EXPRESSION

16. The past participle *written* should be used in place of the present participle *writing*. The past participle is used to reduce (shorten) a relative clause with a passive verb. *In an essay written in 1799* is a short way to say *In an essay that was written in 1779.*

17. A singular pronoun (*itself*) must be used because the pronoun refers to a singular noun phrase (*a metallic object*).

18. An adverb (*abruptly*) must be used in place of the adjective *abrupt* because this word is used to modify a verb (*occurs*).

19. The preposition *of* has been omitted from the phrase *by means of*.

20. A plural verb form (*bounce*) is required because the subject of the clause (*sound waves*) is plural.

21. The correct word form is *carpenter*. (*Carpentry* refers to the field; *carpenter* refers to a person who works in that field.)

22. The relative pronoun *who* is used to refer to persons. The pronoun *which* should be used to refer to inanimate things.

23. A possessive adjective (*her*) should be used in place of *the* to indicate that this is the career of a particular person (*Mary Gardner*).

24. The correct work order is *the sky is*. (The expression *when the sky is clear* is an adverb clause, not a direct question; therefore, the word order is subject + verb, not verb + subject as in direct questions.)

25. The correct word pattern is *both . . . and*.

26. To be parallel with the other verbs in the series (*makes* and *lines*) another full verb (*closes*) is needed in place of the *-ing* form *closing*.

27. The noun *loss* should be used in place of the verb *lost*.

28. The verb *made* should be used in place of the verb *done*; the verb means "constructed" in this sentence.

29. To be parallel with the other items in the series (*status* and *love*), the noun *wealth* should be used in place of the adjective *wealthy*.

30. The singular verb *is* should be used in place of the plural verb *are* to agree with the singular subject *coloring*. (The nouns *red, orange,* and *brown* are adjectives modifying the subject, but are not subjects themselves.)

31. The word *also* cannot be used by itself to connect parts of a sentence; *and* or *and also* should be used.

32. The verb *ripen* must be used in place of the adjective *ripe*.

33. The correct preposition is *Since*. (This is indicated by the use of the present perfect verb form *have devoted*.)

34. In a passive verb phrase, a past participle (*found*) must be used rather than the simple form of the verb (*find*).

35. The correct form is *another*.

36. The correct verb form is *took place*.

37. *Machinery* is properly a noncount noun and cannot be pluralized; the plural-count noun *machines* is correct.

38. The word *many* must be used in place of *much* before a plural noun such as *people*. (Although the noun *people* does not end in the letter -*s*, it is still a plural word.)

39. The correct word order is *almost entirely*.

40. The adjective *native* is followed by the preposition *to*. (However, the noun *native* is often used with the preposition *of*; for example, "She's a native of Texas.")

SECTION 3: READING COMPREHENSION

Answer Key

1. D	11. D	21. B	31. A	41. C
2. C	12. C	22. C	32. C	42. A
3. A	13. B	23. B	33. D	43. A
4. D	14. A	24. C	34. C	44. A
5. A	15. A	25. D	35. D	45. C
6. B	16. B	26. A	36. B	46. D
7. C	17. C	27. D	37. B	47. B
8. B	18. A	28. B	38. C	48. D
9. D	19. B	29. A	39. B	49. A
10. B	20. D	30. C	40. D	50. B

1. The passage deals with the medical uses of optical fibers.

2. The passage states that optical fibers "have opened a window into the living tissues of the body" (line 2) and that with the use of this technology, "physicians can look into the lungs, intestines, and other areas that were formerly inaccessible" lines 4–5.

3. *Formerly* means *previously*.

4. The reference is to the physicians in line 4.

5. According to the passage, "the illuminating bundle, carries light to the tissues" (line 7).

6. The word *cores* is closest in meaning to *centers*.

7. Lines 11–13 state that "During the last five years improved methods of fabricating optical fibers have led to . . . an increase in the number of fibers."

8. In the context of the passage, *resolution* means *sharpness* (the sharpness of the image).

9. Whether fiber-optics techniques are easy to teach to doctors is not mentioned. Choices (A), (B), and (C) are all mentioned in the last paragraph.

10. A basic description of the fiberscope—"[it] consists of two bundles of fibers"—is provided in line 6.

11. The passage primarily deals with Alice Walker's book *The Color Purple* and with critical and popular reaction to the book.

12. *The Color Purple* is a novel and thus a work of fiction.

13. The word *vividly* means *graphically, distinctly*.

14. *Drudgery* means *hard work*—it is usually low-paying, uninteresting work as well.

15. Lines 9–10 indicate that eighteenth-century novelists used the epistolary style; in other words, their books told their stories through the use of letters. Line 12 says that Alice Walker also used this style in *The Color Purple*.

16. The author says that "Celie, like William Faulkner's character Dilsey, does not simply survive, but prevails" (line 14). The two characters are alike in that way.

17. The word *prevail* means *triumph, succeed, win*.

18. The author uses a number of positive terms in connection with the novel, such as "vividly narrates" (line 2) and "special flavor" (line 8). The author mentions that the novel was attacked by some critics but balances that by saying that it was praised by others, that it was a bestseller, and that it won some important literary awards (lines 4–7). All in all, the author's attitude is admiring.

19. According to the first paragraph, the changing colors of the blossoms tell insects which blossoms are full of pollen. Since the insects do not have to visit each blossom, they can gather pollen more efficiently.

20. The word *woo* means *attract, allure*.

21. The reference is to an insect.

22. The word *hue* means *color, shade*.

23. The word *Thus* means *therefore, consequently*.

24. A flower on the lantana plant "starts out . . . as yellow" (line 9) but "turns orange on the second day and red on the third" (lines 11–12).

25. The word *triggering* means *activating, stimulating*.

26. According to the passage, "a flower starts out on the first day as yellow" (line 9) and "insects visited the yellow flowers at least 100 times more than would be expected from haphazard visitation" (lines 14–15). Clearly, the flowers are most attractive to the insects on the first day.

27. Lines 15–17 indicate that the purpose of the experiments was to show that insects were responding to colors rather than to other stimuli, such as the scent (smell) of the nectar.

28. The word *haphazard* means *random, arbitrary*.

29. Lines 18–19 say that "In other types of plants, blossoms change from white to red, others from yellow to red, and so on." This indicates that these plants follow a variety of color-change sequences.

30. According to the passage, the phenomenon has been seen in "74 families of plants" (line 19).

31. The passage begins "The 1960s, however, saw a rising dissatisfaction with the Modernist movement." This indicates that the previous paragraph contained a description of Modernism, because this paragraph challenges the concepts of Modernism.

32. The word *highlighting* means *emphasizing, featuring*.

33. The reference is to Modernist structures (line 5).

34. The passage states that the Modernist movement's "failings were exposed" in the two books mentioned in the first paragraph, indicating that both Jacobs and Venturi were critical of Modernism.

35. According to the second paragraph, the event that signaled the beginning of post-Modernism was the demolition of Modernist buildings in St. Louis in 1972.

36. Venturi's design for the Brant-Johnson house in Vail, Colorado, "owes something to the Italian Renaissance" (lines 14–15).

37. The word *disciple* means *follower, pupil*.

38. Lines 17–18 indicates that these two buildings "incorporate historical souvenirs." This means that they include architectural features from the past that would generally not be associated with skyscrapers.

39. Line 21 says that "[this building is the] most complete instance of historical accuracy."

40. The main topic of the passage is nineteenth-century model communities. Choice (A) is not mentioned; choice (B) is too general; choice (C) is too specific.

41. The author states that "many nineteenth-century reformers hoped to bring about reform through education . . ." (line 1). However, these are not the "communitarian reformers" on whom the passage focuses.

42. Line 6 say that "A number of religious groups, most notably the Shakers, practiced communal living."

43. The word *impetus* means *stimulus, motivation*.

44. The word *thriving* means *prospering, flourishing*.

45. Lines 14–16 say that Fourier's theories influenced Americans through the writings of Albert Brisbane and that Fourierism involved self-sufficient associations called "phalanxes."

46. According to line 18, Hawthorne was "an early member of the latter" ("the latter" refers to Brook Farm).

47. According to lines 18–19, "Noyes founded the most enduring . . . of the utopian communities, the Oneida Community" (*enduring* means *long lasting*).

48. The word *oddest* (the superlative form of the adjective "odd") means *strangest, most unusual*.

49. The author begins the concluding sentence (the last sentence of the passage) with the phrase "needless to say . . . ," which means *obviously*.

50. The author presents an overview of the concept of model communities in the first paragraph and specific examples of this concept (New Harmony, Brook Farm, and the Oneida Community) in the second.

Practice Test 2

Answer Key

1. C	11. D	21. D	31. B	41. B
2. C	12. A	22. B	32. C	42. A
3. A	13. C	23. B	33. A	43. B
4. D	14. B	24. B	34. D	44. C
5. B	15. A	25. D	35. D	45. B
6. C	16. B	26. C	36. A	46. D
7. A	17. C	27. D	37. D	47. B
8. B	18. D	28. C	38. A	48. A
9. D	19. A	29. C	39. A	49. D
10. B	20. C	30. A	40. C	50. C

PART A

TAPESCRIPT*

1. F1: Have you seen my suitcase?
M2: I kept tripping over it, so I put it in the closet.
F2: What does the man mean?

2. F1: That's all you're having for dinner?
M1: I had a late lunch.
F2: What does the man imply?

3. M2: I thought Mary Ann would have a hard time getting used to college life.
M1: Were you ever wrong!
F2: What is learned from this conversation about Mary Ann?

4. F1: George, don't feel so bad. It's not your fault your brother failed that class.
M2: I don't know. I could have encouraged him to study more.
F2: How does George feel?

5. M1: Pamela made quite a few mistakes in the laboratory.
F1: Well, she wouldn't have if she hadn't been in such a hurry to get finished.
F2: What does the woman say about Pamela?

6. F1: Excuse me—I'm trying to get to the courthouse and I think I'm going the wrong way. Should I have turned left on Monroe Street?
M2: No, no you're all right. Just keep going straight on Fourth Avenue until you get to the Post Office, and turn left there.
F2: What is the woman's destination?

7. F1: Mitch and Lynn must have a lot in common since they're both economics majors.
M2: Oh, I didn't realize that Mitch was an economics major too.
F2: What does the man imply?

---

* Note: M1 = first male voice   M2 = second male voice   F1 = first female voice   F2 = second female voice

8. M1: I've got to call Tony right away.
F1: Yeah? How come?
F2: What does the woman ask the man?

9. F2: So, did you have a busy afternoon, Emory?
M1: Well, I watered the tomatoes and corn, and I did some weeding.
F2: What did Emory do this afternoon?

10. M2: Whom should we ask to introduce the guest speaker?
F1: What about Professor Welch?
F2: What does the woman imply about Professor Welch?

11. M2: Would you like milk or sugar in your coffee?
F1: Neither, thank you.
F2: What does the woman want?

12. F1: Did you find that movie exciting?
M1: Exciting! To put it mildly!
F2: What does the man say about the movie?

13. F1: Doug, are you looking forward to moving this weekend?
M1: Well, there are a couple of other ways I'd rather spend my weekend!
F2: What does Doug mean?

14. M2: I won't be able to come to rehearsal this evening.
F1: Arthur can't either. Maybe we should call it off.
F2: What does the woman mean?

15. F1: There's plenty of lemonade. Have another glass.
M1: Thanks, I believe I will.
F2: What will the man probably do?

16. F1: Do you know where Dean Nicholson's office is?
M2: There's a directory in the entrance way.
F2: What does the man imply about Dean Nicholson's office?

17. F2: Hotel rooms along the beach must be very expensive.
M1: Not now. During the off-season, they're dirt cheap.
F2: What does the man say about the hotel rooms?

18. M1: Hi Nora. I was just walking over to the cafeteria for lunch. Care to join me?
F1: I can't. I've got to go to a meeting. It's in the same building as the cafeteria though.
F2: What will Nora probably do?

19. M2: If we hurry, we'll be at the stadium in half an hour.
F1: At best.
F2: What does the woman mean?

20. F1: Joan is *not* what I'd call easygoing.
M1: I know. People find it hard to believe that she's my sister.
F2: What does the man imply?

21. F1: That sure is a catchy song.
M1: You're telling me. The melody's been running through my head all week.
F2: What can be concluded about the song?

22. F1: This stamp you found is pretty rare. I'd like to have one like it myself.
M1: Oh, an expert, are you?
F2: What does the man say about the woman?

23. M1: This schedule says we have to attend an orientation session before we can register.
    M2: Look at it again. That's just for new students.
    F2: What can be inferred about these two speakers?

24. F1: How's your research project coming, Mike?
    M2: So far, so good.
    F2: What does Mike mean?

25. F1: I won't be able to take a vacation this summer. I have to work.
    M1: Guess we're in the same boat.
    F2: What can be inferred about the two speakers?

26. M1: Professor Phillips's class seems pretty interesting.
    F1: I couldn't agree with you more!
    F2: What does the woman mean?

27. M2: Mind if I take your picture?
    F1: No, not at all.
    F2: What does the woman mean?

28. M1: I'm going to buy Julie a book of poems. I know she loves poetry.
    F1: But you can't just get her any book of poems!
    F2: What does the woman imply about Julie?

29. M2: We need to discuss our presentation some time in the next few days.
    F1: Fine. How about over lunch today?
    F2: When does the woman want to talk about the presentation?

30. M1: I drove my motorcycle to work today. It was a great day for a ride.
    F1: Oh, you mean you *did* buy that motorcycle after all!
    F2: What had the woman assumed?

PART B

Questions 31 to 34: Listen to a conversation between two friends.

    F1: Tim, did you get your ticket for the concert Friday?
    M1: I tried to. I stopped by the ticket office on the way back from campus, but they wouldn't take my check.
    F1: Why not?
    M1: The cashier said I didn't have enough identification with me—a student ID card wasn't enough. He said I needed a driver's license, too.
    F1: What happened to yours? Did you lose it, or just forget to bring it with you?
    M1: I don't have one. You know me—I ride my bicycle everywhere I go, so why do I need a driver's license?
    F1: You could still get an official identification card from the state and use that to cash checks.
    M1: Where do I get one of those?
    F1: At the same place you get a driver's license, the Bureau of Motor Vehicles.
    M1: Is that office downtown?
    F1: No, it's out on Southland Parkway, next to the Midvale Shopping Mall.
    M1: What do you think I'll need to do to get one?
    F1: Just bring some official document that has your date of birth on it. You could use a passport, for example.
    M1: I'll ride out there tomorrow.
    F1: Good idea. And I'll tell you what, Tim—if you promise to cash a check as soon as you can, I'll let you borrow some money, and you can go get that ticket.

31. F2: According to the conversation, why was Tim unable to buy the ticket?

32. F2: According to the woman, where is the Bureau of Motor Vehicles?

33. F2: What does the woman suggest Tim bring when he goes to the Bureau of Motor Vehicles?

34. F2: What does the woman offer to do for Tim?

Questions 35 to 38: Listen to a conversation at a student health clinic.

F1: The doctor should be able to see you in a few minutes. I just need some information from you first. What seems to be the problem?

M2: Well, as you can see, I've got a rash on my hands and arms. I think it might be some kind of allergic reaction. My roommate just got a new cat. Maybe I'm allergic to cats.

F1: Hmm. Usually, allergies to animals don't cause rashes on your hands.

M2: Well, maybe I'm allergic to some kind of food, or . . .

F1: When did your rash first develop?

M2: On Monday. By Tuesday, it was worse, and on Tuesday night I could hardly sleep.

F1: Tell me, have you been out in the woods lately?

M2: Out in the woods? I went hiking Saturday. Why? Oh, I get it—you think my rash might be caused by poison ivy, right?

F1: Well, it *looks* like that. The doctor can tell you for sure. Do you know if you came in contact with poison ivy?

M2: No, but then I have no idea what poison ivy looks like.

F1: It grows in clusters of three leaves, and the leaves are waxy looking.

M2: Well, if I *do* have poison ivy, what can the doctor do for me?

F1: He can prescribe a lotion that will relieve the itching. But if I were you, I'd go to the library and look for some color photos of poison ivy, and try to avoid it the next time you go into the woods.

35. F2: What is the probable relationship between the two speakers?

36. F2: According to the conversation, when did the man go hiking?

37. F2: What does the woman believe is the probable source of the man's problem?

38. F2: What does the woman suggest that the man do?

PART C

Questions 39 to 41: Listen to a talk given by a tour guide.

F1: Welcome back to your Northwest Holidays tour bus. I hope you enjoyed your visit to Redwood National Park. We'll be leaving the park in just a few more minutes and heading for Tall Trees Lodge, where we'll spend the night.

I want to tell you a little about tomorrow's destination—Crater Lake National Park. Crater Lake is located in an extinct volcano. A cone-shaped island, Wizard Island seems to float on its surface. One of the first things you'll notice when we get there is the deep-blue color of the water of the lake. The water will be that color whether the sky is clear or cloudy. Once it was thought that the color was due to an unusual mineral content, but chemical analysis showed no such thing. It's now believed that the lake water is so clear and deep that it separates and reflects the blue rays of sunlight and absorbs the other colors.

Oh, and here's another interesting fact about Crater Lake—it has neither an outlet nor an inlet, yet it maintains almost exactly the same level of water, with only slight variations from season to season and year to year. Somehow, gains from snow and rain are perfectly balanced by losses from evaporation and seepage.

We should be arriving at Crater Lake early tomorrow afternoon. We'll be spending the rest of the day in the park, and then on to our next stop, the city of Portland, Oregon. For now, sit back and relax, and we'll be at our hotel in about 20 minutes.

39. F2: Where does this conversation take place?

40. F2: According to the speaker, which of the following makes the water of Crater Lake appear to be such an intense shade of blue?

41. F2: What does the speaker say about the water level of Crater Lake?

Questions 42 to 46: Listen to a lecture given in a U.S. History course.

M2: Good morning, students. Today we'll be continuing to talk about the development of rapid communications in the United States. No discussion of communications is complete without a mention of a particularly dramatic means of delivering the mail: the Pony Express. It was founded in 1860, the year before the Civil War, to carry mail from St. Joseph, Missouri, to the gold fields of California. Racing across Nebraska, Wyoming, Utah, and Nevada, these horsemen covered 2,000 miles in ten days. Every 10 miles, there was a relay station where a fresh horse waited. Each man rode a total of five relays—that's 50 miles!—before he was replaced by a fresh rider. The riders galloped summer and winter, day and night, through rain and wind and snow. Now, let me read to you from a newspaper advertisement that was used to recruit Pony Express riders: "Wanted . . . thin, wiry young fellows—preferably orphans." Can you imagine yourself answering an ad for a job where orphans were preferred! That should give you some idea of the nature of the work. Only eighteen months after the Pony Express was founded, the transcontinental telegraph was opened and put the company out of business—it had been losing money anyway. In its day, though, it provided an extremely useful service. Any questions before we go on?

42. F2: What has the class been studying?

43. F2: According to the speaker, what was the final destination of Pony Express riders?

44. F2: According to the speaker, how many miles did each rider cover before being replaced by another rider?

45. F2: The speaker would probably use which of the following words to describe the work of Pony Express riders?

46. F2: According to the speaker, which of the following caused the end of the Pony Express?

Questions 47 to 50: Listen to a talk given at a meeting of the drama club.

M1: As president of the University Drama Club, I'd like to welcome all our members. Today we have a special guest speaker, Molly Quinn. Molly was a member of the Drama Club herself when she was a student here, and she went on to great success. First, she won parts in several New York plays, and then she made guest appearances on a number of television shows. Most recently, she completed work on her first role in a feature movie. She also hopes to start directing soon; she told me that she might try to get a start by directing television commercials. Molly is going to talk to us today about getting into the acting profession, but before we hear from her, I want to remind everyone that next weekend the Drama Department is holding tryouts for parts in the play *A Doll's House,* so mark that on your calendars. Given her own experience, I'm sure Molly would agree that appearing in campus plays is a great way to learn the basics of acting. Now, let's give Molly a big welcome!

47. F2: What is the speaker's primary purpose in giving the talk?

48. F2: When is this talk being given?

49. F2: According to the speaker, what is Molly Quinn's most recent accomplishment?

50. F2: The speaker implies that Molly Quinn did which of the following when she was a student?

SECTION 2: STRUCTURE AND WRITTEN EXPRESSION

Answer Key

1.	A	11.	B	21.	A	31.	C
2.	B	12.	C	22.	C	32.	A
3.	A	13.	B	23.	B	33.	C
4.	D	14.	C	24.	D	34.	A
5.	C	15.	D	25.	D	35.	D
6.	D	16.	A	26.	A	36.	D
7.	A	17.	D	27.	D	37.	C
8.	B	18.	D	28.	C	38.	B
9.	C	19.	C	29.	C	39.	A
10.	A	20.	D	30.	B	40.	B

EXPLANATION: WRITTEN EXPRESSION

16. Before a plural count noun (such as *superstitions*) the word *many* must be used. (*Much* is used before noncount nouns.)

17. The participle *illuminated* is needed in place of the noun *illumination*.

18. The plural pronoun *them* should be used to refer to the plural noun *joints*.

19. The word *percentage* must be used if there is no preceding number ("the *percentage* is growing" but "fifteen *percent*").

20. The word *ago* is used unnecessarily; the phrase should read *for over 5,000 years*.

21. The adjective form, *outer*, is required.

22. The comparative form of a two-syllable adjective ending in -*y* (such as *easy*) is -*ier*; *more* is not used; *easier* is therefore the correct form.

23. The correct word order is preposition + relative pronoun (*in which*).

24. A noun (*warmth*) must be used in place of the adjective *warm*.

25. In this sentence, *editorial* is the first word of a compound noun (*editorial staffs*) and should not be pluralized.

26. The past tense (*began*) should be used in place of the past participle *begun*. (By itself, a past participle such as *begun* can never serve as a main verb.)

27. The word *as* has been omitted; the phrase should read *such as rayon*.

28. The subject and verb of the second clause, *it is*, are missing; the phrase should read *but it is not*.

29. The correct word order is *much too*. (Or the word *much* may be omitted.)

30. The noun *economics* is required in place of the adjective *economic*.

31. The correct word order is adjective + *enough*: *smooth enough*.

32. *Whatever* should replace *however*.

33. The correct form is *other*. (*Another* is not usually used before plural nouns such as *types*.)

34. The noun *depth* is needed in place of the adjective *deep*.

35. The correct pattern is *from . . . to*.

36. The word *it* is used unnecessarily and should be omitted. (The subject of that clause is the relative pronoun *that*.)

37. The word *relatively* cannot be used with an intensifying modifier such as *very*; the word *very* should be omitted.

38. The adjective *formal* should replace the adverb *formally*.

39. The word *sunshine* is a noncount noun and cannot be pluralized.

40. The article *the* should be omitted: *by hand*.

SECTION 3: READING COMPREHENSION

		Answer Key		
1. D	11. B	21. C	31. B	41. C
2. A	12. A	22. A	32. C	42. D
3. C	13. A	23. D	33. A	43. A
4. B	14. D	24. C	34. D	44. B
5. D	15. B	25. B	35. B	45. C
6. A	16. C	26. D	36. B	46. C
7. A	17. A	27. D	37. C	47. D
8. B	18. D	28. A	38. A	48. C
9. C	19. A	29. C	39. B	49. A
10. D	20. B	30. D	40. B	50. C

EXPLANATION

1. Choice (A) is only a detail; there is no comparison between clippers and steamships, so (B) is not correct; there is no mention of shipbuilding techniques in the passage, so (C) is not correct; the best answer is (D).

2. The word *swiftest* means *fastest, quickest*.

3. The passage says that "most were constructed in the shipyards of New England."

4. In the context of the passage, a vessel is a ship.

5. Line 6 states that "clippers took gold seekers from the East Coast to the West."

6. The second paragraph indicates that clippers were "built for speed" (line 8) and that other considerations, such as operating costs (B) and cargo capacity (C), were sacrificed for this purpose (lines 8-9). A large crew (D) was necessary for the speedy operation of clippers (lines 11-12).

7. The word *slanted* means *tilted, angled*.

8. According to the passage, clipper ships "sometimes (used) skysails and moonrakers," indicating that clipper ships did not always use these sails.

9. According to lines 14-15, this record was held by the clipper ship *Lightning*.

10. The *Cutty Sark* was a British tea clipper, and according to the passage, these ships were "composites" (line 18); in other words, they were built with iron frames and wooden planking.

11. Choices (A), (C), and (D) are all discussed in the final paragraph; there is no mention of competition with British ships.

12. The passage ends with a mention of the end of the age of sail; it is logical that the next paragraph will concern the beginnings of the next age, that of ships powered by steam.

13. The passage primarily discusses Ralph Earl's career. There is no comparison between Earl's art and that of Gainsborough's (B); there is no specific reference to Earl's influences (C); there is no description of the art scene in New York City in the late eighteenth century (D).

14. It is mentioned in several points in the passage that Earl painted portraits (A); in the first paragraph, it is mentioned that Earl painted landscapes (B) and scenes from the battles of Lexington and Concord (C); there is no evidence that he painted pictures of fruit and flowers—still lifes (D).

15. According to the passage, Earl went to London "to study with Benjamin West" (line 4), so West must have been Earl's teacher.

16. In the context of the passage, *outstanding* means *unpaid*.

17. The word *itinerant* means *traveling, wandering*.

18. The phrase *sprang from the same roots* means *having the same general background*.

19. In the third paragraph, the author discusses the "counterpoint" (contrast) between "the severity of the couple" and "the relative luxury of the Ellsworth's interior furnishings."

20. According to the passage, *Reclining Hunter* is an anomaly (something uncharacteristic or unusual) because it "uncharacteristically shows Earl's wit (humor)." This indicates that most of Earl's paintings were more serious than this one.

21. The reference is to the "well-dressed gentleman"—that is, the hunter.

22. The author mentions a number of positive qualities in the passage about Earl; for example, "his uncommon technical skills." No negative attributes are mentioned.

23. The passage discusses the phenomenon of sparks on the Moon and offers an explanation for this phenomenon.

24. According to the first line of the passage, the sparks of light have been seen "for centuries" (hundreds of years).

25. The word *sporadically* means *occasionally*.

26. According to the passage, evidence for the theory is provided when the rocks are "fractured in the lab" (line 8).

27. The reference is to the lunar rocks.

28. In the context of the passage, *stray* means *loose* or *escaped* (from the rocks).

29. The passage explains that thermal cracking is caused by "a sudden change in temperature" (line 11). Choice (C) is the best example of this.

30. There is no mention in the passage that gas pressure can fracture lunar rocks.

31. The passage mainly deals with guyots—one feature of the undersea world.

32. The word *conceal* means *hide, obscure*.

33. According to line 4, Harry H. Hess discovered guyots while serving "on a ship equipped with a fathometer," implying that this device was used in the discovery.

34. Lines 5-6 state that Guyot "served on the faculty of Princeton University for thirty years."

35. Lines 6-7 state that guyots "have been found in every ocean but the Arctic."

36. According to lines 7-8, "like offshore canyons, guyots present a challenge to oceanographic theory." Guyots are not necessarily found near continental shelves (A); there is no evidence that offshore canyons are of volcanic origin (C) or that they were ever above the surface of the sea (D).

37. Line 11 states that "most lie between 3,200 feet and 6,500 feet."

38. Rubble is rough, broken fragments (pieces) of stone or other material.

39. According to lines 11-12, "their tops are not really flat but slope upward to a low pinnacle at the center." Choice (B) best depicts this description.

40. According to the passage, the two processes were the depression of the sea floor beneath the volcanoes and rising level of the sea (lines 15-16).

41. Lines 16-17 indicate that the sea level rose "especially when the last Ice Age ended, some 8,000 to 11,000 years ago."

42. The passage primarily concerns the effort by women to secure the right to vote; choices (A) and (B) are mentioned only as details, and there is little discussion of the effect of the Nineteenth Amendment (C).

43. The phrase *in earnest* means *seriously, earnestly*.

44. According to the passage, the National Women's Suffrage Association worked "on the federal level" (lines 3-4) while the American Women's Suffrage Association worked "through state legislation" (lines 4-5).

45. Lines 6-7 indicate that Wyoming enfranchised women in 1869 "while still a territory."

46. The phrase *most astute* means *cleverest, wisest*.

47. According to lines 11-12, Alice Paul founded the National Women's Party.

48. In the context of the passage, *province* refers to the sphere of activities of a certain group—in this case, men's jobs.

49. Since both of the newly enfranchised women and the men voted for Harding (lines 20-21) the clear implication is that Harding was elected.

50. The author mentions the growth of women in the workforce in line 15.

Practice Test 3

SECTION 1: LISTENING COMPREHENSION

Answer Key

1.	C	11.	B	21.	D	31.	A	41.	D	51.	D	61.	A	71.	D
2.	A	12.	D	22.	A	32.	D	42.	C	52.	B	62.	B	72.	B
3.	A	13.	C	23.	C	33.	B	43.	B	53.	C	63.	B	73.	C
4.	C	14.	D	24.	C	34.	A	44.	A	54.	B	64.	C	74.	C
5.	D	15.	D	25.	B	35.	C	45.	B	55.	A	65.	C	75.	A
6.	B	16.	B	26.	D	36.	D	46.	A	56.	D	66.	C	76.	B
7.	C	17.	D	27.	A	37.	A	47.	D	57.	A	67.	B	77.	C
8.	B	18.	A	28.	B	38.	B	48.	D	58.	C	68.	D	78.	D
9.	C	19.	A	29.	C	39.	C	49.	A	59.	A	69.	C	79.	D
10.	A	20.	B	30.	C	40.	D	50.	C	60.	C	70.	C	80.	A

PART A

TAPESCRIPT*

1. M1: Why did it take them so long to fix your car?
   F1: Well, for one thing, they had to remove the engine.
   M2: What does the woman mean?

2. F2: So Patrick, now that your final exams are over, what are you going to do?
   M1: I plan to take it easy for a couple of weeks or so.
   M2: What does Patrick tell the woman?

3. F1: I'm going to ask Greg to help me learn this computer program.
   M1: Greg's pretty busy now. But I know a thing or two about this program myself.
   M2: What does the man imply?

4. M1: How often does the bus go to Springsdale?
   F2: Only twice a day.
   M2: What does the woman mean?

5. M1: Professor Cassini, can we write our term paper on any topic we like?
   F1: As long as you talk it over with me first.
   M2: What is learned from this conversation?

6. F2: I just found an old photo of this dormitory.
   M1: It looks so different!
   M2: What can be inferred from this conversation?

7. M1: I saw Rudy in chemistry class, and boy, he looked upset.
   F1: Yeah? I wonder how come.
   M2: What would the woman like to know about Rudy?

---
* Note: M1 = first male voice   M2 = second male voice   F1 = first female voice   F2 = second female voice

8. F1: Why isn't Patty going to the party tonight?
　　F2: Oh, you know Patty—she hates loud parties.
　　M2: What can be inferred about Patty?

9. F2: You can change planes in either Chicago or Denver.
　　M1: You mean there's no direct flight from New York to Phoenix?
　　M2: Where does the man want to go?

10. M1: Cindy, did you like that movie you saw last night?
　　F1: Oh yes, but you know what? Halfway through it, I realized I'd seen it years before.
　　M2: What does Cindy tell the man?

11. F2: Ted used to ask so many questions in Professor Beasley's class.
　　F1: Yeah, and then, for some reason, he just stopped asking her anything.
　　M2: What do the speakers say about Ted?

12. F2: So Harry, were you able to solve the puzzle?
　　M1: Yes, but I'll tell you, it's a lot harder than it looks.
　　M2: What does Harry tell the woman?

13. M1: Kelly, I thought you were going skiing this weekend.
　　F1: I was hoping to, but that plan fell through.
　　M2: What does Kelly tell the man?

14. F2: How's your cold, Ron?
　　M1: It's gone from bad to worse, I'm afraid.
　　M2: What does Ron mean?

15. F1: I picked up a few flowers for the dinner party.
　　M1: A few! The dining room looks like a florist shop!
　　M2: What does the man imply about the woman?

16. F1: I wasn't in class the day Professor Mitchie gave out the schedule. Can I see yours?
　　M1: Oh, sure. But he told us that there are a couple of mistakes on it.
　　M2: What does the man mean?

17. F1: Now, this one shows the view right out of my hotel room.
　　F2: Wow—it looks just like a postcard!
　　M2: What are the speakers probably doing?

18. M1: Steve left us some directions for finding the campground.
　　F2: I saw them, and if these are the best directions we can get, we'll never find it!
　　M2: What does the woman imply?

19. F1: You're wearing that old blue jacket to the theater tonight?
　　M1: What else?
　　M2: What does the man mean?

20. M1: Walter told me that he was late because he had a flat tire.
　　F2: That's a likely story!
　　M2: What does the woman mean?

21. M1: I'm sorry, Laura, but something's come up—I won't be able to meet with you today.
　　F1: Well, how about the same time tomorrow. We can meet at that new coffee shop on Fourteenth Street because this place will be closed then.
　　M2: What does Laura mean?

22. M2: How did you get that big dent in your door?
　　F1: I have no idea. Yesterday, I went into the shopping mall, and when I came back out to the parking lot, there it was.
　　M2: What are the speakers discussing?

23.   F1:   I heard you're taking an advanced physics class. How's it going?
     M1:   I'm out of my depth, I'm afraid.
     M2:   What does the man mean?

24.   F2:   Hope you can make it to the dinner tonight. We're serving fish and salad and some fresh corn from my garden.
     M1:   Oh, you decided to have fish after all.
     M2:   What had the man assumed?

25.   F1:   What's the matter, Rob?
     M1:   I just locked my keys in my car and I have to be at work in half an hour.
     M2:   What is Rob's problem?

26.   M1:   Kathy, I want to hang this new picture—do you have a hammer I can borrow?
     F2:   No—but you could use this old shoe.
     M2:   What does Kathy suggest the man do with the shoe?

27.   M1:   I can't decide which of these two articles would be more useful to read.
     F1:   As far as I'm concerned, you can't go wrong.
     M2:   What does the woman mean?

28.   F2:   I'd love to be up in the mountains where it's cool.
     M1:   So you're not enjoying our weather this month?
     M2:   What can be inferred from the man's remark?

29.   F1:   I just got some change from the change machine upstairs.
     M1:   Oh, so someone finally fixed that?
     M2:   What had the man originally assumed before talking to the woman?

30.   M1:   This is a great restaurant. You can get anything you want here.
     F2:   Anything except good service!
     M2:   What is the woman's opinion of the restaurant?

31.   M1:   You know, at first, I didn't realize what a comedian Howard is!
     F1:   Oh, I know—he fools a lot of people!
     M2:   How would the speakers describe Howard?

32.   M1:   I'm having a lot of trouble writing this paper.
     F2:   If I were you, I'd go back to the drawing board.
     M2:   What does the woman suggest the man do?

33.   F1:   What delicious salad!
     M1:   How about another helping?
     M2:   What does the man ask the woman about the salad?

34.   F1:   I didn't know you were interested in geology, Sam.
     M1:   Well, it's a requirement to take at least one science course, and geology seemed like the easiest one.
     M2:   Why is Sam taking the geology course?

35.   F2:   Have you ever seen a professional basketball game?
     M1:   Only on television.
     M2:   What does the man mean?

36.   F1:   Connie asked you a lot of questions, didn't she?
     M1:   Yeah, she sure did, and I'd like to know what she was driving at.
     M2:   What does the man wonder about Connie?

37.   F1:   Well, we found something nice for Jill. Now what about Allen?
     M1:   Let's stop by the sporting goods store and get an archery target. Allen loves archery.
     M2:   What are these two probably doing?

38. F2: Gary, do you know when the work on that new road will be done?
    M1: The sooner the better, as far as I'm concerned.
    M2: What does Gary say about the new road?

39. M1: I had to wait 3 hours to see the doctor.
    F1: Oh, come on, Jim—I just heard you tell your roommate that you had a 2-hour wait!
    M2: What does the woman imply about Jim?

40. F1: Andy sure has a hot temper, doesn't he?
    F2: He does fly off the handle easily.
    M2: What do the speakers say about Andy?

41. M1: Professor Pottinger, you'll be giving your lecture on the causes of the Civil War next week, right?
    F1: The week after, actually.
    M2: What does Professor Pottinger say about the lecture?

42. F2: See you later. I'm going to the bank to deposit my check.
    M1: Oh, Marie, I really need some laundry detergent. If I give you some money, do you think you can pick up some on the way back?
    M2: What does the man ask Marie to do?

43. F1: What did you say when you were introduced to the author?
    M1: To tell you the truth, I was so tongue-tied, I could hardly say a word to her.
    M2: What does the man mean?

44. M1: Are you going to buy that car you looked at this afternoon?
    F2: Well, maybe. It's got a lot of miles on it. But I need a car with a lot of room and it sure has that.
    M2: What does the woman like about the car?

45. M1: Look at these photos I took. They're terrible! I've got to try another camera.
    F1: Or take some photography lessons!
    M2: What does the woman imply?

46. M1: That was a difficult passage to translate.
    F2: I'll say. Even David had trouble with this one!
    M2: What does the woman imply about David?

47. F1: What kind of music would you like to hear?
    M1: Well, I haven't heard any good jazz for awhile.
    M2: What does the man imply?

48. M1: Who was that woman you were talking to at the party?
    F2: Oh, that was Wendy Donovan. She was my roommate's best friend in high school.
    M2: How does the woman know Wendy Donovan?

49. M1: Did you see that notice from the landlord?
    F1: Yes, and I could hardly believe my eyes!
    M2: What does the woman say about the notice?

50. M1: Alice, what would you say if I told you that I asked a few more people to join our study group?
    F2: Oh, I wouldn't mind a bit!
    M2: What does Alice mean?

PART B

Questions 51 to 54: Listen to a conversation between two friends.

> F1: Kirk, I understand your jazz band is going to play at the Student Center Ballroom. I just saw a poster advertising the event, and I called to tell you I'll be there.
>
> M1: Oh, thanks, but I'm not in that band anymore. In fact, I'm not in a group at all right now.
>
> F1: That's too bad—you're such a talented musician. Why did you leave the group?
>
> M1: I just couldn't be a full-time student and still rehearse with the band every night. I missed a couple of practice sessions during my midterm exams, and I thought I'd better quit before the bandleader fired me.
>
> F1: Say, you know my friend Charlie, don't you? He plays saxophone and trumpet, and he and some of his friends are getting a band together. I bet they could use a good drummer.
>
> M1: I wouldn't have time for that, either.
>
> F1: Oh, I don't think they'll practice very often. Charlie and his friends are all students, too.
>
> M1: Do they plan to perform?
>
> F1: No, I don't think so. They just enjoy playing jazz. Here, I'll give you his number, and you can get in touch with him.

51. M2: What prompted the woman to call the man?

52. M2: The man implies that he left the band for which of the following reasons?

53. M2: What role did the man probably play in the band?

54. M2: What does the woman suggest that the man do in order to contact her friend?

Questions 55 to 58: Listen to a telephone conversation.

(RING . . . RING . . . SOUND OF PHONE BEING PICKED UP.)

> M1: Hello, *Campus Daily,* advertising department. This is Mark speaking.
>
> F2: Hi. I'm calling to place a couple of ads.
>
> M1: Sure. Under what classification?
>
> F2: Well, I'd like one in the "Roommates Wanted" section.
>
> M1: All right. And how would you like your ad to read?
>
> F2: It should read "Female roommate wanted for pleasant, sunny two-bedroom apartment on Elliewood Avenue, three blocks from campus. Share rent and utilities. Available September first. Call between 5 and 9 p.m. and ask for Cecilia."
>
> M1: Fine. And what about your other ad?
>
> F2: That one I'd like under "Merchandise for Sale," and I'd like it to read "Matching blue sofa and easy chair for sale, excellent condition, $350 or best offer. Call between 5 and 9 p.m. and ask for Cecilia." Did you get all that?
>
> M1: Uh huh. You'll want your phone number on these, right?
>
> F2: Oh sure. Thanks for reminding me. It's 555-6792.
>
> M1: And how long do you want these ads to run?
>
> F2: For a week, I guess. How much would that be?
>
> M1: Let's see—it's $5.00 a week per line. Your two ads will both take up three lines, so that's $15 per ad.

55. M2: Where does Mark work?

56. M2: Which of the following is Cecilia trying to find?

57. M2: Which of the following did Cecilia initially forget to tell Mark?

58. M2: What is the total amount that the woman has to spend for the two advertisements?

Questions 59 to 63: Listen to a conversation between two friends.

M1: Hi, Shelly! How was your vacation?

F1: Great! I went to New Orleans.

M1: Really? Why did you decide to go there?

F1: Well, I have a cousin who lives there. She's been trying to get me to take a vacation down there for a long time, and so finally, she talked me into it.

M1: How did you get there?

F1: Well, at first I was going to drive, but my cousin said parking is a big problem there, so I flew. Once I was there, I took buses and streetcars.

M1: I've seen some pictures of New Orleans—the architecture there is really interesting, isn't it?

F1: Yeah, it's incredible, especially in the French Quarter and in the Garden District where my cousin lives. And I love the spicy food there, and the music, of course. My cousin took me to some great little restaurants and jazz clubs.

M1: How was the weather when you were there?

F1: That's about the only thing I *didn't* enjoy. It was really hot and sticky.

M1: Wasn't New Orleans originally a French city?

F1: Yes, the French founded it. And then the king of France gave it to the king of Spain, and later the French took it over again. And then the French sold it to the United States along with the rest of the Louisiana Purchase.

M1: I remember reading in a history book about the battle of New Orleans. That was during the War of 1812, wasn't it?

F1: Right. The Americans under Andrew Jackson fought a battle with the British near there. In fact, Jackson Square in the French Quarter is named after him.

M1: Well, it sure sounds like you had a great time.

F1: Oh, I sure did. And I plan to go back there next spring for the Mardi Gras festival!

59. M2: What are these people primarily discussing?

60. M2: According to the conversation, how did the woman get to New Orleans?

61. M2: What was one aspect of New Orleans that the woman did NOT enjoy?

62. M2: Which of the following groups originally founded New Orleans?

63. M2: According to the woman, what role did Andrew Jackson play in the history of New Orleans?

End of Tape 1.

PART C

Questions 64 to 67: Listen to part of a lecture given in a class of film students.

M1:   Class, today we're going to continue our discussion of special genres of film. In our last class, we talked about Westerns, and saw some excerpts from some of those movies, such as *High Noon* and *Duel in the Sun.* Today we'll shift our attention to science fiction films. Most people think of science fiction as a fairly modern genre, but in fact, one of the first commercial films ever made was about a trip to the moon. In the 1930s there were some excellent prophetic films about the future, including *Things to Come,* which is based on a story by the famous author H. G. Wells. The so-called "Golden Age" of science fiction movies took place in the 1950s when hundreds of such films were made. Some of these turned out to be unforgettable classics. Some of these, frankly, were awful films, and the only reason we watch them today is that they seem quaint and sometimes unintentionally funny, with their low-budget special effects and wooden dialogue.

   A renaissance in science fiction films took place in the late 1970s when George Lucas released his first *Star Wars* film. It had a fast pace, interesting characters, and, finally, special effects came of age. It was widely popular then and remains popular now, and many similar films have followed.

   Now, I think you'll find your homework for this weekend rather enjoyable. The Paramount Theater is holding a science fiction film festival over the weekend. They're showing a dozen films, all made during the "Golden Age" of science fiction. They're showing some of the real classics, including my personal favorite, *The Day the Earth Stood Still,* as well as some movies that have seldom been seen since they were first released back in the 1950s. I'd like all of you to attend at least two or three of these films and be prepared to talk about your reactions to them in class on Monday.

64.   M2:   What is the main topic of this lecture?

65.   M2:   According to the speaker, which of the following is a Western film?

66.   M2:   What can be inferred about the movies being shown this weekend at the Paramount Theater?

67.   M2:   What does the speaker ask the audience to be ready to do on Monday?

Questions 68 to 71: Listen to a talk about hydrogen fueled vehicles.

F2:   It's the goal of nearly all automakers to produce a car that causes no air pollution at all—a zero-emission vehicle, or ZEV. Some states have even mandated that manufacturers make ZEVs available by a certain deadline. So far, most research has been done on electric cars, but such battery operated cars have certain disadvantages. The biggest drawback is that electric cars must have their batteries recharged every 100 miles or so. Recently, engineers have completed some encouraging research on the use of hydrogen as a fuel. They believe that vehicles with internal combustion engines can become ZEVs if they switch from gasoline to hydrogen. When hydrogen is mixed with oxygen and burned, it produces no toxic fumes—only water vapor. However, because it is such a volatile gas, engines burning hydrogen are always backfiring. The engineers learned that if rotary engines are used instead of conventional piston-driven engines, there is no backfiring—just smooth acceleration. Some people wonder if hydrogen-fueled cars would be safe. As it turns out, they are safer than gasoline-fueled cars. That's because they don't store free hydrogen in tanks. The hydrogen is bound to metal, and released as needed. The main problem with hydrogen is that there's simply not enough available. If hydrogen-fueled cars become popular, there will be a need to build hundreds of massive hydrogen-producing plants.

68.   M2:   How does the speaker probably feel about the development of hydrogen-fueled cars?

69.   M2:   According to the speaker, researchers trying to develop zero-emission vehicles have concentrated until recently on which of the following?

70.   M2:   According to the speaker, hydrogen-fueled cars produce which of the following?

71. M2: According to the speaker, which of the following is the primary problem with large-scale use of hydrogen-fueled cars?

Questions 72 to 75: Listen to a talk about parrots.

F1: First off, I'd like to clear up a couple of popular misconceptions about parrots. For one thing, they do not all have brilliant, colorful plumage. In fact, some are quite plain-looking birds with dull-colored feathers. Another misconception is that parrots all live in hot tropical forests. Some species live high in the mountains. One species, the kea parrot, lives near the highland glaciers of New Zealand. The only type of climate that parrots cannot tolerate is an extremely dry one. There are 816 types of parrots, and all of them can speak at least a few words when kept as pets. The champion talker is the gray parrot, which can learn two or three hundred words. Parrots also have remarkable singing skills. Among us humans, the ability to sing exactly on key is called perfect pitch, and only one out of about 500 of us have it. All parrots are born with this knack. Parrots also have a perfect sense of rhythm, never missing a beat.

72. M2: What is the speaker's first purpose in giving this talk?

73. M2: Which of the following environments would be least favorable for parrots?

74. M2: What does the speaker say about the gray parrot?

75. M2: What ability are all parrots born with?

Questions 76 to 80: Listen to part of a classroom lecture.

M2: Today, class, we're going to talk about the traditional homes of the Innuit people of the Arctic. The Innuit—or Eskimos, as they are sometimes called, generally had two homes, one for summer and one for winter. During the summer, they usually lived in tents made of either canvas or animal skin. The Innuit built three types of winter homes, depending on where they lived. In northern Alaska, where driftwood is plentiful, most winter homes were domes of wood covered with earth. In Labrador and Greenland, winter homes were generally constructed of flat stones. Only in the Central Canadian Arctic did they generally build houses of snow. Canadians of European descent called these igloos, but to the Innuit, any kind of house is called an igloo. To make a snow house, the Innuit stacked blocks of wind-packed ice in a rising spiral of ever-smaller circles. They filled in the cracks with loose snow. A skilled Innuit could build a snow house in around 2 hours. The Innuit are the only people who built such domes without support underneath. Heat from a lamp warmed the house, while the bitter outside air prevented it from melting. An Innuit family ate and slept on a platform of packed snow covered with furs. The snow house also featured an entrance tunnel that was lower than the floor. This served as a trap for cold outside air. There was also a small opening in the roof, covered with seal skin, that could be opened to let out stale air and ventilate the house. Today, almost all Innuit live in permanent all-year housing, but they sometimes build these wonderful, traditional houses of snow and a few even continue to live in them.

76. M1: Which of the following was used by the Innuit as the main material for a summer house?

77. M1: Where were snow houses the main form of winter house?

78. M1: What does the word *igloo* mean to an Innuit?

79. M1: What was one unique feature of the snow houses built by the Innuit?

80. M1: How was seal skin used in snow houses?

SECTION 2: STRUCTURE AND WRITTEN EXPRESSION

Answer Key

Structure

1. C	6. D	11. B	16. A	21. D
2. C	7. C	12. D	17. A	22. C
3. B	8. A	13. D	18. B	23. A
4. C	9. D	14. B	19. D	
5. A	10. C	15. D	20. C	

Written Expression

24. A	32. D	40. A	47. B	54. C
25. B	33. C	41. A	48. B	55. A
26. C	34. B	42. B	49. A	56. C
27. B	35. D	43. B	50. D	57. D
28. A	36. A	44. C	51. D	58. A
29. B	37. B	45. D	52. B	59. B
30. C	38. D	46. A	53. D	60. A
31. C	39. C			

EXPLANATION: WRITTEN EXPRESSION

24. The word *like* must be used in place of *alike*. (The correct patterns are ''Like A, B . . .'' and ''A and B are alike.'')

25. The full passive verb *are needed* should be replaced by a past participle (*needed*) or by a relative clause (*that are needed*).

26. The plural possessive *their* must be used in place of *its* because it refers to the plural noun phrase *blind snakes.*

27. The verb *do* should be used in place of *make.*

28. The word *so* is required in place of *too.* (The correct pattern is *so* + adjective + *that* clause.)

29. A main verb (*include*) must be used in place of the participle. (Used alone, an *-ing* form can never serve as a main verb.)

30. An adverb (*efficiently*) is needed rather than the noun *efficiency.*

31. The plural form, *thousands,* is required.

32. To be parallel with the other items in the series (*beaten, melted,* and *pured*) another past participle (*drawn*) is required.

33. The adjective *high* is needed in place of the noun *height.* (The phrase *in height* could also be used to correct the sentence.)

34. The present perfect tense (*have worn*) is required in place of the past tense (*wore*). (The present perfect is usually used in sentences that contain the expression *since* + time word.)

35. The noun *use* is needed in place of the gerund *using.*

36. The definite article *the* cannot be used before a fraction; the phrase should correctly read *one third* or *a third.*

37. A comparative form (*more beautiful*) is needed in place of the superlative (*most beautiful*).

38. The noun *biography* should be used in place of the adjective *biographical*.

39. The singular verb *has* must be used to agree with the subject. (After the phrase *each of the* + plural noun, a singular verb is always used.)

40. The word *because* must be used before a clause. (*Because of* is used only before a noun phrase.)

41. Before a noun phrase (*Martha Graham's first dance lesson*) the word *after* must be used rather than *afterwards*.

42. The word *to* has been omitted; the phrase should read *due to the*.

43. In this sentence, the preposition *for* must be used after *responsible*. (It is possible to use *responsible to* + person).

44. The singular pronoun *it* should replace the pronoun *they* because the pronoun refers to the singular phrase *Costume jewelry*.

45. In order to be parallel with the other words in the series (*scientific practices* and *superstitions*) a noun (*beliefs*) is needed in place of the verb *believes*.

46. The noun *sculptures* should be used in place of the noun *sculptors*. (A *sculptor* is a person who makes a *sculpture*.)

47. The relative pronoun *who* is properly used to refer only to a person; the relative pronouns *that* or *which* should be used to refer to a profession.

48. The word *apples* should not be pluralized; it is part of a compound noun. (*Apple and pear trees* means *apple trees and pear trees*.)

49. The preposition *at* is unnecessary and should be omitted.

50. At the end of a clause, this phrase should be *as well*, not *as well as*. (The correct patterns are *A as well as B* and *A and B as well*.)

51. The adverb *suddenly* is needed in place of the adjective *sudden*.

52. The preposition *by* is omitted; the phrase should read *formed by the* . . .

53. The reflexive pronoun *themselves* should be used in place of the personal pronoun *them*.

54. The definite article *the* has been omitted; the phrase should correctly read *the course of*.

55. The correct word order is adverb + participle (*widely spaced*).

56. The noun *loss* should be used in place of the verb/participle *lost*.

57. Before a noun (*distortions*) the negative word *no* should be used in place of *not*.

58. In this sentence, the verb *takes* should be used in place of the verb *is*. (The correct pattern is *it* + *takes* + time period + infinitive.)

59. The singular pronoun *that* should be used, because it refers to the singular noun phrase *fossil record*.

60. The word *as* should be used in place of *that*. (*As* in this sentence means *in the way that* . . .)

SECTION 3: READING COMPREHENSION

Answer Key

1. C	11. D	21. A	31. A	41. A	51. D	61. D
2. A	12. C	22. B	32. C	42. C	52. B	62. D
3. B	13. A	23. C	33. C	43. A	53. B	63. C
4. D	14. D	24. C	34. C	44. C	54. D	64. D
5. A	15. B	25. C	35. B	45. B	55. A	65. C
6. B	16. C	26. A	36. B	46. A	56. B	66. A
7. C	17. D	27. B	37. D	47. D	57. C	67. D
8. A	18. A	28. B	38. C	48. B	58. A	68. C
9. D	19. A	29. C	39. A	49. C	59. D	69. A
10. B	20. B	30. B	40. D	50. A	60. C	70. B

1. There is no mention in the passage that lighthouses are used as weather stations to report bad weather to sailors. The other functions of lighthouses are given in lines 1–2.

2. The reference is to *mariners (sailors)* in line 1.

3. The word *prominent* is closest in meaning to *conspicuous*.

4. According to the passage, a characteristic is a "distinctive pattern of light" (line 4).

5. According to lines 8–9, "a group-occulting signal consists of a fixed light with two or more periods of darkness at regular intervals."

6. A catoptric apparatus is one "in which metal is used to reflect the light" (line 11).

7. There is no specific example provided for a lighthouse with day-marker patterns. There *are* examples of a lighthouse in the shape of a pyramid (the Bastion Lighthouse), a lighthouse made of steel (American Shoal Lighthouse), and a lighthouse that resembles a house on a platform (Race Rock Light).

8. The word *tapering* means *becoming narrower*.

9. According to lines 17–18, "Where lighthouses might be confused in daylight, they can be distinguished by day-marker patterns." It is logical that lighthouses would be confused in daylight because they have similar structures.

10. The author said that, in the past, "lighthouse keepers put in hours of tedious work maintaining the lights." Today, however, humans supply "only occasional maintenance."

11. There is no information to support (A); the passage says that the number of lighthouses has declined greatly since 1900. There is no information about the number of lighthouses in any single country other than the United States, so (B) could not be correct. Nor is there information about (C)—the specific numbers of functioning lighthouses or lighthouses that have been converted into historical monuments. There IS information to support (D); there were 1,500 lighthouses in the United States in 1900, more than the 1,400 lighthouses existing outside the United States today.

12. The passage compares the scientific accomplishments and methodologies of Luther Burbank and George Washington Carver. The products created by the two scientists (A) are mentioned, but only as details. There is very little information about their influence as scientists (B), and only Burbank is mentioned as being influenced by Darwin (D).

13. The word *drastically* is closest in meaning to *dramatically*.

14. According to line 2, they "were close friends."

15. This potato still "bears his name" (line 5), so it must be called the Burbank potato.

16. The reference is to Burbank's work.

17. The word *thwarted* means *defeated, obstructed*.

18. The word *thorough* means *complete*.

19. Line 12 states that Burbank "kept records only for his own use." Line 14 states that "Carver, on the other hand, was a careful researcher who took thorough notes."

20. Lines 15–16 indicate that Carver earned his master's degree at Iowa State College.

21. There is no mention that Carter developed new uses for cotton. In fact, according to lines 19–20, these other products were developed to "free Southern agriculture from the tyranny of cotton."

22. The word *tyranny* is closest in meaning to the word *control*.

23. The reference to his weaknesses as a researcher starts on line 11, beginning "However, the value of his contributions was diminished . . ."

24. The focus of the passage is on Prince Edward Island's two main remaining natural habitats, sand dunes and salt marshes.

25. The quotation marks are used because the scenery looks unspoiled to visitors but has actually been tampered with since the eighteenth century.

26. The word *hamlets* is closest in meaning to *villages*.

27. The phrase *tampering with* is closest in meaning to *interfering with*.

28. The second paragraph states that 80 percent of the trees had been cut down by 1900 to clear the land for farming and that more had been killed off by disease. However, the paragraph goes on to say that some of the farmland has been abandoned and returned to forest, so there must be more forest now than there was in 1900.

29. Maple, birch, and oak are given as examples of the original climax forest. "Opportunist species," especially spruce (line 8) replaced these trees and would be more likely to be seen today.

30. According to lines 15–16, beach pea and bayberry take root after marram grass stabilizes the dunes.

31. According to lines 16–17, when marram grass is broken down, "the dunes may spread inland and inundate agricultural lands . . ."

32. The word *trampled* is closest in meaning to *stepped on*.

33. The word *bogs* is given as a synonym of the word *marshes* in line 22.

34. According to line 19, "in the south are red dunes."

35. Lines 20–21 state that "the dunes were once used as cattle pasture . . . but were abandoned." Line 25 states that marsh hay grown in the salt marshes was "used by the early settlers" but that "like the dunes, though, the marshes were soon dismissed as wasteland and escaped development" (lines 25–26).

36. The author describes the destruction of one ecosystem—the original forest cover—in paragraph 2.

37. The first paragraph discusses the many environments in which lichens can live. Choice (A) is incorrect because lichens can live in the "driest desserts" (line 2). Choice (B) is incorrect because they can live in "steaming tropical rain forests" (line 1) and in hot springs. Choice (C) is incorrect because lichens can live "on the bricks of big-city buildings" (lines 1–2).

38. The author refers to lichens as pioneers because they start "the formation of soil in which mosses, then ferns, and then other plants can take root."

39. The word *barren* means *lifeless*.

40. *Symbiosis* is defined in the passage as a relationship in which two organisms "live together to the benefit of both" (lines 7–8). In choice (A) the tiger and the grass do not actually live together, and while the tiger may benefit, the grass is unaffected. The same is true in choice (B), in which there is no mention that the shark benefits. In choice (C) the mistletoe benefits, but the trees are harmed. (This relationship is known as *parasitism*.) In choice (D), both the protozoa and the termites benefit by obtaining nutrition.

41. Line 9 state that fungi "shelter the tender algae from direct sunlight," indicating that direct sunlight could damage the algae.

42. The fungi are considered strange because they are "unlike any species that live independently" (line 12).

43. The paragraph explains why lichens' characteristics as double organisms make them difficult to classify. Choice (B) is only a detail of the paragraph; there is no reason to believe that the author thinks choice (C) is true; choice (D) is too general to be the main idea of the paragraph, and there is no information in the passage to support this idea.

44. The word *splendid* means *excellent, fine*.

45. The passage primarily deals with the conflict between the states supporting the Large State Plan and those supporting the Small State Plan, and the Great Compromise that worked out the differences between the two groups.

46. According to line 1, there were representatives from all thirteen states except Rhode Island—a total of twelve.

47. The first paragraph indicates that the delegates to the Constitutional Convention had been told to revise the Articles of Confederation but that most delegates "believed that a strong central government was needed" (lines 3–4). This implies that the Articles provided for only a weak form of government.

48. According to lines 6–7, in 1787 Virginia was the largest state in population; its population was twice that of New York, four times that of New Jersey, and ten times that of Delaware. Delaware, therefore, had the smallest population of the four states listed.

49. The phrase refers to the Large State Plan.

50. Angry debate was "heightened by a stifling heat wave" (line 13) while "a cooling of temperatures seemed to come with lower temperatures" (line 14).

51. The word *shrewd* means *clever, cunning*.

52. There is no mention in the passage of how the president would be chosen under the compromise plan.

53. The phrase *broke the logjam* means that problems were cleared up and progress became possible.

54. The primary purpose of the passage is to discuss the development of balloon-frame houses, a "revolution in building" (line 11).

55. Lines 7–8 indicate that the balloon-frame house was "invented . . . by a carpenter from Hartford, Connecticut."

56. Choice (A) is answered: it was invented in Chicago (line 8). Choice (C) is answered: it was 2 × 4 and 2 × 6 inches (line 9). Choice (D) is answered: it was invented in 1833 (line 7). However, the inventor is not named in the passage.

57. Choices (A) and (B) are colonial wooden homes, and, according to the passage, most of these "could be built with simple tools and minimal skills" (lines 3–4). Choice (D) "could be assembled by any careful worker who could saw in a straight line and drive a nail" (lines 9–10). Choice (C), however, "required highly-skilled workers with special tools" (line 7).

58. Choices (B), (C), and (D) are listed in the third paragraph. Choice (A) is not given. In fact, the author implies that sophisticated tools were not needed to build this type of house.

59. Because of the lightweight materials used to build balloon-frame houses, "skeptics predicted that a strong wind would send such houses flying through the air like balloons" (lines 13–14).

60. The word *derision* means *ridicule, mockery*.

61. The passage concentrates on the books written by Rachel Carson and on her career as a writer.

62. Lines 1–2 state that Carson studied zoology at Johns Hopkins University.

63. Carson was born in 1907 (line 1) and published *Under the Sea Wind* in 1941 (line 4), so she must have been about 34 years of age at the time of publication.

64. According to lines 4–5, when *Under the Sea Wind* was first published, "it received excellent reviews, but sales were poor until it was reissued in 1952."

65. There is no mention that Rachel Carson took part in a research expedition. The other sources are given in lines 7–9.

66. Carson "realized the limitations of her nontechnical readers" (line 9), implying that the book was not highly technical. It did have a poetic quality (line 7), and it was fascinating (interesting), according to line 6, and well researched (lines 7–9).

67. The word *reckless* is closest in meaning to *irresponsible*.

68. Line 11 states that the book *Silent Spring* "proved how much harm was done by the reckless use of insecticides."

69. The word *faulty* is closest in meaning to the word *flawed*.

70. Carson's work "was vindicated" by the report (lines 14–15), implying that the report contradicted the chemical industry's claims and supported her ideas.

Practice Test 4

SECTION 1: LISTENING COMPREHENSION

Answer Key

1. B	11. A	21. C	31. D	41. B
2. D	12. A	22. C	32. B	42. A
3. C	13. B	23. B	33. B	43. A
4. D	14. A	24. C	34. D	44. B
5. D	15. C	25. A	35. C	45. C
6. A	16. B	26. C	36. D	46. C
7. C	17. A	27. D	37. A	47. C
8. C	18. D	28. A	38. C	48. A
9. A	19. B	29. B	39. D	49. D
10. D	20. B	30. D	40. D	50. B

PART A

TAPESCRIPT*

1. **F1:** We need someone to put together a slide show for our class presentation.
   M1: How about Donna?
   F2: What does the man mean?

2. **F1:** Could you hand me a teaspoon, please?
   M2: Hang on, let me wash one.
   F2: What is the man going to do?

3. **M1:** Steve hasn't been himself lately, has he?
   F1: Well, no, he hasn't—he's had a lot on his mind.
   F2: What do the speakers say about Steve?

4. **F1:** What's Nancy doing this afternoon?
   M1: Playing golf, probably. She never wants to do anything else.
   F2: What does the man say about Nancy?

5. **F1:** How's that soup you ordered, Max?
   M2: Not as warm as I'd like it to be.
   F2: What does Max say about the soup?

6. **M1:** So, where are the books being stored?
   M2: In a warehouse somewhere.
   F2: What is learned from this conversation?

7. **F1:** Have you heard the good news about Marilyn?
   M1: You mean that she won a prize for her poetry?
   F2: What has the man heard about Marilyn?

8. **F1:** You sure checked a lot of books out of the library.
   M2: Oh, these aren't library books. I went to a used book sale. They were practically giving them away!
   F2: What does the man imply about the books?

---
* Note: M1 = first male voice   M2 = second male voice   F1 = first female voice   F2 = second female voice

9. M1: I heard your guitar was damaged.
    F1: Yes, but thanks to Mr. Benson, now it's as good as new.
    F2: What can be inferred about Mr. Benson from the conversation?

10. F1: All my papers almost blew away.
    M1: Windy out there today, isn't it?
    F2: What does the man mean?

11. F1: You know, whenever I read a book, I always wonder what the author looks like. For example, I'd like to see a picture of Robert Kurtz.
    M1: Well, if you're that interested, there's a photograph of him on the back of his new book.
    F2: What does the man say about Robert Kurtz?

12. F1: You don't know how to set up the printer? Try reading the manual, why don't you?
    M1: I did, and I'm still in the dark.
    F2: What is the man's problem?

13. (RING . . . RING . . . SOUND OF PHONE BEING PICKED UP.)
    M2: Hello?
    F1: Hello, is Rita there?
    M2: Hang on a minute—I'll see.
    F2: What does the man imply about Rita?

14. F1: I should have spent more time practicing the piano to get ready for the concert. I don't think I played well at all.
    M2: If I were you, I wouldn't dwell on it another minute.
    F2: What does the man suggest the woman do?

15. F1: I can't understand why Harold changed majors. He would have made a great mathematician.
    M1: I don't know either. He loved the subject, and his grades were good.
    F2: What can be concluded about Harold from this conversation?

16. M1: Robin, do you realize you had a dental appointment an hour ago?
    F1: I *did?*
    F2: What is Robin's reaction to the man's remark?

17. M1: Oh, so Charlene *was* able to get reservations for dinner here tonight.
    F1: Yes, just at the last minute.
    F2: What had the man initially assumed?

18. M1: I don't suppose you're free to go bowling Saturday evening, are you?
    F1: As a matter of fact, I *am.* I was planning to go to a lecture with my sister, but it was called off.
    F2: What will the woman probably do on Saturday evening?

19. M1: I just bought a camcorder. It's used, but it's in pretty good condition.
    F1: What's a good used camcorder going for these days?
    F2: What does the woman ask the man?

20. F1: These new glasses are giving me headaches.
    M1: Mine did, too, as first. That should wear off soon.
    F2: What does the man tell the woman?

21. F1: Today's the first of the month. Isn't your rent due today?
    M1: Yes, but I always pay it the day before it's due.
    F2: What does the man say about his rent?

22. M2: Is Roberta at home yet?
    F1: No, she had to work late again today.
    F2: What does the woman say about Roberta?

23.   M1: I've never taken a class as hard as the first half of the accounting course.
   F1: You think *that* was hard—wait till you take the second half!
   F2: What does the woman imply about the accounting course?

24.   M2: Have you ever read the book *The Great Gatsby*?
   F1: Only a couple of dozen times!
   F2: What does the woman imply about the book?

25.   M2: I understand you intend to become a research biologist.
   F1: My dream is that someday, I'll discover something as important as penicillin.
   F2: What does the woman want to do?

26.   F1: A lot of people were planning to attend the debate.
   M1: Not many were there, though.
   F2: What does the man mean?

27.   F1: I need to pay my check and leave.
   M1: I'll try to catch the waiter's eye.
   F2: What does the man intend to do?

28.   F1: I heard someone say that Sally needs a lot of improvement if she hopes to win the tennis match on Saturday.
   M2: Whoever said that obviously hasn't seen her out on the court recently!
   F2: What does the man imply about Sally?

29.   M1: Wow, your apartment looks great! I've never seen it so clean.
   F1: Well, my roommates pitched in and helped me, and the work was done in no time.
   F2: What does the woman say about her roommates?

30.   M1: Professor Atkinson, can I see you after this class?
   M2: I'm due at a faculty meeting then—how about the same time on Friday?
   F2: When does Professor Atkinson suggest that they meet?

PART B

Questions 31 to 33: Listen to a conversation between two students.

   M1: Want to go out and get something to eat?
   F1: I can't. I have a chemistry midterm on Monday and a German exam on Tuesday.
   M1: I have a geology exam Monday myself, but I think I'm ready for it.
   F1: What kind of exam is it going to be—multiple choice or essay?
   M1: Neither. The professor is going to give us a mineral sample and we have to identify it.
   F1: How do you do that? I mean, a rock's a rock, isn't it?
   M1: Actually, there are a lot of tests you can perform on minerals to help you figure out what they are. Probably the first tests I'll do are scratch tests. When you do a scratch test, you rub the sample on a known mineral to see if the unknown mineral scratches the known mineral or vice versa. That tells you the relative hardness of the sample.
   F1: What other tests will you do?
   M1: I'll probably do a streak test next. In that test, you rub an unknown mineral against a piece of unglazed porcelain to see what color the streak is.
   F1: Why can't you just *look* at the mineral to see what color it is?
   M1: Well, you can, but sometimes a mineral has a lot of impurities, and they can change its color, but a streak test shows the mineral's true color. Then there's always the specific gravity test, the blowpipe test . . . oh, and the ultraviolet test, and . . .
   F1: And after you've done all these tests, you can positively identify any mineral?
   M1: Well, usually . . . but not always. I just hope I can on Monday!

31.   F2: What type of exam is the man taking on Monday?

32. F2: According to the man, what does a streak test show about a mineral?

33. F2: What does the man imply about the tests used to identify minerals?

Questions 34 to 37: Listen to a telephone conversation.

(RING . . . RING . . . SOUND OF PHONE BEING PICKED UP.)

M2: Hello?

F1: Hi, Mike, this is Polly at Via Tours. Hope I didn't catch you at a bad time. I just wanted to give you an update on your travel plans for next week.

M2: No, no—I'm glad you called. What have you found out?

F1: Well, I've made hotel reservations for you in Key West at the Beachcomber Hotel.

M2: Oh, great—that's my favorite hotel there.

F1: And I've got you a rental car so that you can get from the Miami airport down to Key West.

M2: Perfect. And what about the airline reservations?

F1: That's the problem. There aren't any direct flights from here to Miami, you know. You'll have to fly through either Minneapolis or Chicago. I went ahead and put you on a flight from here to Chicago for next Monday, and I've got you on stand-by from Chicago to Miami.

M2: Stand-by? You mean I don't have confirmed reservations to Miami?

F1: I'm afraid not, but I'm pretty confident that something will open up and we'll be able to get you on a flight.

M2: I hope so. Well, let me know as soon as you hear something. And next year, I've got to be sure to book my flights earlier.

34. F2: What is Polly's probable occupation?

35. F2: According to the conversation, where does Mike hope to spend his vacation?

36. F2: For which of the following does Mike not have confirmed reservations?

37. F2: What does Mike tell Polly he will do next year?

PART C

Questions 38 to 42: Listen to a talk given at an art exhibit.

M2: I'd like to take this opportunity to welcome all of you to the opening of the American Folk Art Exhibit here at the Hotchkiss Museum. Some of the pieces in this exhibit have been displayed in other museums, but this is the first time they've all been shown together. Of course, most folk artists would be surprised to find their work in a museum. That's because folk artists created their art for practical purposes, or sometimes simply for the pleasure of creating art, but *not* because they expected their work to wind up in an exhibit in a museum, in a private gallery, or in the home of a collector.

As you look around, you'll see that the work of these early American artists is delightful if simple and it still feels fresh. Our exhibit includes many types of folk art, but I suggest we begin with a look at the work of sign painters from the eighteenth and nineteenth centuries. Although the paint on these signs has faded, they were surely painted in bright colors to catch the eye or prospective customers. Keep in mind that before around 1870, the majority of Americans couldn't read. Shopkeepers wanted practical signs to advertise their wares. This sign, for example, with its picture of a steaming soup kettle, once hung in front of a restaurant in colonial Boston. This one, in the shape of a horseshoe, hung in front of a blacksmith's shop. You can probably guess where that sign with a picture of a boot on it once hung.

You may have noticed that there are no plaques to tell you the names of these sign painters. Sometimes we do know the names of folk artists because they signed their work or had a particularly distinctive style, but there were no signatures on any of these signs, and the artists' names have long since been forgotten.

38. F2: Where is this talk being given?

39. F2: What does the speaker say about the art that appears in this exhibit?

40. F2: What can be inferred about the sign with the picture of a boot on it?

41. F2: Which of the following words would the speaker probably use to describe American folk art?

42. F2: Why does the speaker not mention the names of the sign painters?

Questions 43 to 46: Listen to a talk given at an academic awards ceremony.

M1: Good evening. I'd like to welcome the president of Colton College, the chancellors, the administrators, my fellow faculty members, and the students to the Academic Excellence Awards Night. Our first award, for Faculty Member of the Year, goes to Professor Patricia Callaghan. I'm particularly pleased that this year's winner is from my own department. Professor Callaghan has been at Colton College for a total of eight years now—two as a graduate student and six as a faculty member. She has consistently received top evaluations from the students as well as from her department head. Her papers on historical economics are well respected by all of her colleagues—including myself, if I may say so—and this year she received a government grant to continue her work on generating computer models of the economy. Please join me, ladies and gentlemen, in giving a round of applause to Professor Callaghan.

43. F2: What is the purpose of this talk?

44. F2: Who is the speaker?

45. F2: What subject does Professor Callaghan probably teach?

46. F2: For how many years has Professor Callaghan been a teacher at Colton College?

Questions 47 to 50: Listen to part of a lecture given in a class of American Literature.

F1: Good morning, class. In our last class, we talked about Walt Whitman, and said he was one of the two greatest voices of American poetry in the nineteenth century. The other was Emily Dickinson. Now, their poetry could not have been more different. Dickinson claimed that she never even read Whitman's poems. Their lifestyles could not have been more different. But they were both important innovators.

Now, I said before that Whitman became well known around the world. Dickinson was famous only in her own village—Amherst, Massachusetts—and that was not for her poetry but for her mysterious ways. You see, she almost never left the house of her father, who was a wealthy lawyer. When she did appear, she always wore white dresses. Although this may not seem too strange to us today, it was pretty unusual for Amherst in the 1800s!

For a woman who lived such an uneventful life, though, she wrote amazingly perceptive poems about nature, love, and death. Her poems are all short and untitled. What I particularly admire about these poems is their economy—she was able to say so much in so few words!

She never intended her poems to be published. At least ten of them were published during her lifetime, but that was against her will. After her death in 1886, her family discovered that she had written over 1,700 poems. They published a collection of about thirty of her poems a few years later, and eventually, all of them appeared in print.

Now, we'll take a look at some of her poems, but first . . . questions, anyone?

47. F2: What point does the speaker make about Walt Whitman?

48. F2: Why was Emily Dickinson famous in her hometown?

49. F2: What does the speaker say she particularly admires about the poems of Emily Dickinson?

50. F2: About how many of Emily Dickinson's poems were published when she was alive?

SECTION 2: STRUCTURE AND WRITTEN COMPREHENSION

Answer Key

1. D	11. B	21. C	31. A
2. A	12. C	22. B	32. B
3. B	13. A	23. D	33. D
4. D	14. C	24. B	34. B
5. C	15. B	25. A	35. A
6. A	16. B	26. D	36. C
7. A	17. D	27. D	37. C
8. D	18. C	28. A	38. D
9. B	19. C	29. D	39. D
10. A	20. D	30. C	40. A

16. The possessive adjective *its* should replace *one's*.

17. A noun (*sanitation*) is needed in place of the adjective *sanitary*.

18. When used before a noun, a number + measurement is not pluralized; the correct phrase is *60-mile*.

19. The correct word order is *long before*.

20. The noun *humor* is needed in place of the adjective *humorous*.

21. Before a clause (*bacteria are the chief decomposers of grassland soil*) the word *as* must be used instead of *like*. (*Like* is only used before noun phrases.)

22. The correct superlative form of the one-syllable adjective *safe* is *safest*.

23. The plural possessive form *their* must be used to refer to the plural noun phrase *ballpoint pens*.

24. The definite article *the* should not be used before the names of fields of study, such as *archaeology*.

25. The word *such* should replace the word *so*.

26. The noun *life* should be used in place of *live*.

27. For parallelism, an *-ing* form (*hiking*) is needed in place of the plural noun *hikes*.

28. The noun *ability* should be used in place of the adjective *able*.

29. The correct pattern is *not only . . . but also*.

30. The plural verb *do* should be used in place of the singular *does* in order to agree with the plural subject *gases*.

31. The word *Most* should be used in place of *Almost*. (This sentence could also be corrected by using the phrase *Almost all*.)

32. The expression *both . . . and* is used to join two words or phrases, but this sentence contains a series of three words: *nails, claws,* and *hooves*. Therefore, the word *both* should be eliminated.

33. The correct word order is *did they*. Sentences beginning with negative adverbials (such as *not until*) follow the question pattern: auxiliary + subject + main verb.

34. The expression *percent* must be used in place of *percentage*.

35. The plural noun *Mathematicians* (people who study mathematics) must be used in place of the singular noun *Mathematics* (the field); this is clear because the verb *have* is plural.

36. An adjective (*wild*) is needed in place of the adverb *wildly*. (The word *lovely* is an adjective that ends with *-ly*, not an adverb.)

37. The definite article *the* is needed in place of the indefinite article *a*.

38. After the adjective *essential* the preposition *to* or *for* should be used.

39. The correct word choice in this sentence is *earliest*.

40. A noun (*marriage*) is needed in place of the participle *married*.

SECTION 3: READING COMPREHENSION

Answer Key

1. C	11. B	21. B	31. B	41. C
2. A	12. D	22. A	32. D	42. A
3. B	13. C	23. B	33. D	43. C
4. D	14. A	24. A	34. A	44. A
5. B	15. D	25. D	35. D	45. D
6. C	16. A	26. C	36. A	46. B
7. C	17. B	27. B	37. C	47. A
8. B	18. C	28. A	38. C	48. C
9. B	19. D	29. C	39. A	49. D
10. A	20. C	30. D	40. D	50. B

1. The first paragraph presents an overall definition of cooperation. Choice (A) is incorrect because the first paragraph explains what cooperation has in common with competition and conflict, but not how it differs from them. Choice (B) is incorrect because examples of specific forms of cooperation are given in the second, third, and fourth paragraphs, not the first. Choice (D) is incorrect; at no point in the passage does the author urge readers to cooperate.

2. The word *cherished* means *prized, loved.*

3. The word *fuse* means *unite, join together.*

4. According to line 8, primary cooperation "is most often characteristic of preliterate societies" —in other words, societies in which people have generally not developed the ability to read and write.

5. Lines 11–12 state that "members perform tasks so that they can *separately* enjoy the fruits of their cooperation in terms of salary, prestige, or power."

6. The passage states that in tertiary cooperation, "latent conflict underlies the shared work" and that it "involves common means to achieve antagonistic goals." The situation described in choice (C) best fits this definition. Choice (A) is an example of secondary cooperation; choice (B) is an example of competition; choice (D) is an example of primary (or perhaps secondary) competition.

7. In the fourth paragraph, the author calls the third type *tertiary cooperation,* or *accommodation* (line 14). At the end of that paragraph, the author states that "the term *antagonistic cooperation* is sometimes used for this relationship" as well. Latent conflict is NOT another term for this relationship; it is a characteristic of it.

8. The word *fragile* means *weak* or *easily broken.*

9. In this passage, *common* means *shared* or *jointly held.*

10. The author defines a concept *(cooperation)* by discussing each of its three forms in the second, third, and fourth paragraphs of the passage.

11. Only one of Schaefer's contributions to science is noted and that only briefly in the first paragraph. There is no description in the passage of the process by which snow crystals are formed. The effects of cloud seeding are not directly discussed. The passage is mainly an introduction to the basics of cloud seeding or weather modification.

12. In this passage, the word *spawned* means *created, generated.* (It literally means to give birth to.)

13. According to the first paragraph, farmers and ranchers first felt optimism (lines 3–4). However, because it was not clear whether "the cloud-seeding operations of the late 1940s and 1950s . . . had any effect" it is reasonable to believe that the farmers' and ranchers' optimism must have turned to disappointment.

14. Line 7 states that cloud seeding came to be called "weather modification," indicating that cloud seeding is the older term.

15. According to lines 10–11, winter orographic clouds are "formed when air currents encounter a mountain slope and rise."

16. The reference is to water droplets (line 17).

17. The passage states that in ground-based seeding, silver iodide is burned in ground generators and that the "smoke rises into the clouds where the tiny silver iodide particles act as nuclei for the formation of ice crystals" (lines 13–15).

18. Choice (A) is not correct because seeding from planes is "more expensive" (line 18). Choice (B) is not correct; when clouds are seeded from airplanes, the process of spontaneous nucleation is employed (lines 17–18). Choice (D) cannot be correct; there is no information about the effect of temperature on cloud-seeding operations. Choice (B) is best because the passage says that seeding from airplanes is "more efficient" (line 18).

19. Line 21 states, "About 85 percent of the waters in the rivers of the West comes from melted snow."

20. The author quotes an expert in lines 22–23 who says that "the water problems of the future may make the energy problem of the 1970s seem like child's play to solve." (*Child's play* means a simple problem.)

21. In line 24, the author mentions "private interests such as ski areas and agricultural cooperatives."

22. In line 28, the author calls the effort to produce precipitation in 1976–77 a "crash program" (meaning an urgent or emergency program) and later classes it with "hurry-up programs" (line 29).

23. The passage begins "The biological community changes once again as one moves from the city to the suburbs," indicating that the probable subject of the previous paragraph was the biological community in the city.

24. Most of the trees "have been deliberately planted" (lines 2–3) while mammals "have moved in from the surrounding countryside" (lines 3–4).

25. The word *thoroughfares* means *streets* or *roads.*

26. Line 6 states that "usually only one species" of squirrel is found "in any given suburb."

27. The word *thrive* means *flourish, prosper.*

28. The word *odd* means *strange, unusual.*

29. The topic of the second paragraph is "the odd biological sameness in these suburban communities" (line 10).

30. The author states in lines 13–14 that "unlike the natural biomes, the urban and suburban communities exist in spite of, not because of, the climate." This means that the climate actually creates the conditions in the natural biomes, so the effect there is much more noticeable.

31. The passage mainly discusses the potential use of Hot Dry Rock. There is no mention in the passage of the drawbacks (disadvantages) of using Hot Dry Rock nor does the passage explain how Hot Dry Rock was discovered; choice (D) is merely a detail of the third paragraph.

32. The term *pressurized reservoir* refers to a supply of water that has been superheated by Hot Dry Rock. The other terms refer to Hot Dry Rock itself.

33. The word *adjacent* means *side-by-side* or *next to*.

34. Lines 4–5 state that "the concept . . . is quite simple, at least in theory," indicating that putting the concept into practice might be difficult.

35. The reference is to the surface of the Earth.

36. According to the second paragraph, the heat energy of the water "is transferred to a volatile liquid which in turn drives an electric power-producing turbine."

37. According to lines 10–12, Duchane thinks that a 1-megawatt plant will be built "in around two decades" (twenty years) and that "a small prototype station will be built in half that time" (ten years).

38. The "grander dream" refers to the possibility of pumping seawater into the Hot Dry Rock, turning some of it to vapor, and thus obtaining pure water while producing electricity at the same time (lines 12–15).

39. The reference is to seawater (line 13).

40. The passage mainly focuses on historic houses in Taos that have been restored and are now open to the public.

41. The word *meticulously* means *carefully, painstakingly*.

42. The word *imposing* means *striking, impressive*.

43. According to line 7, "Its twenty-one rooms and two courtyards now house a living museum."

44. Bent was "a trader who later became governor of the New Mexico territory" (lines 9–10) and was thus a merchant and a politician.

45. According to lines 10–11, "Carson's house was built in 1843, Bent's three years later"—in other words, 1846.

46. The term *bigger sister* indicates that Sante Fe is similar to Taos but has a larger population.

47. The author mentions "the works of Jack London and other bestselling authors," (lines 14–15), so in this context, *works* means *books*.

48. Line 15 states that Blumenschein was on a "Denver-to-Mexico City sketching tour."

49. The artist Nicolai Fechin was "Russian-born" (line 18) and he carved and decorated the furniture and so on to look like that "of a traditional country house in his homeland" (line 20). The style must have been traditional Russian.

50. Jack London is not given in the passage as a resident of Taos. He is mentioned because Ernest Blumenschein illustrated his books.

Practice Test 5

Answer Key

1. D	11. B	21. C	31. D	41. D
2. D	12. A	22. A	32. C	42. C
3. C	13. B	23. D	33. C	43. B
4. A	14. B	24. A	34. A	44. D
5. B	15. C	25. A	35. A	45. C
6. B	16. A	26. D	36. B	46. D
7. D	17. A	27. D	37. C	47. B
8. D	18. D	28. D	38. B	48. D
9. C	19. B	29. C	39. D	49. C
10. A	20. D	30. A	40. A	50. B

PART A

TAPESCRIPT*

1. F1: I thought you were going to pick up some strawberries to have after dinner.
   M1: I went by Bailey's Market to get some, but they were fresh out.
   M2: What does the man mean?

2. M1: That has to be one of the worst lectures Professor Fowles has ever given.
   F2: It certainly wasn't up to his usual standards.
   M2: What do the speakers say about Professor Fowles?

3. M1: I *hate* missing breakfast!
   F1: Me too, but if we'd stopped for breakfast, we would have missed the appointment.
   M2: What did the speakers do this morning?

4. M1: I bought a new bicycle this week.
   F2: Glad to hear it. What kind?
   M2: What does the woman ask the man about the bicycle?

5. M1: Have you ever watched that program *Family Tree* on television?
   F2: Well, I *tried* to a couple of times.
   M2: What does the woman imply about the program?

6. F2: Let's make some sandwiches before we go. Then we won't have to eat lunch at the ski lodge.
   M1: That's not a bad idea—the restuarant there is *so* expensive!
   M2: What will the speakers probably do?

7. M1: I had to miss Dr. Hudson's first class. What was the lecture about?
   F2: For one thing, she talked about the differences between planets and stars.
   M2: What course does Professor Hudson probably teach?

---
* Note:　M1 = first male voice　　M2 = second male voice　　F1 = first female voice　　F2 = second female voice

215

8. M1: If you'd like to sing along, here are the lyrics for that song.
   F1: Oh, I already know them by heart!
   M2: What does the woman mean?

9. F1: Excuse me—do you know where the Admiral Hotel is?
   M1: I can't say that I do. Why don't you walk over and ask that taxi driver? He should know.
   M2: What does the man suggest the woman do?

10. F1: Tim sure got these clean!
   F2: I'll say! You can hardly tell that there are panes of glass in them.
   M2: What are the two speakers probably discussing?

11. F2: What time is Dean Metzger's reception tonight? Seven?
   M1: That's *tonight*?
   M2: What had the man NOT been aware of?

12. F2: Weren't you in my advanced math class last semester?
   M1: Me? You must be joking—I can barely add 2 and 2 together.
   M2: What does the man imply?

13. M1: You let Vince plan this event?
   F1: This time—but never again!
   M2: What does the woman imply about Vince?

14. F2: What was the matter with Jack last night?
   F1: I don't know—he was a nervous wreck, though, wasn't he?
   M2: What do the speakers say about Jack?

15. F1: I just walked by Professor Dixon's classroom, and there was no one in there.
   M1: That's because he always takes his class outside when the weather is nice.
   M2: What can be inferred from this conversation?

16. M1: On second thought, I'm going to take statistics instead of computer science.
   F2: Are you *sure* this time?
   M2: What does the *man* tell the woman?

17. F1: What did you think of the opera you saw Saturday night?
   M1: Frankly, I don't have much to compare it with.
   M2: What does the man imply?

18. F1: Here's the tape, some scissors, and some brown paper.
   M1: Thanks. Now I just need to find Richard's address.
   M2: What is the man probably going to do?

19. M1: Bob was late for the dinner because he was helping his roommate.
   F2: Isn't that just like Bob?
   M2: What does the woman imply about Bob?

20. F2: What did you think of Brenda's story?
   M1: To tell you the truth, I found it hard to keep a straight face while she was telling it.
   M2: How did the man feel about the story?

21. M1: Is this Dr. Goldsmith's office?
   F2: No, this is room 301. Dr. Goldsmith's office is right downstairs from here.
   M2: Where is Dr. Goldsmith's office?

22. F1: I saw Suzanne at the meeting this afternoon.
   M1: Yeah—she was the *last* person I expected to see there.
   M2: What does the man imply about Suzanne?

23. M1: Marie's picture was in the newspaper.
F2: Oh? What for?
M2: What does the woman ask?

24. M1: Traffic was so bad on the way to the airport that I almost missed my flight to Boston.
F2: I could have told you that it would be.
M2: What does the woman mean?

25. F1: That seafood restaurant on College Avenue is going to close down after just two months.
M1: So I heard. Too bad.
M2: What does the man mean?

26. F2: Here you are, sir—a hamburger and a large drink.
M1: Wait a second—that's what you call *large*?
M2: What does the man imply?

27. F1: Peter, want to play softball?
M1: No, I have to go down to the lumber yard now. I'm building some bookshelves.
M2: What will Peter probably do next?

28. F2: No, Emma's not here. She went to choir practice.
M1: Oh, she must be feeling much better then.
M2: What had the man assumed about Emma?

29. M1: How did you find out about this lecture series?
F1: Just through word of mouth.
M2: What does the woman say about the lecture series?

30. F1: Have you decided whether you're staying at the Buckley House or the Sherman Hotel during the conference?
M1: I didn't have to decide—the Buckley was already completely booked.
M2: What can be inferred from this conversation?

PART B

Questions 31 to 33: Listen to a conversation between two students.

M1: Hey, Amy, where are you off to?
F2: To the Recreation Center. I've got a physical education class.
M1: What course are you taking?
F2: Fencing.
M1: Oh, really? Is it hard?
F2: I was in the fencing club in high school, so for me it's mostly review.
M1: I once heard someone call fencing "the thinking person's sport." Would you agree with that?
F2: It *does* require lots of concentration, and if you want to win matches, tactics are important—just like in a game of chess.
M1: And I suppose you have to be fast and strong to win.
F2: Speed is important, and agility, but you don't have to be particularly strong to be a good fencer. The main reason I like fencing, though, is that it's great exercise. I find an hour of fencing is as good a workout as, say, an hour of tennis.

31. M2: What is the woman going to do?

32. M2: Which of the following does the woman say is *not* particularly important in fencing?

33. M2: Why does the woman compare fencing to tennis?

Questions 34 to 37: Listen to a conversation in a university bookstore.

F1: That comes to $160.

M1: One hundred and sixty dollars! I just can't believe how expensive textbooks are. And that's just for required texts. Why, if I had to buy all the books on my suggested reading lists, I'd have to take out a bank loan!

F1: You could save some money if you bought used texts, you know.

M1: I suppose, but it's hard for me to study from a text that's been marked up. Tell me, if I don't need some of these books, can I get a full refund?

F1: Sure, if the professor changes his mind about a book or if you drop a course, just return it and we'll give you your money back—but only for the first three weeks of class. So don't write your name in the text or mark it up until you're sure you're going to keep it all semester.

M1: And what about at the end of the semester? What's your buy-back policy?

F1: As long as the books are in reasonably good condition, and they're going to be used in class the next semester, we'll give you 50 percent of their original value—even if you didn't buy them at this store. Of course, if a professor changes texts or if a new edition comes out, we won't buy them back at all.

M1: Fifty percent—that's all?

F1: Well, I suppose that doesn't sound like much, but that's the store policy.

34. M2: What is the man buying?

35. M2: At what point in the semester does this conversation take place?

36. M2: If the man sells all the books that he buys today back to the store at the end of the semester, how much money will he receive?

37. M2: Why would the bookstore NOT buy back the man's books at any price?

PART C

Questions 38 to 42: Listen to a presentatoin given in an architecture class.

F1: Good afternoon, everyone. As you all know, our class project was to investigate some unconventional styles of housing and report on one. The one I chose is called the Earthship. It was developed by an architect named Michael Reynolds about twenty-five years ago, and there are about a thousand of them in existence today. One remarkable thing about the Earthship is that it is built almost entirely of recycled materials. The exterior walls are made of used tires packed with soil. Aluminum cans are tucked between the tires and the exterior walls are coated with straw and mud. Interior walls are made of cement and glass bottles. This may not sound very attractive, but, to learn more about these houses, I visited one not too far from here and, I can tell you, the finished building is very beautiful. And these houses use no outside electricity. They generate electricity from rooftop solar panels. They produce no sewage and don't pump water from the ground. So, what about costs? You can buy a book describing the building process for around $25 and architectural drawings for $2,000. A small, basic house—called a "nest"—can be built for about $35,000. Larger Earthships can cost hundreds of thousands of dollars. Now, I've brought a small model of an Earthship that I built myself. I hope that when I graduate and am designing houses myself, I can incorporate some of these ideas into my own designs. So come on up and take a close look at it.

38. F2: Who is the speaker?

39. F2: Which of these would NOT be needed to build an Earthship?

40. F2: What did the speaker do to research her project?

41. F2: According to the speaker, what is a "nest"?

42. F2: What did the speaker bring with her?

Questions 43 to 46: Listen to an announcement made on a university radio station.

M1: The Central State University School of Engineering invites you to go fly a kite—that is, once you've designed it. This weekend, the Third Annual Kite Competition will take place. Building a kite poses a number of engineering problems, and we want to see how you solve them. As in the two previous years, there are lots of prizes. There will be prizes for the kite with the largest surface area and for the kite with the smallest; for the kite that can lift the heaviest load and for the kite made from the most unusual material; there's even one for the funniest kite. Of course, all winning kites must be working models; you must be able to fly them at least 100 feet in the air. You don't have to be an engineering student to compete—all interested students at Central State are invited to enter. Preliminary events take place Saturday in the commons south of the Engineering Tower. Final events will be held at the stadium on Sunday afternoon.

43. M2: According to the speaker, how many times has the kite competition been held before this year?

44. M2: Which of the following would win a prize in the kite competition?

45. M2: According to the speaker, who is eligible to enter the kite competition?

46. M2: According to the speaker, when and where will the final portion of the kite competition be held?

Questions 47 to 50: Listen to part of a lecture given in an anthropology class.

F2: Students, have you ever been to a potluck dinner, where all the guests bring a different dish? The English word *potluck* is believed to come from an American Indian word *potlatch*. Today we're going to continue our discussion of Native American ceremonies by taking a look at this fascinating ceremonial activity—the potlatch. The potlatch was practiced among all the tribes of Native Americans who lived in the Pacific Northwest region of North America. Among members of these cultures, the concepts of prestige and rank were very important, and potlatches were the primary way to advance their social position. The potlatch reached its most elaborate form among a tribe called the Kwakiutl, who lived in British Columbia, Canada.

Potlatches were held to commemorate important events in the families of the hosts, such as births, naming ceremonies, or marriages. After feasting and dancing, the host would give away valuable gifts, such as blankets, jewelry, or food.

So—potlatches were a little like our birthday parties in reverse! At potlatches, the host might also throw copper money into the sea and destroy some of his most valuable possessions, such as canoes. As for the guests at potlatches—well, it was their turn next. They were required to hold potlatches of their own and to give away even more valuable gifts than they had received. As you can see, potlatches were a form of investment.

47. M2: What is the speaker primarily describing in this talk?

48. M2: According to the speaker, which of the following groups held potlatches?

49. M2: According to the speaker, what was a host's primary purpose for having a potlatch?

50. M2: Why does the speaker refer to a potlatch as a form of investment?

End of Tape 2.

SECTION 2: STRUCTURE AND WRITTEN EXPRESSION

Answer Key

1. B	11. A	21. D	31. D
2. D	12. A	22. A	32. D
3. B	13. B	23. C	33. B
4. C	14. D	24. C	34. A
5. B	15. B	25. A	35. A
6. A	16. C	26. C	36. D
7. C	17. C	27. A	37. B
8. D	18. D	28. C	38. B
9. A	19. B	29. D	39. D
10. C	20. B	30. C	40. D

EXPLANATION: WRITTEN EXPRESSION

16. The correct pattern is *either . . . or*.

17. The word *other* should not be pluralized when used before a plural noun.

18. For parallelism, a superlative form (*heaviest*) is needed.

19. The noun *replica* should be pluralized. (After the word *many*, a plural noun is used.)

20. The preposition *during* should be used in place of *when* before a noun phrase (*construction of . . .*); the word *when* is used before clauses.

21. The noun *development* should be used in place of the verb *develop*.

22. After a modal auxiliary verb (*must*), the simple form of the verb (*learn*) should be used in place of the *-ing* form.

23. The pronoun *it* is an unnecessary repetition of the subject and should be omitted.

24. With the verb *derived*, the preposition *from* should be used in place of the preposition *of*.

25. The verb *differ* is needed in place of the adjective *different*.

26. The adverb *primarily* should be used in place of the adjective *primary*.

27. The word *runners* should be used in place of *running* to be parallel with *walkers*.

28. The adjective *simple* should be used in place of the adverb *simply* to modify the noun *existence*.

29. The correct word order is *future time*. (The phrase *at some time in the future* would also be correctly used here.)

30. The gerund form (*understanding*) is needed in place of the simple form *understand*.

31. The correct word choice is *twice*.

32. The possessive form *his* should replace the definite article *the*.

33. The noun *part* is needed in place of the adverb *partly* after the preposition *in*.

34. The correct word order is *Of all mammals*.

35. To be parallel with the other items in the series (*rhythm* and *melody*), a noun (*harmony*) is needed in place of the verb *harmonize*.

36. The correct word is *them* because the pronoun refers to *objects* not to *babies*.

37. The plural verb *have* should be used in place of the singular form *has* in order to agree with the plural subject *loblolly pines*.

38. Because the information in the second clause is in contrast with the information in the first clause, the two clauses should be joined with the word *but* instead of the word *and*.

39. The plural form *humans* should be singular (*human*) because in a compound noun such as *human beings*, only the second noun is pluralized.

40. In a passive verb phrase, the past participle *polished* must be used in place of the simple form.

SECTION 3: READING COMPREHENSION

Answer Key

1. A	11. D	21. B	31. C	41. A
2. A	12. B	22. D	32. A	42. A
3. D	13. B	23. D	33. A	43. C
4. B	14. A	24. C	34. C	44. C
5. C	15. C	25. A	35. A	45. A
6. D	16. B	26. C	36. B	46. D
7. D	17. A	27. B	37. D	47. B
8. C	18. A	28. D	38. A	48. A
9. C	19. C	29. C	39. B	49. D
10. B	20. A	30. D	40. C	50. D

1. The passage mainly describes clusters and superclusters of galaxies. There is no information about the other three choices.

2. The word *evenly* means *uniformly*.

3. Lines 1–2 state that "a few are found alone, but almost all are grouped in formations termed *galactic clusters.*" Therefore, solo galaxies must be outnumbered by galaxies in clusters.

4. The word *globular* means shaped like a globe—in other words, *spherical*.

5. Line 6 states that "It is surmised that even clusters of superclusters are possible." Since their existence is possible but not proven, the author would probably describe them as theoretical.

6. Line 8 says that the Local Group "is typical in terms of the types of galaxies it contains."

7. This question involves some simple arithmetic: the Local Group contains twenty galaxies (line 8); there are three large spirals, four medium-size spiral galaxies, and four regular elliptical galaxies. The total of these three types is eleven. Since "the remainder are dwarf ellipticals," (line 12) there must be nine of those, making dwarf ellipticals," the most numerous.

8. According to lines 8–14, in addition to our own galaxy (the Milky Way), only Andromeda and the Clouds of Magellan can be seen from somewhere on the Earth with the naked eye (i.e., without a telescope). Therefore, the Triangulum Spiral must be invisible to the unaided eye.

9. Lines 17–18 state that "the Local Group . . . and the Virgo Cluster form part of a much larger cluster of clusters—the Local Supercluster."

10. The word *riddle* means *puzzle, mystery*.

11. Lines 22–23 state that "galaxies contain great amounts of 'dark matter,'" indicating that dark matter does NOT lie between galaxies but inside them. The fourth paragraph provides information to show that choices (A), (B), and (C) ARE true.

12. The word *members* is used throughout the passage to refer to members of galactic clusters—in other words, to galaxies.

13. The passage deals mainly with Sequoyah's accomplishment—especially the creation of the Cherokee alphabet. The passage supplies only a little information about choices (A), (C), and (D).

222

14. Lines 2-3 indicate that the invention of the Cherokee alphabet was accomplished in just a dozen (twelve) years.

15. The first paragraph indicates that Sequoyah was a hunter, a silversmith, and an intrpreter as a young man. He did not serve as a representative in Washington until "his later life" (lines 18-19).

16. According to lines 6-7, Sequoyah used the term "talking leaves" to refer to the books of white people.

17. Lines 7-8 state that "his chief aim was to record their ancient tribal customs."

18. The word *cumbersome* means *awkward, clumsy*.

19. Lines 10-11 state that "he made symbols for the sounds of the Cherokee language."

20. There is no mention that Sequoyah borrowed symbols from the Egyptian alphabet. The other choices are given in line 12.

21. The word *wholeheartedly* means *enthusiastically, eagerly*.

22. Lines 21-22 state that "a statue of Sequoyah represents Oklahoma in the Statuary Hall in the Capitol building in Washington, D.C."

23. Lines 23-24 indicate that Sequoyah is rembered today chiefly because the sequoia trees of California are named in his honor.

24. The reaction to the alphabet is given in lines 13-14 in the sentence "The response was phenomenal."

25. The passage offers a basic definition and description of the amphibian class of animals.

26. Line 3 states that "unlike reptiles, amphibians never have claws on their toes." The other characteristics are listed in the first paragraph.

27. In the context of the passage, the term *scales* refers to the plates that cover certain animals, such as fish.

28. According to lines 10-11, amphibians that undergo a double metamorphosis change "not only from gill breathers to lung breathers but also from vegetarians to insectivores."

29. Amphibians' ability to breathe through their skin is most useful when they are in hibernation "during the coldest months"; i.e., in the winter (lines 8-9).

30. The first paragraph deals with the similarities and differences between amphibians and reptiles. Line 2 says that "some amphibians, such as salamanders, are even shaped like lizards," indicating that lizards must not be amphibians. The other three choices are mentioned as amphibians in the third paragraph.

31. The word *stubby* means *short and thick*.

32. The reference is to toads.

33. The passage is basically a history of animated film from its beginnings in 1906 to the 1990s. Choice (B) is briefly described in the passage, but is not the main idea. Choice (C) is incorrect because the passage discusses the development of animation in general, not of one specific film. Choice (D) is mentioned in the last paragraph but is not the main idea of the whole passage.

34. According to line 4, McCay's films "featured . . . characters with individual personalities."

35. The word *streamlined* means *simplified, made easier and faster*.

36. The reference is to the cartoon character Felix the Cat.

37. Since the first cartoon with sound (*Steamboat Willie*) was made in 1928, earlier cartoons must have been silent films.

38. Lines 13-14 state, "The results of this are apparent in *Snow White and the Seven Dwarfs*." (The word *this* refers to the training in anatomy, acting, drawing, and motion studies.)

39. The phrase *splintered off from* means *broke away from*. (A splinter is a small piece that breaks off a larger piece.)

40. The author DOES mention characters used by Disney (Mickey Mouse, Snow White), by Hanna and Barbera (Yogi Bear, the Flintstones), and Warner Brothers (Bugs Bunny, Daffy Duck). There is NO mention of any of the characters used by United Productions of America.

41. The phrase *blurred the lines* means *eliminated the distinctions*.

42. Lines 27-28 state that animators first experimented with computer animation in the 1950s, but the first full-length computer-animated film was not made until the 1990s.

43. The word *heyday* means *prime, peak*.

44. The first mention of animation on television is in lines 20-21, in the sentence beginning "In the 1950s children's cartoons began to be broadcast . . ."

45. The first paragraph deals mostly with the dangers created by fog.

46. The word *catastrophic* means *disastrous, calamitous*.

47. According to line 10, "This type of fog (advection fog) often occurs along the California coast . . ."

48. Advection fog occurs when "a warm ocean current blows across the surface of a cold current" (lines 11-12). This type of fog occurs off Newfoundland, where the Labrador Current meets the Gulf Stream. Since the Gulf Stream is identified as warm (line 13) the Labrador Current must be cold.

49. The author first discusses "the most common type of fog," radiation fog. He then describes advection fog—"another common type." Finally, he mentions two kinds of fog that "are somewhat more unusual"—frontal fog and steam fog.

50. Since fog is a weather phenomenon, it is likely that the passage was written by an expert in meteorology (the study of weather).

Practice Tests 1-5
Answer Sheets

Answer Sheet

Practice Test 1

Section 1: Listening Comprehension

Part A

1. Ⓐ Ⓑ Ⓒ Ⓓ
2. Ⓐ Ⓑ Ⓒ Ⓓ
3. Ⓐ Ⓑ Ⓒ Ⓓ
4. Ⓐ Ⓑ Ⓒ Ⓓ
5. Ⓐ Ⓑ Ⓒ Ⓓ
6. Ⓐ Ⓑ Ⓒ Ⓓ
7. Ⓐ Ⓑ Ⓒ Ⓓ
8. Ⓐ Ⓑ Ⓒ Ⓓ
9. Ⓐ Ⓑ Ⓒ Ⓓ
10. Ⓐ Ⓑ Ⓒ Ⓓ
11. Ⓐ Ⓑ Ⓒ Ⓓ
12. Ⓐ Ⓑ Ⓒ Ⓓ
13. Ⓐ Ⓑ Ⓒ Ⓓ
14. Ⓐ Ⓑ Ⓒ Ⓓ
15. Ⓐ Ⓑ Ⓒ Ⓓ
16. Ⓐ Ⓑ Ⓒ Ⓓ
17. Ⓐ Ⓑ Ⓒ Ⓓ
18. Ⓐ Ⓑ Ⓒ Ⓓ
19. Ⓐ Ⓑ Ⓒ Ⓓ
20. Ⓐ Ⓑ Ⓒ Ⓓ

21. Ⓐ Ⓑ Ⓒ Ⓓ
22. Ⓐ Ⓑ Ⓒ Ⓓ
23. Ⓐ Ⓑ Ⓒ Ⓓ
24. Ⓐ Ⓑ Ⓒ Ⓓ
25. Ⓐ Ⓑ Ⓒ Ⓓ
26. Ⓐ Ⓑ Ⓒ Ⓓ
27. Ⓐ Ⓑ Ⓒ Ⓓ
28. Ⓐ Ⓑ Ⓒ Ⓓ
29. Ⓐ Ⓑ Ⓒ Ⓓ
30. Ⓐ Ⓑ Ⓒ Ⓓ

Part B

31. Ⓐ Ⓑ Ⓒ Ⓓ
32. Ⓐ Ⓑ Ⓒ Ⓓ
33. Ⓐ Ⓑ Ⓒ Ⓓ
34. Ⓐ Ⓑ Ⓒ Ⓓ
35. Ⓐ Ⓑ Ⓒ Ⓓ
36. Ⓐ Ⓑ Ⓒ Ⓓ
37. Ⓐ Ⓑ Ⓒ Ⓓ
38. Ⓐ Ⓑ Ⓒ Ⓓ

Part C

39. Ⓐ Ⓑ Ⓒ Ⓓ
40. Ⓐ Ⓑ Ⓒ Ⓓ
41. Ⓐ Ⓑ Ⓒ Ⓓ
42. Ⓐ Ⓑ Ⓒ Ⓓ
43. Ⓐ Ⓑ Ⓒ Ⓓ
44. Ⓐ Ⓑ Ⓒ Ⓓ
45. Ⓐ Ⓑ Ⓒ Ⓓ
46. Ⓐ Ⓑ Ⓒ Ⓓ
47. Ⓐ Ⓑ Ⓒ Ⓓ
48. Ⓐ Ⓑ Ⓒ Ⓓ
49. Ⓐ Ⓑ Ⓒ Ⓓ
50. Ⓐ Ⓑ Ⓒ Ⓓ

Practice Test 1

Section 2: Structure and Written Expression

1.	(A)	(B)	(C)	(D)	21.	(A)	(B)	(C)	(D)
2.	(A)	(B)	(C)	(D)	22.	(A)	(B)	(C)	(D)
3.	(A)	(B)	(C)	(D)	23.	(A)	(B)	(C)	(D)
4.	(A)	(B)	(C)	(D)	24.	(A)	(B)	(C)	(D)
5.	(A)	(B)	(C)	(D)	25.	(A)	(B)	(C)	(D)
6.	(A)	(B)	(C)	(D)	26.	(A)	(B)	(C)	(D)
7.	(A)	(B)	(C)	(D)	27.	(A)	(B)	(C)	(D)
8.	(A)	(B)	(C)	(D)	28.	(A)	(B)	(C)	(D)
9.	(A)	(B)	(C)	(D)	29.	(A)	(B)	(C)	(D)
10.	(A)	(B)	(C)	(D)	30.	(A)	(B)	(C)	(D)
11.	(A)	(B)	(C)	(D)	31.	(A)	(B)	(C)	(D)
12.	(A)	(B)	(C)	(D)	32.	(A)	(B)	(C)	(D)
13.	(A)	(B)	(C)	(D)	33.	(A)	(B)	(C)	(D)
14.	(A)	(B)	(C)	(D)	34.	(A)	(B)	(C)	(D)
15.	(A)	(B)	(C)	(D)	35.	(A)	(B)	(C)	(D)
					36.	(A)	(B)	(C)	(D)
16.	(A)	(B)	(C)	(D)	37.	(A)	(B)	(C)	(D)
17.	(A)	(B)	(C)	(D)	38.	(A)	(B)	(C)	(D)
18.	(A)	(B)	(C)	(D)	39.	(A)	(B)	(C)	(D)
19.	(A)	(B)	(C)	(D)	40.	(A)	(B)	(C)	(D)
20.	(A)	(B)	(C)	(D)					

Practice Test 1

Section 3: Reading Comprehension

1. (A) (B) (C) (D)
2. (A) (B) (C) (D)
3. (A) (B) (C) (D)
4. (A) (B) (C) (D)
5. (A) (B) (C) (D)
6. (A) (B) (C) (D)
7. (A) (B) (C) (D)
8. (A) (B) (C) (D)
9. (A) (B) (C) (D)
10. (A) (B) (C) (D)

11. (A) (B) (C) (D)
12. (A) (B) (C) (D)
13. (A) (B) (C) (D)
14. (A) (B) (C) (D)
15. (A) (B) (C) (D)
16. (A) (B) (C) (D)
17. (A) (B) (C) (D)
18. (A) (B) (C) (D)

19. (A) (B) (C) (D)
20. (A) (B) (C) (D)
21. (A) (B) (C) (D)
22. (A) (B) (C) (D)
23. (A) (B) (C) (D)
24. (A) (B) (C) (D)
25. (A) (B) (C) (D)
26. (A) (B) (C) (D)
27. (A) (B) (C) (D)
28. (A) (B) (C) (D)
29. (A) (B) (C) (D)
30. (A) (B) (C) (D)

31. (A) (B) (C) (D)
32. (A) (B) (C) (D)
33. (A) (B) (C) (D)
34. (A) (B) (C) (D)
35. (A) (B) (C) (D)
36. (A) (B) (C) (D)
37. (A) (B) (C) (D)
38. (A) (B) (C) (D)
39. (A) (B) (C) (D)

40. (A) (B) (C) (D)
41. (A) (B) (C) (D)
42. (A) (B) (C) (D)
43. (A) (B) (C) (D)
44. (A) (B) (C) (D)
45. (A) (B) (C) (D)
46. (A) (B) (C) (D)
47. (A) (B) (C) (D)
48. (A) (B) (C) (D)
49. (A) (B) (C) (D)
50. (A) (B) (C) (D)

Answer Sheet

Practice Test 2

Section 1: Listening Comprehension

Part A

1. Ⓐ Ⓑ Ⓒ Ⓓ
2. Ⓐ Ⓑ Ⓒ Ⓓ
3. Ⓐ Ⓑ Ⓒ Ⓓ
4. Ⓐ Ⓑ Ⓒ Ⓓ
5. Ⓐ Ⓑ Ⓒ Ⓓ
6. Ⓐ Ⓑ Ⓒ Ⓓ
7. Ⓐ Ⓑ Ⓒ Ⓓ
8. Ⓐ Ⓑ Ⓒ Ⓓ
9. Ⓐ Ⓑ Ⓒ Ⓓ
10. Ⓐ Ⓑ Ⓒ Ⓓ
11. Ⓐ Ⓑ Ⓒ Ⓓ
12. Ⓐ Ⓑ Ⓒ Ⓓ
13. Ⓐ Ⓑ Ⓒ Ⓓ
14. Ⓐ Ⓑ Ⓒ Ⓓ
15. Ⓐ Ⓑ Ⓒ Ⓓ
16. Ⓐ Ⓑ Ⓒ Ⓓ
17. Ⓐ Ⓑ Ⓒ Ⓓ
18. Ⓐ Ⓑ Ⓒ Ⓓ
19. Ⓐ Ⓑ Ⓒ Ⓓ
20. Ⓐ Ⓑ Ⓒ Ⓓ

21. Ⓐ Ⓑ Ⓒ Ⓓ
22. Ⓐ Ⓑ Ⓒ Ⓓ
23. Ⓐ Ⓑ Ⓒ Ⓓ
24. Ⓐ Ⓑ Ⓒ Ⓓ
25. Ⓐ Ⓑ Ⓒ Ⓓ
26. Ⓐ Ⓑ Ⓒ Ⓓ
27. Ⓐ Ⓑ Ⓒ Ⓓ
28. Ⓐ Ⓑ Ⓒ Ⓓ
29. Ⓐ Ⓑ Ⓒ Ⓓ
30. Ⓐ Ⓑ Ⓒ Ⓓ

Part B

31. Ⓐ Ⓑ Ⓒ Ⓓ
32. Ⓐ Ⓑ Ⓒ Ⓓ
33. Ⓐ Ⓑ Ⓒ Ⓓ
34. Ⓐ Ⓑ Ⓒ Ⓓ
35. Ⓐ Ⓑ Ⓒ Ⓓ
36. Ⓐ Ⓑ Ⓒ Ⓓ
37. Ⓐ Ⓑ Ⓒ Ⓓ
38. Ⓐ Ⓑ Ⓒ Ⓓ

Part C

39. Ⓐ Ⓑ Ⓒ Ⓓ
40. Ⓐ Ⓑ Ⓒ Ⓓ
41. Ⓐ Ⓑ Ⓒ Ⓓ
42. Ⓐ Ⓑ Ⓒ Ⓓ
43. Ⓐ Ⓑ Ⓒ Ⓓ
44. Ⓐ Ⓑ Ⓒ Ⓓ
45. Ⓐ Ⓑ Ⓒ Ⓓ
46. Ⓐ Ⓑ Ⓒ Ⓓ
47. Ⓐ Ⓑ Ⓒ Ⓓ
48. Ⓐ Ⓑ Ⓒ Ⓓ
49. Ⓐ Ⓑ Ⓒ Ⓓ
50. Ⓐ Ⓑ Ⓒ Ⓓ

Practice Test 2

Section 2: Structure and Written Expression

1.	Ⓐ Ⓑ Ⓒ Ⓓ		21.	Ⓐ Ⓑ Ⓒ Ⓓ
2.	Ⓐ Ⓑ Ⓒ Ⓓ		22.	Ⓐ Ⓑ Ⓒ Ⓓ
3.	Ⓐ Ⓑ Ⓒ Ⓓ		23.	Ⓐ Ⓑ Ⓒ Ⓓ
4.	Ⓐ Ⓑ Ⓒ Ⓓ		24.	Ⓐ Ⓑ Ⓒ Ⓓ
5.	Ⓐ Ⓑ Ⓒ Ⓓ		25.	Ⓐ Ⓑ Ⓒ Ⓓ
6.	Ⓐ Ⓑ Ⓒ Ⓓ		26.	Ⓐ Ⓑ Ⓒ Ⓓ
7.	Ⓐ Ⓑ Ⓒ Ⓓ		27.	Ⓐ Ⓑ Ⓒ Ⓓ
8.	Ⓐ Ⓑ Ⓒ Ⓓ		28.	Ⓐ Ⓑ Ⓒ Ⓓ
9.	Ⓐ Ⓑ Ⓒ Ⓓ		29.	Ⓐ Ⓑ Ⓒ Ⓓ
10.	Ⓐ Ⓑ Ⓒ Ⓓ		30.	Ⓐ Ⓑ Ⓒ Ⓓ
11.	Ⓐ Ⓑ Ⓒ Ⓓ		31.	Ⓐ Ⓑ Ⓒ Ⓓ
12.	Ⓐ Ⓑ Ⓒ Ⓓ		32.	Ⓐ Ⓑ Ⓒ Ⓓ
13.	Ⓐ Ⓑ Ⓒ Ⓓ		33.	Ⓐ Ⓑ Ⓒ Ⓓ
14.	Ⓐ Ⓑ Ⓒ Ⓓ		34.	Ⓐ Ⓑ Ⓒ Ⓓ
15.	Ⓐ Ⓑ Ⓒ Ⓓ		35.	Ⓐ Ⓑ Ⓒ Ⓓ
			36.	Ⓐ Ⓑ Ⓒ Ⓓ
16.	Ⓐ Ⓑ Ⓒ Ⓓ		37.	Ⓐ Ⓑ Ⓒ Ⓓ
17.	Ⓐ Ⓑ Ⓒ Ⓓ		38.	Ⓐ Ⓑ Ⓒ Ⓓ
18.	Ⓐ Ⓑ Ⓒ Ⓓ		39.	Ⓐ Ⓑ Ⓒ Ⓓ
19.	Ⓐ Ⓑ Ⓒ Ⓓ		40.	Ⓐ Ⓑ Ⓒ Ⓓ
20.	Ⓐ Ⓑ Ⓒ Ⓓ			

Practice Test 2

Section 3: Reading Comprehension

1.	(A)	(B)	(C)	(D)
2.	(A)	(B)	(C)	(D)
3.	(A)	(B)	(C)	(D)
4.	(A)	(B)	(C)	(D)
5.	(A)	(B)	(C)	(D)
6.	(A)	(B)	(C)	(D)
7.	(A)	(B)	(C)	(D)
8.	(A)	(B)	(C)	(D)
9.	(A)	(B)	(C)	(D)
10.	(A)	(B)	(C)	(D)
11.	(A)	(B)	(C)	(D)
12.	(A)	(B)	(C)	(D)
13.	(A)	(B)	(C)	(D)
14.	(A)	(B)	(C)	(D)
15.	(A)	(B)	(C)	(D)
16.	(A)	(B)	(C)	(D)
17.	(A)	(B)	(C)	(D)
18.	(A)	(B)	(C)	(D)
19.	(A)	(B)	(C)	(D)
20.	(A)	(B)	(C)	(D)
21.	(A)	(B)	(C)	(D)
22.	(A)	(B)	(C)	(D)

23.	(A)	(B)	(C)	(D)
24.	(A)	(B)	(C)	(D)
25.	(A)	(B)	(C)	(D)
26.	(A)	(B)	(C)	(D)
27.	(A)	(B)	(C)	(D)
28.	(A)	(B)	(C)	(D)
29.	(A)	(B)	(C)	(D)
30.	(A)	(B)	(C)	(D)
31.	(A)	(B)	(C)	(D)
32.	(A)	(B)	(C)	(D)
33.	(A)	(B)	(C)	(D)
34.	(A)	(B)	(C)	(D)
35.	(A)	(B)	(C)	(D)
36.	(A)	(B)	(C)	(D)
37.	(A)	(B)	(C)	(D)
38.	(A)	(B)	(C)	(D)
39.	(A)	(B)	(C)	(D)
40.	(A)	(B)	(C)	(D)
41.	(A)	(B)	(C)	(D)

42.	(A)	(B)	(C)	(D)
43.	(A)	(B)	(C)	(D)
44.	(A)	(B)	(C)	(D)
45.	(A)	(B)	(C)	(D)
46.	(A)	(B)	(C)	(D)
47.	(A)	(B)	(C)	(D)
48.	(A)	(B)	(C)	(D)
49.	(A)	(B)	(C)	(D)
50.	(A)	(B)	(C)	(D)

Answer Sheet

Practice Test 3 (Long Form)

Section 1: Listening Comprehension

Part A

1. Ⓐ Ⓑ Ⓒ Ⓓ
2. Ⓐ Ⓑ Ⓒ Ⓓ
3. Ⓐ Ⓑ Ⓒ Ⓓ
4. Ⓐ Ⓑ Ⓒ Ⓓ
5. Ⓐ Ⓑ Ⓒ Ⓓ
6. Ⓐ Ⓑ Ⓒ Ⓓ
7. Ⓐ Ⓑ Ⓒ Ⓓ
8. Ⓐ Ⓑ Ⓒ Ⓓ
9. Ⓐ Ⓑ Ⓒ Ⓓ
10. Ⓐ Ⓑ Ⓒ Ⓓ
11. Ⓐ Ⓑ Ⓒ Ⓓ
12. Ⓐ Ⓑ Ⓒ Ⓓ
13. Ⓐ Ⓑ Ⓒ Ⓓ
14. Ⓐ Ⓑ Ⓒ Ⓓ
15. Ⓐ Ⓑ Ⓒ Ⓓ
16. Ⓐ Ⓑ Ⓒ Ⓓ
17. Ⓐ Ⓑ Ⓒ Ⓓ
18. Ⓐ Ⓑ Ⓒ Ⓓ
19. Ⓐ Ⓑ Ⓒ Ⓓ
20. Ⓐ Ⓑ Ⓒ Ⓓ
21. Ⓐ Ⓑ Ⓒ Ⓓ
22. Ⓐ Ⓑ Ⓒ Ⓓ
23. Ⓐ Ⓑ Ⓒ Ⓓ
24. Ⓐ Ⓑ Ⓒ Ⓓ
25. Ⓐ Ⓑ Ⓒ Ⓓ

26. Ⓐ Ⓑ Ⓒ Ⓓ
27. Ⓐ Ⓑ Ⓒ Ⓓ
28. Ⓐ Ⓑ Ⓒ Ⓓ
29. Ⓐ Ⓑ Ⓒ Ⓓ
30. Ⓐ Ⓑ Ⓒ Ⓓ
31. Ⓐ Ⓑ Ⓒ Ⓓ
32. Ⓐ Ⓑ Ⓒ Ⓓ
33. Ⓐ Ⓑ Ⓒ Ⓓ
34. Ⓐ Ⓑ Ⓒ Ⓓ
35. Ⓐ Ⓑ Ⓒ Ⓓ
36. Ⓐ Ⓑ Ⓒ Ⓓ
37. Ⓐ Ⓑ Ⓒ Ⓓ
38. Ⓐ Ⓑ Ⓒ Ⓓ
39. Ⓐ Ⓑ Ⓒ Ⓓ
40. Ⓐ Ⓑ Ⓒ Ⓓ
41. Ⓐ Ⓑ Ⓒ Ⓓ
42. Ⓐ Ⓑ Ⓒ Ⓓ
43. Ⓐ Ⓑ Ⓒ Ⓓ
44. Ⓐ Ⓑ Ⓒ Ⓓ
45. Ⓐ Ⓑ Ⓒ Ⓓ
46. Ⓐ Ⓑ Ⓒ Ⓓ
47. Ⓐ Ⓑ Ⓒ Ⓓ
48. Ⓐ Ⓑ Ⓒ Ⓓ
49. Ⓐ Ⓑ Ⓒ Ⓓ
50. Ⓐ Ⓑ Ⓒ Ⓓ

Part B

51. Ⓐ Ⓑ Ⓒ Ⓓ
52. Ⓐ Ⓑ Ⓒ Ⓓ
53. Ⓐ Ⓑ Ⓒ Ⓓ
54. Ⓐ Ⓑ Ⓒ Ⓓ
55. Ⓐ Ⓑ Ⓒ Ⓓ
56. Ⓐ Ⓑ Ⓒ Ⓓ
57. Ⓐ Ⓑ Ⓒ Ⓓ
58. Ⓐ Ⓑ Ⓒ Ⓓ
59. Ⓐ Ⓑ Ⓒ Ⓓ
60. Ⓐ Ⓑ Ⓒ Ⓓ
61. Ⓐ Ⓑ Ⓒ Ⓓ
62. Ⓐ Ⓑ Ⓒ Ⓓ
63. Ⓐ Ⓑ Ⓒ Ⓓ

Part C

64. Ⓐ Ⓑ Ⓒ Ⓓ
65. Ⓐ Ⓑ Ⓒ Ⓓ
66. Ⓐ Ⓑ Ⓒ Ⓓ
67. Ⓐ Ⓑ Ⓒ Ⓓ
68. Ⓐ Ⓑ Ⓒ Ⓓ
69. Ⓐ Ⓑ Ⓒ Ⓓ
70. Ⓐ Ⓑ Ⓒ Ⓓ
71. Ⓐ Ⓑ Ⓒ Ⓓ
72. Ⓐ Ⓑ Ⓒ Ⓓ
73. Ⓐ Ⓑ Ⓒ Ⓓ
74. Ⓐ Ⓑ Ⓒ Ⓓ
75. Ⓐ Ⓑ Ⓒ Ⓓ
76. Ⓐ Ⓑ Ⓒ Ⓓ
77. Ⓐ Ⓑ Ⓒ Ⓓ
78. Ⓐ Ⓑ Ⓒ Ⓓ
79. Ⓐ Ⓑ Ⓒ Ⓓ
80. Ⓐ Ⓑ Ⓒ Ⓓ

Practice Test 3

Section 2: Structure and Written Expression

1. Ⓐ Ⓑ Ⓒ Ⓓ
2. Ⓐ Ⓑ Ⓒ Ⓓ
3. Ⓐ Ⓑ Ⓒ Ⓓ
4. Ⓐ Ⓑ Ⓒ Ⓓ
5. Ⓐ Ⓑ Ⓒ Ⓓ
6. Ⓐ Ⓑ Ⓒ Ⓓ
7. Ⓐ Ⓑ Ⓒ Ⓓ
8. Ⓐ Ⓑ Ⓒ Ⓓ
9. Ⓐ Ⓑ Ⓒ Ⓓ
10. Ⓐ Ⓑ Ⓒ Ⓓ
11. Ⓐ Ⓑ Ⓒ Ⓓ
12. Ⓐ Ⓑ Ⓒ Ⓓ
13. Ⓐ Ⓑ Ⓒ Ⓓ
14. Ⓐ Ⓑ Ⓒ Ⓓ
15. Ⓐ Ⓑ Ⓒ Ⓓ
16. Ⓐ Ⓑ Ⓒ Ⓓ
17. Ⓐ Ⓑ Ⓒ Ⓓ
18. Ⓐ Ⓑ Ⓒ Ⓓ
19. Ⓐ Ⓑ Ⓒ Ⓓ
20. Ⓐ Ⓑ Ⓒ Ⓓ

21. Ⓐ Ⓑ Ⓒ Ⓓ
22. Ⓐ Ⓑ Ⓒ Ⓓ
23. Ⓐ Ⓑ Ⓒ Ⓓ
24. Ⓐ Ⓑ Ⓒ Ⓓ
25. Ⓐ Ⓑ Ⓒ Ⓓ
26. Ⓐ Ⓑ Ⓒ Ⓓ
27. Ⓐ Ⓑ Ⓒ Ⓓ
28. Ⓐ Ⓑ Ⓒ Ⓓ
29. Ⓐ Ⓑ Ⓒ Ⓓ
30. Ⓐ Ⓑ Ⓒ Ⓓ
31. Ⓐ Ⓑ Ⓒ Ⓓ
32. Ⓐ Ⓑ Ⓒ Ⓓ
33. Ⓐ Ⓑ Ⓒ Ⓓ
34. Ⓐ Ⓑ Ⓒ Ⓓ
35. Ⓐ Ⓑ Ⓒ Ⓓ
36. Ⓐ Ⓑ Ⓒ Ⓓ
37. Ⓐ Ⓑ Ⓒ Ⓓ
38. Ⓐ Ⓑ Ⓒ Ⓓ
39. Ⓐ Ⓑ Ⓒ Ⓓ
40. Ⓐ Ⓑ Ⓒ Ⓓ

41. Ⓐ Ⓑ Ⓒ Ⓓ
42. Ⓐ Ⓑ Ⓒ Ⓓ
43. Ⓐ Ⓑ Ⓒ Ⓓ
44. Ⓐ Ⓑ Ⓒ Ⓓ
45. Ⓐ Ⓑ Ⓒ Ⓓ
46. Ⓐ Ⓑ Ⓒ Ⓓ
47. Ⓐ Ⓑ Ⓒ Ⓓ
48. Ⓐ Ⓑ Ⓒ Ⓓ
49. Ⓐ Ⓑ Ⓒ Ⓓ
50. Ⓐ Ⓑ Ⓒ Ⓓ
51. Ⓐ Ⓑ Ⓒ Ⓓ
52. Ⓐ Ⓑ Ⓒ Ⓓ
53. Ⓐ Ⓑ Ⓒ Ⓓ
54. Ⓐ Ⓑ Ⓒ Ⓓ
55. Ⓐ Ⓑ Ⓒ Ⓓ
56. Ⓐ Ⓑ Ⓒ Ⓓ
57. Ⓐ Ⓑ Ⓒ Ⓓ
58. Ⓐ Ⓑ Ⓒ Ⓓ
59. Ⓐ Ⓑ Ⓒ Ⓓ
60. Ⓐ Ⓑ Ⓒ Ⓓ

Practice Test 3

Section 3: Reading Comprehension

1. Ⓐ Ⓑ Ⓒ Ⓓ
2. Ⓐ Ⓑ Ⓒ Ⓓ
3. Ⓐ Ⓑ Ⓒ Ⓓ
4. Ⓐ Ⓑ Ⓒ Ⓓ
5. Ⓐ Ⓑ Ⓒ Ⓓ
6. Ⓐ Ⓑ Ⓒ Ⓓ
7. Ⓐ Ⓑ Ⓒ Ⓓ
8. Ⓐ Ⓑ Ⓒ Ⓓ
9. Ⓐ Ⓑ Ⓒ Ⓓ
10. Ⓐ Ⓑ Ⓒ Ⓓ
11. Ⓐ Ⓑ Ⓒ Ⓓ

12. Ⓐ Ⓑ Ⓒ Ⓓ
13. Ⓐ Ⓑ Ⓒ Ⓓ
14. Ⓐ Ⓑ Ⓒ Ⓓ
15. Ⓐ Ⓑ Ⓒ Ⓓ
16. Ⓐ Ⓑ Ⓒ Ⓓ
17. Ⓐ Ⓑ Ⓒ Ⓓ
18. Ⓐ Ⓑ Ⓒ Ⓓ
19. Ⓐ Ⓑ Ⓒ Ⓓ
20. Ⓐ Ⓑ Ⓒ Ⓓ
21. Ⓐ Ⓑ Ⓒ Ⓓ
22. Ⓐ Ⓑ Ⓒ Ⓓ
23. Ⓐ Ⓑ Ⓒ Ⓓ

24. Ⓐ Ⓑ Ⓒ Ⓓ
25. Ⓐ Ⓑ Ⓒ Ⓓ
26. Ⓐ Ⓑ Ⓒ Ⓓ
27. Ⓐ Ⓑ Ⓒ Ⓓ
28. Ⓐ Ⓑ Ⓒ Ⓓ
29. Ⓐ Ⓑ Ⓒ Ⓓ
30. Ⓐ Ⓑ Ⓒ Ⓓ
31. Ⓐ Ⓑ Ⓒ Ⓓ
32. Ⓐ Ⓑ Ⓒ Ⓓ
33. Ⓐ Ⓑ Ⓒ Ⓓ
34. Ⓐ Ⓑ Ⓒ Ⓓ
35. Ⓐ Ⓑ Ⓒ Ⓓ
36. Ⓐ Ⓑ Ⓒ Ⓓ

37. Ⓐ Ⓑ Ⓒ Ⓓ
38. Ⓐ Ⓑ Ⓒ Ⓓ
39. Ⓐ Ⓑ Ⓒ Ⓓ
40. Ⓐ Ⓑ Ⓒ Ⓓ
41. Ⓐ Ⓑ Ⓒ Ⓓ
42. Ⓐ Ⓑ Ⓒ Ⓓ
43. Ⓐ Ⓑ Ⓒ Ⓓ
44. Ⓐ Ⓑ Ⓒ Ⓓ

45. Ⓐ Ⓑ Ⓒ Ⓓ
46. Ⓐ Ⓑ Ⓒ Ⓓ
47. Ⓐ Ⓑ Ⓒ Ⓓ
48. Ⓐ Ⓑ Ⓒ Ⓓ
49. Ⓐ Ⓑ Ⓒ Ⓓ
50. Ⓐ Ⓑ Ⓒ Ⓓ
51. Ⓐ Ⓑ Ⓒ Ⓓ
52. Ⓐ Ⓑ Ⓒ Ⓓ
53. Ⓐ Ⓑ Ⓒ Ⓓ

54. Ⓐ Ⓑ Ⓒ Ⓓ
55. Ⓐ Ⓑ Ⓒ Ⓓ
56. Ⓐ Ⓑ Ⓒ Ⓓ
57. Ⓐ Ⓑ Ⓒ Ⓓ
58. Ⓐ Ⓑ Ⓒ Ⓓ
59. Ⓐ Ⓑ Ⓒ Ⓓ
60. Ⓐ Ⓑ Ⓒ Ⓓ

61. Ⓐ Ⓑ Ⓒ Ⓓ
62. Ⓐ Ⓑ Ⓒ Ⓓ
63. Ⓐ Ⓑ Ⓒ Ⓓ
64. Ⓐ Ⓑ Ⓒ Ⓓ
65. Ⓐ Ⓑ Ⓒ Ⓓ
66. Ⓐ Ⓑ Ⓒ Ⓓ
67. Ⓐ Ⓑ Ⓒ Ⓓ
68. Ⓐ Ⓑ Ⓒ Ⓓ
69. Ⓐ Ⓑ Ⓒ Ⓓ
70. Ⓐ Ⓑ Ⓒ Ⓓ

Answer Sheet

Practice Test 4

Section 1: Listening Comprehension

Part A

1. (A) (B) (C) (D)
2. (A) (B) (C) (D)
3. (A) (B) (C) (D)
4. (A) (B) (C) (D)
5. (A) (B) (C) (D)
6. (A) (B) (C) (D)
7. (A) (B) (C) (D)
8. (A) (B) (C) (D)
9. (A) (B) (C) (D)
10. (A) (B) (C) (D)
11. (A) (B) (C) (D)
12. (A) (B) (C) (D)
13. (A) (B) (C) (D)
14. (A) (B) (C) (D)
15. (A) (B) (C) (D)
16. (A) (B) (C) (D)
17. (A) (B) (C) (D)
18. (A) (B) (C) (D)
19. (A) (B) (C) (D)
20. (A) (B) (C) (D)

21. (A) (B) (C) (D)
22. (A) (B) (C) (D)
23. (A) (B) (C) (D)
24. (A) (B) (C) (D)
25. (A) (B) (C) (D)
26. (A) (B) (C) (D)
27. (A) (B) (C) (D)
28. (A) (B) (C) (D)
29. (A) (B) (C) (D)
30. (A) (B) (C) (D)

Part B

31. (A) (B) (C) (D)
32. (A) (B) (C) (D)
33. (A) (B) (C) (D)
34. (A) (B) (C) (D)
35. (A) (B) (C) (D)
36. (A) (B) (C) (D)
37. (A) (B) (C) (D)

Part C

38. (A) (B) (C) (D)
39. (A) (B) (C) (D)
40. (A) (B) (C) (D)
41. (A) (B) (C) (D)
42. (A) (B) (C) (D)
43. (A) (B) (C) (D)
44. (A) (B) (C) (D)
45. (A) (B) (C) (D)
46. (A) (B) (C) (D)
47. (A) (B) (C) (D)
48. (A) (B) (C) (D)
49. (A) (B) (C) (D)
50. (A) (B) (C) (D)

Practice Test 4

Section 2: Structure and Written Expression

1. Ⓐ Ⓑ Ⓒ Ⓓ	21. Ⓐ Ⓑ Ⓒ Ⓓ
2. Ⓐ Ⓑ Ⓒ Ⓓ	22. Ⓐ Ⓑ Ⓒ Ⓓ
3. Ⓐ Ⓑ Ⓒ Ⓓ	23. Ⓐ Ⓑ Ⓒ Ⓓ
4. Ⓐ Ⓑ Ⓒ Ⓓ	24. Ⓐ Ⓑ Ⓒ Ⓓ
5. Ⓐ Ⓑ Ⓒ Ⓓ	25. Ⓐ Ⓑ Ⓒ Ⓓ
6. Ⓐ Ⓑ Ⓒ Ⓓ	26. Ⓐ Ⓑ Ⓒ Ⓓ
7. Ⓐ Ⓑ Ⓒ Ⓓ	27. Ⓐ Ⓑ Ⓒ Ⓓ
8. Ⓐ Ⓑ Ⓒ Ⓓ	28. Ⓐ Ⓑ Ⓒ Ⓓ
9. Ⓐ Ⓑ Ⓒ Ⓓ	29. Ⓐ Ⓑ Ⓒ Ⓓ
10. Ⓐ Ⓑ Ⓒ Ⓓ	30. Ⓐ Ⓑ Ⓒ Ⓓ
11. Ⓐ Ⓑ Ⓒ Ⓓ	31. Ⓐ Ⓑ Ⓒ Ⓓ
12. Ⓐ Ⓑ Ⓒ Ⓓ	32. Ⓐ Ⓑ Ⓒ Ⓓ
13. Ⓐ Ⓑ Ⓒ Ⓓ	33. Ⓐ Ⓑ Ⓒ Ⓓ
14. Ⓐ Ⓑ Ⓒ Ⓓ	34. Ⓐ Ⓑ Ⓒ Ⓓ
15. Ⓐ Ⓑ Ⓒ Ⓓ	35. Ⓐ Ⓑ Ⓒ Ⓓ
	36. Ⓐ Ⓑ Ⓒ Ⓓ
16. Ⓐ Ⓑ Ⓒ Ⓓ	37. Ⓐ Ⓑ Ⓒ Ⓓ
17. Ⓐ Ⓑ Ⓒ Ⓓ	38. Ⓐ Ⓑ Ⓒ Ⓓ
18. Ⓐ Ⓑ Ⓒ Ⓓ	39. Ⓐ Ⓑ Ⓒ Ⓓ
19. Ⓐ Ⓑ Ⓒ Ⓓ	40. Ⓐ Ⓑ Ⓒ Ⓓ
20. Ⓐ Ⓑ Ⓒ Ⓓ	

Practice Test 4

Section 3: Reading Comprehension

1. Ⓐ Ⓑ Ⓒ Ⓓ
2. Ⓐ Ⓑ Ⓒ Ⓓ
3. Ⓐ Ⓑ Ⓒ Ⓓ
4. Ⓐ Ⓑ Ⓒ Ⓓ
5. Ⓐ Ⓑ Ⓒ Ⓓ
6. Ⓐ Ⓑ Ⓒ Ⓓ
7. Ⓐ Ⓑ Ⓒ Ⓓ
8. Ⓐ Ⓑ Ⓒ Ⓓ
9. Ⓐ Ⓑ Ⓒ Ⓓ
10. Ⓐ Ⓑ Ⓒ Ⓓ

11. Ⓐ Ⓑ Ⓒ Ⓓ
12. Ⓐ Ⓑ Ⓒ Ⓓ
13. Ⓐ Ⓑ Ⓒ Ⓓ
14. Ⓐ Ⓑ Ⓒ Ⓓ
15. Ⓐ Ⓑ Ⓒ Ⓓ
16. Ⓐ Ⓑ Ⓒ Ⓓ
17. Ⓐ Ⓑ Ⓒ Ⓓ
18. Ⓐ Ⓑ Ⓒ Ⓓ
19. Ⓐ Ⓑ Ⓒ Ⓓ
20. Ⓐ Ⓑ Ⓒ Ⓓ

21. Ⓐ Ⓑ Ⓒ Ⓓ
22. Ⓐ Ⓑ Ⓒ Ⓓ
23. Ⓐ Ⓑ Ⓒ Ⓓ
24. Ⓐ Ⓑ Ⓒ Ⓓ
25. Ⓐ Ⓑ Ⓒ Ⓓ
26. Ⓐ Ⓑ Ⓒ Ⓓ
27. Ⓐ Ⓑ Ⓒ Ⓓ
28. Ⓐ Ⓑ Ⓒ Ⓓ
29. Ⓐ Ⓑ Ⓒ Ⓓ
30. Ⓐ Ⓑ Ⓒ Ⓓ

31. Ⓐ Ⓑ Ⓒ Ⓓ
32. Ⓐ Ⓑ Ⓒ Ⓓ
33. Ⓐ Ⓑ Ⓒ Ⓓ
34. Ⓐ Ⓑ Ⓒ Ⓓ
35. Ⓐ Ⓑ Ⓒ Ⓓ
36. Ⓐ Ⓑ Ⓒ Ⓓ
37. Ⓐ Ⓑ Ⓒ Ⓓ
38. Ⓐ Ⓑ Ⓒ Ⓓ
39. Ⓐ Ⓑ Ⓒ Ⓓ

40. Ⓐ Ⓑ Ⓒ Ⓓ
41. Ⓐ Ⓑ Ⓒ Ⓓ
42. Ⓐ Ⓑ Ⓒ Ⓓ
43. Ⓐ Ⓑ Ⓒ Ⓓ
44. Ⓐ Ⓑ Ⓒ Ⓓ
45. Ⓐ Ⓑ Ⓒ Ⓓ
46. Ⓐ Ⓑ Ⓒ Ⓓ
47. Ⓐ Ⓑ Ⓒ Ⓓ
48. Ⓐ Ⓑ Ⓒ Ⓓ
49. Ⓐ Ⓑ Ⓒ Ⓓ
50. Ⓐ Ⓑ Ⓒ Ⓓ

b) **Romans 5:3,4** "And not only this, but we also exult in our tribulations, knowing that tribulation brings about perseverance; [4] and perseverance, proven character; and proven character, hope;"

c) **Colossians 1:11** "strengthened with all power, according to His glorious might, for the attaining of all steadfastness and patience; joyously,"

d) **James 1:2** "Consider it all joy, my brethren, when you encounter various trials,"

For more information on being cheerful in trials, read Tip #18 – Become an Optimist.

9B - Our Problems Don't Even Compare

Here we see that our present sufferings are not worth comparing to the glory that is waiting for us.

Romans 8:18 "For I consider that the sufferings of this present time are not worthy to be compared with the glory that is to be revealed to us."

9C - View Problems Differently

To the Christian, problems can also be referred to as "blessings in disguise." That's because God has ways of taking problems and making them work out for our benefit.

Indeed, challenges don't have to get us anxious or depressed. However, this can only happen when we keep our spiritual focus on God and His Word. We don't want to be like Peter, in Matthew 14:23-32, when he was walking on the water with Jesus, he began to take his eyes off of Jesus and started looking at the wind and the waves, and he began to sink. Instead, we want to learn to keep our thoughts on God's Word, and on the promises He has for us.

9D - What's Our Job?

Our job as Christians is to <u>believe</u>. It is God's job to answer our prayers. The only way to truly believe, is to be hopeful, trusting and optimistic. Thankfully, we can learn how not to be disturbed by the challenges in our lives. We can learn to stay in control of our responses to our problems instead of reacting to them. We can learn to keep our peace of mind no matter what obstacles come our way!

Question 9: Can you tell us of a recent problem in your life and how you responded to it?

10A - Natural Reactions to Pain

A woman experienced prolonged labor while giving birth to her first child. Five hours, 10 hours, 15 hours; after 20 hours she began thinking of reasons why God was giving her such a difficult delivery. Her mind took her back through her life, and she started to remember all the times she hurt people, even in a small way. She became convinced that the reason she was in this difficult situation was because of the mistakes she had made. Others tried to tell her differently, but she couldn't see it. Fortunately, God helped her get through the delivery.

10B - Pain Can Be a Good Thing

A natural reaction to pain can be self-inspection. When pain makes us think about our past experiences, we can assess the circumstances to determine if we were guilty or not. If so, we can repent of it, and move on with our lives.

Pain, with its natural reaction of self-assessment, isn't a bad thing. It can cause us to do a thorough "house-cleaning" of our heart. After it is complete, we are ready to aim for new successes in our life!

Question 10: Has your pain ever caused you to do self-inspection?

11A - <u>King David Arrives Home in Ziklag</u>

In 1 Samuel 30, we read of the time when King David and his army came home to Ziklag, only to find that their city was burning, and their wives and children carried off by the Amalekite army. David and his men were overcome with terrible grief. They wept until they had no more strength to weep. The men even considered stoning David. David was greatly distressed. Then he asked God for advice. God's answer was: "Pursue and overtake." So they did, and they got their families back!

Question 11: After coming home from battle, and seeing their burnt and vacant city, could David have inquired of God <u>before</u> his distress set in, and thereby have avoided the emotional pain?

12A - <u>Natural Reactions When Somebody Hurts Us</u>

When somebody hurts us, the natural reaction is to want to hurt them back. But we should be careful when dealing with vengeance. Some people who have fought back have been injured, and even killed. Sometimes, the best thing to do is just forgive the person who hurt us and go on.

12B - When we refuse to forgive, we imprison ourselves. Thus, the act of forgiveness is more for the person who got hurt, rather than the person who injured us. It may *feel* like we cannot forgive the person, however, like love, forgiveness is an act of the will. *We can choose to forgive the person.* By doing so, we let God handle the person who hurt us, in His way and in His time. That is faith. We will know we truly have forgiven the person when we no longer obsess about the incident. If we are having difficulty forgiving someone, sometimes it is helpful to begin praying for the person, asking God to bless their life in every way.

Matthew 5:44 "But I say to you, love your enemies and pray for those who persecute you,"

Question 12: Is there someone in your life with whom you have vengeful thoughts? If so, what do you think about making a quality decision to forgive them?

13A - <u>Natural Reaction When You Feel Depressed</u>

Sometimes when we feel down, we make the mistake of trying hard not to *look* depressed. This can cause more anxiety because we are trying to be somebody we are not. Like the person who breaks their leg, a doctor will tell them not to put too much weight on it for a few weeks. The same goes for someone who is troubled emotionally. We shouldn't try too hard to look happy. Instead, we should become more of a spectator of life for a while until we heal up emotionally. In due time, our healing will come, and we will rejoice genuinely!

Question 13: Have you ever tried too hard to hide your emotional pain?

14A - <u>Avoid Isolation</u>

Another natural reaction when experiencing emotional pain can be to isolate ourselves from others. By keeping our problem a secret, we can rob ourselves of good people who can help us resolve our issue. It is best to go against our natural reaction and tell our doctor and loved ones how we are feeling. Then together, search for the help that is needed. For more on this, see Tip #5 – Form a Support Team.

Question 14: Have you ever withheld information from people who you knew could help solve your problem?

15A - <u>Natural Reaction When Life Gets Hard</u>

When life gets difficult, the natural reaction is to flee from a situation. We can get caught up in the mindset, *"The grass is greener on the other side."* If we feel compelled to move on, it is sometimes best to stay in a situation until we achieve victory in it. Then move on to something else. What we don't want, is to *"jump out of the frying pan and into the fire."* This will further complicate our problem.

Question 15: Have you ever tried to get out of a difficult situation by moving to something else, only to end up in worse circumstances?

16A - <u>Seeing Ourselves in Others</u>

Sometimes, when we begin seeing areas in our lives improve; we tend to see them in other people's lives as well. The temptation can be to tell others what their areas of weakness are. This can possibly hurt them, and can hurt us as well. It is best to be careful when sharing information related to someone else's recovery. Doing so with gentleness and humility will give us greater success in passing on the valuable truths we have learned.

The following verses give us tips on how to reach out to others.

a) **Matthew 7:5** "You hypocrite, first take the log out of your own eye, and then you will see clearly to take the speck out of your brother's eye."

b) **1 Corinthians 14:3** "But one who prophesies speaks to men for edification and exhortation and consolation."

c) **Galatians 6:1** "Brethren, even if anyone is caught in any trespass, you who are spiritual, restore such a one in a spirit of gentleness; *each one* looking to yourself, so that you too will not be tempted."

Question 16: Have you ever tried to help a person see a certain truth, but hurt yourself, and them, by doing so?

17A - <u>Natural Reaction When Healed from Fear</u>

Sometimes, when we get free from fear, we can become overly confident. Our new-found confidence can cause us to boldly do things that *may seem right to us*, but can lead us to more pain. We need to use our new found freedom wisely. Boldness should be tempered with wisdom. When recovering from fear, it is best to get feedback from others before making important decisions in our life.

Question 17: Have you ever been overly confident and tried to do something that eventually caused you pain?

18A - <u>Busyness</u>

Sometimes, when we become anxious, a natural reaction can be that we become overly busy. Our busyness can act as a distraction, preventing us from pursuing our healing, and thus prolonging our illness.

Question 18: Have you ever avoided facing problems in your life by getting overly busy?

19A - <u>Hurt by People at Church</u>

Because people make mistakes, the day may come when someone at our church hurts us. Our judgment toward someone at church can grow by causing us to pass judgment toward the church, and even God Himself. We shouldn't let the natural reaction to this hurt cause us to lose our church friendships, or our walk with God. It is best to resolve the hurt as soon as possible. We should be gracious and forgive. We should forgive people as if we ourselves made the mistake and would need forgiveness. For more on this, see Tip #21 – Collect "Grace Doors."

Question 19: Have you ever found yourself being judgmental toward a person, a church, a denomination, or even God Himself?

20A - With God's help we can learn how to <u>respond, rather than react</u> to the challenges of life.

* * * * * * *

TIP #11

****

Know Yourself

****

1A - Life has a way of leading us away from God's best for our lives. The problem is that change in our heart can happen so slowly that we aren't aware we are drifting away from God. What complicates this problem further is that we have inherent weaknesses that we may not be aware of, or not paying attention to. Not being aware of our weaknesses can be a serious problem. Our enemy, the devil, knows us better than we know ourselves, and he can use this knowledge against us. Let's take some time to identify our strengths and weaknesses, so we'll be ready for any challenge that comes our way.

1B - People in the Bible had weaknesses. God has given us their stories so we can learn from them.

Eve was too naïve when she was speaking with the serpent (Satan).

Genesis 3:1-6 "Now the serpent was more crafty than any beast of the field which the LORD God had made. And he said to the woman, "Indeed, has God said, 'You shall not eat from any tree of the garden'?" [2] The woman said to the serpent, "From the fruit of the trees of the garden we may eat; [3] but from the fruit of the tree which is in the middle of the garden, God has said, 'You shall not eat from it or touch it, or you will die.'" [4] The serpent said to the woman, "You surely will not die! [5] For God knows that in the day you eat from it your eyes will be opened, and you will be like God, knowing good and evil." [6] When the woman saw that the tree was good for food, and that it was a delight to the eyes, and that the tree was desirable to make *one* wise, she took from its fruit and ate; and she gave also to her husband with her, and he ate."

1C - Adam's weakness was his impulsiveness to take the fruit from Eve.

Question 1: Does anyone come to mind that is naïve like Eve, or impulsive like Adam?

2A - King Saul became jealous of young David.

1 Samuel 18:7-9 "The women sang as they played, and said, "Saul has slain his thousands, And David his ten thousands." [8] Then Saul became very angry, for this saying displeased him; and he said, "They have ascribed to David ten thousands, but to me they have ascribed thousands. Now what more can he have but the kingdom?" [9] Saul looked at David with suspicion from that day on."

Question 2: Can you think of anyone who gets jealous easily?

3A - King Solomon became addicted to women, and began marrying non-Jewish (Gentile) women.

When we start spending too much time with worldly people, it can reduce our love for God, and our service for Him. Solomon's story is very sad when you consider how he began his reign as king, with great humility and uprightness of heart toward God.

1 Kings 11:1-4 "Now King Solomon loved many foreign women along with the daughter of Pharaoh: Moabite, Ammonite, Edomite, Sidonian, and Hittite women, ² from the nations concerning which the LORD had said to the sons of Israel, "You shall not associate with them, nor shall they associate with you, *for* they will surely turn your heart away after their gods." Solomon held fast to these in love. ³ He had seven hundred wives, princesses, and three hundred concubines, and his wives turned his heart away. ⁴ For when Solomon was old, his wives turned his heart away after other gods; and his heart was not wholly devoted to the LORD his God, as the heart of David his father *had been*."

Question 3: Do any Christians come to mind that spend too much time with non-Christian people?

4A - In Joshua Chapter 7, we read how the Israelite army suffered a devastating defeat. This caused Joshua to fall on his face before God to find out why they lost the battle. God said that there was sin in the camp. The camp was searched, and Achan confessed to stealing some of the booty from a previous battle. He suffered a terrible loss for doing so.

Joshua 7:24,25 "Then Joshua and all Israel with him, took Achan the son of Zerah, the silver, the mantle, the bar of gold, his sons, his daughters, his oxen, his donkeys, his sheep, his tent and all that belonged to him; and they brought them up to the valley of Achor. ²⁵ Joshua said, "Why have you troubled us? The LORD will trouble you this day." And all Israel stoned them with stones; and they burned them with fire after they had stoned them with stones."

Question 4: Does anyone come to mind who likes nice things a little too much?

5A - One day King Nebuchadnezzar was in the middle of a prideful speech of how he built such a grand kingdom by his own might. Suddenly, God humbled him in a very dramatic way. For seven long years, King Nebechadnezzar lived like an ox in the field, grazing on grass.

Daniel 4:30-33 "The king reflected and said, 'Is this not Babylon the great, which I myself have built as a royal residence by the might of my power and for the glory of my majesty?' ³¹ While the word *was* in the king's mouth, a voice came from heaven, *saying*, 'King Nebuchadnezzar, to you it is declared: sovereignty has been removed from you, ³² and you will be driven away from mankind, and your dwelling place *will be* with the beasts of the field. You will be given grass to eat like cattle, and seven periods of time will pass over you until you recognize that the Most High is ruler over the realm of mankind and bestows it on whomever He wishes.' ³³ Immediately the word concerning Nebuchadnezzar was fulfilled; and he was driven away from mankind and began eating grass like cattle, and his body was drenched with the dew of heaven until his hair had grown like eagles' *feathers* and his nails like birds' *claws*."

Question 5: Do you know anyone who is prideful? Did their pride cause them a downfall?

6A - Samson was one of the judges of Israel, and especially gifted by God to help liberate Israel from a forty year reign of the Philistines.

Judges 13:1-5 "Now the sons of Israel again did evil in the sight of the LORD, so that the LORD gave them into the hands of the Philistines forty years. [2] There was a certain man of Zorah, of the family of the Danites, whose name was Manoah; and his wife was barren and had borne no *children*. [3] Then the angel of the LORD appeared to the woman and said to her, "Behold now, you are barren and have borne no *children*, but you shall conceive and give birth to a son. [4] Now therefore, be careful not to drink wine or strong drink, nor eat any unclean thing. [5] For behold, you shall conceive and give birth to a son, and no razor shall come upon his head, for the boy shall be a Nazirite to God from the womb; and he shall begin to deliver Israel from the hands of the Philistines."

6B - Samson was born with the gift of strength. His strength was due to his long hair which had never been cut. But Samson had a weakness. He was careless about the secret of his power. After years of causing havoc for the Philistines, the Philistines convinced Samson's girlfriend, Delilah, to inquire of Samson the source of his great strength. Samson toyed with her for a while, giving her false sources. However, after Delilah's ongoing and tearful inquiries, Samson did the unthinkable; he told her the real source of his strength - his long hair. While sleeping that night, his hair was cut, and when he awoke, he was powerless to defend himself, and he became a slave of the Philistines.

> **Judges 16:17** "So he told her all *that was* in his heart and said to her, "A razor has never come on my head, for I have been a Nazirite to God from my mother's womb. If I am shaved, then my strength will leave me and I will become weak and be like any *other* man.""

Question 6: Does anyone come to mind that treats their natural gift with casual disinterest, to a point where they allow Satan to play havoc in their lives?

7A - Now that we see how flawed Bible characters can be, it may be easier for us to confess our own areas of weakness.

Question 7: Do you know of any weaknesses in your life? Would you like to share any with the group?

8A - God sometimes uses other people to tell us what our weaknesses are. We would do well to take note of what people are telling us to see if there is any truth to what they are saying. We could also ask people who know us if they see any weaknesses in our lives.

Question 8: Has anyone ever talked to you about areas of weakness in your life, either in a serious, joking, or mean way? What was your reaction? What did you learn about yourself?

9A - Once we know our weaknesses, we can begin to work on improving those areas, so they become less of a handicap in our lives. A good strategy is to have accountability people in our lives, people we can confess our shortcomings to, and who can inspire us to be our best.

Question 9: Have you ever had an accountability person or group in your life? How did it help you?

10A - <u>Know Your Strengths</u>

God has given us strengths. He challenges us to find out our gifts.

Proverbs 25:2 "It is the glory of God to conceal a matter, But the glory of kings is to search out a matter."

Question 10: Has anyone ever told you, you were gifted in some way? How did you respond to it?

11A - Our gifts can bring us a measure of joy when we operate in them.

Question 11: In what ways have you been energized by your talents?

12A - Sometimes when we discover what our strengths are, we can become prideful. We can even use our gift for unjust gain. For instance, a salesperson that has a warm, caring personality can begin selling products that will benefit them more than the customer.

Question 12: Have you ever got a little prideful or careless after finding out what your gifts were? If so, can you tell us about it?

13A - Often, God uses our natural talents in the church.

Question 13: In what ways could you make use of your gifts in the church?

14A - Having an accurate understanding of our strengths and weaknesses can give us an edge in life. Becoming a life-long student of ourselves will help us to make right choices in our life, and will help us produce fruitful service for God, as well as happiness and peace for ourselves.

* * * * * * *

TIP #12

****

Don't Judge

****

1A - One major cause of anxiety and depression is the act of passing judgment on others. You might ask, *"Do I just turn a blind eye to anyone that does wrong to me?"* That depends on the situation. Every circumstance is different, and every person we come in contact with is different, thus requiring a particular response. Having a pastor or a support team in our life will give us people we can speak with, who can give us suggestions on how to best respond to a given situation.

1B - If it is an abusive situation we should first try to remove ourselves from the abuse. By doing so, we can better assess the hurtful action. We will then be better able to respond properly to it if it happens again. (To recognize abuse more readily, see the *"Types of Abuse"* section at the end of the book.)

1C - When someone abuses us it is natural to pass judgment on them. However, Jesus tells us not to judge others. Here are two such verses.

   a) **Matthew 7:1,2** (Jesus is speaking) "Do not judge so that you will not be judged. [2] For in the way you judge, you will be judged; and by your standard of measure, it will be measured to you."

   b) **Luke 6:37** "Do not judge, and you will not be judged; and do not condemn, and you will not be condemned; pardon, and you will be pardoned."

1D - When Jesus tells us not to judge, does that mean we can't judge the action? We know that judicial judges judge actions all the time. We also know that Jesus gives permission to judge people's actions when He says, *"Do not give what is holy to dogs, and do not throw your pearls before swine,"* (Matthew 7:6) and *"Beware of false prophets"* (Matthew 7:15-16). How do we determine who the dogs and pigs are, and the false prophets are if we not allowed to judge?

1E - When we share with people how sin is so damaging, how can we warn people who may be engaged in sinful actions such as *immorality, impurity, sensuality,* [20] *idolatry, sorcery, enmities, strife, jealousy, outbursts of anger, disputes, dissensions, factions (heresies),* [21] *envying, drunkenness, carousing,* (Galatians 5:19-21)? Won't listing these sins sound like we are passing judgment? It's a delicate issue.

1F - In **John 7:24**, Jesus tells us *"Do not judge according to appearance, but judge with righteous judgment."* Examining the above references would make it appear it is permissible to judge a person's actions.

1G - For sure, we ought not judge the person. We ought not to judge them because we all have blind spots. Plus, it is only by God's grace that we aren't as mixed up as the person who wronged us.

Forms of Judging

Judgment Toward People

Often we get into the habit of passing judgment on others because we ourselves were judged in the past. Let's take some time to see in what ways others have judged us.

Question 1: Looking back at your youth, can you remember being judged by your parents? If yes, can you tell us why, and are they still passing judgment on you today?

Question 2: Did your parents pass judgment on others? If yes, can you tell us on whom?

Question 3: Can you remember being judged by kids at school? If yes, can you tell us why?

Question 4: Can you remember being judged by teachers or other adult leaders? If yes, can you tell us why?

5A - Judgment toward Institutions

Sometimes we face problems at school that cause us to pass judgment on schools.

Question 5: Looking back over your school years, can you remember passing judgment on your schools for any reason? If yes, can you tell us why?

6A - Sometimes we face problems on the job that cause us to pass judgment on companies that employ us.

Question 6: Can you remember passing judgment on companies or workers for any reason? If yes, can you tell us why?

7A - Judgment Toward Ideologies

Sometimes we are influenced by people who are prejudiced for one reason or another.

Question 7: Can you remember judging people who were different than you (race, ethnicity, religion, political persuasion, ideologies, etc.)? If yes, can you tell us why?

8A - Avoid this Kind of Judgment

One of the most damaging acts of judgment to our emotional health is that of judging ourselves. These kinds of judgments are characterized by critical, condemning, self-shaming, and other demeaning thoughts and feelings.

Question 8: Can you remember ever passing judgment on yourself? If yes, can you tell us why, and do you still pass judgment on yourself today?

10A - Judgment Scriptures

The scriptures are very clear on not passing judgment on other people. See the scriptures below.

a) **Luke 6:37** "Do not judge, and you will not be judged; and do not condemn, and you will not be condemned; pardon, and you will be pardoned."

b) **James 2:3,4** "and you pay special attention to the one who is wearing the fine clothes, and say, "You sit here in a good place," and you say to the poor man, "You stand over there, or sit down by my footstool," [4] have you not made distinctions among yourselves, and become judges with evil motives?"

c) **James 4:11,12** "Do not speak against one another, brethren. He who speaks against a brother or judges his brother, speaks against the law and judges the law; but if you judge the law, you are not a doer of the law but a judge *of it.* [12] There is *only* one Lawgiver and Judge, the One who is able to save and to destroy; but who are you who judge your neighbor?"

d) **1 Peter 2:23** "and while being reviled, He did not revile in return; while suffering, He uttered no threats, but kept entrusting *Himself* to Him who judges righteously;"

10B - The Cure for Being Hurt When Being Judged

The way out of the pain of having been judged by others is through the act of forgiveness. Our natural reaction to those who have hurt us is to hurt them back, but that will only keep us in emotional distress. We must go against our natural reaction and consciously forgive the person who has hurt us. We do not have to *feel* like forgiving them. We forgive them not by our emotions, instead, as an act of our will, knowing it is the right thing to do. For more on this, see Tip #10 – Respond Rather Than React.

10C - One Important Reason to Forgive

After we have forgiven someone their hurtful action toward us, and the pain of it has gone, we will then have a story to share with others of how God has helped us through the act of forgiveness. That's why one of the slogans of the program is: *Don't focus on what you lost, focus on what you gained.* When we forgive someone who has hurt us, we gain a "platform" with which we can use to tell our story and inspire others to forgive, especially if what they are struggling with is a similar offense. Others will be helped by realizing they aren't the only ones who have suffered hurt, and they will be challenged to forgive their trespassers too.

Question 10: Do you have a trauma that God could use to help others with? Would you like to share that with us?

11A - A Helpful Skill to Learn

After recovering from the hurtful words spoken to us, we can ask God to help us to no longer care what people think of us. Faith in God will give us greater confidence. We will be better able to shrug off unkind words spoken to us or about us. We can be like Jesus when He spoke these words from the cross, *"Father, forgive them, for they do not know what they are doing."* (Luke 23:34)

Question 11: Is there an area of your life in which you would like God to help you be more carefree?

12A - Learning to be non-judgmental will help us keep our peace of mind, and will help our personalities become more attractive, thus giving us greater happiness with those around us.

* * * * * * *

TIP #13

****

Be "Good Ground"

****

1A - Jesus tells us that the parable of the sower is a "stand-alone" parable. He asks, how will you know any parable if you don't know this one? Thus, it is good for us to read it, and glean everything we can from it. The title of this Tip comes from the soil types described in the parable. May God teach us something valuable as we read it.

1B - **Mark 4:3-20**

"Listen *to this*! Behold, the sower went out to sow; [4] as he was sowing, some *seed* fell beside the road, and the birds came and ate it up. [5] Other *seed* fell on the rocky *ground* where it did not have much soil; and immediately it sprang up because it had no depth of soil. [6] And after the sun had risen, it was scorched; and because it had no root, it withered away. [7] Other *seed* fell among the thorns, and the thorns came up and choked it, and it yielded no crop. [8] Other *seeds* fell into the good soil, and as they grew up and increased, they yielded a crop and produced thirty, sixty, and a hundredfold." [9] And He was saying, "He who has ears to hear, let him hear." [10] As soon as He was alone, His followers, along with the twelve, *began* asking Him *about* the parables."

1C - "[11] And He was saying to them, "To you has been given the mystery of the kingdom of God, but those who are outside get everything in parables, [12] so that WHILE SEEING, THEY MAY SEE AND NOT PERCEIVE, AND WHILE HEARING, THEY MAY HEAR AND NOT UNDERSTAND, OTHERWISE THEY MIGHT RETURN AND BE FORGIVEN." [13] And He *said to them, "Do you not understand this parable? How will you understand all the parables? [14] The sower sows the word. [15] These are the ones who are beside the road where the word is sown; and when they hear, immediately Satan comes and takes away the word which has been sown in them."

1D - "[16] In a similar way these are the ones on whom seed was sown on the rocky *places*, who, when they hear the word, immediately receive it with joy; [17] and they have no *firm* root in themselves, but are *only* temporary; then, when affliction or persecution arises because of the word, immediately they fall away. [18] And others are the ones on whom seed was sown among the thorns; these are the ones who have heard the word, [19] but the worries of the world, and the deceitfulness of riches, and the desires for other things enter in and choke the word, and it becomes unfruitful. [20] And those are the ones on whom seed was sown on the good soil; and they hear the word and accept it and bear fruit, thirty, sixty, and a hundredfold."

Question 1: What kind of ground are you when you hear God's Word taught?

a) **Hard Ground - Do you dismiss it quickly?**

b) **Stony Ground – Are you interested in God's Word initially, but then let it slip away soon after?**

c) **Thorny Ground – Are you enthusiastic about God's Word, but easily allow the cares of life to limit you from getting closer to God and doing His work?**

d) **Good Ground – Are you really interested in God's Word and looking for every opportunity to read it and tell people the message of eternal life through Jesus?**

* * * * * * *

Tip #14

****

Develop a Conqueror Mentality

****

1A - God wants each of us to be strong and able to handle any problem that comes our way. A good example of this is the young man David, who found out about a giant named, Goliath, who was making fun of the Israelite army. When the time came, David marched up in great boldness and he defeated the giant!

1B - Here is the account:

1 Samuel 17:20 – 51 "So David arose early in the morning and left the flock with a keeper and took *the supplies* and went as Jesse had commanded him. And he came to the circle of the camp while the army was going out in battle array shouting the war cry. [21] Israel and the Philistines drew up in battle array, army against army. [22] Then David left his baggage in the care of the baggage keeper, and ran to the battle line and entered in order to greet his brothers. [23] As he was talking with them, behold, the champion, the Philistine from Gath named Goliath, was coming up from the army of the Philistines, and he spoke these same words; and David heard *them*."

1C - "[24] When all the men of Israel saw the man, they fled from him and were greatly afraid. [25] The men of Israel said, "Have you seen this man who is coming up? Surely he is coming up to defy Israel. And it will be that the king will enrich the man who kills him with great riches and will give him his daughter and make his father's house free in Israel." [26] Then David spoke to the men who were standing by him, saying, "What will be done for the man who kills this Philistine and takes away the reproach from Israel? For who is this uncircumcised Philistine, that he should taunt the armies of the living God?" [27] The people answered him in accord with this word, saying, "Thus it will be done for the man who kills him.""

1D - "Now Eliab his oldest brother heard when he spoke to the men; and Eliab's anger burned against David and he said, "Why have you come down? And with whom have you left those few sheep in the wilderness? I know your insolence and the wickedness of your heart; for you have come down in order to see the battle." [29] But David said, "What have I done now? Was it not just a question?" [30] Then he turned away from him to another and said the same thing; and the people answered the same thing as before."

1E - "**31** When the words which David spoke were heard, they told *them* to Saul, and he sent for him. **32** David said to Saul, "Let no man's heart fail on account of him; your servant will go and fight with this Philistine." **33** Then Saul said to David, "You are not able to go against this Philistine to fight with him; for you are *but* a youth while he has been a warrior from his youth."

1F - "**34** But David said to Saul, "Your servant was tending his father's sheep. When a lion or a bear came and took a lamb from the flock, **35** I went out after him and attacked him, and rescued *it* from his mouth; and when he rose up against me, I seized *him* by his beard and struck him and killed him. **36** Your servant has killed both the lion and the bear; and this uncircumcised Philistine will be like one of them, since he has taunted the armies of the living God." **37** And David said, "The LORD who delivered me from the paw of the lion and from the paw of the bear, He will deliver me from the hand of this Philistine." And Saul said to David, "Go, and may the LORD be with you."

1G - "**38** Then Saul clothed David with his garments and put a bronze helmet on his head, and he clothed him with armor. **39** David girded his sword over his armor and tried to walk, for he had not tested *them*. So David said to Saul, "I cannot go with these, for I have not tested *them*." And David took them off. **40** He took his stick in his hand and chose for himself five smooth stones from the brook, and put them in the shepherd's bag which he had, even in *his* pouch, and his sling was in his hand; and he approached the Philistine."

1H - "**41** Then the Philistine came on and approached David, with the shield-bearer in front of him. **42** When the Philistine looked and saw David, he disdained him; for he was *but* a youth, and ruddy, with a handsome appearance. **43** The Philistine said to David, "Am I a dog, that you come to me with sticks?" And the Philistine cursed David by his gods. **44** The Philistine also said to David, "Come to me, and I will give your flesh to the birds of the sky and the beasts of the field."

1J - "**45** Then David said to the Philistine, "You come to me with a sword, a spear, and a javelin, but I come to you in the name of the LORD of hosts, the God of the armies of Israel, whom you have taunted. **46** This day the LORD will deliver you up into my hands, and I will strike you down and remove your head from you. And I will give the dead bodies of the army of the Philistines this day to the birds of the sky and the wild beasts of the earth, that all the earth may know that there is a God in Israel, **47** and that all this assembly may know that the LORD does not deliver by sword or by spear; for the battle is the LORD'S and He will give you into our hands."

1K - "**48** Then it happened when the Philistine rose and came and drew near to meet David, that David ran quickly toward the battle line to meet the Philistine. **49** And David put his hand into his bag and took from it a stone and slung *it*, and struck the Philistine on his forehead. And the stone sank into his forehead, so that he fell on his face to the ground. **50** Thus David prevailed over the Philistine with a sling and a stone, and he struck the Philistine and killed him; but there was no sword in David's hand."

1L - "**51** Then David ran and stood over the Philistine and took his sword and drew it out of its sheath and killed him, and cut off his head with it. When the Philistines saw that their champion was dead, they fled."

Question 1: What thoughts come to your mind after reading the story of David?

Question 2: In what area of your life do you need to develop a conqueror mentality?

3A - We, too, can have boldness like young David had. One way is by reading the following scriptures out loud over and over. By making it a priority in our lives to speak God's Word, we'll develop a connection with God that nothing else can. We can go one step further by memorizing the verses.

1) **Joshua 1:5** "No man will *be able to* stand before you all the days of your life. Just as I have been with Moses, I will be with you; I will not fail you or forsake you. ."

2) **2 Samuel 22:29-31** "For You are my lamp, O LORD; And the LORD illumines my darkness. [30] "For by You I can run upon a troop; By my God I can leap over a wall. [31] "As for God, His way is blameless; The word of the LORD is tested; He is a shield to all who take refuge in Him."

3) **2 Chronicles 16:9** "For the eyes of the LORD move to and fro throughout the earth that He may strongly support those whose heart is completely His. You have acted foolishly in this. Indeed, from now on you will surely have wars."

4) **Psalm 18:32-40** "The God who girds me with strength And makes my way blameless? [33] He makes my feet like hinds' *feet*, And sets me upon my high places. [34] He trains my hands for battle, So that my arms can bend a bow of bronze. [35] You have also given me the shield of Your salvation, And Your right hand upholds me; And Your gentleness makes me great. [36] You enlarge my steps under me, And my feet have not slipped. [37] I pursued my enemies and overtook them, And I did not turn back until they were consumed. [38] I shattered them, so that they were not able to rise; They fell under my feet. [39] For You have girded me with strength for battle; You have subdued under me those who rose up against me. [40] You have also made my enemies turn their backs to me, And I destroyed those who hated me."

5) **Psalm 28:7** "The Lord is my strength and my shield; My heart trusts in Him, and I am helped; Therefore my heart exults, And with my song I shall thank Him."

6) **Psalm 44:5-7** "Through You we will push back our adversaries; Through Your name we will trample down those who rise up against us. [6] For I will not trust in my bow, Nor will my sword save me. [7] But You have saved us from our adversaries, And You have put to shame those who hate us."

7) **Psalm 68:35** "O God, You are awesome from Your sanctuary. The God of Israel Himself gives strength and power to the people. Blessed be God!"

8) **Psalm 138:3** "On the day I called, You answered me; You made me bold with strength in my soul."

9) **Psalm 144:1,2** "Blessed be the LORD, my rock, Who trains my hands for war, *And* my fingers for battle; [2] My lovingkindness and my fortress, My stronghold and my deliverer, My shield and He in whom I take refuge, Who subdues my people under me."

10) **Proverbs 3:26** "For the Lord will be your confidence And will keep your foot from being caught."

11) **Job 17:9** "Nevertheless the righteous will hold to his way, And he who has clean hands will grow stronger and stronger."

12) **Isaiah 40:29** "He gives strength to the weary, And to *him who* lacks might He increases power."

13) **Isaiah 54:17** "No weapon that is formed against you will prosper; And every tongue that accuses you in judgment you will condemn. This is the heritage of the servants of the LORD, And their vindication is from Me," declares the LORD."

14) **Daniel 11:32** "By smooth *words* he will turn to godlessness those who act wickedly toward the covenant, but the people who know their God will display strength and take action."

15) **Hosea 11:10** "They will walk after the LORD, He will roar like a lion; Indeed He will roar And *His* sons will come trembling from the west."

16) **Zechariah 4:6** "Then he said to me, "This is the word of the LORD to Zerubbabel saying, 'Not by might nor by power, but by My Spirit,' says the LORD of hosts."

17) **Matthew 10:1** "Jesus summoned His twelve disciples and gave them authority over unclean spirits, to cast them out, and to heal every kind of disease and every kind of sickness."

18) **Matthew 10:6-8** "but rather go to the lost sheep of the house of Israel. [7] And as you go, preach, saying, 'The kingdom of heaven is at hand.' [8] Heal *the* sick, raise *the* dead, cleanse *the* lepers, cast out demons. Freely you received, freely give."

19) **Mark 6:7,13** "And He summoned the twelve and began to send them out in pairs, and gave them authority over the unclean spirits;… And they were casting out many demons and were anointing with oil many sick people and healing them."

20) **Mark 16:20** "And they went out and preached everywhere, while the Lord worked with them, and confirmed the word by the signs that followed."

21) **Luke 9:1** "And He called the twelve together, and gave them power and authority over all the demons and to heal diseases."

22) **Luke 10:19** "Behold, I have given you authority to tread on serpents and scorpions, and over all the power of the enemy, and nothing will injure you."

23) **Acts 1:8** "but you will receive power when the Holy Spirit has come upon you; and you shall be My witnesses both in Jerusalem, and in all Judea and Samaria, and even to the remotest part of the earth."

24) **Acts 2:43** "Everyone kept feeling a sense of awe; and many wonders and signs were taking place through the apostles."

25) **Acts 4:33** "And with great power the apostles were giving testimony to the resurrection of the Lord Jesus, and abundant grace was upon them all."

26) **Romans 15:19** "in the power of signs and wonders, in the power of the Spirit; so that from Jerusalem and round about as far as Illyricum I have fully preached the gospel of Christ."

27) **1 Corinthians 4:20** "For the kingdom of God does not consist in words but in power."

28) **2 Corinthians 12:12** "The signs of a true apostle were performed among you with all perseverance, by signs and wonders and miracles."

29) **Philippians 4:13** "I can do all things through Him who strengthens me."

30) **1 Thessalonians 1:5** "for our gospel did not come to you in word only, but also in power and in the Holy Spirit and with full conviction; just as you know what kind of men we proved to be among you for your sake."

31) **Hebrews 2:4** "God also testifying with them, both by signs and wonders and by various miracles and by gifts of the Holy Spirit according to His own will."

32) **1 John 2:20** "But you have an anointing from the Holy One, and you all know."

33) **1 John 2:27** "As for you, the anointing which you received from Him abides in you, and you have no need for anyone to teach you; but as His anointing teaches you about all things, and is true and is not a lie, and just as it has taught you, you abide in Him."

Question 3: How do you feel after reading these verses out loud?

* * * * * * *

TIP #15

****

Eliminate Wasted Thinking

****

1A - As we journey toward peace and happiness, we'll need to look at all the ways wasted thinking takes up room in our daily thoughts. In this Tip, we'll explore the various negative ways our mind can think. Then we'll look at ways to disarm these negative thought patterns when they come up.

1B - Types of Wasted Thinking

The following webpage describes 15 ways in which our thinking can be hindered. Please refer to psychcentral.com/lib/15-common-cognitive-distortions and read the introduction.

1C - Filtering

Please read the "Filtering" description at psychcentral.com/lib/15-common-cognitive-distortions.

1D - "Filtering" in the Bible

In 1Samuel 18, we see that even though the shepherd boy, David, killed a giant enemy of Israel, King Saul became angry because the boy became more famous than he.

1 Samuel 18:6-11 "It happened as they were coming, when David returned from killing the Philistine, that the women came out of all the cities of Israel, singing and dancing, to meet King Saul, with tambourines, with joy and with musical instruments. [7] The women sang as they played, and said, "Saul has slain his thousands, And David his ten thousands." [8] Then Saul became very angry, for this saying displeased him; and he said, "They have ascribed to David ten thousands, but to me they have ascribed thousands. Now what more can he have but the kingdom?"

1E - "[9] Saul looked at David with suspicion from that day on. [10] Now it came about on the next day that an evil spirit from God came mightily upon Saul, and he raved in the midst of the house, while David was playing *the harp* with his hand, as usual; and a spear *was* in Saul's hand. [11] Saul hurled the spear for he thought, "I will pin David to the wall." But David escaped from his presence twice."

1F - Saul Filtered Out the Positives

David did become more famous than King Saul; however, David was not a threat to Saul's Kingdom. David was a young boy who fully loved God and the King. Saul had become David's father-in-law, so David was not a threat to King Saul; but Saul "filtered out" the positives. Saul's filtering caused him great stress in his mind, so much so that he needed David to play music to calm him down. It was a horrible existence for Saul; on one hand, he needed David to play for him, while on the other hand, he was furious with David's abilities and his fame.

1G - Acknowledge Other People's Gifts

Saul needed to accept David for who he was. David had developed a close relationship with God through the songs he was writing and singing while watching the sheep. He was likely meditating on what his Rabbi preached every Sabbath. He heard how Godly men should pray, praise and work, and he believed what he heard and practiced it. All of this helped transform David, a boy, into a "Giant" of a man, on the inside.

1H - Saul Was Fear-Driven

Saul needed to trust God that He would protect him. Instead, he let his fear of David stealing his throne, ruin his life. This burdened Saul with a lot of wasted thinking and emotional pain.

1J - Conquering Filtering

If we struggle with Filtering, it may be helpful to first see if fear is a root cause. If yes, then we would benefit from admitting we have a problem with fear. At this point, it would be helpful to find a couple of people we could contact when the fear begins causing us unrest. The next time our emotions are bothered, we could contact one of these people for support. See Tip #5 - Form A Support Team, for more on this. Meanwhile we could also read out loud, multiple times daily, the Affirmation #1 – I do Not Fear, as well as Core Belief #3 – I Believe God Wants Me to Live in Perfect Peace at All Times.

Noticing fear in our life, and responding to it effectively, will help us conquer Filtering.

Question 1: Can you think of an example of Filtered Thinking, or someone who has Filtered Thinking?

2A - Polarized Thinking

Please read the "Polarized Thinking" description at psychcentral.com/lib/15-common-cognitive-distortions.

2B - "Polarized Thinking" In the Bible

The Apostles

Here is a story of the disciples getting prideful with power.

Luke 9:51-55 "When the days were approaching for His ascension, He was determined to go to Jerusalem; [52] and He sent messengers on ahead of Him, and they went and entered a village of the Samaritans to make arrangements for Him. [53] But they did not receive Him, because He was traveling toward Jerusalem. [54] When His disciples James and John saw *this*, they said, "Lord, do You want us to command fire to come down from heaven and consume them?" [55] But He turned and rebuked them, [and said, "You do not know what kind of spirit you are of,"

2C - At this point, the disciples had become accustomed to being empowered by Jesus to heal people of diseases and the ability to cast out of evil spirits. It would appear they got carried away with that power and felt it was OK to kill these people because they were not welcoming Jesus and His disciples.

Question 2: Can you tell us a time when you got carried away with power?

3A - Elijah and the Prophets of Baal

Another example in the Bible of someone struggling with the effects of Polarized Thinking is the story of Elijah after he defeated the prophets of Baal.

1 Kings 19:13-14,18 "When Elijah heard *it*, he wrapped his face in his mantle and went out and stood in the entrance of the cave. And behold, a voice *came* to him and said, "What are you doing here, Elijah?" [14] Then he said, "I have been very zealous for the LORD, the God of hosts; for the sons of Israel have forsaken Your covenant, torn down Your altars and killed Your prophets with the sword. And I alone am left; and they seek my life, to take it away. [18] Yet I will leave 7,000 in Israel, all the knees that have not bowed to Baal and every mouth that has not kissed him."

3B - Elijah's Amazing Feat

Elijah, indeed, had been busy for God, proving that the prophets of Baal (Satan) were no match for the living God. In one of the most dramatic events of a man of God, Elijah, single-handedly, humiliates and kills 450 false prophets.

3C - Elijah's Depression

Then remarkably, Elijah loses all faith in himself and in God, when he learned of Jezebel's anger toward him for killing all of her prophets. This unusual reaction from a mighty man of God could've occurred because he was physically exhausted after the events of the previous days. After Jezebel's threat to kill Elijah, Elijah ran for his life until he finally stopped twenty-four hours later. He then begged God to kill him.

3D - Elijah's Pride

After resting a couple of days, Elijah went on a 40-day journey in the wilderness. Then God spoke to him. And we find out that Elijah was full of pride as he described to God all he had been doing the previous days for God. He also thought he was the only one left who served God. God had to let him know He still had 7,000 priests who hadn't bowed the knee to Baal.

3E - Tip for God's Workers

All of our godly activity is good, but when it begins to make us think we are better than the next person, we need to step back and renew our humility, and remember that we are nothing without God's help in our lives.

3F - Conquering Polarized Thinking

If we struggle with Polarized Thinking, we could benefit from stepping back and praying about situations before reacting to them. We could benefit from reading Tip #12 – Don't Judge, Tip #25 – Collect Grace Doors, and Tip #20 – Practice Humility, as well as reading, multiple times daily, Affirmation #3 – I Flow in Harmony and Love.

Question 3: Can you tell us a time where you were experiencing some major victories in your life and how those victories drained you physically, or distorted your thinking?

Question 4: Can you think of someone who struggles with Polarized Thinking (black or white thinking)?

5A - Over-Generalization

Please read the "Over-Generalization" description at psychcentral.com/lib/15-common-cognitive-distortions.

5B - Conquering Over-Generalization

Here is an example of Over-Generalization and some possible tips to conquer it:

Let's imagine someone is preparing to learn how to drive a car, and they watch a show on television about a new driver who gets into an accident during their first time behind the wheel. The viewer might now be fearful of learning how to drive a car. To conquer that fear, they might want to check the statistics of how many people get into car accidents during their first time driving. The odds are very low. They could also begin to meditate on the truth that God wants His people to live by faith, and not by fear. They could help themselves by reading out loud, multiple times daily, Affirmation #1 – I Do Not Fear. Finally, they could get into the car, in a safe area, and boldly start learning how to drive a car. It might be difficult, but it can be done.

Question 5: Can you think of someone who struggles with Over-Generalization?

6A - Jumping to Conclusions

Please read the Jumping to Conclusions description at psychcentral.com/lib/15-common-cognitive-distortions.

6B - An example of someone who struggles with Jumping to Conclusions could be if we started a new friendship, and that person suddenly stops texting us and refuses to answer our calls. We could negatively assume that we have offended the other person. Later, we find out that the person had lost their cell phone, which prevented them from texting us or calling us back. Meanwhile, we would have wasted time feeling badly, and needlessly trying to figure out how we offended this person.

6C - Jumping To Conclusions in the Bible

In Joshua Chapter 22, the Israelites were ready to go to war with the Tribes of Reuben, Gad, and Manasseh, because they wrongly assumed that the altar they built was a sign that they were rebelling against God. Here is God's advice:

Proverbs 25:8 "Do not go out hastily to argue *your case*; Otherwise, what will you do in the end, When your neighbor humiliates you?"

Good advice.

6D - Conquering Jumping To Conclusions

If we struggle with Jumping To Conclusions, we could first consider Slogan #28 - Sleep On It. Sometimes, time has a way of resolving problems.

We could also take time to reflect on the idea that we don't have to care what people think about us. If people leave our circle of friendship, there could be a good reason for it, and we don't need to know the reason; we can leave that in God's hands. We could benefit from saying, multiple times daily, Affirmation #3 – I Flow in Harmony and Love.

Question 6: Can you think of someone who wastes time jumping to conclusions?

7A - <u>Catastrophizing</u>

Please read the Catastrophizing description at <u>psychcentral.com/lib/15-common-cognitive-distortions</u>.

7B - <u>Catastrophizing in the Bible</u>

In Numbers Chapter 13, God told Moses to send twelve leaders of Israel, to spy out the land that God wanted the Children of Israel to own and to live in. Ten of the twelve men came back fearful, and gave bad reports.

> **Numbers 13:30-33** "Then Caleb quieted the people before Moses and said, "We should by all means go up and take possession of it, for we will surely overcome it." [31] But the men who had gone up with him said, "We are not able to go up against the people, for they are too strong for us." [32] So they gave out to the sons of Israel a bad report of the land which they had spied out, saying, "The land through which we have gone, in spying it out, is a land that devours its inhabitants; and all the people whom we saw in it are men of *great* size. [33] There also we saw the Nephilim (the sons of Anak are part of the Nephilim); and we became like grasshoppers in our own sight, and so we were in their sight."

7C - The result of having so many fearful leaders was that Israel had to wander in the wilderness 40 years! God wanted all the fearful and disobedient people to die off before helping them move into their new homeland. There can be dire consequences to being fearful!

7D - <u>Conquering Catastrophizing</u>

If we struggle with the habit of thinking that catastrophes are always coming our way, we need God's help to calm down. We need to realize that God is well able to prevent bad things from happening, and if He doesn't, we need to have faith that He can bring good out of any negative situation (See Romans 8:28 below). A good place to start in conquering Catastrophizing is by reading out loud, multiple times daily, Affirmation #1 – I Do Not Fear, and Tip #9 – Develop Your Faith.

> **Romans 8:28** "And we know that God causes all things to work together for good to those who love God, to those who are called according to *His* purpose."

Question 7: Can you think of someone who wastes time thinking that disasters are coming their way?

8A - <u>Personalization</u>

Please read the Personalization description at <u>psychcentral.com/lib/15-common-cognitive-distortions</u>.

8B - <u>Conquering Personalization</u>

If we struggle with Personalization, it is helpful to realize that life does not revolve around us. We can learn to step back from a situation and not get emotionally involved in everything that goes on around us. We could also learn that it's OK to be more of an observer of life, and not feel guilty for doing so. In addition, we could realize that whatever happens to us or others around us is completely fixable by God. We can learn to give everything to God and let Him direct the events of people's lives as He sees fit, and we can learn to be OK with that. We could benefit from reading all six Affirmations multiple times daily.

Question 8: Can you think of someone who wastes time thinking and talking about a mysterious link between their lives and other people's lives (Personalization)?

9A - <u>Control Fallacies</u>

Please read the Control Fallacies description at psychcentral.com/lib/15-common-cognitive-distortions.

9B - <u>Conquering Control Fallacies</u>

If we struggle with Control Fallacies, we could realize we don't have to be controlled by other people. In the example used on the webpage, the person could have slowed down and done a better job instead of rushing through it. We could also realize that other people's happiness is not our responsibility. Reading the Affirmations, multiple times daily, would be helpful in conquering this condition, as well.

Question 9: Can you think of someone who wastes time thinking they don't measure up, or that other people's happiness is dependent on them?

10A - <u>Types of Wasted Thinking – Fallacy of Fairness</u>

Please read the Fallacy of Fairness description at psychcentral.com/lib/15-common-cognitive-distortions.

10B - <u>Conquering Fallacy of Fairness</u>

If we struggle with Fallacy of Fairness we could realize that life simply isn't fair, and that it is helpful to accept what is handed to us, and make the best of it. We could also consider that we don't need everyone around us to agree with our point of view. It can also be helpful to realize that we only have a limited understanding; and that there are many things we can learn from others. If we struggle with this, we can help ourselves by considering that we sometimes win people to our way of thinking, and sometimes we don't, and to be OK with that. We could benefit from saying, multiple times daily, Affirmation #3 – I Flow in Harmony and Love.

Question 10: Can you think of someone who wastes time thinking and talking about how unfair life is?

11A - <u>Blaming</u>

Please read the Blaming description at psychcentral.com/lib/15-common-cognitive-distortions.

11B - <u>Blaming in the Bible</u>

Below we see how Adam blamed Eve, and Eve blamed the serpent for deceiving her. Blaming got in the way of them taking responsibility for their actions.

a) **Genesis 3:11,12** "And He said, "Who told you that you were naked? Have you eaten from the tree of which I commanded you not to eat?" [12] The man said, "The woman whom You gave *to be* with me, she gave me from the tree, and I ate."

b) **Genesis 3:13** "Then the LORD God said to the woman, "What is this you have done?" And the woman said, "The serpent deceived me, and I ate."

11C - <u>Conquering Blaming</u>

If we struggle with blaming, we could benefit by realizing that it is normal to make mistakes. We are fallible creatures. That's why we need God to help us live our lives. We could also realize that when we do make mistakes, it is good to quickly admit where we went wrong. Doing so, can give us greater respect from others when they see we are willing to accept responsibility for our mistakes. We can learn to embrace our humanity, and the grace that we need when we make mistakes. To conquer Blaming, it can be helpful to read out loud, multiple times daily, Affirmation #1 - I Do Not Fear, and Affirmation #3 - I Flow in Harmony and Love.

11D - Here are some scriptures on being quick to admit guilt.

a) **Leviticus 5:5** "So it shall be when he becomes guilty in one of these, that he shall confess that in which he has sinned."

b) **2 Samuel 24:10** "Now David's heart troubled him after he had numbered the people. So David said to the LORD, "I have sinned greatly in what I have done. But now, O LORD, please take away the iniquity of Your servant, for I have acted very foolishly.""

Question 11: Can you think of someone who wastes time blaming others for their mistakes and their unhappiness?

12A - Shoulds

Please read the Shoulds description at psychcentral.com/lib/15-common-cognitive-distortions.

12B - Conquering Shoulds

If we struggle with Shoulds, we could benefit from realizing that God wants us to relax. God does have guidelines for us, but one of His main directives is for us not to fret. This includes, not worrying, or judging people who do not keep our list of rules. It's great that we have high expectations for ourselves and others, but we should first model such standards in our own lives. Our actions can speak *for* us. If we feel compelled to share our expectations with others, we could do it in love, gentleness, and humility. This will give us better results. We would benefit from saying, multiple times daily, Affirmation #3 – I Flow in Harmony and Love.

Question 12: Can you think of someone who wastes time being prideful about what they do, or judgmental about what other people do?

13A - Emotional Reasoning

Please read the Emotional Reasoning description at psychcentral.com/lib/15-common-cognitive-distortions.

13B - Conquering Emotional Reasoning

If we struggle with Emotional Reasoning, we could realize that feelings a fickle. They are subject to change depending on various factors, usually by our fears! Therefore we could first benefit from reading Tip #9 – Develop Your Faith, and reading, multiple times daily, Affirmation #1 – I Do Not Fear. We would also benefit from meditating on **2 Corinthians 5:7** *"for we walk by faith, not by sight."* A person who walks by faith doesn't pay too much attention to how things look or how they feel, they base what they want, upon God's willingness to answer prayer, and they hold on, in patience, until they receive what they've asked for. If we don't like how things feel, we change our situation, or ourselves, using our faith.

Question 13: Can you think of someone who wastes time being misdirected by feelings?

14A - Fallacy of Change

Please read the Fallacy of Change description at psychcentral.com/lib/15-common-cognitive-distortions.

14B - <u>Conquering Fallacy of Change</u>

If we struggle with Fallacy of Change, we could benefit from realizing that we can be perfectly happy even if circumstances or people around us don't change for the better. We could give people around us the grace to learn in their own time, and in their own way. We could also benefit from saying, multiple times daily, Affirmation #3 - I Flow in Harmony and Love, as well as saying Core Belief #3 – I Believe God Wants Me to Live in Perfect Peace.

Question 14: Can you think of someone who wastes time thinking of ways to make people change?

15A - <u>Global Labeling</u>

Please read the Global Labeling description at <u>psychcentral.com/lib/15-common-cognitive-distortions</u>.

15B - <u>Conquering Global Labeling</u>

If we struggle with Global Labeling, we could benefit from realizing we don't have to try so hard to sound impressive or make a point. We can relax and not judge. That way we can enjoy our lives, and make it enjoyable for others. We could also benefit by saying, multiple times daily, Affirmation #3 - I Flow in Harmony and Love.

Question 15: Can you think of someone who wastes time coming up with damaging comparisons and judgments – Global Labeling?

16A - <u>Always Being Right</u>

Please read the Always Being Right description at <u>psychcentral.com/lib/15-common-cognitive-distortions</u>.

16B - <u>Conquering Always Being Right</u>

If we struggle with always having to be right, we would benefit from realizing that as humans we all make mistakes occasionally, and thus it isn't worth getting upset over. We just have to keep trying to do our best without getting stressed out about it. We could also benefit from saying, multiple times daily, Affirmation #3 - I Flow in Harmony and Love, as well as Affirmation #1 - I Do Not Fear.

Question 16: Can you think of someone who wastes time trying to always be right?

17A - <u>Heaven's Reward Fallacy</u>

Please read the Heaven's Reward Fallacy description at <u>psychcentral.com/lib/15-common-cognitive-distortions</u>.

17B - <u>Conquering Heaven's Reward Fallacy</u>

If we struggle with Heaven's Reward Fallacy, we can benefit from remembering that the greatest person we could make sacrifices for is God, and that we can't "out-give" God. Eventually, He will reward us. We can ask God to help us keep our eyes on Him, and do all things for God, rather than having our eyes on others and doing things for them.

Question 17: Can you think of someone who wastes time expecting approval from people and working overly hard to get it?

18A - Other Kinds of Wasted Thinking

Appearance

A lot of advertising is focused around people's looks. It is natural to want to present ourselves in the best way possible; and it can also be enjoyable. The problem comes in when we obsess about our looks. Any thinking that goes beyond basic, everyday grooming could be wasted thinking. Questions we can ask ourselves can include: Do I dislike anything about my looks? Do I spend time thinking about how to change the features of my looks? Is my value as a person dependent on my looks? Am I focused on these features because I feel people will like me more if I change them? If we answer yes to any of these questions, we might want to work on resolving this issue in our lives.

18B - The Unimportance of Appearance in the Bible

The following are Bible verses that teach that, in God's eyes, a person's looks is unimportant. Notice what attribute *is* important, is having a loving heart.

a) **1 Samuel 16:7** "But the LORD said to Samuel, "Do not look at his appearance or at the height of his stature, because I have rejected him; for God *sees* not as man sees, for man looks at the outward appearance, but the LORD looks at the heart.""

b) **Proverbs 31:30** "Charm is deceitful and beauty is vain, *But* a woman who fears the LORD, she shall be praised."

c) **1 Peter 3:3,4** "Your adornment must not be *merely* external—braiding the hair, and wearing gold jewelry, or putting on dresses; [4] but *let it be* the hidden person of the heart, with the imperishable quality of a gentle and quiet spirit, which is precious in the sight of God."

18C – Below, are scriptures about our immense value, just the way we are.

a) **Psalm 139:13,14** "For You formed my inward parts; You wove me in my mother's womb. [14] I will give thanks to You, for I am fearfully and wonderfully made; Wonderful are Your works, And my soul knows it very well."

b) **Isaiah 43:4** "Since you are precious in My sight, *Since* you are honored and I love you, I will give *other* men in your place and *other* peoples in exchange for your life."

c) **Luke 12:7** "Indeed, the very hairs of your head are all numbered. Do not fear; you are more valuable than many sparrows."

Question 18: Can you think of someone who wastes time thinking about how to improve their looks?

19A - Income Ability

Sometimes we dislike ourselves because we feel we don't earn enough money. It's natural to want to earn enough money to meet all of our financial needs. The problem comes in when we obsess about how to make more and more money. Some questions to ask ourselves might be: Is my value as a person dependent on my income? Do I dislike myself because I cannot earn enough money? Would the extra money I earn be spent on things I don't need? If we answered yes to any of these questions, we might want to work on resolving this issue in our lives. Here are some Bible verses to consider.

a) **Luke 3:14** "*Some* soldiers were questioning him, saying, "And *what about* us, what shall we do?" And he said to them, "Do not take money from anyone by force, or accuse *anyone* falsely, and be content with your wages.""

b) **1 Timothy 6:6** "But godliness *actually* is a means of great gain when accompanied by contentment."

c) **2 Timothy 2:4** "No soldier in active service entangles himself in the affairs of everyday life, so that he may please the one who enlisted him as a soldier."

Question 19: Can you think of someone who wastes time thinking of ways to earn more money?

20A - <u>Our Spouse</u>

Sometimes we waste time being upset at our spouse. We don't realize we have the ability to help our spouse become a great person. We also may not realize we have the power to love our spouse in spite of past conflicts we've had with them, as well as, in spite of existing weaknesses they might have. Some questions to ask ourselves might be: Do I spend time being angry with my spouse? Do I spend time looking at other people and wish they were my spouse? Do I think I am too good for my spouse? If we answered yes to any of these questions, we might want to work on resolving this issue in your life.

Question 20: Can you think of someone who wastes time being judgmental toward their spouse?

21A - <u>Addiction</u>

Sometimes we develop addictions that cause us to waste time thinking about how to get our next fix. Addictions can be conquered. The Victory Tips Program can help in conquering an addiction. We have a short Tip on conquering an addiction, #23. Our daily telephone support calls can also help in conquering an addiction.

Question 21: Can you think of someone who wastes time thinking about how and when to get their next fix?

22A - The bottom line is that God wants us to live with peace of mind. We should never settle for a mind that is tossed to and fro with the cares of life. We can learn how to tame our mind and live in peace.

* * * * * * *

TIP #16

****

Develop a Disciplined Lifestyle

****

1A - The essence of discipline is denying ourselves things of low value to gain something of greater value. Few great things in life are accomplished without discipline. Every athlete will tell you it took discipline of diet, exercise and practice to become good at what they do. Every successful business person will tell you it took long hours and hard work to get to where they got in the business world. Discipline is a key ingredient to living a successful life.

Question 1: Can you think of a person who is successful and disciplined? If so, can you tell us in what way they are disciplined?

2A - <u>Bible Verses on Being Disciplined and Self-Controlled</u>

a) **Galatians 5:22-23** "But the fruit of the Spirit is love, joy, peace, patience, kindness, goodness, faithfulness, gentleness, self-control; against such things there is no law."

b) **1 Thessalonians 5:6** "so then let us not sleep as others do, but let us be alert and sober."

c) **Titus 1:8** "but hospitable, loving what is good, sensible, just, devout, self-controlled,"

d) **1 Peter 1:13** "Therefore, prepare your minds for action, keep sober *in spirit*, fix your hope completely on the grace to be brought to you at the revelation of Jesus Christ."

e) **1 Peter 5:8** "Be of sober *spirit*, be on the alert. Your adversary, the devil, prowls around like a roaring lion, seeking someone to devour:"

Question 2: Can you recall anyone in your life who taught you to be disciplined? If so, what did they say to you?

3A - Following, are instructions Paul gave to Titus on how Christians should live. Much of it relates to being disciplined.

<u>Discipline Tips for Older Men</u>

Titus 2:2 "Older men are to be temperate, dignified, sensible, sound in faith, in love, in perseverance."

3B - <u>Discipline Tips for Older and Younger Women</u>

Titus 2:3-5 "Older women likewise are to be reverent in their behavior, not malicious gossips nor enslaved to much wine, teaching what is good, so that they may encourage the young women to love their husbands, to love their children, *to be* sensible, pure, workers at home, kind, being subject to their own husbands, so that the word of God will not be dishonored."

3C - <u>Discipline Tips for Young Men</u>

Titus 2:6-8 "Likewise urge the young men to be sensible; in all things show yourself to be an example of good deeds, with purity in doctrine, dignified, sound in speech which is beyond reproach, so that the opponent will be put to shame, having nothing bad to say about us."

3D - <u>Discipline Tips for Employees</u>

a) **Titus 2:9** "*Urge* bondslaves to be subject to their own masters in everything, to be well-pleasing, not argumentative."

b) **Ephesians 6:5-8** "Slaves, be obedient to those who are your masters according to the flesh, with fear and trembling, in the sincerity of your heart, as to Christ; [6] not by way of eyeservice, as men-pleasers, but as slaves of Christ, doing the will of God from the heart. [7] With good will render service, as to the Lord, and not to men, [8] knowing that whatever good thing each one does, this he will receive back from the Lord, whether slave or free."

3E - <u>Discipline and Children</u>

Another aspect of life requiring discipline is in the area of raising children. The following verses talk about the need to "punish" (discipline) our children when they do wrong, demonstrating that true love must sometimes be tough.

a) **Proverbs 13:24** "He who withholds his rod hates his son, but he who loves him disciplnes him diligently."

b) **Proverbs 19:18** "Discipline your son while there is hope, and do not desire his death."

c) **Proverbs 23:13** "Do not hold back discipline from the child, Although you strike him with the rod, he will not die."

d) **Proverbs 29:17** "Correct your son, and he will give you comfort; He will also delight your soul."

Question 3: Can you think of anyone's children who would benefit from better discipline? If so, how are they trying to discipline their children presently?

4A **-** <u>Discipline and Diet</u>

a) **Proverbs 23:21** "For the heavy drinker and the glutton will come to poverty, And drowsiness will clothe *one* with rags."

b) **Philippians 3:19** "whose end is destruction, whose god is *their* appetite, and *whose* glory is in their shame, who set their minds on earthly things."

Question 4: Can you think of someone who would benefit from being disciplined in the area of diet?

5A - <u>Discipline and Exercise</u>

With factories becoming more automated and people spending more time online, the general population is reducing the amount of physical activity they do. Yet, the human body was made to do manual labor, to be physically fit. Physical work and exercise, develops muscles, accelerates the heart, and clears the mind. Not prioritizing physical activity can place a person at risk of premature death, due to high blood pressure, heart disease, obesity, and other silent killers. It also puts a person at risk of injury, due to occasional over-exertion.

Below, are some scriptures about maintaining our physical bodies.

a) **Proverbs 24:5** "A wise man is strong, And a man of knowledge increases power."

b) **Proverbs 31:17** "She girds herself with strength, And makes her arms strong."

c) **Isaiah 40:31** "Yet those who wait for the Lord Will gain new strength; They will mount up *with* wings like eagles, They will run and not get tired, They will walk and not become weary."

d) **Romans 12:1** "Therefore I urge you, brethren, by the mercies of God, to present your bodies a living and holy sacrifice, acceptable to God, which is your spiritual service of worship."

e) **1 Corinthians 6:19-20** "Or do you not know that your body is a temple of the Holy Spirit who is in you, whom you have from God, and that you are not your own? For you have been bought with a price: therefore glorify God in your body."

f) **1 Corinthians 9:27** "but I discipline my body and make it my slave, so that, after I have preached to others, I myself will not be disqualified."

g) **1 Corinthians 10:31** "Whether, then, you eat or drink or whatever you do, do all to the glory of God."

Question 5: Can you think of someone who would benefit from an exercise program?

6A - <u>Jesus Chose Disciples</u>

When Jesus walked the earth, He chose for Himself, twelve disciples. The word "disciple" is the root word, for the word "discipline."

6B - <u>An Analogy of Discipline in Nature</u>

A nicely landscaped yard got that way because someone took the time to get rid of weeds, trim the bushes, plant beautiful flowers, and so on. All of this took time and hard work, but in the end it makes for a beautiful yard. So too with mental well-being; it can take effort to identify and uproot wrong beliefs and replace them with proper, life-giving beliefs. But in due time, a happy, peaceful life will emerge and be a joy for the person, and for those around them.

Question 6: In what way can you see yourself improving your self-discipline?

* * * * * * *

Tip #17

****

Develop a Lifestyle of Holiness

****

Just as He chose us in Him before the foundation of the world, that we
would be holy and blameless before Him. In love. Ephesians 1:4

1A - The central theme of the Bible is to show us how to have a relationship with God and the forgiveness we need through our Lord Jesus Christ. In the Old Testament, we read about God's high standards for daily living. They were so high that no one was able to achieve it. People sinned. The only thing that could pay the penalty for sin was blood. Thus, in the Old Testament God instructed His people to sacrifice animals once a year to pay for the sins of the people.

1B - Then a better sacrifice came, the Lord Jesus Christ. Two thousand years ago, the blood of a sinless man, Jesus Christ, was spilled, to pay the penalty for the sin of all of humanity. It was a horrendous day - but a monumental day, the day Jesus allowed Himself to be nailed to a cross. Because of Jesus, we can trade our sin nature for a new nature. Thank God for Jesus!

1C - Why did Jesus have to die? Why did animals have to die? Because of sin.

If sin is so terrible that it cost the lives of numerous animals, and the life of a perfect human being - Jesus Christ, shouldn't we be living holy lives? Absolutely.

The problem is that living holy lives rarely comes up in people's minds. Most people end up living half-hearted, semi-holy lives. This kind of lifestyle can become a hindrance to our happiness.

1D - We should understand, however, that our motive for living a holy life is not so that we can *buy* ourselves a place in heaven after we die. The Bible says that our best works are like filthy rags in God's sight (See Isaiah 64:6 below). Our good works could never be good enough to save our souls. We need the sacrifice of Jesus to cleanse our souls of sin.

Isaiah 64:6 "For all of us have become like one who is unclean, And all our righteous deeds are like a filthy garment; And all of us wither like a leaf, And our iniquities, like the wind, take us away."

1E - Our holy living is a bi-product of living a life connected with God.

God is very gracious. He has an end goal for us to achieve, as far as holy living is concerned; however, He also extends grace to those who are just starting their Christian walk, and have difficulties in their behavior. God understands the challenges that people have to work through before they develop a life of holiness. Thus, for most people change happens gradually.

1F - Our reason for living a holy life is to honor God for saving our souls, and to be an example to others.

Also, a holy life helps us to share the good news of Jesus's sacrifice more effectively.

Do you care what God cares about? God cares about people, people who need to hear the Gospel of Jesus Christ. Thus, He needs faithful people willing to let Him live His life through them. It is an amazing experience. Are you one of these people? Then, consider developing a lifestyle of holiness.

Question 1: Have you ever considered the importance of living a holy life?

2A - At this point, it is important to outline what a Christian should do if they sin. Eventually, we will all miss the mark in trying to live a God-honoring life. When this happens, we need to come to God in humility, and confess our sin, and ask Him to forgive us, based on the sacrifice Jesus made, for us, on the cross. See the verse below.

1 John 1:9 "If we confess our sins, he is faithful and just to forgive us our sins, and to cleanse us from all unrighteousness."

By faith, we receive our forgiveness, and we go on. We should also take steps, to prevent us from falling into that same sin again. Otherwise, it becomes a habit or an addiction. With the right support and direction, we can learn to overcome our negative behaviors. (See Tip #23 – Conquer The Addiction, for more on this.)

Question 2: Have you developed the habit of going straight to God for His forgiveness, and for His help in the weak areas of your life?

3A - Below are some verses about God's ultimate goal for us relating to holy living.

a) **2 Timothy 1:9** "who has saved us and called us with a holy calling, not according to our works, but according to His own purpose and grace which was granted us in Christ Jesus from all eternity,"

b) **2 Timothy 2:19** "Nevertheless, the firm foundation of God stands, having this seal, "The Lord knows those who are His," and, "Everyone who names the name of the Lord is to abstain from wickedness."

c) **Titus 1:7-8** "For the overseer must be above reproach as God's steward, not self-willed, not quick-tempered, not addicted to wine, not pugnacious, not fond of sordid gain, but hospitable, loving what is good, sensible, just, devout, self-controlled,"

d) **Titus 2:12** "instructing us to deny ungodliness and worldly desires and to live sensibly, righteously and godly in the present age,"

e) **James 1:19-20** "This you know, my beloved brethren. But everyone must be quick to hear, slow to speak and slow to anger; for the anger of man does not achieve the righteousness of God."

f) **James 1:21** "Therefore, putting aside all filthiness and all that remains of wickedness, in humility receive the word implanted, which is able to save your souls."

g) **1 Peter 2:11** "Beloved, I urge you as aliens and strangers to abstain from fleshly lusts which wage war against the soul."

h) **2 Peter 3:11** "Since all these things are to be destroyed in this way, what sort of people ought you to be in holy conduct and godliness,"

Question 3: Is God asking for too much of His people, to live upright lives?

4A - Verses Relating to Purity

a) **1 Tim 5:1-2** "Do not sharply rebuke an older man, but rather appeal to him as a father, to the younger men as brothers, the older women as mothers, and the younger women as sisters, in all purity."

b) **1 Tim 5:20, 22** "Those who continue in sin, rebuke in the presence of all, so that the rest also will be fearful of sinning…Do not lay hands upon anyone too hastily and thereby share responsibility for the sins of others; keep yourself free from sin."

c) **1 Peter 1:22** "Since you have in obedience to the truth purified your souls for a sincere love of the brethren, fervently love one another from the heart:"

Question 4: Do you think you might like the challenge of trying to live a pure life?

5A - Knowledge Can Help Us Stay Pure

Proverbs 2:11 "Discretion shall preserve thee, understanding shall keep thee:"

The Bible Talks About Our "Old Self" and Our "New Self"

a) **Galatians 5:24** "And they that are Christ's have crucified the flesh with the affections and lusts."

b) **Colossians 3:9-10** "Lie not one to another, seeing that ye have put off the old man with his deeds; [10] And have put on the new man, which is renewed in knowledge after the image of him that created him."

c) **1 Peter 1:14-16** "As obedient children, do not be conformed to the former lusts which were yours in your ignorance, but like the Holy One who called you, be holy yourselves also in all your behavior; because it is written, "You shall be holy, for I am holy.""

d) **2 Timothy 2:21** "If a man therefore purge himself from these, he shall be a vessel unto honour, sanctified, and meet for the master's use, and prepared unto every good work."

5B - Verses on the Lusts of the Flesh

a) **Romans 13:14** "But put on the Lord Jesus Christ, and make no provision for the flesh in regard to its lusts."

b) **Galatians 5:16** "But I say, walk by the Spirit, and you will not carry out the desire of the flesh."

5C - <u>Verses on Sexual Purity</u>

a) **Proverbs 5:20** "For why should you, my son, be exhilarated with an adulteress And embrace the bosom of a foreigner?"

b) **Ephesians 5:3** "But immorality or any impurity or greed must not even be named among you, as is proper among saints;"

c) **Ephesians 5:5,6** "For this you know with certainty, that no immoral or impure person or covetous man, who is an idolater, has an inheritance in the kingdom of Christ and God. Let no one deceive you with empty words, for because of these things the wrath of God comes upon the sons of disobedience."

d) **1 Thessalonians 4:3-7** "For this is the will of God, your sanctification; that is, that you abstain from sexual immorality; that each of you know how to possess his own vessel in sanctification and honor, not in lustful passion, like the Gentiles who do not know God; and that no man transgress and defraud his brother in the matter because the Lord is the avenger in all these things, just as we also told you before and solemnly warned you. For God has not called us for the purpose of impurity, but in sanctification."

Question 5: Do you know someone who has a problem with sexual purity?

6A - <u>Shame is Associated with Sin</u>

Ephesians 5:12 "For it is disgraceful even to speak of the things which are done by them in secret."

Question 6: Have you experienced shame with some of the things you've done?

7A - <u>Holy Living Includes Holy Speaking</u> (For more on this, see Tip #7 – Speak Right Words)

a) **Ephesians 5:4** "and there must be no filthiness and silly talk, or coarse jesting, which are not fitting, but rather giving of thanks."

b) **James 1:26** "If anyone thinks himself to be religious, and yet does not bridle his tongue but deceives his own heart, this man's religion is worthless."

c) **1 Peter 3:10-11** 'For, "The one who desires life, to love and see good days, Must keep his tongue from evil and his lips from speaking deceit. "He must turn away from evil and do good; He must seek peace and pursue it."

Question 7: Do you know anyone whose speech needs to be improved?

8A - <u>Reckless Living Can Prevent Us From Getting To Heaven</u>

a) **Ephesians 5:5-7** "For this ye know, that no whoremonger, nor unclean person, nor covetous man, who is an idolater, hath any inheritance in the kingdom of Christ and of God. ⁶ Let no man deceive you with vain words: for because of these things cometh the wrath of God upon the children of disobedience. ⁷ Be not ye therefore partakers with them."

b) **Hebrews 12:14** "Follow peace with all men, and holiness, without which no man shall see the Lord:"

Question 8: Is spending eternity with God in heaven something you want, and worth living holy for?

9A - <u>We are a Light With Holy Lives</u>

Ephesians 5:8-10 "for you were formerly darkness, but now you are Light in the Lord; walk as children of Light [9] (for the fruit of the Light consists in all goodness and righteousness and truth), [10] trying to learn what is pleasing to the Lord."

9B - We should keep our minds on good things.

Colossians 3: 1-3 "Therefore if you have been raised up with Christ, keep seeking the things above, where Christ is, seated at the right hand of God. [2] Set your mind on the things above, not on the things that are on earth. [3] For you have died and your life is hidden with Christ in God."

Question 9: What are good ways to help keep our minds on good things?

10A - <u>Develop these Traits</u>

a) **Colossians 3:12** "But women will be preserved through the bearing of children if they continue in faith and love and sanctity with self-restraint."

b) **2 Timothy 2:22** "Now flee from youthful lusts and pursue righteousness, faith, love and peace, with those who call on the Lord from a pure heart."

c) **Titus 2:2** "Older men are to be temperate, dignified, sensible, sound in faith, in love, in perseverance."

d) **Titus 2:3-5** "Older women likewise are to be reverent in their behavior, not malicious gossips nor enslaved to much wine, teaching what is good, so that they may encourage the young women to love their husbands, to love their children to be sensible, pure, workers at home, kind, being subject to their own husbands, so that the word of God will not be dishonoured."

e) **Titus 2:6-8** "Likewise urge the young men to be sensible; [7] in all things show yourself to be an example of good deeds, *with* purity in doctrine, dignified, [8] sound *in* speech which is beyond reproach, so that the opponent will be put to shame, having nothing bad to say about us."

f) **2 Peter 1:5-9** "Now for this very reason also, applying all diligence, in your faith supply moral excellence, and in *your* moral excellence, knowledge, [6] and in *your* knowledge, self-control, and in *your* self-control, perseverance, and in *your* perseverance, godliness, [7] and in *your* godliness, brotherly kindness, and in *your* brotherly kindness, love. [8] For if these *qualities* are yours and are increasing, they render you neither useless nor unfruitful in the true knowledge of our Lord Jesus Christ. [9] For he who lacks these *qualities* is blind *or* short-sighted, having forgotten *his* purification from his former sins."

Question 10: Which of these traits seem appealing to you? How would you develop them?

11A - Live a Life Worthy of God

a) **Colossians 1:10** "so that you will walk in a manner worthy of the Lord, to please Him in all respects, bearing fruit in every good work and increasing in the knowledge of God."

b) **1 Thessalonians 2:11,12** "just as you know how we were exhorting and encouraging and imploring each one of you as a father would his own children, so that you would walk in a manner worthy of the God who calls you into His own kingdom and glory."

c) **2 Thessalonians 1:5** "This is a plain indication of God's righteous judgment so that you will be considered worthy of the kingdom of God, for which indeed you are suffering."

d) **2 Thessalonians 1:11** "To this end also we pray for you always, that our God will count you worthy of your calling, and fulfill every desire for goodness and the work of faith with power:"

11B - Live Blameless Lives

a) **Proverbs 20:7** "A righteous man who walks in his integrity—How blessed are his sons after him."

b) **1 Thessalonians 3:13** "so that He may establish your hearts without blame in holiness before our God and Father at the coming of our Lord Jesus with all His saints."

c) **1 Thessalonians 5:21-23** "But examine everything *carefully*; hold fast to that which is good; [22] abstain from every form of evil. [23] Now may the God of peace Himself sanctify you entirely; and may your spirit and soul and body be preserved complete, without blame at the coming of our Lord Jesus Christ."

d) **2 Peter 3:14** "Therefore, beloved, since you look for these things, be diligent to be found by Him in peace, spotless and blameless."

Question 11: Striving for a blameless life can seem like a daunting task. How do you feel about this?

12A - Our Good Life is a Testimony to Others

a) **2 Corinthians 9:13** "Because of the proof given by this ministry, they will glorify God for your obedience to your confession of the gospel of Christ and for the liberality of your contribution to them and to all,"

b) **1 Peter 2:12** "Keep your behavior excellent among the Gentiles, so that in the thing in which they slander you as evildoers, they may because of your good deeds, as they observe *them*, glorify God in the day of visitation."

12B - An effective way to attain and maintain holy living is by memorizing scripture, then speaking it to ourselves throughout our day. Contact us for computer files that can be used to print Bible verse cards to help with this.

* * * * * * *

TIP #18

****

Become an Optimist

****

1A - Can you think of someone who is always optimistic? Is that a good way to be? In this Tip, we will learn how optimism relates to the Christian life. The definition of **optimism** in the Merriam-Webster dictionary is: *"The tendency to be hopeful and to emphasize or think of the good part in a situation rather than the bad part, or the feeling that in the future good things are more likely to happen than bad things:"*

Question 1: In general, what is your level of optimism?

2A - Below, are some quotes on optimism.

a) "Optimism is the faith that leads to achievement. Nothing can be done without hope and confidence." – Helen Keller

b) "One of the things I learned the hard way was that it doesn't pay to get discouraged. Keeping busy and making optimism a way of life can restore your faith in yourself." – Lucille Ball

c) "Be fanatically positive and militantly optimistic. If something is not to your liking, change your liking." – Rick Steves

d) "A healthy attitude is contagious but don't wait to catch it from others. Be a carrier." – Author Unknown

Question 2: What thoughts come to your mind after reading the above quotes on optimism?

3A - The Book of Galatians give an overview of the character traits of people who follow Christ. Some burst with optimism, others not so readily at first glance. Let's see how they relate.

Galatians 5:22,23 "But the fruit of the Spirit is love, joy, peace, patience, kindness, goodness, faithfulness, gentleness, self-control; against such things there is no law."

3B - **Love** – An optimistic person loves people. No matter what the person has done, they still love them. They believe that person will improve when they are treated with love, so they step out in faith to love them. They may not *trust* them immediately, but they show good faith by associating with them and offering them unconditional love.

3C - **Joy** – An optimistic person has joy. They believe the best is yet to come. They have confidence in God's blessings upon their life, and they have confidence in themselves that they can do all things through Christ. They have seen how circumstances and people have turned around because of their joy, so they continually operate in joy. Circumstances may challenge their joy but they swerve around them and keep right on going.

Question 3: How does your optimism show forth in love and joy?

4A - **Peace** – An optimistic person has peace. They believe God has everything in control. They know God blesses those who live righteous lives, and they have peace knowing that there is no sin blocking them from God's flow of blessings. If they do sin, they know they can quickly repent of it, and, once again, live in a state of peace and favor in God's kingdom. Their optimism gives them peace!

4B - **Longsuffering** (Patience) – An optimistic person is patient. They believe in God's ability to help them do everything at the right time. They are busy, but at the same time they are at rest on the inside, trusting God. If things slow them down, they don't get flustered, they look at it as an opportunity to learn from the hindrance, or to help someone in need at that moment. Their optimism gives them peace as they wait.

4C - **Gentleness** – An optimistic person is gentle. They know the valuable truth Jesus taught, *"Treat others the same way you want them to treat you."* (**Luke 6:31**) They know that people respond better to gentleness than to aggression, so they model gentleness. Gentleness is a hallmark of maturity, and it keeps the social atmosphere happier.

Question 4: How does your optimism show forth in peace, patience, and gentleness?

5A - **Goodness** – Two definitions of good or goodness is 'honorable' and 'favorable.' Optimism can feed both of these attributes for the optimistic person. Optimism attracts honor and favor. Optimists "raise the bar" of what is possible and causes people to see challenges in a different light, giving the optimist increased honor and favor. This helps spur growth and advancement. Optimists feed their spirit with God's Word, which saturates them with goodness. This sets them apart from others.

5B - **Faith** – An optimistic person naturally operates in an atmosphere of faith. Their positive disposition draws blessings toward them. Now, give a natural optimist teaching on biblical faith, and you have a person who is unstoppable. They know that big problems are no match for them and God, and they boldly embrace challenges until their desired goal is achieved. The optimist, with faith, stands in a league of their own.

Question 5: How does your optimism show forth in goodness and faith?

6A - **Meekness** – The Merriam-Webster dictionary defines meekness as: *"enduring injury with patience and without resentment."* An optimistic person knows there is value in suffering and does not shy away from it. They know that some of humanities greatest feats have come from great suffering. To the optimist, not a second of God's grace is lost in the midst of life's challenges. They endure with patience for as long as it takes, and always without resentment.

6B - **Temperance** (Self-control) – An optimistic person has good self-control. They know it is wise to forego a small pleasure now to reap a great blessing in the future. They know how easy it is for someone to _react_ to a problem and further complicate their problems. An optimist's self-control protects them. They respond rather than react. Self-control is their best investment for a bright future, and they guard it well.

Question 6: How does your optimism show forth in meekness and temperance?

7A - <u>Optimism in the Bible</u>

<u>Taking the Promised Land</u>

In Tip #15 – Eliminate Wasted Thinking, we saw how ten of the twelve Israelite leaders said they could not beat the giants in a war to take the Promised Land that God had given them (Numbers Chapter 13). The other two, Joshua and Caleb, said, they were well able to beat the giants. Below, is Caleb's appeal to go in and take the land.

> **Numbers 11:30** "Then Moses returned to the camp, both he and the elders of Israel."

7B - Joshua and Caleb were optimistic, the others were pessimistic. Because the pessimistic people persuaded the others to hold back, all of Israel had to wander in the wilderness for 40 years until the pessimistic people all died. Associating with well-meaning, pessimistic people can bring problems in our lives.

Question 7: Can you think of pessimistic people in your life who are negatively affecting you? What do you think of reducing your contact with them?

8A - <u>The Optimism of David</u>

In Tip #14 – Develop a Conqueror Mentality, we talked about the shepherd boy, David, finding out about the giant, Goliath, how he was taunting the Israelite army. David became bold and spoke the following words.

> **1 Samuel 17:43-47** "The Philistine said to David, "Am I a dog, that you come to me with sticks?" And the Philistine cursed David by his gods. [44] The Philistine also said to David, "Come to me, and I will give your flesh to the birds of the sky and the beasts of the field.""

8B - "[45] Then David said to the Philistine, "You come to me with a sword, a spear, and a javelin, but I come to you in the name of the LORD of hosts, the God of the armies of Israel, whom you have taunted. [46] This day the LORD will deliver you up into my hands, and I will strike you down and remove your head from you. And I will give the dead bodies of the army of the Philistines this day to the birds of the sky and the wild beasts of the earth, that all the earth may know that there is a God in Israel, [47] and that all this assembly may know that the LORD does not deliver by sword or by spear; for the battle is the LORD'S and He will give you into our hands."

8C - Sure enough, David killed Goliath, and everyone was amazed at his feat of power, as well as his faith in God. David was optimistic; everyone else was pessimistic. David's optimism attracted God's power in his life and helped him defeat Goliath.

Question 8: Can you think of a "giant" in your life that God is waiting to help you conquer?

9A - <u>Healing the Lame Man</u>

In Acts Chapter 3, scripture records the story of the apostle Peter healing the lame man at the temple.

Acts 3:1-9 "Now Peter and John were going up to the temple at the ninth *hour*, the hour of prayer. [2] And a man who had been lame from his mother's womb was being carried along, whom they used to set down every day at the gate of the temple which is called Beautiful, in order to beg alms of those who were entering the temple. [3] When he saw Peter and John about to go into the temple, he *began* asking to receive alms."

9B - [4] But Peter, along with John, fixed his gaze on him and said, "Look at us!" [5] And he *began* to give them his attention, expecting to receive something from them. [6] But Peter said, "I do not possess silver and gold, but what I do have I give to you: In the name of Jesus Christ the Nazarene—walk!" [7] And seizing him by the right hand, he raised him up; and immediately his feet and his ankles were strengthened. [8] With a leap he stood upright and *began* to walk; and he entered the temple with them, walking and leaping and praising God. [9] And all the people saw him walking and praising God;"

9C - Peter was boldly optimistic that God would heal the paralytic man.

Peter and John had received extraordinary power from God to start the Christian church. The miracles were evidence that God was with the apostle's, to prove that their message about Jesus Christ was true.

Question 9: Is there a ministry that God wants you to start, for which you need His help?

10A - In Acts Chapter 16, we see how praising God caused Paul and Silas to be freed from prison.

Acts 16:18-26 "She continued doing this for many days. But Paul was greatly annoyed, and turned and said to the spirit, "I command you in the name of Jesus Christ to come out of her!" And it came out at that very moment. [19] But when her masters saw that their hope of profit was gone, they seized Paul and Silas and dragged them into the market place before the authorities, [20] and when they had brought them to the chief magistrates, they said, "These men are throwing our city into confusion, being Jews, [21] and are proclaiming customs which it is not lawful for us to accept or to observe, being Romans.""

10B - "[22] The crowd rose up together against them, and the chief magistrates tore their robes off them and proceeded to order *them* to be beaten with rods. [23] When they had struck them with many blows, they threw them into prison, commanding the jailer to guard them securely; [24] and he, having received such a command, threw them into the inner prison and fastened their feet in the stocks. [25] But about midnight Paul and Silas were praying and singing hymns of praise to God, and the prisoners were listening to them; [26] and suddenly there came a great earthquake, so that the foundations of the prison house were shaken; and immediately all the doors were opened and everyone's chains were unfastened."

10C - Paul and Silas chose to be optimistic and praised God while they suffered for His name, and God miraculously freed them from prison.

Question 10: Is there a problem in your life in which God wants you to be optimistic and praise Him in?

11A - <u>Ways to Become an Optimist</u>

<u>Speak Your Way to Optimism</u>

The Bible says in **Romans 4:17** *"(As it is written, "A father of many nations have I made you") in the presence of Him whom he believed, even God, who gives life to the dead and <u>calls into being that which does not exist.</u>"*

11B - This principle of speaking things into existence, shows us that when we pray for something, we can help it along by speaking faith-affirming words that depict the item we want, has already come into existence. That's what God does – He speaks things into existence. So, we can start saying:

a) My life is great.

b) My job is great.

c) My spouse is great.

d) My church is great.

e) My pastor is great.

f) My apt (or house) is great.

g) My school is great.

h) My teachers are great.

i) My parents are great.

j) My siblings are great.

k) My neighbors are great.

l) My vehicle is great.

m) My job search is great.

n) My city has great employers.

o) My public transportation is great.

11C - All of these statements can be true when we compare them with other people's experience.

Our words can have a significant influence on our beliefs. Our beliefs are important because they influence our automatic thinking. With positive beliefs, our minds automatically think positive. For more on this principle, read Tip #7 - Speak Right Words.

Question 11: Do you speak positive words to improve optimism in your life?

12A - <u>Be Thankful</u>

Another way to maintain optimism is by being thankful.

For example, when we consider everything we do with the help of modern appliances, we can be thankful for each appliance. Below are a few verses on being thankful. For more information on gratitude, read Tip #25 – Be Thankful.

a) **Psalm 107:1** "Oh give thanks to the Lord, for He is good, For His lovingkindness is everlasting."

b) **Ephesians 5:20** "always giving thanks for all things in the name of our Lord Jesus Christ to God, even the Father;"

c) **Colossians 3:15** "Let the peace of Christ rule in your hearts, to which indeed you were called in one body; and be thankful.

d) **1 Thessalonians 5:18** "in everything give thanks; for this is God's will for you in Christ Jesus."

Question 12: What are you in the habit of being thankful for?

13A - <u>Make Friends with Optimists</u>

The Bible has a lot to say about the people we associate with. Below are some verses about relationships.

a) **Proverbs 1:10** "My son, if sinners entice you, Do not consent."

b) **Proverbs 13:20** "He who walks with wise men will be wise, But the companion of fools will suffer harm."

c) **Proverbs 14:7** "Leave the presence of a fool, Or you will not discern words of knowledge."

d) **Proverbs 22:24-25** "Do not associate with a man given to anger; Or go with a hot-tempered man, Or you will learn his ways, And find a snare for yourself."

e) **1 Corinthians 15:33** "Do not be deceived: "Bad company corrupts good morals.""

Question 13: Can you think of any optimistic people you could get to know more?

Question 14: What do you think of making optimism something to strive for in your life?

* * * * * * *

TIP #19

****

Eliminate Anger

****

1A - Anger is a definite hindrance to happiness. Many of us have triggers that bring on our anger. It is helpful to take time to assess the root causes of our anger and learn how to disarm it.

In a June 29, 2017 article in Time Magazine entitled, "The Rage Flu - Why All This Anger is Contagious and Making Us Sick, Dr. Gary Slutkin, founder of Cure Violence, and a faculty member of the University of Illinois at Chicago is quoted as saying *"Violence and violent speech meet the criteria of disease... Like a virus, violence makes more of itself. Rage begets more rage. And it spreads because we humans are wired to follow our peers."*

1B - The author of the magazine article, Susanna Schrobsdorff, adds that *"...if extreme speech becomes acceptable in one realm, it's likely to spread to overlapping realms – from the dinner table, to social feeds, to a political demonstration. ...And for the more vulnerable, those who are mentally unstable or disenfranchised, this sickness can lead to actual violence directed at the person or institution that symbolizes their disappointment."* Ms. Schrobsdorff also quotes Dr. Slutkin as saying *"Undesirable social norms are becoming more prevalent."*

1C - <u>Anger and Anxiety</u>

Something to note is that there can be a link between anxiety and anger. If we've never learned how to calm ourselves down, and problems come up, they can trigger an anger response in us. When we see that our anger can "freeze" those around us, we can use it to influence others to do what we want - whenever we want. However, our anger can stop us from developing emotionally.

Question 1: What tends to trigger your anger?

2A - Jesus was very much against anger.

Matthew 5-22 "But I say to you that everyone who is angry with his brother shall be guilty before the court; and whoever says to his brother, 'You good-for-nothing,' shall be guilty before the supreme court; and whoever says, 'You fool,' shall be guilty *enough to go* into the fiery hell."

2A - Anger is so destructive that the Bible advises us to get rid of it before bedtime.

Ephesians 4:26 "Be angry, and yet do not sin; do not let the sun go down on your anger,"

Question 2: Do you make it a habit to forgive everyone before sunset?

3A - The Bible implies that there is a link between anger and the devil. Right after the above verse, it says, "and do not give the devil an opportunity." (**Ephesians 4:27**)

3B - The following verses link anger to evil.

a) **Psalms 37:8** "Cease from anger and forsake wrath; Do not fret; it leads only to <u>evildoing</u>."

b) **Ephesians 4:31** "Let all bitterness and wrath and anger and clamor and slander be put away from you, along with all malice:"

3C - The following scripture shows how anger in King Saul's life brought about torment from an evil spirit.

1 Samuel 18:9-11 " Now it came about on the next day that an evil spirit from God came mightily upon Saul, and he raved in the midst of the house, while David was playing *the harp* with his hand, as usual; and a spear *was* in Saul's hand. [11] Saul hurled the spear for he thought, "I will pin David to the wall." But David escaped from his presence twice."

Question 3: Have you ever witnessed anger that made you see a connection between anger and the devil?

4A - <u>Four Synonyms</u>

Ephesians 4:31 "Let all bitterness and wrath and anger and clamor and slander be put away from you, along with all malice."

The above verse gives us four synonyms for the word anger: bitterness, wrath, clamor, and malice.

Question 4: Is there anything in your life that you are bitter about?

5A - The Bible verse below gives us a unique verb for what to do with anger.

Psalms 37:8 "Cease from anger and <u>forsake</u> wrath; Do not fret; it leads only to evildoing."

The meanings of the word "forsake" are 1) to quit or leave entirely; <u>abandon</u>; desert; and, 2) to give up or <u>renounce</u> (a habit, way of life, etc.).

Question 5: Can you see yourself forsaking (abandoning) anger? Can you see yourself renouncing anger, and committing to living a whole new life free of anger?

6A - The same verse links anger with fretting and worrying.

Psalms 37:8 "Cease from anger and forsake wrath; Do not fret; it leads only to evildoing."

Question 6: Do you have any worries that contribute to you getting angry?

7A - Ephesians 4:31 *(above),* gives us another adjective for the word anger: Malice. It is defined as the desire to inflict injury, harm, or suffering on another, either because of a hostile impulse or deep-seated meanness.

Question 7: Have you ever wanted to inflict pain on someone?

8A - Here is another scripture on synonyms for anger and to not be associated with it.

> **Colossians 3:8** "But now you also, put them all aside: anger, wrath, malice, slander, and abusive speech from your mouth."

8B - The Bible tells us that anger is something that fools have a problem with.

> **Ecclesiastes 7:9** "Do not be eager in your heart to be angry, For anger resides in the bosom of fools."

Question 8: Has anyone told you that you were foolish? If so, was it in connection with anger?

9A - On the contrary, people who are slow to wrath are looked upon as wise, with great understanding.

> **Proverbs 14:29** "He who is slow to anger has great understanding, But he who is quick-tempered exalts folly."

Question 9: Do people tell you that you are wise?

10A - The following verse gives two tips on how to avoid anger.

> **James 1:19-20** "This you know, my beloved brethren. But everyone must be quick to hear, slow to speak and slow to anger; for the anger of man does not achieve the righteousness of God."

Question 10: When conflict arises, do you give people adequate time to state their case?

11A - A hot-tempered person attracts conflict.

> **Proverbs 15:18** "A hot-tempered man stirs up strife, But the slow to anger calms a dispute."

Soft speech can remove anger in a situation.

> **Proverbs 15:1** "A gentle answer turns away wrath, But a harsh word stirs up anger."

Question 11: Do you make it a point to soften your speech when anger is building up in you or those around you?

12A - A Wise Man Watches How He Responds

There is a saying that says, "Choose your battles wisely." In the following scripture, we see the benefits of backing off from tense situations.

> **Proverbs 19:11** "A man's discretion makes him slow to anger, And it is his glory to overlook a transgression."

Here we see that a wise man can defer his anger. That means wise people can tell when it isn't a good time to discuss a problem with someone, so they put it off for a while. A wise person will sometimes even pass over someone's mistake, giving the other person grace.

Question 12: Can you see yourself not reacting to a problem, and even letting a matter go?

13A - The following verse states that anger is not from God.

James 1:20 "for the anger of man does not achieve the righteousness of God."

13B - <u>This Can Cause Anger</u>

Many times anger occurs because we are passing judgment on people. The Bible has much to say about not passing judgment on people. The way we judge others will be the way God judges us.

a) **Matthew 7:1,2** (Jesus is speaking) "Do not judge so that you will not be judged. For in the way you judge, you will be judged; and by your standard of measure, it will be measured to you."

b) **Luke 6:37** "Do not judge, and you will not be judged; and do not condemn, and you will not be condemned; pardon, and you will be pardoned."

Refer to Tip #12 – Don't Judge, for more information on not passing judgment.

Question 13: Would you like God to judge you the way you judge others?

14A - Knowing how to prevent anger has great value.

Proverbs 16:32 "He who is slow to anger is better than the mighty, And he who rules his spirit, than he who captures a city.."

Question 14: Are you happy with the way you disarm anger in your life?

15A - Anger can hinder us from making friends with emotionally healthy people.

Proverbs 22:24-25 "Do not associate with a man given to anger; Or go with a hot-tempered man, Or you will learn his ways And find a snare for yourself."

Question 15: Do you know of angry people who could benefit from making friends with healthier individuals?

Are you up for the challenge of learning how to disarm anger in your life? To help you do this, consider giving people a dollar for every time they see you angry. It will be a good investment in your life!

* * * * * * *

TIP #20

****

Practice Humility

****

1A - Learning to be humble is one of the most attractive attributes we can develop. The word "humble" is defined as having, or showing, a modest or low estimate of one's importance.

We don't have to *be* lower in importance; rather we give others the privilege of being higher than us.

Jesus taught the paradox, to become great, one must become humble.

a) **Matthew 18:4** "Whoever then humbles himself as this child, he is the greatest in the kingdom of heaven."

b) **Matthew 23:12** "Whoever exalts himself shall be humbled; and whoever humbles himself shall be exalted."

1B - Jesus taught us humility by displaying it in a number of ways.

First, He was born in a humble place, a barn.

Luke 2:16 "So they came in a hurry and found their way to Mary and Joseph, and the baby as He lay in the manger."

1C - Second, He was humble toward His parents.

Luke 2:51 "And He went down with them and came to Nazareth, and He continued in subjection to them; and His mother treasured all these things in her heart."

1D - Third, Jesus never had a house.

Luke 9:58 "And Jesus said to him, "The foxes have holes and the birds of the air have nests, but the Son of Man has nowhere to lay His head."

1E - Fourth, Jesus spent His teaching days as a servant.

a) **Matthew 20:28** "just as the Son of Man did not come to be served, but to serve, and to give His life a ransom for many."

b) **Luke 22:27** "For who is greater, the one who reclines at the table or the one who serves? Is it not the one who reclines at the table? But I am among you as the one who serves."

c) **Philippians 2:7** "but emptied Himself, taking the form of a bond-servant, and being made in the likeness of men"

d) **Philippians 2:8** "Being found in appearance as a man, He humbled Himself by becoming obedient to the point of death, even death on a cross."

1F - Jesus was not self-willed.

John 6:38 "For I have come down from heaven, not to do My own will, but the will of Him who sent Me."

1G - The apostle Paul told us to be humble.

Colossians 3:12 "So, as those who have been chosen of God, holy and beloved, put on a heart of compassion, kindness, humility, gentleness and patience;"

1H - The writer of Proverbs spoke highly of humility.

a) **Proverbs 15:33** "The fear of the Lord is the instruction for wisdom, And before honor comes humility."

b) **Proverbs 18:12** "Before destruction the heart of man is haughty, But humility goes before honor."

Question 1: Can you think of someone who portrays humility?

Question 2: How would you rate your level of humility?

3A - We can see a greater importance of humility when we understand how negative the opposite is - pride.

a) **Proverbs 8:13** "The fear of the Lord is to hate evil; Pride and arrogance and the evil way; And the perverted mouth, I hate."

b) **Proverbs 16:5** "Everyone who is proud in heart is an abomination to the Lord; Assuredly, he will not be unpunished."

c) **Proverbs 16:18** "Pride goes before destruction, And a haughty spirit before stumbling"

3B - Humility is a very attractive character trait, and can be displayed with very little effort. Notice the easy-going sense we feel in the following quote from Jesus.

Matthew 11:29, 30 "Take My yoke upon you and learn from Me, for I am gentle and humble in heart, and you will find rest for your souls. For My yoke is easy and My burden is light."

Question 3: Can you think of anyone who is humble, and would you agree that their demeanor feels effortless?

4A - When we don't humble ourselves, sometimes God will humble us, through life events.

Deuteronomy 8:2 "You shall remember all the way which the Lord your God has led you in the wilderness these forty years, that He might humble you, testing you, to know what was in your heart, whether you would keep His commandments or not."

4B - Our humility can cause God to lift us out of evil.

a) **1 Kings 21:29** "Do you see how Ahab has humbled himself before Me? Because he has humbled himself before Me, I will not bring the evil in his days, but I will bring the evil upon his house in his son's days."

b) **2 Chronicles 7:14** "and My people who are called by My name humble themselves and pray and seek My face and turn from their wicked ways, then I will hear from heaven, will forgive their sin and will heal their land."

c) **2 Chronicles 12:7** "When the Lord saw that they humbled themselves, the word of the Lord came to Shemaiah, saying, "They have humbled themselves so I will not destroy them, but I will grant them some measure of deliverance, and My wrath shall not be poured out on Jerusalem by means of Shishak."

d) **2 Chronicles 12:12** "And when he humbled himself, the anger of the Lord turned away from him, so as not to destroy him completely; and also conditions were good in Judah."

e) **2 Chronicles 32:26** "However, Hezekiah humbled the pride of his heart, both he and the inhabitants of Jerusalem, so that the wrath of the Lord did not come on them in the days of Hezekiah."

Question 4: Can you think of a time that God was humbling you?

5A - Sometimes we need to show humility.

a) **2 Kings 22:19** "because your heart was tender and you humbled yourself before the Lord when you heard what I spoke against this place and against its inhabitants that they should become a desolation and a curse, and you have torn your clothes and wept before Me, I truly have heard you," declares the Lord."

b) **Psalms 35:13** "But as for me, when they were sick, my clothing was sackcloth; I humbled my soul with fasting, And my prayer kept returning to my bosom."

Question 5: Have you ever done something to show your humility toward God?

6A - God will hear the prayers of the humble.

a) **2 Kings 22:19** "because your heart was tender and you humbled yourself before the Lord when you heard what I spoke against this place and against its inhabitants that they should become a desolation and a curse, and you have torn your clothes and wept before Me, I truly have heard you," declares the Lord."

b) **2 Chronicles 34:27** "Because your heart was tender and you humbled yourself before God when you heard His words against this place and against its inhabitants, and because you humbled yourself before Me, tore your clothes and wept before Me, I truly have heard you," declares the Lord."

6B - God's rescuing power can come to the humble person.

> **Job 22:29** "When you are cast down, you will speak with confidence, And the humble person He will save."

6C - Do this when you are in trouble with people.

> **Proverbs 6:3** "Do this then, my son, and deliver yourself; Since you have come into the hand of your neighbor, Go, humble yourself, and importune your neighbor."

6D - God will dwell with you when you are humble.

> **Isaiah 57:15** "For thus says the high and exalted One Who lives forever, whose name is Holy, "I dwell on a high and holy place, And also with the contrite and lowly of spirit In order to revive the spirit of the lowly And to revive the heart of the contrite."

6E - The humble person can become the greatest person.

a) **Proverbs 29:23** "A man's pride will bring him low, But a humble spirit will obtain honor."

b) **Luke 14:11** "For everyone who exalts himself will be humbled, and he who humbles himself will be exalted."

c) **Luke 18:14** "I tell you, this man went to his house justified rather than the other; for everyone who exalts himself will be humbled, but he who humbles himself will be exalted."

d) **James 4:10** "Humble yourselves in the presence of the Lord, and He will exalt you."

e) **1 Peter 5:6** "Therefore humble yourselves under the mighty hand of God, that He may exalt you at the proper time,"

Question 6: What are some ways you can be humble?

* * * * * * *

TIP #21

****

Collect "Grace Doors"

****

1A - It was Thanksgiving weekend, and a gentleman was waiting his turn to drive out of a grocery store parking lot. To his left, he saw an older woman backing out of her parking spot heading straight for his driver's door. It looked like she wasn't going to stop, so the man honked his horn, but her car kept going and hit his door. The two drivers got out of their vehicles to assess the damage, and to exchange driver's licenses and insurance information. The gentleman could smell alcohol on the breath of the other driver.

1B - About an hour later, the gentleman called the woman driver and told her, "I've decided not to pursue the insurance claim on the dented door. I am a handy person, so repairing the door is not a big deal for me. Plus, I know one day I'm going to make a mistake and will need grace, so I am "paying it forward" by giving you grace for the dented door. I hope you have a nice Thanksgiving weekend."

1C - The woman was speechless. Her husband had to come on the phone to finish the call. The gentleman explained to the husband what he had just told his wife. The husband said his wife was speechless and thanked the man very much for the call.

1D - This example shows what we mean by the term "Grace Door," a situation in which we give someone grace for a mistake they have made.

Question 1: Have you ever given someone grace like this? If so, can you tell us about it?

2A - The truth is, we all make mistakes, and it's only a matter of time before we make our next mistake. Thus, it's good to be prepared for them. One way to be prepared is to have "Grace Doors" in our "account." That means having a number of past instances where we have given grace to people for the mistakes they made that affected us.

2B - The Bible says that we reap what we sow. If we have given grace to others, we *ourselves* can expect to receive grace when *we* make a mistake. See the following scriptures about us reaping what we sow.

  a) **2 Corinthians 9:6** "Now this I say, he who sows sparingly will also reap sparingly, and he who sows bountifully will also reap bountifully."

b) **Galatians 6:7** "Do not be deceived, God is not mocked; for whatever a man sows, this he will also reap."

Question 2: Can you think of a time when you reaped what you sowed? Are you in a situation now in which you could give grace to someone?

3A - Grace Was God's Idea

Below are stories of grace in the Bible.

Noah was a righteous man living in a world of sinners. At the time, God wanted to destroy the human race and start again. Noah was the only righteous man living. Noah's history of right living caused him to find grace with God.

Genesis 6:8,9 "But Noah found grace in the eyes of the Lord. [9] These are the generations of Noah: Noah was a just man and perfect in his generations, and Noah walked with God."

3B - Lot

Another example of God giving grace to someone is the story of Lot and his family. They lived in the cities of Sodom and Gomorrah. These cities had become so filled with sin that many people were suffering because of it. God decided He had no choice but to destroy the cities.

In contrast, God gave grace to Lot and his family who lived there, by allowing them to escape before His fierce anger wiped out the cities.

Genesis 19:19 "Behold now, thy servant hath found grace in thy sight, and thou hast magnified thy mercy, which thou hast shewed unto me in saving my life;"

3C - Jacob

God gave Jacob twelve sons. His eleventh son was named Joseph; Joseph became Jacob's favorite son. Thus, the other brothers didn't like Joseph. One day they sold him to slave traders and then told Jacob a lion killed Joseph. Jacob was heart-broken. Joseph went through some ups and downs in a foreign country, but in the end he became a top leader in Egypt. When a famine gripped the area, Jacob and his family traveled to the one area with food – Egypt. There Jacob was reacquainted with his lost son Joseph – such grace from God! God also gave grace to Jacob by keeping him and his family alive during a famine.

Genesis 46:30 "And Israel said unto Joseph, Now let me die, since I have seen thy face, because thou art yet alive."

3D - God's Grace Toward Us

The most notable example of grace is when God, our Father, sent His only begotten son, Jesus, to pay the penalty for our sin, by dying on a cross. We deserved death because of our sin, but Jesus willingly died in our place. That is profound grace.

Romans 5:8 says, "*And Israel said unto Joseph, Now let me die, since I have seen thy face, because thou art yet alive.*"

Only a sinless man could pay the penalty of our sin, and that was Jesus.

3E - <u>Our Grace toward Others</u>

Just as God gave us grace through Jesus, God expects us to give grace to others.

a) **Matthew 6:12** "And forgive us our debts, as we also have forgiven our debtors."

b) **Ephesians 4:32** "Be kind to one another, tender-hearted, forgiving each other, just as God in Christ also has forgiven you."

c) **Colossians 3:13** "bearing with one another, and forgiving each other, whoever has a complaint against anyone; just as the Lord forgave you, so also should you."

If it is within our power to forgive someone, we should forgive them.

3F - However, it is good to keep in mind that we sometimes hurt people by letting them *off the hook* too easily. They could start feeling entitled to our forgiveness, thus abuse our good nature. Each case is different; so we need to pray for wisdom that God will help us know when to use "tough love," and when to freely forgive. For the most part, live a lifestyle of grace, and you will be given grace yourself.

* * * * * * *

TIP #22

****

Volunteer

****

1A - When our day-to-day life becomes a constant struggle, it can be tempting to just stay home and do nothing. However, great blessings await us if we will move out of our comfort zone and help make a difference in other people's lives. A great way to do this is through volunteering. Real benefits can be had, even if we only volunteer for an hour a week.

1B - It can be surprising how God uses our volunteering to direct us to new people who can enrich our lives. He can also use our past experiences to help us to do a good job in a volunteer position. Volunteering has a way of expanding our vision to new ideas we could never have come up with otherwise. Here's how volunteering can help us.

a) Volunteering can help take our mind off whatever is bothering us.

b) Volunteering helps us network with others.

c) Volunteering can lead to promotions.

d) Volunteering can advance our career.

e) Volunteering can help us live a more active lifestyle.

f) Volunteering can add a sense of fun and excitement to our lives.

Question 1: Can you tell us in what ways you've volunteered in the past? If so, how did it help you?

2A - <u>A Good Distraction</u>

Volunteering can help distract us from thinking negatively. This is a huge benefit for people who struggle with anxiety or depression. Choosing a volunteer position that entails meeting new people and learning new skills helps this further.

Question 2: Can you tell us about the people you've met and things you've learned while volunteering?

3A - <u>Networking for Employment</u>

Volunteering can help us network with others. People who watch us volunteer may know an employer who is looking to hire for a paid position.

3B - <u>Promotion</u>

Doing a good job as a volunteer prepares us for greater responsibility in the future. The Bible says, if we are faithful in little, God can entrust us with greater.

a) **Matthew 25:23** "His master said to him, 'Well done, good and faithful slave. You were faithful with a few things, I will put you in charge of many things; enter into the joy of your master."

b) **Luke 16:10** "He who is faithful in a very little thing is faithful also in much; and he who is unrighteous in a very little thing is unrighteous also in much."

So get ready for promotion!

3C - <u>Above the Rest</u>

More than ever employers are looking to give back to their communities. Thus, some of them look for people who like to volunteer. If our resume shows volunteer work, it can put us ahead of other candidates who haven't volunteered.

Question 3: Has volunteering helped you meet key people or led to a promotion in your career?

4A - <u>More Active</u>

For someone who struggles with depression, a volunteer position that requires physical activity can help them feel more productive, improve their physical health, and improve their sleep.

Question 4: Have you ever had a physically active volunteer position? If so, how did it help you?

5A - <u>Fun</u>

Some volunteer positions require us to do activities with people. Some of these activities can lead to some great fun, making the exercise beneficial for both the volunteer and the people being helped.

Question 5: Have you ever had enjoyable times volunteering?

6A - <u>Volunteering (Serving) in the Bible</u>

There are a lot of Bible verses on being of service to others.

a) **Proverbs 11:25** "The generous man will be prosperous, And he who waters will himself be watered."

b) **Matthew 20:26** "It is not this way among you, but whoever wishes to become great among you shall be your servant,"

c) **Mark 9:35** "Sitting down, He called the twelve and *said to them, "If anyone wants to be first, he shall be last of all and servant of all.""

d) **Mark 10:42-44** "Calling them to Himself, Jesus *said to them, "You know that those who are recognized as rulers of the Gentiles lord it over them; and their great men exercise authority over them. [43] But it is not this way among you, but whoever wishes to become great among you shall be your servant; [44] and whoever wishes to be first among you shall be slave of all.""

e) **Mark 10:45** "For even the Son of Man did not come to be served, but to serve, and to give His life a ransom for many.""

f) **John 12:26** "If anyone serves Me, he must follow Me; and where I am, there My servant will be also; if anyone serves Me, the Father will honor him.""

g) **Galatians 5:13** "For you were called to freedom, brethren; only do not turn your freedom into an opportunity for the flesh, but through love serve one another.""

h) **1 Corinthians 4:1-2** "Let a man regard us in this manner, as servants of Christ and stewards of the mysteries of God. In this case, moreover, it is required of stewards that one be found trustworthy.""

i) **Ephesians 2:10** "For we are His workmanship, created in Christ Jesus for good works, which God prepared beforehand so that we would walk in them.""

j) **Philippians 2:5-7** "Have this attitude in yourselves which was also in Christ Jesus, [6] who, although He existed in the form of God, did not regard equality with God a thing to be grasped, [7] but emptied Himself, taking the form of a bond-servant, and being made in the likeness of men:""

6B - A Key Place to Volunteer

A great place to volunteer is at church. Here are some reasons why.

a) We get to know some of the nicest people around.

b) We work together to achieve a common goal.

c) We get a sense of purpose.

d) We can be used of God to inspire someone who may be struggling.

e) We position ourselves to meet God in a very special way – serving in His house.

f) We encourage our pastor and the leadership team by volunteering.

g) We become good role models to those around us.

6C - The Nicest People

Many older people have been church members for a long time and have developed into strong, cheerful Christians. Their love for God, for their church, and for the community is attractive. Serving at church puts us into direct contact with these amazing people, and it positions us to be blessed by their Christ-filled lives. This blessing is especially helpful when we are recovering from an emotional wound.

Also, these fine Christian people become great candidates for the role of support team members in our life. See more on this in Tip #5 – Form a Support Team.

Question 6: Have you made some quality friendships at a local church? If so, can you tell us about them?

7A - Achieving a Common Goal

A popular saying is, "Teamwork makes the dream work." This can apply to church life. Every church member has unique, God-given strengths, and when church members are operating in their gifts together, the results can be remarkable.

7B - Teamwork in the Bible

Below is a profound story that perfectly demonstrates the power of unity.

Genesis 11:1-8 "Now the whole earth used the same language and the same words. [2] It came about as they journeyed east, that they found a plain in the land of Shinar and settled there. [3] They said to one another, "Come, let us make bricks and burn *them* thoroughly." And they used brick for stone, and they used tar for mortar. [4] They said, "Come, let us build for ourselves a city, and a tower whose top *will reach* into heaven, and let us make for ourselves a name, otherwise we will be scattered abroad over the face of the whole earth." [5] The LORD came down to see the city and the tower which the sons of men had built."

7C - "[6] The LORD said, "Behold, they are one people, and they all have the same language. And this is what they began to do, and now nothing which they purpose to do will be impossible for them. [7] Come, let Us go down and there confuse their language, so that they will not understand one another's speech." [8] So the LORD scattered them abroad from there over the face of the whole earth; and they stopped building the city."

7D - These people had discovered the power of unity. But because the goal was something that displeased God, God decided to confuse their languages and scatter them all over the earth. Indeed, there is great power in teamwork.

Question 7: Have you ever helped out on a big project at church? If so, how did it feel?

8A - Sense of Purpose

One of the easiest ways to breathe new life into a depressed person is by helping them choose an inspirational goal. This also applies to churches. A good church leader can help a church maintain vibrancy by choosing great goals for the church to reach for.

8B - Volunteering at Church

A church should take time to help members see the importance of the various jobs that need to be done for the church, and they should gladly take time to explain thoroughly the tasks at hand. As well, the leaders should take time to see that the job was done properly, and if needed, lovingly offer helpful tips on how to improve the job next time. They should also express appreciation for all that has been done. All of this validates the church members and gives them a sense of importance for their contribution to the church.

Question 8: Have you ever felt a sense of purpose for the tasks you have taken on at your church?

Question 9: Have you ever been sincerely thanked for your contribution at your church? How did it feel?

10A - <u>Inspire Someone</u>

When we take time to help at church, we can meet new people. Some of these people may be struggling. Even people who look as if everything is going well could be good at hiding their pain. God has a way of letting us know who these hurting people are, so we can befriend them and inspire them.

Question 10: Has God ever helped you meet people at church who needed a friend?

11A - <u>Meeting God in a Very Special Way</u>

In essence, the body of believers is God's home. His holiness and love should be evident in a local church. When it is, this draws God's presence. Whenever we walk into a church, or volunteer at a church, we should have a sense of optimism that in some way we will meet with God and receive an impartation of His power and grace in our life. When you go to church, be expectant! That is faith!

Here is a Bible story of a miracle that happened at a local church.

11B - **Acts 3:1-8** "Now Peter and John were going up to the temple at the ninth *hour*, the hour of prayer. [2] And a man who had been lame from his mother's womb was being carried along, whom they used to set down every day at the gate of the temple which is called Beautiful, in order to beg alms of those who were entering the temple. [3] When he saw Peter and John about to go into the temple, he *began* asking to receive alms. [4] But Peter, along with John, fixed his gaze on him and said, "Look at us!"

11C - And he *began* to give them his attention, expecting to receive something from them. [6] But Peter said, "I do not possess silver and gold, but what I do have I give to you: In the name of Jesus Christ the Nazarene—walk!" [7] And seizing him by the right hand, he raised him up; and immediately his feet and his ankles were strengthened. [8] With a leap he stood upright and *began* to walk; and he entered the temple with them, walking and leaping and praising God."

Question 11: Do you go to church with a sense of optimism that God is going to reveal Himself to you?

12A - <u>Encourage Your Pastor</u>

Being a pastor or an elder in a local church can be a difficult job. Volunteering our time to help the church can mean so much to a pastor and others in leadership. It can help energize them to be all that God needs them to be, at that church.

Question 12: Have you ever taken time to show appreciation to your pastor and the church staff?

13A - <u>Beware of Complaining at Church</u>

It is important when we serve at our church that we do not fall into the habit of complaining about the church or its members. Gossip in a church can be extremely harmful. We should be ready to take someone aside to explain this truth to them if we see they are bothered by a church-related problem. We should even consider helping the person resolve the issue at hand. For more on this, go to Tip #7 – Speak Right Words, and Tip #12 – Don't Judge. Below are some scriptures that caution us to avoid complaining.

a) **Ephesians 4:29** "Let no unwholesome word proceed from your mouth, but only such a word as is good for edification according to the need of the moment, so that it will give grace to those who hear."

b) **Philippians 2:14** "Do all things without grumbling or disputing;"

c) **James 5:9** "Do not complain, brethren, against one another, so that you yourselves may not be judged; behold, the Judge is standing right at the door."

Question 13: Have you ever helped a person resolve an issue they had about the church?

14A - Become a Role Model

Churches, in general, and growing churches especially, need good role models for people it be inspired by, and to follow. Here are two scriptures on being a good example.

a) **Matthew 5:16** "Let your light so shine before men, that they may see your good works, and glorify your Father which is in heaven."

b) **1 Timothy 4:12** "Let no man despise thy youth; but be thou an example of the believers, in word, in conversation, in charity, in spirit, in faith, in purity."

Question 14: Have you ever been inspired by someone at your church? What was it about them that caught your attention?

15A - In the verse below, Jesus tells us that the harvest is plenteous but the laborers are few. Therefore, churches often need more volunteers.

Matthew 9:37-38 "Then He said to His disciples, "The harvest is plentiful, but the workers are few. Therefore beseech the Lord of the harvest to send out workers into His harvest."

New people will be attracted to the church when they see members doing their best to share the gospel message, either one-to-one, or by volunteering in larger evangelistic projects.

15B - Jesus gave us the Great Commission, to go out and make disciples of all men and women, teaching them all that Jesus taught us. Some churches are taking this very seriously, and are developing movie-producing skills in order to create impressive, full-length movies. These movies present the gospel in ways that everyday people can relate to. Whatever methods our church uses to promote the gospel, it will require people to be committed to the tasks, people willing to be good role models where they are.

Question 15: Has your church talked about big ways in which to spread the gospel of Jesus Christ?

16A - Volunteering is definitely a helpful strategy to improve your mood and aim your life in the direction of success.

* * * * * * *

TIP #23

****

Conquer the Addiction

****

1A - Addictions are fast becoming a major problem in our communities, with some areas reaching crisis levels. Therefore the church should be ready to meet the needs of people caught in a cycle of defeat due to addictions.

1B - Any activity we feel compelled to do regularly, to feel better, could be an addiction. We shouldn't be fooled by the low statistics of a behavior. If we need something to dull emotional pain, we should assess the root cause of this urge to see if it is an addiction. Some of the more common addictions are over-eating, alcohol, drugs, pornography, sex, shopping, gambling, video gaming, television, and work. Sadly, addictions are even prevalent in the church. We need God to help us in this regard.

Below are some scriptures related to addiction.

a) **Deuteronomy 21:20** "They shall say to the elders of his city, 'This son of ours is stubborn and rebellious, he will not obey us, he is a glutton and a drunkard."

b) **Proverbs 23:21** "For the heavy drinker and the glutton will come to poverty, And drowsiness will clothe one with rags."

c) **Matthew 11:19** "The Son of Man came eating and drinking, and they say, 'Behold, a gluttonous man and a drunkard, a friend of tax collectors and sinners!' Yet wisdom is vindicated by her deeds."

d) **Luke 7:34** "The Son of Man has come eating and drinking, and you say, 'Behold, a gluttonous man and a drunkard, a friend of tax collectors and sinners!"

Question 1: What addictions do people, you know, struggle with today?

2A - <u>Reasons to Break an Addiction</u>

<u>Financial Loss</u>

One significant loss that can come from addictions is financial. Life *without* an addiction can be difficult enough when it comes to managing our money; add an addiction and our financial stability is further weakened.

The Bible advises us to stay clear of debt.

a) **Deuteronomy 15:6** "For the Lord your God will bless you as He has promised you, and you will lend to many nations, but you will not borrow; and you will rule over many nations, but they will not rule over you."

b) **Proverbs 22:7** "The rich rules over the poor, And the borrower becomes the lender's slave."

c) **Luke 14:28** "For which one of you, when he wants to build a tower, does not first sit down and calculate the cost to see if he has enough to complete it?"

d) **Romans 13:8** "Owe nothing to anyone except to love one another; for he who loves his neighbor has fulfilled the law."

Question 2: Can you think of anyone who is in debt because of an addiction?

3A - Loss of Relationships

Many families have been torn apart because of a loved one who is entrenched in an addiction. Although there are many support groups in almost every community, there are still people who are not getting the help they need to break free of their addiction.

Question 3: Can you think of anyone who is going through great stress because of a loved one caught in an addiction?

4A - Loss of Time

Another loss, is the loss of time that we spend engrossed in our addiction. The family of a famous lead singer of a 1970s music group reported that the singers dying words were, "So much wasted time..." Wasted time can be something we *all* could assess in our lives, more so, for those with addiction.

4B - Below we see the Bible cautions us to beware of wasting time.

a) **Psalms 90:12** "So teach us to number our days, That we may present to You a heart of wisdom."

b) **Ephesians 5:16** "making the most of your time, because the days are evil."

c) **Colossians 4:5** "Conduct yourselves with wisdom toward outsiders, making the most of the opportunity."

Question 4: Can you think of anyone who wastes time because of an addiction?

5A - Loss of Public Services

Another consequence of addictions is the toll it takes on police services, first responders, and hospital staff. It isn't just the cost of their time; it is also the emotional toll it takes on these public service providers while doing their jobs. They see people at their worst, and it can cause them to develop PTSD (Post Traumatic Stress Disorder), a debilitating mental illness that can lead to suicide.

Question 5: Can you think of anyone who is in public service and has to provide care for those with addictions? How does their job affect them?

6A - <u>Toll on Children</u>

Nobody wants to see children get hurt, but this can happen because of addictions. Children don't know how to mentally process something like an angry parent or sibling who is fighting an addiction. The frightening experiences children are exposed to can have a profound, negative effect on them for the rest of their lives. Further, an addiction can be inherited by the child, and thus become a generational problem within families.

Question 6: Can you think of any children who have been traumatized because of addiction?

7A - <u>Toll on Industry</u>

A notable council on drug addiction states that drug abuse alone costs employers $80 billion a year. High employee turnover rates, lower quality of work, workplace theft, absenteeism, accidents, and sick time, all play a part in reducing profitability for corporations. Losses corporately can mean fewer finances going to community endeavors.

Question 7: Can you think of anyone who works in human resources, or owns a company, and deals with employees who have addictions? What do they say about helping employees with addictions?

8A - <u>Breaking the Addiction</u>

Addictions can be challenging to break. There needs to be a sincere desire to quit the addiction. From a Christian standpoint, we could see the addiction as sin. We must reach a point where we are so turned off by our *sin,* that we want to do something about it.

8B - Jesus said, if you want to follow Him, you have to deny yourself. People with addictions find it difficult to deny themselves. See scriptures below.

a) **Mark 8:34** "And He summoned the crowd with His disciples, and said to them, "If anyone wishes to come after Me, he must deny himself, and take up his cross and follow Me.""

b) **Luke 9:23 & Matthew 16:24** "And He was saying to them all, "If anyone wishes to come after Me, he must deny himself, and take up his cross daily and follow Me.""

Question 8: In what way do you deny yourself?

9A - The Bible says that one of the fruits of the Spirit is self-control.

Galatians 5:22-23 "But the fruit of the Spirit is love, joy, peace, patience, kindness, goodness, faithfulness, gentleness, self-control; against such things there is no law."

Most addicts will admit nonetheless that they have very little self-control.

Question 9: How would you rate your level of self-control?

10A - Below are some steps we can take that can help us break an addiction.

<u>Step 1 - Ask Ourselves "Why Do We Do It?"</u>

Often there is a mental health condition causing us to have an addiction. Many people need relief from symptoms of guilt, anxiety, or depression. Once we resolve the mental health issue, our addiction will be easier to beat.

Question 10: Do you know anyone who has pinpointed the root cause of why they have an addiction?

11A - <u>Step 2 - Think Rationally About the Addiction</u>

Many people don't think rationally about their addiction. They tell themselves it isn't as bad as it is. They minimize the significance of the addiction and its effect on their life.

Question 11: Do you know anyone who minimizes the effects of their addiction?

12A - <u>Step 3 - Pray</u>

It is helpful to ask God for His assistance in breaking our addiction. Some people testify that God miraculously healed them of their addiction instantaneously. Since this is possible, we, too, can aim our faith toward God to give us a complete and instant healing from our addiction. It may seem too large a task to ask, but we remind ourselves that God takes great pleasure in people who are bold enough to ask Him for big things. (For more on this read Tip #9 – Develop Your Faith.)

12B - When we pray a prayer of this nature, it is helpful to couple our prayer with action. We might want to write out our prayer and the date we prayed it, as a memorial to ourselves and to God that we have invited Him into this great need we have, and that we are expecting Him to give us this healing.

12C - We could also ask the elders of our church to anoint us with oil and pray a prayer of healing. The Bible instructs us to do this for those who need healing in their physical bodies, but it can also be used for breaking an addiction.

> **James 5:14** "Is anyone among you sick? Then he must call for the elders of the church and they are to pray over him, anointing him with oil in the name of the Lord:"

12D - Another way to couple our prayer with action is by disposing of any of the addictive substance we may still have in our possession.

Another way to couple our prayer with action is by giving a donation. We aren't *buying* our healing; giving a donation is just another way to show God we are serious about our request and that we are willing to sacrifice for it. If our finances are low, we can volunteer our time to help someone.

12E - <u>Our Prayer</u>

The actual prayer that we pray doesn't have to be long or perfect. It can be as simple as, *"God, I believe Jesus died for my sins, and for the healing of my body. My body (or mind) needs to be set free from this addiction. Please heal me, so I am no longer controlled by this substance (or action). I ask this in Jesus's name."*

12F - We could then call someone from our church and tell them what we have just prayed and done, and ask them to help us keep our commitment to God, to never go back to the addiction.

Whether our healing is instant or gradual, below are some practical steps we can take to help ourselves stay free of our addiction.

Question 12: Do you know anyone who God has set free from addiction?

13A - <u>Step 3 - Replace Bad Habits with Good Habits</u>

The Victory Tips Program suggests that we take up memorizing Bible verses. We can become so busy learning new verses that we distract ourselves from the thoughts of the addiction. This also is a great way to get closer to God.

Question 13: Do you know anyone who successfully replaced bad habits with good habits?

14A - <u>Step 4 - Identify Trigger Times</u>

There can be times during our day when we are more prone to give in to our addiction, such as break times, meal times, evenings, pay-days, holidays, etc. We can prepare for these times by having other activities to do in place of the negative habit; perhaps something healthy like focused breathing, an exercise routine, a relaxation routine, prayer or Bible study.

Question 14: Can you suggest activities to do in place of addictive behaviors?

15A - <u>Step 5 - Limit Access to the Substance</u>

One way to cut off access to our substance is by not carrying cash. Not having money can prevent us from purchasing our drug of choice. If we have an online addiction, we could consider removing the computer from our home.

We could also avoid going near places we used to go to for our "fix."

As well, we could also break off friendships with those who have addictions, and make friends with people who don't have addictions. A church can be a great place to meet people without addictions.

Question 15: Can you think of other ways a person might cut off access to their drug of choice?

16A - <u>Step 6 - Be Accountable to People</u>

It can be helpful to find people we can call every day, to let them know how we're doing. If we have the person's permission, we don't have to feel bad if we need to contact them multiple times a day. It can be helpful to find several people in our lives to call, in case one isn't available when we need to speak with them. Surrounding ourselves with people who care about us, and who never feel we have contacted them too much, is very helpful. We shouldn't let shame prevent us from getting the help we need. We may need a lot of support at present, but we should realize that someday we can be the support person for someone else in need. For more on this topic see Tip #5 – Form a Support Team.

Question 16: If you have an addiction, can you think of people who may be helpful in providing accountability for you? How might you find others?

17A - <u>Step 7 – Learn About the Addiction</u>

Knowledge is power. We can do research online, or we can get books, CDs, or DVDs, at the library.

We could also find good recovery groups and start attending meetings regularly. We can also learn much by speaking with people who have conquered a similar addiction.

Question 17: Do you know of good resources to help people with addictions?

18A - <u>Step 8 – Reward Yourself</u>

We can be our own best friend by rewarding ourselves when we make even the slightest progress in our attempts to conquer our addiction.

Question 18: What are good ways you reward yourself?

19A - With God's help we can become overcomers in every way of or lives, including conquering addictions. We can begin to see ourselves as a conqueror. For more on this concept see Tip #14 – Develop a Conqueror Mentality. For more practical help in breaking an addiction, contact us.

* * * * * * *

TIP #24

****

Have a Vision for Your Life

****

1A - God has created us for a purpose. The Bible says He laid out the purpose for our lives before we were even born. **Ephesians 2:10** says, *"For we are His workmanship, created in Christ Jesus for good works, which God prepared beforehand so that we would walk in them."*

Our life's purpose will eventually begin manifesting at some point in our life. We call this birthing stage of a mission, a vision. It is a captivating, irresistible sense of something we must do. It can come suddenly, or it can happen slowly, over days, weeks, and months. The following scripture gives us a sense of the importance of a vision.

Proverbs 29:18 "Where there is no vision, the people are unrestrained, But happy is he who keeps the law."

Question 1: Have you ever had a vision or a sense of what you were supposed to do?

2A - <u>Begin with a Prayer</u>

Life can have a way of *"knocking the wind out of us."* The challenges of life can sometimes seem impossible to conquer, and we are tempted to adopt a defeatist attitude. But just because one door of opportunity closes on us, doesn't mean new doors can't open. If a dream we've been holding on to falls apart, we can ask God for a new purpose for our life, and He will give it to us. Here is a well known Bible verse on getting guidance. We can use it to help steer us to our next vision, or goal, in life.

Proverbs 3:5-6 "Trust in the Lord with all your heart And do not lean on your own understanding.
In all your ways acknowledge Him, And He will make your paths straight."

Question 2: Have you ever felt like you couldn't go any further? If so, would you like to share with us what happened?

3A - <u>Become Unstoppable!</u>

It may surprise us what new directions God has for us. When they come, they will infuse us with a new zest for life. The following are some people in the Bible who had a vision for their life, and it caused them to become unstoppable.

a) Noah had a vision of building a large boat for God. Doing so took him a very long time (120 years), but he didn't give up. It gave him purpose, and it saved him and his family! (Genesis 6 & 7)

b) Moses had a vision of setting the Israelites free from the Egyptians. After God met him at a burning bush, He sent Moses to complete the mission. Doing so was stressful, but he kept at it until the Israelites were free. (Exodus 3)

c) Joseph had a vision of his family bowing down to him. Life became very difficult for him but he kept living for God, and God eventually made him Prime Minister of Egypt! Amazingly, his family did bow down before him! (Genesis 37)

d) Paul had a vision of preaching the gospel for Jesus all over the world. No matter how hard it was, he kept at it, and eventually, God used his preaching and his letters to reach millions of people for Christ. His letters make up most of the New Testament!

Question 3: Have you ever received new direction for your life? If so, how did it make you feel?

4A - <u>Beware of Some Visions</u>

The peculiar thing about a vision is that it can either be a positive, life-giving goal, or it can be a negative, hurtful purpose. An example of a negative vision is in the life of Haman, a vizier under King Ahasuerus of Persia, who lived around 465 B.C. Haman took offense to Mordecai, a Jew, for not bowing down to him when he went by.

Esther 3:6 "But he disdained to lay hands on Mordecai alone, for they had told him who the people of Mordecai were; therefore Haman sought to destroy all the Jews, the people of Mordecai, who were throughout the whole kingdom of Ahasuerus."

4B - Haman built a set of gallows 50 feet high, and a 75 foot high sharpened, impaling pole, with which to impale Mordecai. These were eventually used to impale Haman, himself. Haman's vision cost him his life.

Question 4: Have you ever had an irresistible sense of what you were supposed to do, but had it hurt you?

5A - <u>Check Your Vision</u>

So we've prayed for direction. We've gotten an answer. It feels good. What do we do next? We can check our vision by asking ourselves the following questions. Answers to these questions can help determine the value of the new goal we have in mind.

a) What does God's Word say about this new vision?

b) What do my church friends say about this new direction?

c) What do respected church leaders think of the idea?

6B - <u>Heavenly Value</u>

In evaluating a vision, something to consider is the spiritual value of the work we would like to do. The following verses tell us our works will one day, "be burned," to see if there is any spiritual value in them.

1 Corinthians 3:13-15 "each man's work will become evident; for the day will show it because it is *to be* revealed with fire, and the fire itself will test the quality of each man's work. [14] If any man's work which he has built on it remains, he will receive a reward. [15] If any man's work is burned up, he will suffer loss; but he himself will be saved, yet so as through fire."

Question 5: Have you ever told others about your vision? If so, how did they respond?

6A - Once the concept of the vision is affirmed, take time to write it out in more detail. The following verse tells us to write out our vision.

Habakkuk 2:2-3 "Then the LORD answered me and said, "Record the vision And inscribe *it* on tablets, That the one who reads it may run. [3] "For the vision is yet for the appointed time; It hastens toward the goal and it will not fail. Though it tarries, wait for it; For it will certainly come, it will not delay."

Most visions can only be accomplished with help from others. Writing out the vision gives new people a way of understanding what the vision is and how to help bring it into reality.

Question 6: Have you ever had a yearning desire to do something in which you took time to write it out?

7A - Getting Help

Next, we'll want to create a plan of how to bring this vision to reality. It is a good idea to contact people who have some skill in the kind of work that the vision requires. The Bible says a lot about getting good counsel.

a) **Proverbs 12:15** "The way of a fool is right in his own eyes, But a wise man is he who listens to counsel."

b) **Proverbs 15:22** "Without consultation, plans are frustrated, But with many counselors they succeed."

c) **Proverbs 24:6** "For by wise guidance you will wage war, And in abundance of counselors there is victory."

7B - At this point, it's important to be careful who we share our vision with. Some "would-be" helpers might only see reasons why our vision could never come to pass. This can cause doubt in our mind and discourage us from going any further with the goal.

Question 7: Have you ever contacted someone for advice about a vision you had? How did they respond?

8A - Set Goals

It's important to start setting goals so we can track our progress. This will also help us accomplish tasks in a shorter time frame. Our counselors can help us with this. The following scriptures challenge us to work hard at completing our God-given tasks.

a) **2 Chronicles 15:7** "But you, be strong and do not lose courage, for there is reward for your work."

b) **Proverbs 21:5** "The plans of the diligent lead surely to advantage, But everyone who is hasty comes surely to poverty."

c) **Philippians 3:14** "I press on toward the goal for the prize of the upward call of God in Christ Jesus."

8B - <u>Stay in Prayer</u>

It is helpful to stay close to God in prayer throughout our work so we can detect any adjustments we may need to make along the way.

As an example, after Jesus was born, Joseph received a change of course from an angel in a dream.

Matthew 2:13 "Now when they had gone, behold, an angel of the Lord appeared to Joseph in a dream and said, "Get up! Take the Child and His mother and flee to Egypt, and remain there until I tell you; for Herod is going to search for the Child to destroy Him.""

8C - We should stay in prayer, so we don't waste time doing something we weren't supposed to do.

Psalm 127:1 "Unless the Lord builds the house, They labor in vain who build it; Unless the Lord guards the city, The watchman keeps awake in vain."

Enjoy the excitement of creating something new! God is the "Great Creator," so we'll be in good company when we include God in our project!

* * * * * * *

TIP #25

****

Be Thankful

****

1A - Another helpful attribute to develop in our lives is that of being thankful. Scientific research shows that thankfulness boosts the immune system and increases blood supply, both of which contribute to improved physical and emotional health. Research also shows that it enhances alertness, enthusiasm, energy, and sleep improvements. All of these benefits contribute to less stress, anxiety, and depression.

The Bible refers to thanksgiving many times. Below are some of the key verses for gratitude.

Question 1: How would you rate your level of thankfulness?

2A - Below is a verse that tells us to be thankful for all things. Does the Apostle Paul mean for us to be thank for bad things that happen to us, as well? Good question.

Ephesians 5:20 "always giving thanks for all things in the name of our Lord Jesus Christ to God, even the Father;"

Below is a verse that tells us to be thankful "in" all things. This is something we can definitely do, if not the above.

1 Thessalonians 5:18 "in everything give thanks; for this is God's will for you in Christ Jesus."

Question 2: Can you think of a time when you were thankful "for" or "in" a negative event in your life?

3A - <u>A Good Reason To Be Thankful – God's Mercy</u>

The Bible doesn't just say "give thanks," sometimes it says "O give thanks."

a) **Psalms 106:1** "Praise the Lord! Oh give thanks to the Lord, for He is good; For His lovingkindness is everlasting."

b) **Psalms 118:1** "Give thanks to the Lord, for He is good; For His lovingkindness is everlasting."

That means His mercy is so good; it implies, "Look! See how great it is!"

Question 3: How highly do you value God's mercy in your life? Can you tell us a time He showed great mercy to you?

4A - <u>Thankful In Times of Loss</u>

Life can also include times of loss. And while these losses can try to derail our lives, we can help offset the loss by, remembering, and, being thankful for, the times *before* the loss. Such as a loved one passing away or becoming ill. We can remember the good times before the loss of our loved one.

Or in the case of an automobile becoming too expensive to repair, we can throw a party for the years of service that we *did* get out of it.

Question 4: Has your life ever been derailed by a loss, but you found something to be thankful for in spite of it?

5A - A loss can be a difficult time in our lives. It is the perfect time to prove Christ's words that He spoke to the Apostle Paul, in **2 Corinthians 12:9**, *"...My grace is sufficient for you, for power is perfected in weakness..."* We can find hidden strength in Christ.

Question 5: Have you ever found unexpected grace to get through a hard time in your life?

6A - The verse below talks about the things we do and say, how we should do it all in the name of the Lord Jesus, and with thanksgiving to God.

> **Colossians 3:17** "Whatever you do in word or deed, do all in the name of the Lord Jesus, giving thanks through Him to God the Father."

6B - The scripture below tells us to present our requests to God with thanksgiving.

> **Philippians 4:6** "Be anxious for nothing, but in everything by prayer and supplication with thanksgiving let your requests be made known to God."

Here are other verses on thanksgiving.

a) **Colossians 2:6,7** "Therefore as you have received Christ Jesus the Lord, so walk in Him, having been firmly rooted and now being built up in Him and established in your faith, just as you were instructed, and overflowing with gratitude."

b) **Colossians 3:15** "Let the peace of Christ rule in your hearts, to which indeed you were called in one body; and be thankful."

c) **Colossians 4:2** "Devote yourselves to prayer, keeping alert in it with an attitude of thanksgiving."

Question 6: Are you in the habit of starting your prayer requests with thanksgiving?

7A - The following scripture tells us to enter His presence with thanksgiving.

> **Psalms 100:4** "Enter His gates with thanksgiving And His courts with praise. Give thanks to Him, bless His name."

7B - The following are other scriptures on being thankful.

a) **1 Chronicles 16:34** "O give thanks to the Lord, for He is good; For His lovingkindness is everlasting."

b) **Nehemiah 12:46** "For in the days of David and Asaph, in ancient times, there were leaders of the singers, songs of praise and hymns of thanksgiving to God."

c) **Psalm 26:7** "That I may proclaim with the voice of thanksgiving And declare all Your wonders."

d) **Psalm 50:14** "Offer to God a sacrifice of thanksgiving And pay your vows to the Most High."

e) **Psalm 69:30** "I will praise the name of God with song And magnify Him with thanksgiving."

f) **Psalm 95:2** "Let us come before His presence with thanksgiving, Let us shout joyfully to Him with psalms."

g) **Psalm 107:22** "Let them also offer sacrifices of thanksgiving, And tell of His works with joyful singing."

h) **Psalm 116:17** "To You I shall offer a sacrifice of thanksgiving, And call upon the name of the Lord."

i) **Psalm 147:7** "Sing to the Lord with thanksgiving; Sing praises to our God on the lyre,"

j) **Amos 4:5** "Offer a thank offering also from that which is leavened, And proclaim freewill offerings, make them known. For so you love to do, you sons of Israel," Declares the Lord God."

k) **Jonah 2:9** "But I will sacrifice to You With the voice of thanksgiving. That which I have vowed I will pay. Salvation is from the Lord."

l) **Colossians 3:15** "Let the peace of Christ rule in your hearts, to which indeed you were called in one body; and be thankful."

m) **Colossians 3:17** "Whatever you do in word or deed, do all in the name of the Lord Jesus, giving thanks through Him to God the Father."

n) **1 Timothy 4:4** "For everything created by God is good, and nothing is to be rejected if it is received with gratitude;"

o) **Hebrews 12:28** "Therefore, since we receive a kingdom which cannot be shaken, let us show gratitude, by which we may offer to God an acceptable service with reverence and awe:"

* * * * * * *

Tip #26

****

Welcome MLCs

****

1A - Life can be filled with challenges. Thus, it is good to be prepared when these challenges come around. One way to be prepared is to be able to welcome MLC's. "MLC" stands for Major Life Challenge. They are the more difficult times in our lives such as the death of a loved one, spouse wanting a divorce, negative diagnosis, job loss, serious injury, relocation, lawsuit, and financial loss. Each of these requires an adjustment in our thinking so we keep our peace of mind.

Question 1: Can you think of a time in your life when you were faced with an MLC? If so, how well did you handle it?

2A - Why "Welcome" MLCs?

At first glance, we might wonder why we would want to welcome one of these events in our lives. We will examine the reasons below.

First, as Christians, God requires us to live by faith. That means that we trust God in every aspect of our lives; this includes the difficult times. Our faith tells us that God can heal a negative situation, or bring good out of it.

a) **Romans 1:17** "But the righteous man shall live by faith." (Also found in Habakkuk 2:4, Galatians 3:11 and Hebrews 10:38.)

b) **2 Corinthians 12:9** "And He has said to me, "My grace is sufficient for you, for power is perfected in weakness." Most gladly, therefore, I will rather boast about my weaknesses, so that the power of Christ may dwell in me."

c) **Ephesians 3:20** "Now to Him who is able to do far more abundantly beyond all that we ask or think, according to the power that works within us,"

Question 2: Can you think of a time when your faith helped carry you through a major life challenge?

3A - God Can Replace

Another reason to have faith is that God can *replace* what has been lost, as in the case of Job. We talked briefly about Job in Tip #3 – Admit You Have a Problem.

Job was a very reverent follower of God. Satan told God that surely Job would curse Him if his life were negatively affected. God didn't think so, and He let Satan trouble Job's life to prove His point to Satan.

3B - The first trial was with the loss of farm animals.

Job 1:12-19 "Then the LORD said to Satan, "Behold, all that he has is in your power, only do not put forth your hand on him." So Satan departed from the presence of the LORD.[13] Now on the day when his sons and his daughters were eating and drinking wine in their oldest brother's house, [14] a messenger came to Job and said, "The oxen were plowing and the donkeys feeding beside them, [15] and the Sabeans attacked and took them. They also slew the servants with the edge of the sword, and I alone have escaped to tell you."

3C - "[16] While he was still speaking, another also came and said, "The fire of God fell from heaven and burned up the sheep and the servants and consumed them, and I alone have escaped to tell you." [17] While he was still speaking, another also came and said, "The Chaldeans formed three bands and made a raid on the camels and took them and slew the servants with the edge of the sword, and I alone have escaped to tell you."

3D - Job's second loss was the death of all his children.

"[18] While he was still speaking, another also came and said, "Your sons and your daughters were eating and drinking wine in their oldest brother's house, [19] and behold, a great wind came from across the wilderness and struck the four corners of the house, and it fell on the young people and they died, and I alone have escaped to tell you."

These were terrible losses for Job.

Question 3: Have you ever lost something valuable to you? If so, how did you respond?

4A - Job's Health

Job was then afflicted with boils all over his body.

Job 2:6-8 "So the LORD said to Satan, "Behold, he is in your power, only spare his life."[7] Then Satan went out from the presence of the LORD and smote Job with sore boils from the sole of his foot to the crown of his head. [8] And he took a potsherd to scrape himself while he was sitting among the ashes."

Question 4: Have you ever had a major health problem? If so, how did you handle it?

5A - Job's Relationships

Even Job's wife was no help to him. She told Job to "curse God and die."

Job never cursed God, but he did do something that he shouldn't have – he complained. In fact, the whole of Chapter 3 is a complaint about his misfortune. Following, are four of the verses of Chapter 3 that bear this out.

Job 3:3-6 "Let the day perish on which I was to be born, And the night *which* said, 'A boy is conceived.' [4] "May that day be darkness; Let not God above care for it, Nor light shine on it.[5] "Let darkness and black gloom claim it; Let a cloud settle on it; Let the blackness of the day terrify it. [6] "*As for* that night, let darkness seize it; Let it not rejoice among the days of the year; Let it not come into the number of the months."

Question 5: Have you ever complained about a problem in your life? If so, would you like to share with us what happened?

6A - <u>God Shows Up</u>

Thirty-six chapters later, after much philosophical talk from Job and his well-meaning friends, God corrected everyone's misunderstandings of why things happened as they did. Job repented, and then God began to bless Job. Job ended up getting twice as much back of what he lost.

Job 42:19 "The Lord restored the fortunes of Job when he prayed for his friends, and the Lord increased all that Job had twofold."

The story of Job gives us hope that God can make up for the losses that occur in our lives too.

Question 6: Have you ever experienced a great loss, and then received back more than you lost?

7A - Looking at Job's story, notice who was responsible for Job's loss. Job thought it was God, but it was actually Satan.

Job 1:12 "Then the Lord said to Satan, "Behold, all that he has is in your power, only do not put forth your hand on him." So Satan departed from the presence of the Lord."

Question 7: Have you ever had a loss in your life and blamed God for it?

8A - When Jesus was on earth, He attributed most of the people's problems to the work of Satan.

a) **Matthew 8:16** "When evening came, they brought to Him many who were demon-possessed; and He cast out the spirits with a word, and healed all who were ill."

b) **Matthew 9:33** "After the demon was cast out, the mute man spoke; and the crowds were amazed, and were saying, "Nothing like this has ever been seen in Israel."

c) **Matthew 12:22** "Then a demon-possessed man who was blind and mute was brought to Jesus, and He healed him, so that the mute man spoke and saw."

d) **Matthew 17:18** "And Jesus rebuked him, and the demon came out of him, and the boy was cured at once."

e) **Luke 13:11,16** "And there was a woman who for eighteen years had had a sickness caused by a spirit; and she was bent double, and could not straighten up at all. [16] And this woman, a daughter of Abraham as she is, whom Satan has bound for eighteen long years, should she not have been released from this bond on the Sabbath day?"

Question 8: Do you think your problems have come because of Satan?

9A - <u>What if it's My Fault?</u>

Sometimes our losses in life are brought about by our own poor choices. However, just because we sometimes make poor choices doesn't mean God won't help us. He responds to our faith, not because we always do everything right. Thus, we don't have to be discouraged with our mistakes; we can show God that we are trusting Him, and we become candidates for His help, even if we caused the problem.

Mark 11:24 "Therefore I say to you, all things for which you pray and ask, believe that you have received them, and they will be granted you."

Question 9: What can you do to show God that you are trusting Him to solve your present problem?

10A - Other Reasons to Welcome MLC's

As mentioned above, the first reason is to see the challenge as a way to stretch our faith. We sometimes need difficulties to help us grow spiritually.

Secondly, our correct responses to our challenges can bring pleasure to God as He sees us trust him every step of the way. We believe that no problem is too big for us when we have Jesus by our side, guiding us, and even praying for us. See below.

Romans 8:34 "who is the one who condemns? Christ Jesus is He who died, yes, rather who was raised, who is at the right hand of God, who also intercedes for us."

10B - Thirdly, we welcome MLC's because they teach us how to be victorious even though we have problems. Circumstances don't have to dictate how we feel. They force us to learn how to cast all our cares onto God. See the verses below.

a) **Psalm 55:22** "Cast your burden upon the Lord and He will sustain you; He will never allow the righteous to be shaken."

b) **Philippians 4:6** "Be anxious for nothing, but in everything by prayer and supplication with thanksgiving let your requests be made known to God."

c) **1 Peter 5:7** "casting all your anxiety on Him, because He cares for you."

10C - Fourthly, we welcome MLC's because after God delivers us, we'll have a powerful testimony to share with others who may be going through a similar challenge. In fact, our MLC can be the launch pad for a far-reaching ministry. Millions of people can be helped because of the victory we have found while going through a serious challenge.

10D - Fifthly, we welcome MLC's because we're simply curious about how God is going to deliver us. We picture ourselves as a bystander, someone on the outside looking in, observing how God is going to "fix" this situation at hand. This mindset helps us not to get overly engrossed in our problems.

10E - For any life challenge, it is good not to get overly stressed about it, but rather to trust God to solve it; even more so when it is a Major Life Challenge. True, there may be things we have to do to help solve our problem, but our primary focus is on God to solve it. This makes us candidates for His supernatural help.

10F - Remember that our peace is a reflection of our faith. When we have peace about a situation, we know our faith is intact. The following scriptures give us a sense of peace when we truly believe Jesus is in the middle of our life challenge.

10G - **John 14:1-12** "Do not let your heart be troubled; believe in God, believe also in Me. [2] In My Father's house are many dwelling places; if it were not so, I would have told you; for I go to prepare a place for you. [3] If I go and prepare a place for you, I will come again and receive you to Myself, that where I am, *there* you may be also. [4] And you know the way where I am going." [5] Thomas *said to Him, "Lord, we do not know where You are going, how do we know the way?" [6] Jesus said to him, "I am the way, and the truth, and the life; no one comes to the Father but through Me. [7] If you had known Me, you would have known My Father also; from now on you know Him, and have seen Him."

10H - "[8] Philip said to Him, "Lord, show us the Father, and it is enough for us." [9] Jesus said to him, "Have I been so long with you, and *yet* you have not come to know Me, Philip? He who has seen Me has seen the Father; how *can* you say, 'Show us the Father'? [10] Do you not believe that I am in the Father, and the Father is in Me? The words that I say to you I do not speak on My own initiative, but the Father abiding in Me does His works."

10J - "[11] Believe Me that I am in the Father and the Father is in Me; otherwise believe because of the works themselves. [12] Truly, truly, I say to you, he who believes in Me, the works that I do, he will do also; and greater *works* than these he will do; because I go to the Father. [13] Whatever you ask in My name, that will I do, so that the Father may be glorified in the Son. [14] If you ask Me anything in My name, I will do *it*."

Question 10: Can you recall a stressful situation in which you had complete peace that God was right beside you, helping you get through the ordeal?

11A - Final Reason

The final reason we want to welcome major life challenges is that the way we go through them becomes a testimony of the reality of Jesus and His help. People will take notice when they see us go through a challenge peacefully, knowing that they, themselves, would have difficulty going through it. That helps prove the reality of Jesus Christ, and it may be enough for some people to consider making Jesus the Lord of their lives. Don't be afraid of MLC's, instead welcome them. Squeeze out every bit of good that is in them.

Question 11: Can you think of a time when you went through a difficult situation with grace and peace? Did someone comment on how well you went through it?

12A – MLCs can be difficult to go through, but they can also lead us to some amazing growth spiritually.

* * * * * * *

TIP #27

****

Resolve Delayed Maturity

****

When I was a child, I used to speak like a child, think like a child, reason like a child; when I became a man, I did away with childish things. 1 Corinthians 13:11

1A - It is important for us to attain maturity in all aspects of our life. This is because we influence those around us. If people see us engage in certain behaviors, they will consider doing them as well. Thus it is essential to model maturity - emotionally, intellectually, behaviorally and spiritually. A healthy, thriving society depends on it.

1B - <u>Who is This Tip For?</u>

This Tip is primarily written for young people. Knowing vital information when we are young means we won't have to struggle through some pitfalls that catch young people off guard in today's society. This Tip will also alert us to weaknesses we may not know we have. Knowing our weaknesses, early in life, means we can guard them and work on them before they develop into unmanageable problems later in life.

Finally, knowing what a well-adjusted life looks like, early on, will better prepare us to raise our children successfully when that time comes.

Question 1: Can you think of any young people who are presently struggling in life?

2A - <u>Delayed Maturity</u>

Sometimes unhappiness is linked to areas of our lives that are not fully matured. Delayed maturity can come from early childhood trauma. It can also come from an unhealthy home environment growing up. Thirdly, it can from people we associate with during our adolescent and young adult years. Whatever the cause, delayed maturity can hinder us from developing inner peace, and from building friendships with emotionally healthy peers.

2B - <u>Delayed Maturity is Common</u>

Since it is difficult for anyone to go through childhood and adolescence without some form of negative influence, at home, at school, or within the community, most everyone has delayed maturity to some extent.

Question 2: Can you think of someone who has delayed maturity?

3A - <u>Making a Commitment</u>

The apostle Paul was confronted with this challenge at some point in his life. In our theme verse, it appears he made a conscientious decision to live in maturity. Here it is again.

1 Corinthians 13:11 "When I was a child, I used to speak like a child, think like a child, reason like a child; when I became a man, I did away with childish things."

For our good and the good of those around us, we too can make a conscientious decision that we will live in maturity in every area of our life. God gives us the power of choice. We can choose to make life decisions that lead us to success in all areas our lives. This is one of them.

3B - <u>Childhood Trauma</u>

One of the causes of delayed maturity is childhood trauma. Some examples of childhood trauma are assault, molestation, severe teasing, neglect, and other forms of mental, physical, and emotional abuse. Depending on a child's ability to process trauma, the result can be overwhelming fear that prevents the child from returning to a natural state of calm in their minds. Such ongoing stress can prevent normal emotional growth, thus, delaying their maturity.

Question 3: Can you think of someone who experienced childhood trauma? If so, are there any lingering effects from their past trauma in their life today?

4A - <u>Observations</u>

Occasionally, people will comment on our behavior peculiarities. Sometimes, we mistakenly embrace these peculiarities with a sense of pride, and carry on the behavior. For those of us unsure of our identities, these peculiarities can fill our need for individuality, but in an unhealthy way. We don't realize that the trait that people are noticing in us can hold us back from fully maturing. It is wise to take note of what others are saying about us. Their unwelcome observations may sting, but they illuminate our blind spots and alert us to some self-development needed in our lives.

4B - <u>Compare</u>

One way for us to detect if delayed maturity has affected our life can be by comparing our lives with other people's lives in our age group. To do so, we could compare aspects such as the level of inner peace, social skills, educational achievements, and career success.

This method can be deceiving, however, in that, if the people we are comparing ourselves to, are also lacking in maturity, then the determinations we make about ourselves will not be accurate.

Question 4: Based on successful people in your age range, how do you compare with them as far as level of inner peace, social skills, educational achievements, and career success?

5A - One way to detect delayed maturity in us can be if we tend to be gullible; easily lead away from truth.

Question 5: Can you think of anyone who is easily lead away from truth?

6A - <u>Disrespect</u>

Another way to detect delayed maturity in us can be by examining the comments people make toward us. If we have delayed maturity, we may sometimes be teased or disrespected.It might be difficult for us to see the disrespect since it may have been happening to us our whole life. We may need to ask a trusted person to help us see if there is any disrespect in what others are saying to us. If any exists, we may need to adopt new ways of acting and responding to those who disrespect us.

At this point, we may also want to determine if we are disrespecting ourselves. If so, we'll want to make changes to how we view ourselves, as well.

Question 6: Can you think of any adults who are frequently teased or disrespected? Do you feel they might have delayed maturity?

7A - <u>Respect and Christianity</u>

As Christians, we need to aim for maximum respect. People may not agree with our faith stance, but they should respect us for our commitment to living a godly life. Below are some related verses.

a) **1 Corinthians 4:1** "Let a man regard us in this manner, as servants of Christ and stewards of the mysteries of God."

b) **1 Timothy 4:12** "Let no one look down on your youthfulness, but rather in speech, conduct, love, faith and purity, show yourself an example of those who believe."

c) **Titus 2:15** "These things speak and exhort and reprove with all authority. Let no one disregard you."

7B - <u>Enabling</u>

Sometimes we enable people to carry on in their delayed maturity. For reasons of respect or sympathy, we may detect where people are emotionally, and we lower ourselves to their level of maturity. Doing this permits them to carry on acting the way they do.

7C - Enabling people in this way is particularly hurtful in the church of Jesus Christ. When we communicate the gospel message, it ought to come from a position of maturity. Otherwise, people may not respect the message we give.

Question 7: Can you think of anyone with delayed maturity with whom you lowered yourself to their level of maturity? Can you tell us about it?

8A - <u>Communication</u>

Another way to detect our delayed maturity can be in the content of our communications. In our desire to relate well with others, we can sometimes share too much information about our personal lives.

For example, in a job setting, it is best to present a professional persona that rarely goes into detail about our personal affairs.

Below are some Bible verses about talking too much.

a) **Proverbs 10:19** "When there are many words, transgression is unavoidable, But he who restrains his lips is wise."

b) **Proverbs 17:28** "Even a fool, when he keeps silent, is considered wise; When he closes his lips, he is considered prudent."

c) **Proverbs 21:23** "He who guards his mouth and his tongue, Guards his soul from troubles."

d) **Proverbs 29:20** "Do you see a man who is hasty in his words? There is more hope for a fool than for him."

e) **James 1:19** "This you know, my beloved brethren. But everyone must be quick to hear, slow to speak and slow to anger;"

For more on this subject see Tip #7 – Speak Right Words.

Question 8: Can you think of any adults who share too much personal information? Do you feel they might have delayed maturity?

9A - Speaking Skills

Another way to detect our delayed maturity can be if we have difficulty speaking to people, or have trouble talking to groups of people. Fear can prevent us from developing into calm, pleasant, enjoyable communicators.

Below are Bible verses about not fearing man.

a) **Deuteronomy 1:17** "You shall not show partiality in judgment; you shall hear the small and the great alike. You shall not fear man, for the judgment is God's. The case that is too hard for you, you shall bring to me, and I will hear it."

b) **1 Samuel 15:24** "Then Saul said to Samuel, "I have sinned; I have indeed transgressed the command of the Lord and your words, because I feared the people and listened to their voice.""

c) **Proverbs 29:25** "The fear of man brings a snare, But he who trusts in the Lord will be exalted."

d) **Isaiah 51:12** "I, even I, am He who comforts you. Who are you that you are afraid of man who dies And of the son of man who is made like grass,"

9B - Help with Speaking

A great organization that helps people become better communicators is Toastmasters. There are likely Toastmasters clubs near where you live. To find out where, go to www.toastmasters.org.

Question 9: Can you think of someone who has a speech impediment, or has trouble speaking to groups of people?

10A - Anger

Another way to detect delayed maturity in us can be if our personality is dominated by anger. As adults, we want to communicate in a respectful, mature way, without anger.

Here are two Bible verses telling us to avoid getting angry.

a) **Psalms 37:8** "Cease from anger and forsake wrath; Do not fret; it leads only to evildoing."

b) **Ephesians 4:31** "Let all bitterness and wrath and anger and clamor and slander be put away from you, along with all malice:"

For more information on anger, see Tip #18 - Eliminate Anger.

Question 10: Can you think of anyone who struggles with excessive anger? Do you feel they may have delayed maturity?

11A - Complaining and Being Critical

Another way to detect delayed maturity in us can be if we criticize and complain. As an adult, we want to avoid being critical and complaining. Criticizing and complaining is a quick way to lose good people as friends, and can hinder making new friends. An excellent book on this subject is: *How to Win Friends and Influence People by Dale Carnegie.*

For more on eliminating complaining, see Tip #7 – Speak Right Words, and Affirmation #4 – I Only Speak Right Words.

Below are some scriptures about not complaining.

a) **Numbers 11:1-4** "Now the people became like those who complain of adversity in the hearing of the Lord; and when the Lord heard it, His anger was kindled, and the fire of the Lord burned among them and consumed some of the outskirts of the camp."

b) **1 Corinthians 10:10** "Nor grumble, as some of them did, and were destroyed by the destroyer."

c) **Philippians 2:14** "Do all things without grumblings or disputing:"

Question 11: Can you think of any adults who have a problem with being critical or complaining? Do you feel they may have delayed maturity?

12A - Confidentiality

Another way to detect delayed maturity in us can be if we break confidentiality. This is a serious breach of trust. A mature person considers confidentiality before talking about other people.

The Bible talks about this problem in the verses below.

a) **Psalms 101:5** "Whoever secretly slanders his neighbor, him I will destroy; No one who has a haughty look and an arrogant heart will I endure."

b) **Proverbs 11:13** "He who goes about as a talebearer reveals secrets, But he who is trustworthy conceals a matter."

c) **Proverbs 17:9** "He who conceals a transgression seeks love, But he who repeats a matter separates intimate friends."

d) **Proverbs 20:19** "He who goes about as a slanderer reveals secrets, Therefore do not associate with a gossip."

e) **1 Timothy 5:13** "At the same time they also learn to be idle, as they go around from house to house; and not merely idle, but also gossips and busybodies, talking about things not proper to mention."

Question 12: Can you think of any adults who easily break confidentiality? Do you feel they might have delayed maturity?

13A - <u>Lying</u>

Another way to detect delayed maturity in us can be if we lie. In Tip #7 – Speak Right Words, we list 11 verses that caution us against lying.

Question 13: Can you think of anyone who frequently lies? Do you feel they have delayed maturity?

14A - <u>Entitlement Syndrome</u>

Another way to detect delayed maturity in us may be if we think we are entitled to things. We're not happy until we get what's coming to us. Children will have temper tantrums when they don't get what they want. Adults can sometimes think, act and speak out when they don't get what they want. It can even happen in a Christian context, "I'm God's child, so I deserve thus and thus." When things don't go the way we would like, we should be gracious about it, and trust God to bring things our way in His time.

Question 14: Can you think of anyone who feels the world owes them this or that? Do you feel they have delayed maturity?

15A - <u>Poor Work Attitude</u>

Another way to detect delayed maturity in us can be if we are not giving a 100% at our jobs. One of the reasons we show poor performance on our jobs is that our attitude is negative. A successful worker is one who offers top notch service while on the job. A way to brighten our attitude is to think of our job as a "close personal friend", and that we get to visit that "friend" every day.

Question 15: Can you think of anyone who doesn't want to work or has a negative attitude at work? If so, do you think their poor attitude is rooted in past trauma?

16A - <u>Dress and Hygiene</u>

Another way to detect delayed maturity in us can be how we dress, and how well we maintain our hygiene. We should seek to present ourselves well in public, remembering that we influence those around us. We should take care of our looks and hygiene without getting obsessed about our looks or how people view us.

Question 16: Can you think of any adults who frequently dress shabbily, or do not maintain their hygiene? Do you feel they might have delayed maturity?

17A - <u>Family Needs</u>

Another way to determine delayed maturity in us can be if we are not meeting all the needs of our family. We may have the time and ability to meet these needs, but we prefer to focus on other interests in our life. The Bible has strong words against this behavior.

a) **Ephesians 5:25** "Husbands, love your wives, just as Christ also loved the church and gave Himself up for her,"

b) **Ephesians 5:33** "Nevertheless, each individual among you also is to love his own wife even as himself, and the wife must see to it that she respects her husband."

c) **1 Timothy 5:8** "But if anyone does not provide for his own, and especially for those of his household, he has denied the faith and is worse than an unbeliever."

d) **1 Peter 3:7** "You husbands in the same way, live with your wives in an understanding way, as with someone weaker, since she is a woman; and show her honor as a fellow heir of the grace of life, so that your prayers will not be hindered."

Question 17: Can you think of any adults who aren't meeting the needs of their family members adequately? Do you feel they might have delayed maturity?

18A - <u>Financial Responsibility</u>

Another way to detect delayed maturity in us can be with the spending of our finances. As a responsible adult, we want to live within our means, financially. Preferably, we want to live debt free. Living under a load of debt can impact our happiness. Thus we need to have wisdom in budgeting and using our finances.

The Bible cautions us to stay clear of debt as stated below.

a) **Deuteronomy 15:6** "For the Lord your God will bless you as He has promised you, and you will lend to many nations, but you will not borrow; and you will rule over many nations, but they will not rule over you."

b) **Proverbs 22:7** "The rich rules over the poor, And the borrower becomes the lender's slave."

c) **Luke 14:28** "For which one of you, when he wants to build a tower, does not first sit down and calculate the cost to see if he has enough to complete it?"

d) **Romans 13:8** "Owe nothing to anyone except to love one another; for he who loves his neighbor has fulfilled the law."

18B - Retirement planning is also important for our financial health. As a responsible adult, we need to plan for our retirement. Thus we need to budget and invest so that when the time comes when we can no longer work, finances will be there to carry us through for the rest of our lives.

a) **Proverbs 13:22** "A good man leaves an inheritance to his children's children, And the wealth of the sinner is stored up for the righteous."

b) **1 Timothy 5:8** "But if anyone does not provide for his own, and especially for those of his household, he has denied the faith and is worse than an unbeliever."

Question 18: Can you think of anyone who misspends their finances or neglects to plan for retirement? Do you feel they might have delayed maturity?

19A - Another way to detect delayed maturity in us can be if we have multiple adult partners. It is best to make a commitment to one individual, to be faithful to that person, for life. We do this for our mutual good, the good of our family, and the good of society.

A helpful question to ask ourselves can be: "What would the world be like if everybody lived the way I live?"

Here are some Bible verses on being faithful to one spouse.

a) **Ephesians 5:25** "Husbands, love your wives, just as Christ also loved the church and gave Himself up for her,"

b) **Ephesians 5:33** "Nevertheless, each individual among you also is to love his own wife even as himself, and the wife must see to it that she respects her husband."

c) **1 Peter 3:7** "You husbands in the same way, live with your wives in an understanding way, as with someone weaker, since she is a woman; and show her honor as a fellow heir of the grace of life, so that your prayers will not be hindered."

Question 19: Can you think of any adults who are not committed to one spouse? Do you feel they might have delayed maturity?

20A - <u>Final Notes</u>

If you see someone who is delayed in their maturity, make it a consideration to befriend that individual and keep in touch with them. When the time comes for them to make important decisions in their life, you can be there to offer insight that may not be evident to them, thus helping them to prevent a crisis in their life.

Romans 15:1 "Now we who are strong ought to bear the weaknesses of those without strength and not just please ourselves."

20B - Wikipedia has a good definition of psychological maturity:

"Psychological maturity is the ability to respond to the environment in an appropriate manner. This response is generally learned rather than instinctive."

With God's help, we can learn how to develop into mature individuals who, in turn, become excellent examples for others to follow.

* * * * * * *

TIP #28

****

Sing

****

1A - According to a number of sources*, singing can help us overcome anxiety and depression. One such write-up is the August 16, 2013, *Time Magazine* article entitled, "Singing Changes Your Brain." See quotes below.

"When you sing, musical vibrations move through you, altering your physical and emotional landscape. Group singing, for those who have done it, is the most exhilarating and transformative of all. It takes something incredibly intimate, a sound that begins inside you, shares it with a roomful of people and it comes back as something even more thrilling: harmony."

1B - The article goes on to say, *"The elation may come from endorphins, a hormone released by singing, which is associated with feelings of pleasure. Or it might be from oxytocin, another hormone released during singing, which has been found to alleviate anxiety and stress. Oxytocin also enhances feelings of trust and bonding, which may explain why still more studies have found that singing lessens feelings of depression and loneliness."*

1C - A recent study even attempts to make the case that *"music evolved as a tool of social living,"* and that the pleasure that comes from singing together is our evolutionary reward for coming together cooperatively, instead of hiding alone.

Question 1: Have you experienced an improvement in your mood as a result of singing? What is your favorite style of music?

2A - <u>Singing "Plus God."</u>

Singing is a powerful force for good. Now, couple it to God's truths, and we have the potential for huge improvement in our mood. Here are two Bible examples of the power of singing:

In the Book of 2 Chronicles, we see how singing caused the Israelites to win a war.

2 Chronicles 20:21,22 "When he had consulted with the people, he appointed those who sang to the LORD and those who praised *Him* in holy attire, as they went out before the army and said, "Give thanks to the LORD, for His lovingkindness is everlasting." [22] When they began singing and praising, the LORD set ambushes against the sons of Ammon, Moab and Mount Seir, who had come against Judah; so they were routed."

2B - In Acts 16, we see how singing praises to God opened prison doors where Paul and Silas were imprisoned for preaching the gospel.

Acts 16:22-26 "The crowd rose up together against them, and the chief magistrates tore their robes off them and proceeded to order *them* to be beaten with rods. [23] When they had struck them with many blows, they threw them into prison, commanding the jailer to guard them securely; [24] and he, having received such a command, threw them into the inner prison and fastened their feet in the stocks. [25] But about midnight Paul and Silas were praying and singing hymns of praise to God, and the prisoners were listening to them; [26] and suddenly there came a great earthquake, so that the foundations of the prison house were shaken; and immediately all the doors were opened and everyone's chains were unfastened."

Question 2: Do you have any stories of how singing has helped you?

3A - There are many references in the Bible about singing. The following are scripture references highlighting the importance of singing.

Old Testament References

a) **Psalm 13:6** "I will sing to the Lord, Because He has dealt bountifully with me."

b) **Psalm 59:16** "But as for me, I shall sing of Your strength; Yes, I shall joyfully sing of Your lovingkindness in the morning, For You have been my stronghold And a refuge in the day of my distress."

c) **Psalm 95:1,2** "It is good to give thanks to the Lord And to sing praises to Your name, O Most High; To declare Your lovingkindness in the morning And Your faithfulness by night,"

d) **Psalm 100:1,2** "Shout joyfully to the Lord, all the earth. Serve the Lord with gladness; Come before Him with joyful singing."

e) **Psalm 104:33** "I will sing to the Lord as long as I live; I will sing praise to my God while I have my being."

f) **Psalm 147:1** "Praise the Lord! For it is good to sing praises to our God; For it is pleasant and praise is becoming."

New Testament References

g) **1 Corinthians 14:15** "What is the outcome then? I will pray with the spirit and I will pray with the mind also; I will sing with the spirit and I will sing with the mind also."

h) **Ephesians 5:19** "speaking to one another in psalms and hymns and spiritual songs, singing and making melody with your heart to the Lord;"

i) **Colossians 3:16** "Let the word of Christ richly dwell within you, with all wisdom teaching and admonishing one another with psalms and hymns and spiritual songs, singing with thankfulness in your hearts to God."

j) **James 5:13** "Is anyone among you suffering? Then he must pray. Is anyone cheerful? He is to sing praises."

3B - <u>Martin Luther Highly Endorsed Singing</u>

It may be interesting to know that the great reformer of the church, Martin Luther (1483-1546), highly endorsed singing praises to God. He wrote these words:

"When man's natural ability is whetted and polished to the extent that it becomes an art, then do we note with great surprise the great and perfect wisdom of God in music, which is, after all, His product and His gift; we marvel when we hear music in which one voice sings a simple melody, while three, four, or five other voices play and trip lustily around the voice that sings its simple melody and adorn this simple melody wonderfully with artistic musical effects, thus reminding us of a heavenly dance where all meet in a spirit of friendliness, caress, and embrace. . . ."

3C - *"A person who gives this some thought and yet does not regard it [music] as a marvelous creation of God, must be a clodhopper indeed and does not deserve to be called a human being; he should be permitted to hear nothing but the braying of asses and the grunting of hogs." (Luther, "Preface to Georg Rhau's Symphoniae iucundae," LW 53, cited by Buszin in "Luther on Music," The Musical Quarterly 32, no. 1 [1946]: 85)*

3D - <u>God Sings Over You</u>

It may surprise us to know that God sings over us.

Zephaniah 3:17 "The Lord your God is in your midst, A victorious warrior. He will exult over you with joy, He will be quiet in His love, He will rejoice over you with shouts of joy."

Question 3: Do you sing to the Lord in your daily walk with Him?

4A - <u>An Act of Faith</u>

Singing can be an act of faith. If we are feeling so low that all we want to do is go to bed and pull the covers over us, we can begin to sing God's praises. That is an act of faith, and it gets God's attention.

Here are verses about using our will to sing praises to God.

a) **Numbers 21:17** "Then Israel sang this song: "Spring up, O well! Sing to it!"

b) **Judges 5:3** ""Hear, O kings; give ear, O rulers! I—to the Lord, I will sing, I will sing praise to the Lord, the God of Israel."

c) **2 Samuel 22:50** "Therefore I will give thanks to You, O Lord, among the nations, And I will sing praises to Your name."

d) **Psalm 7:17** "I will give thanks to the Lord according to His righteousness And will sing praise to the name of the Lord Most High."

e) **Psalm 9:2** "I will be glad and exult in You; I will **sing** praise to Your name, O Most High."

f) **Psalm 18:49** "Therefore I will give thanks to You among the nations, O Lord, And I will sing praises to Your name."

g) **Psalm 27:6** "And now my head will be lifted up above my enemies around me, And I will offer in His tent sacrifices with shouts of joy; I will sing, yes, I will sing praises to the Lord."

h) **Psalm 30:12** "That my soul may sing praise to You and not be silent. O Lord my God, I will give thanks to You forever."

i) **Psalm 57:7** "My heart is steadfast, O God, my heart is steadfast; I will sing, yes, I will sing praises!"

j) **Psalm 57:9** "I will give thanks to You, O Lord, among the peoples; I will sing praises to You among the nations."

k) **Psalm 59:16** "But as for me, I shall sing of Your strength; Yes, I shall joyfully sing of Your lovingkindness in the morning, For You have been my stronghold And a refuge in the day of my distress."

l) **Psalm 59:17** "But as for me, I shall sing of Your strength; Yes, I shall joyfully sing of Your lovingkindness in the morning, For You have been my stronghold And a refuge in the day of my distress."

m) **Psalm 61:8** "So I will sing praise to Your name forever, That I may pay my vows day by day."

n) **Psalm 71:22** "I will also praise You with a harp, Even Your truth, O my God; To You I will sing praises with the lyre, O Holy One of Israel."

o) **Psalm 75:9** "But as for me, I will declare it forever; I will sing praises to the God of Jacob."

p) **Psalm 89:1** "I will sing of the lovingkindness of the Lord forever; To all generations I will make known Your faithfulness with my mouth."

q) **Psalm 101:1** "I will sing of lovingkindness and justice, To You, O Lord, I will sing praises."

r) **Psalm 108:1** "My heart is steadfast, O God; I will sing, I will sing praises, even with my soul"

s) **Psalm 108:3** "I will give thanks to You, O Lord, among the peoples, And I will sing praises to You among the nations."

t) **Psalm 146:2** "I will praise the Lord while I live; I will sing praises to my God while I have my being."

Question 4: Have you ever forced yourself to sing when you didn't feel like singing?

5A - <u>Sing With Might!</u>

a) **1 Chronicles 13:8** "David and all Israel were celebrating before God with all their might, even with songs and with lyres, harps, tambourines, cymbals and with trumpets."

b) **2 Chronicles 30:21** "The sons of Israel present in Jerusalem celebrated the Feast of Unleavened Bread for seven days with great joy, and the Levites and the priests praised the Lord day after day with loud instruments to the Lord."

c) **Nehemiah 12:42** "and Maaseiah, Shemaiah, Eleazar, Uzzi, Jehohanan, Malchijah, Elam and Ezer. And the singers sang, with Jezrahiah their leader."

d) **Psalm 51:14** "Deliver me from bloodguiltiness, O God, the God of my salvation; Then my tongue will joyfully sing of Your righteousness."

e) **Psalm 71:23** "My lips will shout for joy when I sing praises to You; And my soul, which You have redeemed."

f) **Psalm 138:1** "I will give You thanks with all my heart;I will sing praises to You before the gods."

Question 5: Have you ever sung praise to God with all your might?

6A - <u>Sing About God's Past Works</u>

a) **Exodus 15:1** "Then Moses and the sons of Israel sang this song to the Lord, and said, "I will sing to the Lord, for He is highly exalted; The horse and its rider He has hurled into the sea.""

b) **1 Chronicles 16:9** "Sing to Him, sing praises to Him; Speak of all His wonders."

c) **Psalm 13:6** "I will sing to the Lord, Because He has dealt bountifully with me."

d) **Psalm 21:13** "Be exalted, O Lord, in Your strength; We will sing and praise Your power."

Question 6: Have you ever sung praise to God for the things He has done in the past?

7A - <u>Sing Until Something Happens</u>

2 Chronicles 5:13 "in unison when the trumpeters and the singers were to make themselves heard with one voice to praise and to glorify the Lord, and when they lifted up their voice accompanied by trumpets and cymbals and instruments of music, and when they praised the Lord saying, "He indeed is good for His lovingkindness is everlasting," then the house, the house of the Lord, was filled with a cloud,"

7B - <u>Tell People to Sing</u>

a) **Numbers 21:17** "Then Israel sang this song: "Spring up, O well! Sing to it!""

b) **1 Chronicles 16:23** "Sing to the Lord, all the earth; Proclaim good tidings of His salvation from day to day."

c) **Psalm 9:11** "Sing praises to the Lord, who dwells in Zion; Declare among the peoples His deeds."

d) **Psalm 30:4** "Sing praise to the Lord, you His godly ones, And give thanks to His holy name."

e) **Psalm 33:3** "Sing to Him a new song; Play skillfully with a shout of joy"

f) **Psalm 47:6** "Sing praises to God, sing praises; Sing praises to our King, sing praises."

g) **Psalm 47:7** "For God is the King of all the earth: **si**ng ye praises with understanding."

h) **Psalm 66:2** " Sing praises to God, sing praises; Sing praises sing to our King, sing praises."

i) **Psalm 68:4** "Sing to God, sing praises to His name; Lift up a song for Him who rides through the deserts, Whose name is the Lord, and exult before Him."

j) **Psalm 68:32** "Sing to God, O kingdoms of the earth, Sing praises to the Lord, Selah."

k) **Psalm 92:1** "Sing to God, O kingdoms of the earth, Sing praises to the Lord, Selah."

l) **Psalm 96:2** "Sing to the Lord, bless His name; Proclaim good tidings of His salvation from day to day."

m) **Psalm 98:5** "Sing praises to the Lord with the lyre, With the lyre and the sound of melody."

n) **Psalm 105:2** "Sing to Him, sing praises to Him; Speak of all His wonders."

o) **Psalm 135:3** "Praise the Lord, for the Lord is good; Sing praises to His name, for it is lovely."

p) **Psalm 147:1** "Praise the Lord! For it is good to sing praises to our God; For it is pleasant and praise is becoming."

q) **Psalm 147:7** "Sing to the Lord with thanksgiving; Sing praises to our God on the lyre,"

r) **Isaiah 12:5** "Praise the Lord in song, for He has done excellent things; Let this be known throughout the earth."

s) **Isaiah 44:23** "Shout for joy, O heavens, for the Lord has done it! Shout joyfully, you lower parts of the earth; Break forth into a shout of joy, you mountains, O forest, and every tree in it; For the Lord has redeemed Jacob And in Israel He shows forth His glory."

t) **Isaiah 54:1** "Shout for joy, O barren one, you who have borne no child; Break forth into joyful shouting and cry aloud, you who have not travailed; For the sons of the desolate one will be more numerous Than the sons of the married woman," says the Lord."

u) **Jeremiah 20:13** "Sing to the Lord, praise the Lord! For He has delivered the soul of the needy one From the hand of evildoers."

v) **Zechariah 2:10** "Sing for joy and be glad, O daughter of Zion; for behold I am coming and I will dwell in your midst," declares the Lord."

w) **Psalm 95:1** "O come, let us sing for joy to the LORD, Let us shout joyfully to the rock of our salvation."

Question 7: Have you ever suggested to people that they sing to God?

8A - <u>Sing with Instruments</u>

a) **Psalm 33:2** "Give thanks to the Lord with the lyre; Sing praises to Him with a harp of ten strings."

b) **Psalm 33:3** "Sing to Him a new song; Play skillfully with a shout of joy."

c) **Psalm 87:7** "Then those who sing as well as those who play the flutes shall say, "All my springs of joy are in you."

d) **Psalm 149:3** "Let them praise His name with dancing; Let them sing praises to Him with timbrel and lyre."

Question 8: Do you play a musical instrument to God? If yes, what do you play?

9A - <u>Sing a New Song</u>

a) **Psalm 33:3** "Sing to Him a new song; Play skillfully with a shout of joy."

b) **Psalm 96:1** "Sing to the Lord a new song; Sing to the Lord, all the earth."

c) **Psalm 98:1** "O sing to the Lord a new song, For He has done wonderful things, His right hand and His holy arm have gained the victory for Him."

d) **Psalm 144:9** "I will sing a new song to You, O God; Upon a harp of ten strings I will sing praises to You,"

e) **Psalm 149:1** "Praise the Lord! Sing to the Lord a new song, And His praise in the congregation of the godly ones."

f) **Isaiah 42:10** "Sing to the Lord a new song, Sing His praise from the end of the earth! You who go down to the sea, and all that is in it. You islands, and those who dwell on them."

9B - <u>Singing and Joy</u>

a) **Psalm 67:4** "Let the nations be glad and sing for joy; For You will judge the peoples with uprightness And guide the nations on the earth. Selah."

b) **Psalm 100:2** "Serve the Lord with gladness; Come before Him with joyful singing."

c) **Psalm 126:2** "Then our mouth was filled with laughter And our tongue with joyful shouting; Then they said among the nations, "The Lord has done great things for them."

d) **Isaiah 49:13** "Shout for joy, O heavens! And rejoice, O earth! Break forth into joyful shouting, O mountains! For the Lord has comforted His people And will have compassion on His afflicted."

e) **Isaiah 51:11** "So the ransomed of the Lord will return And come with joyful shouting to Zion, And everlasting joy will be on their heads. They will obtain gladness and joy, And sorrow and sighing will flee away."

f) **Isaiah 52:9** "Break forth, shout joyfully together, You waste places of Jerusalem; For the Lord has comforted His people, He has redeemed Jerusalem."

g) **Isaiah 55:12** ""For you will go out with joy And be led forth with peace; The mountains and the hills will break forth into shouts of joy before you, And all the trees of the field will clap their hands."

h) **Zephaniah 3:14** "Shout for joy, O daughter of Zion! Shout in triumph, O Israel! Rejoice and exult with all your heart, O daughter of Jerusalem!"

Question 9: Have you ever sung to God with great joy?

*Articles on Singing:
https://www.sciencedaily.com/releases/2017/12/171221101402.htm
https://www.psychologytoday.com/gb/blog/the-athletes-way/201811/feeling-lonely-singing-could-be-joyful-remedy
https://www.rhinegold.co.uk/music_teacher/31600/

* * * * * * *

Tip #29

****

Join a Church

****

1A - In this Tip, we are going to see that the Christian church is the center of the community. We will also look at the purpose of the church, part of which, is to show us how to live above anxiety and depression.

Not every congregation meets in a public building, but wherever a church meets, that is the focus of all of heaven. See below.

Hebrews 12:1 "Therefore, since we have so great a cloud of witnesses surrounding us, let us also lay aside every encumbrance and the sin which so easily entangles us, and let us run with endurance the race that is set before us,"

Thus, heaven has the greatest "reality show" in the universe. They are watching us GO!

1B - <u>How the Church Got Started</u>

After God, the Father, resurrected Jesus from the dead, Jesus commissioned His disciples to go and preach the Gospel of forgiveness through Christ Jesus throughout the whole world.

Mark 16:15, "And He said to them, "Go into all the world and preach the gospel to all creation.""

1C - Before the disciples were to evangelize the world Jesus had them wait for the Holy Spirit to empower them.

Acts 2:1-4 "When the day of Pentecost had come, they were all together in one place. [2] And suddenly there came from heaven a noise like a violent rushing wind, and it filled the whole house where they were sitting. [3] And there appeared to them tongues as of fire distributing themselves, and they rested on each one of them. [4] And they were all filled with the Holy Spirit and began to speak with other tongues, as the Spirit was giving them utterance."

Since then the church has grown in number, and in knowledge of the scriptures.

1D - <u>Esteem Mature Christians</u>

In a local church, we can meet some amazing people, individuals who are eager to help us mature in our walk with God. Remember to value these people. We may not see their real value at the time, but years later we will see how instrumental they were in helping us grow spiritually.

a) **Proverbs 27:17** "Iron sharpens iron, So one man sharpens another."

b) **1 Timothy 5:17** "The elders who rule well are to be considered worthy of double honor, especially those who work hard at preaching and teaching."

Question 1: Have you ever been inspired by someone in your church? If so, how did they help you?

2A - <u>Churches and Unbelievers</u>

As the church mobilizes its members, unbelievers will begin attending church services. Wise churches will always present the simple story of salvation through Christ at the end of the service to give unbelievers the opportunity to receive Jesus as their personal Savior. Once they accept Jesus, they can begin enjoying the benefits of connection to a local church.

2B - <u>New Believers</u>

Something to note about churches is, although they have some great people as members, churches that are growing will also have people who are just at the beginning of their spiritual growth. This means that there may be people who have come into the church with various negative habits, behaviors, and mindsets. As we get to know these new members, we might be negatively affected and hurt by them. This is normal. When this happens, it is best for us to forgive the person who has hurt us. We need to remember that we, ourselves, were once new believers, with problems needing help from our Savior, and His church. We will want to quickly forgive these people so we can continue our growth in Christ.

Question 2: Have you ever been hurt by someone in your church? If so, how did it affect you, and what did you learn from it?

3A - Some people say they don't need to be part of a local church, but the Bible tells us not to neglect meeting together.

Hebrews 10:25 "not forsaking our own assembling together, as is the habit of some, but encouraging one another; and all the more as you see the day drawing near."

Question 3: Do you know an Christians who do not attend a local church?

4A - In the scripture below we see that Jesus intends to build a community of believers, and called it His church. His intention is for the church to be strong and victorious.

Matthew 16:18 "also say to you that you are Peter, and upon this rock I will build My church; and the gates of Hades will not overpower it."

Question 4: Do you know of a church which is vibrant and victorious?

5A - The Bible tells us to be watchful of people who try to bring discord into the church.

Romans 16:17 "Now I urge you, brethren, keep your eye on those who cause dissensions and hindrances contrary to the teaching which you learned, and turn away from them."

Question 5: Can you think of anyone who tends to bring division to a church?

6A - The Bible refers to the church as the body of Christ.

a) **Romans 12:5** "So we, who are many, are one body in Christ, and individually members one of another."

b) **1 Corinthians 12:27** "Now you are Christ's body, and individually members of it."

c) **Ephesians 4:12** "For the equipping of the saints for the work of service, to the building up of the body of Christ;"

d) **Ephesians 4:16** "from whom the whole body, being fitted and held together by what every joint supplies, according to the proper working of each individual part, causes the growth of the body for the building up of itself in love."

6B - Since the church is the Body of Christ, the church should know what is important to Jesus. Preaching and teaching the gospel of salvation is what is important to Jesus. See below.

a) **Matthew 10:32** "Therefore everyone who confesses Me before men, I will also confess him before My Father who is in heaven."

b) **Matthew 28:19** "Go therefore and make disciples of all the nations, baptizing them in the name of the Father and the Son and the Holy Spirit,"

c) **Mark 16:15** "And He said to them, "Go into all the world and preach the gospel to all creation.""

d) **Luke 14:23** "And the master said to the slave, 'Go out into the highways and along the hedges, and compel them to come in, so that my house may be filled.""

e) **John 3:3** "Jesus answered and said to him, "Truly, truly, I say to you, unless one is born again he cannot see the kingdom of God.""

f) **John 3:5** "Jesus answered, "Truly, truly, I say to you, unless one is born of water and the Spirit he cannot enter into the kingdom of God.""

g) **John 15:16** "You did not choose Me but I chose you, and appointed you that you would go and bear fruit, and that your fruit would remain, so that whatever you ask of the Father in My name He may give to you."

Question 6: Can you tell us of a church where preaching the gospel is a priority?

7A - A Unique Term

Jesus used a unique term when talking about how people make it to heaven after they die. He said that a person needs to be "born again."

John 3:3 "Jesus answered and said to him, "Truly, truly, I say to you, unless one is born again he cannot see the kingdom of God.""

7B - Heaven is a place without sin, and only sinless people can get to heaven. An marvelous attribute with man is that we have freedom of choice – we can choose to do right, but we can also choose to do wrong. All of us, at some point in our lives, have chosen wrongly – we have sinned. The Bible tells us that only blood can take away sin.

a) **Leviticus 17:11** "For the life of the flesh is in the blood, and I have given it to you on the altar to make atonement for your souls; for it is the blood by reason of the life that makes atonement."

b) **Hebrews 9:22** "And according to the Law, one may almost say, all things are cleansed with blood, and without shedding of blood there is no forgiveness."

7C - We become born again when we admit we have sinned, and we acknowledge what Jesus did on the cross for us personally – Jesus took the punishment for our sin by allowing Himself to be nailed on the cross.

It's at the cross that a great exchange took place. The Apostle Paul tells us what God did when Christ died.

2 Corinthians 5:21 "He made Him who knew no sin to be sin on our behalf, so that we might become the righteousness of God in Him."

7D - Jesus became sin for us so that we might become righteous (sinless) in God's sight. Our sin killed Jesus. But then God miraculously resurrected Jesus on the third day, and now we can all be forgiven of sin. We can also learn how to live free of sin, and be ready for heaven. Our old life of sin dies, and our new life in Christ begins – hence the term, "born again."

Question 7: Can you tell us of a church that uses the term "born again" when speaking to unbelievers about becoming a Christian?

8A - <u>Church Outreach</u>

The most important part of human life is making it to heaven, thus a church should try to be open as many hours a week as possible so unbelievers can come and find Jesus as Savior. Also, that people can be taught how to live free of all hindrances to happiness. In this way, a church is like a hospital; they help "broken" people.

Indeed, people should be able to come in anytime they feel the need, and be able to speak with someone, or learn how to overcome obstacles in their life.

Question 8: Can you tell us of a church that is open many hours a week, teaching people principles that help them know God, and how to overcome obstacles in their life?

9A - In addition to making the church available throughout the week, a church should have community events that give people in the community an opportunity to hear the Gospel message. Most churches offer a week-long Vacation Bible School during the summer. Some churches will rent a band shell in a park and provide a "Church-in-the-Park" experience. Some churches have live theater presentations during Christmas or Easter.

9B - An effective way for a church to present the gospel is when churches work together on a community outreach event. Jesus prayed that such meetings would be held, so that the world would believe that God sent Jesus.

John 17:21 "that they may all be one; even as You, Father, are in Me and I in You, that they also may be in Us, so that the world may believe that You sent Me."

Question 9: What methods of sharing the gospel have you seen churches use?

10A - In addition to sharing the good news of the gospel, the church should be able to help the community in practical ways. See below.

a) **Matthew 5:42** "Give to him who asks of you, and do not turn away from him who wants to borrow from you."

b) **Matthew 25:35** "For I was hungry, and you gave Me something to eat; I was thirsty, and you gave Me something to drink; I was a stranger, and you invited Me in;"

c) **Matthew 25:44-45** "Then they themselves also will answer, 'Lord, when did we see You hungry, or thirsty, or a stranger, or naked, or sick, or in prison, and did not take care of You?' Then He will answer them, 'Truly I say to you, to the extent that you did not do it to one of the least of these, you did not do it to Me.'"

d) **Ephesians 4:28** "He who steals must steal no longer; but rather he must labor, performing with his own hands what is good, so that he will have something to share with one who has need."

e) **Hebrews 13:16** "And do not neglect doing good and sharing, for with such sacrifices God is pleased."

Question 10: In what ways have you seen churches help people in the community?

11A - Church "In-Reach"

In addition to reaching out to help unbelievers, a church should be helping people who are already members of the church. Here are some verses on the church helping its members.

a) **Acts 20:35** "In everything I showed you that by working hard in this manner you must help the weak and remember the words of the Lord Jesus, that He Himself said, 'It is more blessed to give than to receive.'"

b) **Romans 15:1** "Now we who are strong ought to bear the weaknesses of those without strength and not just please ourselves."

c) **Galatians 6:2** "Bear one another's burdens, and thereby fulfill the law of Christ."

d) **Galatians 6:10** "So then, while we have opportunity, let us do good to all people, and especially to those who are of the household of the faith."

e) **Philippians 2:4** "do not merely look out for your own personal interests, but also for the interests of others."

f) **Hebrews 13:16** "And do not neglect doing good and sharing, for with such sacrifices God is pleased."

g) **James 2:15-17** "If a brother or sister is without clothing and in need of daily food, and one of you says to them, "Go in peace, be warmed and be filled," and yet you do not give them what is necessary for their body, what use is that? Even so faith, if it has no works, is dead, being by itself."

h) **1 John 3:17** "But whoever has the world's goods, and sees his brother in need and closes his heart against him, how does the love of God abide in him?"

11B - As members of the Body of Christ, we are one body, and are to share the joys and the pains of our brothers and sisters in Christ. Social media makes it easy for us to stay connected with our church family and lets us know when help is needed.

Question 11: In what ways have you seen churches help its members?

12A - An effective way to meet the many needs of church members is to organize them into groups that meet outside of church meetings. There are various names given to these groups, for example, Home Groups, Home Fellowships, Life Groups, Connect Groups. These groups offer a relaxed atmosphere to get to know one another and to learn about Christ. They also provide immediate, close-to-home care when someone is struggling.

a) **1 Corinthians 12:26** "And if one member suffers, all the members suffer with it; if one member is honored, all the members rejoice with it."

b) **Hebrews 13:5** "Make sure that your character is free from the love of money, being content with what you have; for He Himself has said, "I will never desert you, nor will I ever forsake you.""

Question 12: Do you know of any churches that have weekly home groups? Have you ever been helped by a home group?

13A - Supporting the Church Financially

Donating money can be a delicate issue. A wise church will be thrifty and transparent with their finances so that if a financial matter arises, it can be quickly resolved, so the church can get back to the job of spreading the Gospel.

Question 13: Can you think of a church that publishes an annual report on how donations were allocated?

14A - The Love of Giving

There is something about Jesus that makes people want to give. Zacchaeus, the despised tax collector, felt it. One day he climbed a tree to watch Jesus walk by. Jesus spotted him and said, *"Zacchaeus, make haste, and come down; for to day I must abide at thy house."* (**Luke 19:5**) That brief time with Jesus prompted Zacchaeus to give away a large sum of money.

Luke 19:8 "Zaccheus stopped and said to the Lord, "Behold, Lord, half of my possessions I will give to the poor, and if I have defrauded anyone of anything, I will give back four times as much."

14B - Other people gave more than Zacchaeus. The Apostles gave up everything to follow Him.

Matthew 19:27 "Then Peter said to Him, "Behold, we have left everything and followed You; what then will there be for us?"

Indeed, one way to spot a child of God is by their generosity.

Question 14: Have you ever felt the desire to give to God, or give to help others?

15A - God has instituted a method of meeting the needs of a local church called tithing. The tithing principle is one in which a person gives to God 10% of any profit they earn. This principle started with Abraham. The Bible says that after a war Abraham paid tithes to Melchizedek.

Genesis 14:19-20 "Blessed be Abram of God Most High, Possessor of heaven and earth; [20] And blessed be God Most High, Who has delivered your enemies into your hand." He gave him a tenth of all."

15B - Many people believe Melchisedek was a type of Jesus because he had no beginning and no end. See verses below.

Hebrews 7:1-6 "For this Melchizedek, king of Salem, priest of the Most High God, who met Abraham as he was returning from the slaughter of the kings and blessed him, [2] to whom also Abraham apportioned a tenth part of all *the spoils*, was first of all, by the translation *of his name*, king of righteousness, and then also king of Salem, which is king of peace. [3] Without father, without mother, without genealogy, having neither beginning of days nor end of life, but made like the Son of God, he remains a priest perpetually."

15C - "[4] Now observe how great this man was to whom Abraham, the patriarch, gave a tenth of the choicest spoils. [5] And those indeed of the sons of Levi who receive the priest's office have commandment in the Law to collect a tenth from the people, that is, from their brethren, although these are descended from Abraham. [6] But the one whose genealogy is not traced from them collected a tenth from Abraham and blessed the one who had the promises."

15D - 430 years later, God gave the Levitical Law to Israel, which was a list of rules for God's people to live by. This included tithing.

a) **Leviticus 27:30** "Thus all the tithe of the land, of the seed of the land or of the fruit of the tree, is the Lord's; it is holy to the Lord."

b) **Leviticus 27:32** "For every tenth part of herd or flock, whatever passes under the rod, the tenth one shall be holy to the Lord."

15E - 1500 years after that, we see that Jesus endorsed tithing.

a) **Matthew 23:23** "Woe to you, scribes and Pharisees, hypocrites! For you tithe mint and dill and cummin, and have neglected the weightier provisions of the law: justice and mercy and faithfulness; but these are the things you should have done without neglecting the others."

b) **Luke 11:42** ""But woe to you Pharisees! For you pay tithe of mint and rue and every kind of garden herb, and yet disregard justice and the love of God; but these are the things you should have done without neglecting the others."

Question 15: Can you tell us of a church that teaches the principle of tithing?

16A - The Promise of Blessing

In the following verse we see that God issues us a challenge.

Malachi 3:10 "Bring the whole tithe into the storehouse, so that there may be food in My house, and test Me now in this," says the Lord of hosts, "if I will not open for you the windows of heaven and pour out for you a blessing until it overflows."

16B - Verse 10 says *"...test Me now in this," says the Lord of hosts, "if I will not open for you the windows of heaven and pour out for you a blessing until it overflows."* God wants us to tithe so we can help others. Helping others is a good enough reward to do so, but God doesn't stop there. He says He will bless us if we tithe. Many people testify that their lives have been blessed financially, and in other ways, because of tithing. That is wonderful, but this isn't why we tithe. We tithe because God tells us to tithe.

16C - Here are other scriptures on blessings that come from giving.

a) **Proverbs 11:24** "There is one who scatters, and yet increases all the more, And there is one who withholds what is justly due, and yet it results only in want."

b) **Luke 6:38** "Give, and it will be given to you. They will pour into your lap a good measure— pressed down, shaken together, and running over. For by your standard of measure it will be measured to you in return."

c) **2 Corinthians 9:6** "Now this I say, he who sows sparingly will also reap sparingly, and he who sows bountifully will also reap bountifully."

d) **2 Corinthians 9:7,8** "Each one must do just as he has purposed in his heart, not grudgingly or under compulsion, for God loves a cheerful giver. And God is able to make all grace abound to you, so that always having all sufficiency in everything, you may have an abundance for every good deed:"

Question 16: Do you know people who have been blessed by tithing?

17A - New Testament Giving

Nothing is said about tithing after Jesus was resurrected, but people in the 1st-century church gave much more than the tithe.

Acts 4:36-37 "Now Joseph, a Levite of Cyprian birth, who was also called Barnabas by the apostles (which translated means Son of Encouragement), and who owned a tract of land, sold it and brought the money and laid it at the apostles' feet."

17B - Communal Living

The New Testament church was a beautiful picture of peace and love amongst its members, with everyone sharing what they had with those in need.

a) **Acts 2:44-45** "And all those who had believed were together and had all things in common; and they began selling their property and possessions and were sharing them with all, as anyone might have need."

b) **Acts 4:32** "And the congregation of those who believed were of one heart and soul; and not one of them claimed that anything belonging to him was his own, but all things were common property to them."

c) **Acts 4:34-35** "For there was not a needy person among them, for all who were owners of land or houses would sell them and bring the proceeds of the sales [35] and lay them at the apostles' feet, and they would be distributed to each as any had need."

d) **2 Corinthians 8:13-15** "For *this* is not for the ease of others *and* for your affliction, but by way of equality— [14] at this present time your abundance *being a supply* for their need, so that their abundance also may become *a supply* for your need, that there may be equality; [15] as it is written, "HE WHO *gathered* MUCH DID NOT HAVE TOO MUCH, AND HE WHO *gathered* LITTLE HAD NO LACK.""

Question 17: Can you tell us of a church that has a communal feel when it comes to sharing?

18A - <u>A Store House</u>

The Bible says that if church members are tithing, their church needs to have a "storehouse" – a place where people can come when they are in need. The following scriptures show the importance of tithing and of having a storehouse.

Malachi 3:8-10 "Will a man rob God? Yet you are robbing Me! But you say, 'How have we robbed You?' In tithes and offerings. ⁹ You are cursed with a curse, for you are robbing Me, the whole nation *of you!* ¹⁰ Bring the whole tithe into the storehouse, so that there may be food in My house, and test Me now in this," says the LORD of hosts, "if I will not open for you the windows of heaven and pour out for you a blessing until it overflows.."

Question 18: Can you think of a church that has a "storehouse" from which to give to those in need?

19A - <u>First Century Church Needs</u>

The 1ˢᵗ-century church had great needs. They were feeding the poor and sending groups of people all over the world to spread the Good News of Jesus Christ. The Apostle Paul had to do everything in his power to meet the many needs. Here is a strategy he used: He offered his preaching for free. He didn't want people to think he was preaching the gospel to make money. The following scriptures reveal this mindset.

a) **1 Corinthians 9:18** "What then is my reward? That, when I preach the gospel, I may offer the gospel without charge, so as not to make full use of my right in the gospel."

b) **1 Thessalonians 2:9** "For you recall, brethren, our labor and hardship, how working night and day so as not to be a burden to any of you, we proclaimed to you the gospel of God."

c) **2 Thessalonians 3:8** "nor did we eat anyone's bread without paying for it, but with labor and hardship we kept working night and day so that we would not be a burden to any of you:"

Question 19: Do you know of a church that is sensitive to people's tendency to think *"churches only want your money"*?

20A - Paul could preach the Gospel for free because he was a tent-maker by trade.

Acts 18:3 "and because he was of the same trade, he stayed with them and they were working, for by trade they were tent-makers."

Question 20: Do you know of anyone who funds their own Christian ministry?

21A - <u>Financial Gain and Godliness</u>

In Paul's day, some people taught that having great wealth was a sign of Godliness. Paul refuted that belief extensively.

1 Timothy 6:5-11 "and constant friction between men of depraved mind and deprived of the truth, who suppose that godliness is a means of gain. ⁶ But godliness *actually* is a means of great gain when accompanied by contentment. ⁷ For we have brought nothing into the world, so we cannot take anything out of it either. ⁸ If we have food and covering, with these we shall be content. ⁹ But those who want to get rich fall into temptation and a snare and many foolish and harmful desires which plunge men into ruin and destruction. ¹⁰ For the love of money is a root of all sorts of evil, and some by longing for it have wandered away from the faith and pierced themselves with many griefs. [11] But flee from these things, you man of God, and pursue righteousness, godliness, faith, love, perseverance *and* gentleness."

21B - <u>Two Opponents</u>

Is it wrong to be a wealthy Christian? No, but Jesus told us that wealth can be a god in our lives. He said that we cannot serve, both, God and money.

Matthew 6:24 "No one can serve two masters; for either he will hate the one and love the other, or he will be devoted to one and despise the other. You cannot serve God and wealth."

21C - Money is not our friend. It seeks to displace God in our lives. We must be careful. We can be at a time in our lives when we are enthralled with God, and busy doing things to further His kingdom, and all of a sudden we get a desire to buy something, or we get a better job offer, or we get a business idea. These are not bad things, but they *can* affect our commitment for God. A person's zeal for God is their most valuable possession. And the devil will go after it, and steal it in any way he can. Here are verses related to losing our focus for God.

a) **Revelation 2:4-5** "But I have *this* against you, that you have left your first love. [5] Therefore remember from where you have fallen, and repent and do the deeds you did at first; or else I am coming to you and will remove your lampstand out of its place—unless you repent."

b) **Revelation 3:16** "So because you are lukewarm, and neither hot nor cold, I will spit you out of My mouth."

21D - Jesus addresses the issue of money on a number of occasions. Let's look at the following verses to get a sense of what money is, from Jesus's perspective.

Below, we read how Jesus advised people not to hoard their wealth, but instead to use their money to help others.

a) **Matthew 6:19-21** "Do not store up for yourselves treasures on earth, where moth and rust destroy, and where thieves break in and steal. [20] But store up for yourselves treasures in heaven, where neither moth nor rust destroys, and where thieves do not break in or steal;"

b) **Luke 12:20,21** "But God said to him, 'You fool! This *very* night your soul is required of you; and *now* who will own what you have prepared?' [21] So is the man who stores up treasure for himself, and is not rich toward God**.**"

c) **Luke 12:33** "Sell that ye have, and give alms; provide yourselves bags which wax not old, a treasure in the heavens that faileth not, where no thief approacheth, neither moth corrupteth."

21E - Below, we read how hard it is for a rich man to enter into the kingdom of heaven.

Matthew 19:23,24 "And Jesus said to His disciples, "Truly I say to you, it is hard for a rich man to enter the kingdom of heaven. [24] Again I say to you, it is easier for a camel to go through the eye of a needle, than for a rich man to enter the kingdom of God."

21F - Following, we read how Jesus warns people who are rich.

Luke 6:24,25 "But woe unto you that are rich! for ye have received your consolation. [25] Woe unto you that are full! for ye shall hunger. Woe unto you that laugh now! for ye shall mourn and weep."

21G - Below, we read how Jesus advised people to be content with their wages.

> **Luke 3:14** *"Some* soldiers were questioning him, saying, "And *what about* us, what shall we do?" And he said to them, "Do not take money from anyone by force, or accuse *anyone* falsely, and be content with your wages."

21H - In Matthew 21:12, Mark 11:15 and John 2:15, we see how Jesus flipped over the tables of the money-changers in the temple.

> **Matthew 21:12,13** "And Jesus entered the temple and drove out all those who were buying and selling in the temple, and overturned the tables of the money changers and the seats of those who were selling doves. [13] And He *said to them, "It is written, 'MY HOUSE SHALL BE CALLED A HOUSE OF PRAYER'; but you are making it a ROBBERS' DEN."

21J - Jesus did not think to highly of money, in fact He despised it. Does that mean we aren't supposed to have a savings account or a retirement plan? It can be wise to have these, so it is a delicate question, and can only be answered by each person individually. As we take time to pray and grow close to God, we will learn how to hear His voice. This will help us see where we should allocate our financial resources.

21K - In the final scene of the movie *Schindler's List*, in which Schindler is surrounded by the 1,100 people he saved from Nazi concentration camps, he says slowly and painfully, *"I could have got more out. I could have sold that car and got ten more people out." "And this pin, it is gold. I could have sold it and got two more people out..."* It is a solemn scene, and it illustrates the love and commitment he had developed to help the Jewish people in need.

21L - What is written on *our* 'Schindler's list'? What are *our* priorities? What do we aspire to with our lives? May our 'Schindler's list' be filled with noble goals and achievements, so that when we come face to face with God, we will stand unashamed, waiting and hoping to hear the words, "Well done, good and faithful servant."

> **Matthew 25:21** "His master said to him, 'Well done, good and faithful slave. You were faithful with a few things, I will put you in charge of many things; enter into the joy of your master."

21M - May each of us be "God-conscious" and "others-conscious" so that God can use us to help those in need. And may those responsible for distributing funds for operating church ministries do it wisely. May those who receive these funds, do their jobs well so that many will be helped, and many will hear the Good News of what Jesus did for them, and be challenged to give their lives to Christ, and be saved.

Question 22: Do you know of a church that is watchful of how they spend their money? Do they have a deep desire to share the Gospel message with unsaved people?

22A - Joining a great church can have a wonderful effect on our lives, ushering us toward happiness and fruitfulness in every area of our lives.

* * * * * * *

The Happiness Basics
Meeting Start

The numbered paragraphs below are to be read by the participants in the meeting. They will direct the content of the conversation during the meeting. The Chairperson will read their own parts marked in ***bold italics font,*** and the meeting participants will read their parts marked in **Bold Arial** font, such as **First Speaker**.

1 - *Chairperson: Welcome everyone to the Victory Tips Recovery Group! My name is* ____(Chairperson name)____ ***, and I will be the Chairperson for our meeting. Before we start, please turn off the ringers on your cell phone. Also, please try to limit background noise during the call. Use the Mute feature if need be.***

2 - *Chairperson: Do we have any new visitors?* *[If so, kindly acknowledge and thank them for joining in, and ask who wants to participate or just listen in.]* ***Our meetings have two main sections: The Happiness Basics, and the Happiness Tips. As we go through the program, I will read from the bold italics text marked 'Chairperson', and I will call on others who wish to have Speaker Roles by reading from the*** **Bold Arial** ***font text. Please keep your comments to about thirty seconds so everyone has a chance to speak. The last fifteen minutes are reserved for Prayer Requests and members praying for each other. We should finish in 90 min.***

3 - *Chairperson: So, let's get started! On behalf of the group, I will read the Recovery Prayer below.*

Recovery Prayer

"Dear God, thank you for giving us your Word to heal us. We joyfully dedicate this time to renew our minds to the truths in your Word. With your help we will use your Word to bring down strongholds of fear and deception. We agree that your Word is a light to our path and it leads us to a place of peace, confidence and happiness. We thank you in advance for everything you have done for us, and will do, in our lives. You have made our future bright, and we praise you for this. In Jesus's name. Amen."

4 - *Chairperson*: *This program promotes confidentiality. We teach its importance so those unfamiliar with it can learn about it and begin abiding by it. Whatever is said in the group stays in the group. Here to read our Confidentiality Commitment is our first speaker* _____(Speaker name)_____ .

5 - Confidentiality Speaker: Thank you, ____(Chairperson name)_____ .

We value your confidentiality. Whatever we hear you say at a group or in private conversation we promise not to repeat to anyone. This includes your contact information. We will never share any information about you without your permission.

6 - *Chairperson: Thank you,* _____(Speaker name)_____ . *[Chairperson now asks each person who wants to participate if they have any Praise Reports.]*

7 - *Chairperson*: *We will now start the Happiness Basics part of the meeting. God wants us to be Happy. To talk more about this, is our Happiness Speaker,* __(Speaker name)__ .

8 – Happiness Speaker: Thank you, ___(Chairperson name)___ . Indeed, God wants us to enjoy our journey in life, as seen in the following verses. I will pick one randomly to read, and speak, briefly, on how it applies to God wanting us to be happy. The verse I choose is _____ .

1) **Psalm 19:8** "The precepts of the Lord are right, <u>rejoicing the heart</u>;The commandment of the Lord is pure, <u>enlightening the eyes</u>."

2) **Psalm 28:7** "The Lord is my strength and my shield; My heart trusts in Him, and I am helped; Therefore <u>my heart exults</u>, And with my song I shall thank Him."

3) **Psalm 30:11,12** "You have turned for me my <u>mourning into dancing</u>; You have loosed my sackcloth and girded me with <u>gladness</u>, That my soul may <u>sing praise</u> to You and not be silent. O Lord my God, I will give thanks to You forever."

4) **Psalm 32:11** "<u>Be glad in the Lord and rejoice</u>, you righteous ones; <u>And shout for joy</u>, all you who are upright in heart."

5) **Psalm 64:10** "<u>The righteous man will be glad</u> in the Lord and will take refuge in Him; And all the upright in heart will <u>glory</u>."

6) **Psalm 89:16** "In Your name they rejoice all the day, And by <u>Your righteousness they are exalted</u>."

7) **Psalm 97:11** "Light is sown like seed for the righteous <u>And gladness for the upright in heart</u>."

8) **Ecclesiastes 2:26** "For to a person who is good in His sight He has given wisdom and knowledge and <u>joy</u>,"

9) **Ecclesiastes. 5:19** "Furthermore, as for every man to whom God has given riches and wealth, He has also empowered him to eat from them and to receive his reward and <u>rejoice in his labor</u>; this is the gift of God."

10) **Ecclesiastes. 11:8** "Indeed, if a man should live many years, let him <u>rejoice</u> in them all…"

11) **Luke 10:20** *(Jesus speaking)* "Nevertheless do not rejoice in this, that the spirits are subject to you, but <u>rejoice</u> that your names are recorded in heaven."

12) **John 10:10** "*(Jesus speaking)* "The thief comes only to steal and kill and destroy; <u>I came that they may have life, and have it abundantly.</u>"

13) **John 15:11** "*(Jesus speaking)* "These things I have spoken to you so that <u>My joy may be in you, and that your joy may be made full.</u>"

14) **Acts 2:25, 26** "For David says of Him, 'I saw the Lord always in my presence; For He is at my right hand, so that I will not be shaken. '<u>Therefore my heart was glad and my tongue exulted; Moreover my flesh also will live in hope;</u>"

15) **Romans 15:13** "Now may the God of hope <u>fill you with all joy</u> and peace in believing, so that you will abound in hope by the power of the Holy Spirit."

16) **1 Corinthians 15:57** "but thanks be to God, <u>who gives us the victory through our Lord Jesus Christ.</u>"

17) **2 Corinthians 2:14** "But thanks be to God, who always <u>leads us in triumph in Christ</u>…"

18) **Galatians 5:22** "But the fruit of the Spirit is love, <u>joy</u>, peace, patience, kindness, goodness, faithfulness",

19) **Philippians 1:25** "Convinced of this, I know that I will remain and continue with you all for your progress and <u>joy in the faith,</u>"

20) **Philippians 4:4** "<u>Rejoice in the Lord always</u>: again I will say, <u>Rejoice</u>."

21) **1 Thessalonians 5:16** "<u>Rejoice always;</u>"

22) **1 John 1:4** "These things we write, so that our <u>joy may be made complete.</u>"

23) **2 John 1:12** "Though I have many things to write to you, I do not want to do so with paper and ink; but I hope to come to you and speak face to face, so that <u>your joy may be made full.</u>"

9 - Happiness Speaker: So, God wants us to be happy. We can even be happy when we have problems in our lives. From the verses below, I will pick one randomly to read, and speak briefly on how it applies to us being happy even when we have problems in our lives. The verse I choose is _____.

1) **Psalm 27:6** "And now <u>my head will be lifted up above my enemies around me,</u> And I will offer in His tent sacrifices with shouts of joy; I will sing, yes, I will sing praises to the Lord."

2) **Psalm 119:143** "Trouble and anguish have come upon me, Yet Your <u>commandments are my delight.</u>"

3) **Luke 6:22,23** "Blessed are you when men hate you, and ostracize you, and insult you, and scorn your name as evil, for the sake of the Son of Man. ²³ <u>Be glad</u> in that day and <u>leap for joy,</u> for behold, your reward is great in heaven. For in the same way their fathers used to treat the prophets."

4) **John 16:33** *(Jesus speaking)* "These things I have spoken to you, so that in Me you may have peace. In the world <u>you have tribulation</u>, but take courage; I have overcome the world."

5) **Romans 5:3-5a** "And not only this, but <u>we also exult in our tribulations</u>, knowing that tribulation brings about perseverance; and perseverance, proven character; and proven character, hope; and hope does not disappoint,"

6) **Romans 8:18** "For I consider that the sufferings of this present time are not worthy to be compared with the <u>glory that is to be revealed to us.</u>"

7) **Romans 8:28** "And we know that <u>God causes all things to work together for good</u> to those who love God, to those who are called according to His purpose."

8) **2 Corinthians 4:17** "For momentary, light affliction <u>is producing for us an eternal weight of glory far beyond all comparison,</u>"

9) **2 Corinthians 7:4** "Great is my confidence in you; great is my boasting on your behalf. I am filled with comfort; <u>I am overflowing with joy in all our affliction.</u>"

10) **2 Corinthians 12:9,10** *(In this passage, Paul was troubled by a 'thorn in his flesh.')* "And He (Jesus) has said to me, "My grace is sufficient for you, for power is perfected in weakness." ¹⁰ <u>Most gladly, therefore, I will rather boast about my weaknesses</u>, so that the power of Christ may dwell in me. Therefore I am well content with weaknesses, with insults, with distresses, with persecutions, with difficulties, for Christ's sake; for when I am weak, then I am strong."

11) **Colossians 1:11** "strengthened with all power, according to His glorious might, for the <u>attaining of all steadfastness and patience; joyously.</u>"

12) **James 1:2** "Consider it all joy, my brethren, when you encounter various trials,"

13) **1 Peter 1:6** "In this you <u>greatly rejoice</u>, even though now for a little while, if necessary, you have been distressed by various trials,"

14) **1 Peter 3:14** "But and if ye suffer for righteousness' sake, <u>happy are ye</u>: and be not afraid of their terror, neither be troubled;"

15) **1 Peter 4:12,13** "Beloved, do not be surprised at the fiery ordeal among you, which comes upon you for your testing, as though some strange thing were happening to you;. [13] but to the degree that you share the sufferings of Christ, <u>keep on rejoicing</u>, so that also at the revelation of His glory <u>you may rejoice with exultation</u>."

16) **1 Peter 4:14** "If you are reviled for the name of Christ, you are blessed, because the Spirit of glory and of God rests on you."

10 - Happiness Speaker**: So even in troubles, we can be happy! Back to you, _(Chairperson name)_ .**

11 - *Chairperson: Thank you, _____(Speaker name)_____. So, it is God's will that we be happy, but it goes deeper than that. God wants us to be strong in our spirit. Here to tell us more on that is our Strong Speaker, _____(Speaker name)_____.*

12 - Strong Speaker**: Thank you, ___(Chairperson name)_____. Indeed, God wants people to be strong in spirit, and from the verses below, I will pick one randomly to read, and speak briefly on how it applies to us being strong in our spirit. The verse I choose is _____.**

1) **Joshua 1:6** "<u>Be strong</u> and courageous, for you shall give this people possession of the land which I swore to their fathers to give them."

2) **Joshua 1:7** "Only <u>be strong</u> and very courageous; be careful to do according to all the law which Moses My servant commanded you; do not turn from it to the right or to the left, so that you may have success wherever you go."

3) **Joshua 1:9** "Have I not commanded you? <u>Be strong</u> and courageous! Do not tremble or be dismayed, for the Lord your God is with you wherever you go."

4) **2 Samuel 22:33** "God is <u>my strong fortress;</u> And He sets the blameless in His way."

5) **2 Samuel 22:40** "For You have girded me with <u>strength for battle;</u> You have subdued under me those who rose up against me."

6) **Psalm 31:24** "<u>Be strong</u> and let your heart <u>take courage</u>, All you who hope in the Lord."

7) **Proverbs 24:5** "A wise man is <u>strong,</u> And a man of knowledge <u>increases power</u>."

8) **Romans 8:37** "But in all these things <u>we overwhelmingly conquer</u> through Him who loved us."

9) **1 Corinthians 16:13** "Be on the alert, stand firm in the faith, act like men, <u>be strong</u>."

10) **Ephesians 1:19** "and what is the surpassing greatness of His power toward us who believe. These are in accordance with the working of <u>the strength of His might</u>"

11) **Ephesians 3:16** "that He would grant you, according to the riches of His glory, to <u>be strengthened</u> with power through His Spirit in the inner man,"

12) **Ephesians 3:20** "Now to Him who is able to do far more abundantly beyond all that we ask or think, <u>according to the power that works within us</u>,"

13) **Ephesians 6:10-11** "Finally, be strong in the Lord and in the strength of His might. 11 Put on the full armor of God, so that you will be able to stand firm against the schemes of the devil."

14) **Philippians 4:13** "I can do all things through Him who strengthens me."

15) **Colossians 1:10-11** "so that you will walk in a manner worthy of the Lord, to please Him in all respects, bearing fruit in every good work and increasing in the knowledge of God; strengthened with all power, according to His glorious might, for the attaining of all steadfastness and patience; joyously…"

16) **2 Timothy 1:7** "For God has not given us a spirit of timidity, but of power and love and discipline."

17) **2 Timothy 2:1** "You therefore, my son, be strong in the grace that is in Christ Jesus."

18) **1 Peter 5:10** "After you have suffered for a little while, the God of all grace, who called you to His eternal glory in Christ, will Himself perfect, confirm, strengthen and establish you."

13 - Strong Speaker: So, God wants us to be strong emotionally, but it goes deeper than that. God wants us to stand firm and steadfast, and to be bold, established, and confident! From the verses below, I will pick one randomly to read, then share briefly on how it ties in to God wanting us to be stedfast, bold, established and confident. The verse I choose is _____.

1) **Psalm 20:8** "They have bowed down and fallen, But we have risen and stood upright."

2) **Psalm 138:3** "On the day I called, You answered me; You made me bold with strength in my soul."

3) **Proverbs 10:25** "When the whirlwind passes, the wicked is no more, But the righteous has an everlasting foundation."

4) **1 Corinthians 15:58** "Therefore, my beloved brethren, be steadfast, immovable, always abounding in the work of the Lord, knowing that your toil is not in vain in the Lord."

5) **1 Corinthians 16:13** "Be on the alert, stand firm in the faith, act like men, be strong."

6) **2 Corinthians 5:6,8** "Therefore, being always of good courage, and knowing that while we are at home in the body we are absent from the Lord. 8 we are of good courage, I say, and prefer rather to be absent from the body and to be at home with the Lord."

7) **2 Corinthians 7:4** "Great is my confidence in you; great is my boasting on your behalf. I am filled with comfort; I am overflowing with joy in all our affliction."

8) **Ephesians 3:12** "In whom we have boldness and confident access through faith in Him."

9) **Ephesians 3:13** "Therefore I ask you not to lose heart at my tribulations on your behalf, for they are your glory."

10) **Ephesians 3:16** "that He would grant you, according to the riches of His glory, to be strengthened with power through His Spirit in the inner man,"

11) **Ephesians 6:13** "Therefore, take up the full armor of God, so that you will be able to resist in the evil day, and having done everything, to stand firm."

12) **Ephesians. 6:19** "and pray on my behalf, that utterance may be given to me in the opening of my mouth, to <u>make known with boldness</u> the mystery of the gospel,"

13) **Philippians 1:6** "For I <u>am confident</u> of this very thing, that He who began a good work in you will perfect it until the day of Christ Jesus."

14) **Philippians 1:20** "according to my earnest expectation and hope, that I will not be put to shame in anything, but that with <u>all boldness,</u> Christ will even now, as always, be exalted in my body, whether by life or by death."

15) **Philippians 1:27** "Only conduct yourselves in a manner worthy of the gospel of Christ, so that whether I come and see you or remain absent, I will hear of you that you are <u>standing firm</u> in one spirit, with one mind striving together for the faith of the gospel;"

16) **Philippians 4:1** "Therefore, my beloved brethren whom I long to see, my joy and crown, in this way <u>stand firm</u> in the Lord, my beloved."

17) **Colossians 1:23** "if indeed you continue in the faith <u>firmly established</u> and <u>steadfast,</u> and <u>not moved</u> away from the hope of the gospel that you have heard, which was proclaimed in all creation under heaven, and of which I, Paul, was made a minister."

18) **Colossians 2:7** "having been firmly rooted and now being built up in Him and <u>established</u> in your faith, just as you were instructed, and overflowing with gratitude."

19) **1 Thessalonians 3:8** "or now we really live, if you <u>stand firm</u> in the Lord."

20) **1 Thessalonians. 3:13** "so that He <u>may establish your hearts</u> without blame in holiness before our God and Father at the coming of our Lord Jesus with all His saints."

21) **2 Thessalonians 2:15** "So then, brethren, <u>stand firm</u> and hold to the traditions which you were taught, whether by word of mouth or by letter from us."

22) **2 Thessalonians 2:16,17** "Now may our Lord Jesus Christ Himself and God our Father, who has loved us and given us eternal comfort and good hope by grace, comfort and <u>strengthen your hearts</u> in every good work and word."

23) **2 Peter 1:12** "Therefore, I will always be ready to remind you of these things, even though you already know them, and have <u>been established</u> in the truth which is present with you."

24) **James 5:8** "You too be patient; <u>strengthen your hearts,</u> for the coming of the Lord is near."

14 - Strong Speaker: So, God wants us to stand firm and steadfast, and to be bold, established and confident. Back to you, ____(Chairperson name)____ .

15 - *Chairperson: Thank you, ____(Speaker name)____ . If God's will is for us to be happy and strong, what do you think gets in the way of us experiencing these attributes in our lives? Hosea 4:6 gives us a clue: It says, "My people are destroyed for a lack of knowledge." Knowledge is powerful. Here to help us understand the importance of gathering knowledge is our Knowledge Speaker, ____(Speaker name)____ .*

16 - Knowledge Speaker: **Thank you, ___(Chairperson name)___.** **God urges us to gain knowledge, and from the verses below, I will pick one randomly to read, and then speak briefly on how it applies to the importance of gathering knowledge. The verse I choose is _____.**

1) King Solomon prayed to God for wisdom and knowledge when he was crowned king.

   2 Chronicles 1:9-12 "Now, O LORD God, let thy promise unto David my father be established: for thou hast made me king over a people like the dust of the earth in multitude. [10] Give me now wisdom and knowledge, that I may go out and come in before this people: for who can judge this thy people, that is so great? [11] And God said to Solomon, Because this was in thine heart, and thou hast not asked riches, wealth, or honour, nor the life of thine enemies, neither yet hast asked long life; but hast asked wisdom and knowledge for thyself, that thou mayest judge my people, over whom I have made thee king: [12] Wisdom and knowledge is granted unto thee; and I will give thee riches, and wealth, and honour, such as none of the kings have had that have been before thee, neither shall there any after thee have the like."

2) **Proverbs 2:3-5** "For if you <u>cry for discernment</u>, <u>Lift your voice for understanding</u>; If you seek her as silver And <u>search for her as for hidden treasures</u>; Then you will discern the fear of the Lord And discover the knowledge of God."

3) **Proverbs 3:13,14** "How blessed is the man who <u>finds wisdom</u> And the man who <u>gains understanding</u>. For her profit is better than the profit of silver And her gain better than fine gold."

4) **Proverbs 3:20-22** "By His <u>knowledge</u> the deeps were broken up And the skies drip with dew. My son, <u>let them not vanish from your sight</u>; <u>Keep sound wisdom and discretion</u>, So they will be life to your soul And adornment to your neck."

5) **Proverbs 4:1** "Hear, O sons, the instruction of a father, And give attention that you may <u>gain understanding</u>,"

6) **Proverbs 4:5-7** "<u>Acquire wisdom</u>! <u>Acquire understanding</u>! Do not forget nor turn away from the words of my mouth. "Do not forsake her, and she will guard you; Love her, and she will watch over you. "The beginning of wisdom is: <u>Acquire wisdom</u>; And with all your acquiring, <u>get understanding</u>."

7) **Proverbs 4:13** "<u>Take hold of instruction</u>; do not let go. Guard her, for she is your life."

8) **Proverbs 8:5** "O naive ones, <u>understand prudence</u>; And, O fools, <u>understand wisdom</u>."

9) **Proverbs 8:10** "<u>Take my instruction</u> and not silver, <u>And knowledge</u> rather than choicest gold."

10) **Proverbs 16:16** "How much better it is to <u>get wisdom</u> than gold! And to <u>get understanding</u> is to be chosen above silver."

11) **Proverbs 18:15** "The mind of the prudent acquires knowledge, And the ear of the wise seeks knowledge"

12) **Proverbs 23:23** "<u>Buy truth</u>, and do not sell it, Get wisdom and instruction and understanding."

13) **Proverbs 24:3-5** "By wisdom a house is built, And by understanding it is established; [4] And by knowledge the rooms are filled With all precious and pleasant riches. [5] A wise man is strong, And a man of knowledge increases power."

14) **Proverbs 24:14** "Know that wisdom is thus for your soul; If you find it, then there will be a future, And your hope will not be cut off."

17 - Knowledge Speaker: **So knowledge is valuable and vital for healing from anxiety and depression. Back to you, ___(Chairperson name)___.**

18 - *Chairperson:* *Thank you, ____(Speaker name)____. This program places a great emphasis on God's Word as our way toward peace and happiness. Here to help us understand the importance of God's Word is our Word Speaker, ____(Speaker name)____.*

19 - Word Speaker: **Thank you, ____(Chairperson name)____. God's Word is very important, and from the verses below, I will pick one randomly to read, and speak briefly on how it applies to the importance God's Word. The verse I choose is _____.**

1) **Psalm 107:20** <u>He sent His word and healed them,</u> And delivered them from their destructions."

2) The longest psalm in the Bible is Psalm 119. It has 176 verses! It is 2 ½ times longer than the next longest Psalm. The whole psalm talks about God's Word, how the writer loves God's Word. Do you think God is trying to teach us something about the importance of His Word?

3) **Psalm 138:2** I will bow down toward Your holy temple And give thanks to Your name for Your lovingkindness and Your truth; For <u>You have magnified Your word according to all Your name.</u>"

4) **Proverbs 4:4** "Then he taught me and said to me, "Let your heart hold fast my words; <u>Keep my commandments and live;</u>"

5) **Isaiah 55:11** "<u>So will My word be</u> which goes forth from My mouth; It will not return to Me empty, Without <u>accomplishing what I desire,</u> And <u>without succeeding in the matter for which I sent it.</u>'"

6) **Luke 6:47-48** "Everyone who comes to Me and hears My words and acts on them, I will show you whom he is like: he is like a man building a house, who dug deep and laid a foundation on the rock; and when a flood occurred, the torrent burst against that house and <u>could not shake it, because it had been well built.</u>"

7) **John 1:1** "<u>In the beginning was the Word,</u> and the <u>Word was with God,</u> and <u>the Word was God.</u>"

8) **John 8:37** Jesus told us how important God's Word is in John 8:37, saying, "I know that you are Abraham's descendants; yet you seek to kill Me, because My word has no place in you."

9) **John 15:7** Jesus told us how important God's Word is in John 15:7, saying, "If you abide in Me, <u>and My words abide in you,</u> ask whatever you wish, and it will be done for you."

10) **John 17:17** "Sanctify them in the truth; Your word is truth." *(God's Word is truth. And we know that the truth sets us free!)*

11) **Ephesians 6:17** "And take the helmet of salvation, and the sword of the Spirit, which is the word of God." *(You have to know the Word before you can use it!)*

20 - Word Speaker: **God's Word is important. But, building God's Word into our hearts, is equally important. From the verses below, I will pick one randomly to read, and speak, briefly, on how it applies to the importance of building God's Word into our hearts. I choose verse ____.**

1) **Exodus 13:9** "And it shall serve as a sign to you on your hand, and as a reminder on your forehead, that <u>the law of the Lord may be in your mouth</u>; for with a powerful hand the Lord brought you out of Egypt."

2) **Deuteronomy 6:6-9** "<u>These words</u>, which I am commanding you today, <u>shall be on your heart.</u> [7] You shall <u>teach them diligently to your sons</u> and shall talk of them when you sit in your house and when you walk by the way and when you lie down and when you rise up. [8] <u>You shall bind them as a sign on your hand</u> and they shall be as frontals on your forehead. [9] <u>You shall write them on the doorposts of your house and on your gates.</u>"

3) **Joshua 1:8** "<u>This book of the law shall not depart from your mouth</u>, but <u>you shall meditate on it day and night</u>, so that you may be careful to <u>do according to all that is written in it</u>; for then you will make your way prosperous, and then you will have success."

4) **Psalm 1:2-3** "<u>But his delight is in the law of the Lord</u>, And in <u>His law he meditates day and night</u>. He will be like a tree firmly planted by streams of water, Which yields its fruit in its season And its leaf does not wither; And in whatever he does, he prospers."

5) **Psalm 119:11** "Your word <u>I have treasured in my heart</u>, That I may not sin against You." *(Memorizing scripture can help us live "sin-free".)*

6) **Proverbs 2:1** "My son, <u>if you will receive my words</u> And <u>treasure my commandments within you, Make your ear attentive to wisdom, Incline your heart to understanding;</u> For <u>if you cry for discernment, Lift your voice for understanding; If you seek her as silver And search for her as for hidden treasures;</u> Then you will discern the fear of the Lord And discover the knowledge of God."

7) **Proverbs 4:4** "Then he taught me and said to me, "Let your heart hold fast my words <u>Keep my commandments and live;</u>"

8) **Proverbs 4:20,21** "My son, <u>give attention to my words; Incline your ear to my sayings. Do not let them depart from your sight; Keep them in the midst of your heart.</u>"

9) **Jeremiah 20:9** "But if I say, "I will not remember Him Or speak anymore in His name," Then <u>in my heart it becomes like a burning fire</u> Shut up in my bones; And I am weary of holding it in, And I cannot endure it."

10) **Luke 4:1-4** *Jesus used God's Word to defend himself when he was tempted by the devil:* Jesus, full of the Holy Spirit, returned from the Jordan and was led around by the Spirit in the wilderness for forty days, being tempted by the devil. And He ate nothing during those days, and when they had ended, He became hungry. And the devil said to Him, "If You are the Son of God, tell this stone to become bread." And Jesus answered him, "<u>It is written</u>, 'Man shall not live on bread alone.'"

11) **Luke 4:5-8** "And he led Him up and showed Him all the kingdoms of the world in a moment of time. And the devil said to Him, "I will give You all this domain and its glory; for it has been handed over to me, and I give it to whomever I wish. Therefore if You worship before me, it shall all be Yours." Jesus answered him, "<u>It is written</u>, 'You shall worship the Lord your God and serve Him only.'"

12) **Luke 4:9-13** "And he led Him to Jerusalem and had Him stand on the pinnacle of the temple, and said to Him, "If You are the Son of God, throw Yourself down from here; for it is written, 'He will command His angels concerning You to guard You,' and, 'On their hands they will bear You up, So that You will not strike Your foot against a stone.'" And Jesus answered and said to him, "<u>It is said</u>, 'You shall not put the Lord your God to the test.'" When the devil had finished every temptation, he left Him until an opportune time."

13) **Luke 6:43-45** "or there is no good tree which produces bad fruit, nor, on the other hand, a bad tree which produces good fruit. For each tree is known by its own fruit. For men do not gather figs from thorns, nor do they pick grapes from a briar bush. The good man out of the <u>good treasure of his heart brings forth what is good;</u> and the evil man out of the evil treasure brings forth what is evil; for his <u>mouth speaks from that which fills his heart</u>."

14) **Luke 6:49** "But the one who has heard and has not acted accordingly, is like a man who built a house on the ground without any foundation; and the torrent burst against it and immediately it collapsed, and the ruin of that house was great."

15) **John 1:14** "And <u>the Word became flesh</u>, and dwelt among us, and we saw His glory, glory as of the only begotten from the Father, full of grace and truth."

16) **John 8:31,32** "So Jesus was saying to those Jews who had believed Him, "<u>If you continue in My word, then you are truly disciples of Mine</u>; and you will know the truth, and the truth will make you free."

17) **Romans 10:8** "But what does it say? "<u>The word is near you, in your mouth and in your heart</u>"—that is, the word of faith which we are preaching,"

18) **Colossians 3:16** "<u>Let the word Christ richly dwell within you,</u> with all wisdom teaching and admonishing one another with psalms and hymns and spiritual songs, singing with thankfulness in your hearts to God."

19) **James 1:21** "Therefore, putting aside all filthiness and all that remains of wickedness, in humility <u>receive the word implanted, which is able to save your souls</u>."

21 - Word Speaker: One cause of emotional pain can be sin. God's Word has an answer for that. From the verses below, I will pick one randomly to read, and speak, briefly, on how it applies to God having an answer for sin. The verse I choose is number _____.

1) **Psalm 119:2,3** "How blessed are those who <u>observe His testimonies</u>, Who seek Him with all their heart. <u>They also do no unrighteousness</u> They walk in His ways."

2) **Psalm 119:9** "How can a young man keep his way pure? By keeping it according to Your word."

3) **Psalm 119:11** "<u>Your word I have treasured in my heart, That I may not sin against You.</u> *(When you memorize God's Word, you are able to recite God's Word throughout your day. By doing so, you are less apt to fall into temptation to sin.)*

4) **Psalm 119:127,128** "Therefore <u>I love Your commandments</u> Above gold, yes, above fine gold. Therefore <u>I esteem right all Your precepts</u> concerning everything, I hate every false way."

22 - Word Speaker: Since God's Word is so important, we should ask ourselves: 1) How much time do I spend each day reading and meditating on God's Word? 2) Could it be that my struggles are tied to: a) a lack of interest in God's Word, or b) a lack of understanding of what it teaches about victorious living. Consider praying this prayer: "God, please give me a hunger for your Word." Back to you, ____(Chairperson name)____.

23 - *Chairperson: Thank you, ____(Speaker name)___ . Three personal attributes we recommend you develop in your life are: Faith, Truth, and Love. Here to help us understand the importance of Faith, is our Faith Speaker, ___(Speaker name)___ .*

24 - Faith Speaker: Thank you, ____(Chairperson name)____ . The attribute of Faith is an amazing tool. It enables us to roll our problems over to God, thus freeing us up to enjoy life while we wait for God to move on our behalf. The following are Biblical principles that can help us live in Faith, and keep us in a state of constant peace. From the principles below, I will pick one randomly to read, and speak, briefly, on how it helps us live by Faith. I choose Principle ____.

The Principles Of Faith

1) Based on Hebrews Chapter 11, we see that God places a strong emphasis on a person's faith. *"And without faith it is impossible to please Him, for he who comes to God must believe that He is and that He is a rewarder of those who seek Him."* **Hebrews 11:6**

2) Based on Galatians 5:6, faith works along side of love. *"For in Christ Jesus neither circumcision nor uncircumcision means anything, but faith working through love."* **Galatians 5:6**

3) Based on James 2:26, faith must be demonstrated. (Belief plus Action = Faith) *"For as the body without the spirit is dead, so faith without works is dead also."* **James 2:26** *"You see that faith was working with his works, and as a result of the works, faith was perfected."* **James 2:22**

4) Based on Hebrews 10:35,36, faith must be patient. *"Therefore, do not throw away your confidence, which has a great reward. For you have need of endurance, so that when you have done the will of God, you may receive what was promised."* **Hebrews 10:35,36** *"so that you will not be sluggish, but imitators of those who through faith and patience inherit the promises."* **Hebrews 6:12**

5) Based on 2 Corinthians 5:7, we do not judge a problem's solvability by how impossible *it looks* or how bad *we feel*. *"For we walk by faith, not by sight:"* **2 Corinthians 5:7**

6) Based on Mark 11:24, we believe we have received the thing we have asked for, even before we actually have it. Jesus says, *"Therefore I say to you, all things for which you pray and ask, believe that you have received them, and they will be granted you."* **Mark 11:24** *"And all things you ask in prayer, believing, you will receive."* **Matthew 21:22**

7) Based on James 5:15, we see that faith can heal a sick body. *"and the prayer offered in faith will restore the one who is sick, and the Lord will raise him up, and if he has committed sins, they will be forgiven him."* **James 5:15**

8) Based on 1 Timothy 6:12 & Ephesians Chapter 6, we understand that the life of faith is a *fight*. But based on Romans 8:37, we believe we are more than able to win this fight. *"Fight the good fight of faith; take hold of the eternal life to which you were called, and you made the good confession in the presence of many witnesses."* **1 Timothy 6:12** *"But in all these things we overwhelmingly conquer through Him who loved us."* **Romans 8:37**

9) Based on James 1:6-8, we see that people who waiver in their faith shouldn't expect to receive anything from God. *"But he must ask in faith without any doubting, for the one who doubts is like the surf of the sea, driven and tossed by the wind. For that man ought not to expect that he will receive anything from the Lord, being a double-minded man, unstable in all his ways."* **James 1:6-8**

10) Based on Romans 10:17, faith must be developed. It does not come naturally. It comes from reading and speaking God's Word. *"So faith comes from hearing, and hearing by the word of Christ."* **Romans 10:17**

25 - Faith Speaker: This principle helps us with _____. Back to you, ___(Chairperson name)___.

26 - *Chairperson: Thank you, ___(Chairperson name)___. Here to help us understand the importance of Truth, is our Truth Speaker, ___(Speaker name)___.*

27 - Truth Speaker: Thank you, ___(Chairperson name)___. The key verses for the Truth Speaker are John 8:31-32, in which Jesus said to the Jews who had believed in Him: *"If you abide in my word, you are truly my disciples, and you will know the truth, and the truth will set you free."* Indeed, the Truth *can* set us free! Circumstances take place in our lives that cause us to believe lies. These lies tell us that problems will never change, habits cannot be broken, loved ones will never change, and so on. The antidote to these lies is Truth. For every problem in our lives there is a Truth that can set us free, emotionally, from the problem. The problem may still be there, but the anxiety related to it is gone. Below are some common lies we sometimes believe. From the lies below, I will pick one randomly to read, and speak, briefly, on how it hinders our happiness, and how the truth can set us free. I will choose lie number ____.

1) God doesn't love me.

2) I could never get married.

3) I could never forgive that person.

4) I could never be healed physically.

5) I could never be happy with my spouse.

6) Nobody would want to be my friend.

7) I need to have a spouse to be happy.

8) I could never be happy in my job.

9) I need money or things to be happy.

10) I'll never progress past this level of success.

11) I need to be loved and accepted to be happy.

12) I could never break free from my addiction.

13) I'll never have what it takes to be gainfully employed.

14) My worrying about problems shows that I am responsible.

15) My past is so bad, I'll never recover from my emotional wounds.

16) I could never be happy without this person. (e.g. A loved one who passes away)

17) I need to change my bodily features to be happy and accepted. *(e.g. weight changes or cosmetic surgery.)*

18) I need to act a certain way to be happy and accepted. *(e.g. "I need to be the life of the party.)"*

28 - Truth Speaker: By seeing these lies for what they are, and using the Truth of God's Word to renew our minds, we can be set free from these lies! Back to you, ___(Chairperson name)___.

29 - *Chairperson: Thank you, ___(Speaker name)___. Here to help us understand the importance of Love, is our Love Speaker, ___(Speaker name)___.*

30 - Love Speaker: Thank you, ___(Chairperson name)___. Love helps us respond properly to life's challenges. We may know *what* we should do, but it is Love that allows us to do it willfully and cheerfully. Love is not based on feelings, but on our commitments. Love is a decision we make each day and is proven by our actions. From the verses below, I will pick one randomly to read, and speak, briefly, on how it applies to the importance of Love. I will choose verse ____.

1) **Romans 13:8** "Owe nothing to anyone except to love one another; for he who loves his neighbor has fulfilled the law."

2) **Matthew 5:43-45** "You have heard that it was said, 'You shall love your neighbor and hate your enemy.' [44]But I say to you, love your enemies and pray for those who persecute you, [45] so that you may be sons of your Father who is in heaven; for He causes His sun to rise on the evil and the good, and sends rain on the righteous and the unrighteous."

3) **1 Corinthians 13:3** "And if I give all my possessions to feed the poor, and if I surrender my body to be burned, but do not have love, it profits me nothing."

4) **1 Corinthians 13:4** "Love is patient, love is kind and is not jealous; love does not brag and is not arrogant,"

5) **1 Corinthians 13:5** "does not act unbecomingly; it does not seek its own, is not provoked, does not take into account a wrong suffered,"

6) **1 Corinthians 13:6** "Love does not rejoice in unrighteousness, but rejoices with the truth;"

7) **1 Corinthians 13:7** "Love bears all things, believes all things, hopes all things, endures all things."

8) **1 Corinthians 13:8** "Love never fails; but if there are gifts of prophecy, they will be done away; if there are tongues, they will cease; if there is knowledge, it will be done away."

9) **1 Corinthians 13:13** "But now faith, hope, love, abide these three; but the greatest of these is love."

10) **Galatians 5:13** "For you were called to freedom, brethren; only do not turn your freedom into an opportunity for the flesh, but through love serve one another."

11) **Galatians 5:14** "For the whole Law is fulfilled in one word, in the statement, "You shall love your neighbor as yourself.""

12) **Galatians 5:22,23** "But the fruit of the Spirit is love, joy, peace, patience, kindness, goodness, faithfulness, gentleness, self-control; against such things there is no law."

13) **Ephesians 4:2** "with all humility and gentleness, with patience, showing tolerance for one another in love,"

14) **1 Peter 1:22** "Since you have in obedience to the truth purified your souls for a sincere love of the brethren, fervently love one another from the heart:"

15) **1 Peter 4:8** "Above all, keep fervent in your love for one another, because love covers a multitude of sins."

16) **1 John 4:7** "Beloved, let us love one another, for love is from God; and everyone who loves is born of God and knows God."

17) **1 John 4:18** "There is no fear in love; but perfect love casts out fear, because fear involves punishment, and the one who fears is not perfected in love."

31 - Love Speaker: **So Love is vital to living a happy fruitful life! Back to you, ___(Chairperson name)___ .**

32 - *Chairperson: Thank you,* ____(Speaker name)____. *Affirmations are designed to be spoken out loud, enabling us to use our own self-help resource, our tongue. Here to help us understand the importance of affirmations is our Affirmations Speaker,* ____(Speaker name)____.

33 - Affirmations Speaker: Thank you, ____(Chairperson name)____. As we hear truth spoken by our own mouth, our belief system begins to change. Positive beliefs spawn positive thoughts, and positive thoughts create and maintain happiness. This program offers both generic and Bible-based affirmations. You can even create your own affirmations, customized for situations you come up against. I will pick a Generic Affirmation to read, and share, briefly, how it helps us. The affirmation I choose is ____.

Generic Affirmations

1) "I am bigger than fear."

2) "I bounce back easily."

3) "I live my life effortlessly."

4) "My job is easy."

5) "I handle change easily."

6) "I love a challenge."

7) "Self-discipline is my strong point."

8) "I always see a silver lining."

9) "I see myself as a peaceful, loving person."

10) "You can't upset me. (I won't let you.)"

11) "I see myself as a winner before I see my victory."

12) "I forgive everybody immediately after they hurt me."

13) "God can bring good out of any of my mistakes."

14) "I see my prayers getting answered before I see the actual answer to my prayers."

15) "I see myself as healed in my body before I see and feel the changes I desire."

34 - Affirmations Speaker: I will now choose one of the Bible-based Affirmations below, in which we will all read 3 statements from. The Affirmation I choose is number ____.

Bible-Based Affirmations

1) "I Do Not Fear" Affirmation (Page 173)

2) "I Am Strong" Affirmation (Page 176)

3) "I Flow in Harmony and Love" Affirmation (Page 179)

4) "I Only Speak Right Words" Affirmation (Page 181)

5) "I Only Think Right Thoughts" Affirmation (Page 183)

6) "I Am Happy Because…" Affirmation (Page 186)

35 - Affirmation Speaker: Positive affirmations spoken boldly, define what we believe is true. Doing so positions us to receive more from God and from life! So speak boldly! Back to you, ____(Chairperson name)____.

36 - *Chairperson: Thank you,* ____(Speaker name)____. *Slogans are thought-provoking statements that challenge us to respond to life's problems positively. To tell us more on Slogans is our Slogans Speaker,* ____(Speaker name)____.

37 - Slogans Speaker: **Thank you, ___(Chairperson name)___. From the slogans below, I will pick one randomly to read, and share, briefly, on how it helps us. The slogan I choose is number____.**

1) "Sleep on it."

2) "Don't enable."

3) "I play to win!"

4) "You can start again."

5) "Knowledge is power."

6) "My job is to believe."

7) "Every day's a good day."

8) "Say it until you believe it."

9) "Respond rather than react."

10) "God is bigger than the facts!"

11) "We live by faith, not by sight."

12) "When we're in a battle, we fight!"

13) "Stop running and start confronting."

14) "It's not my problem, it's God's problem."

15) "Positive believing produces positive thinking."

16) "Faith is a lifestyle I can learn."

17) "Anger can be a sign that you are judging."

18) "God responds to faith, seldom to need."

19) "Don't make their problem, your problem."

20) "Problems are opportunities to see God move."

21) "The best *Defense* is a strong Offense."

22) "There is a stress-cancelling response to every problem."

23) "Don't focus on what you lost, focus on what you gained!"

24) "Life is 10% what happens to you, 90% how you respond to it."

25) "Problems are inevitable, the stress is optional."

38 - Slogans Speaker: **Slogans are quick reminders of the truth. Say them often! Back to you, ___(Chairperson name)_____.**

39 - *Chairperson:* ***Thank you, ___(Speaker name)___. There's an easy way to keep our thinking in check. Here to tell us more on that is our Beliefs Speaker, ___(Speaker name)___.***

40 - Beliefs Speaker: **Thank you, ___(Chairperson name)___. Our thinking is influenced by our beliefs. Positive beliefs help us keep our responses to life's problems positive. We recommend adopting the following six Core Beliefs. The idea is to make these Core Beliefs the final word in our lives. No matter what our feelings say or what the circumstances try to tell us, these foundational beliefs are what we are going to use when thinking about ourselves, and when making decisions in our lives. For any belief that feels untrue, we simply say the scriptures associated with that belief over and over until the belief feels true. I will choose one Core Belief to read 3 verses from. The core belief I pick is number ____.**

Core Beliefs

1) "I Believe God loves me, and that I am valuable." (Pg 195)

2) "I Believe Christ's crucifixion paid for my sin." (Pg 199)

3) "I Believe God wants me to live in perfect peace." (Pg 204)

4) "I Believe I have an enemy – Satan." (Pg 208)

5) "I Believe I have another enemy – my fleshly appetites." (Pg 216)

6) "I Believe God wants me to enjoy good physical health." (Pg 218)

41 - Beliefs Speaker: So, adopting and developing this Core Belief will help us with _____. Back to you, ____(Chairperson name)____.

42 - *Chairperson: Thank you, ____(Speaker name)____. Our unhappiness can sometimes be easily diagnosed by pinpointing what the hindrance is. Here to talk to us about hindrances to happiness is our Hindrance Speaker, ____(Speaker name)____.*

43 - Hindrance Speaker: Thank you, ____(Chairperson name)____. There are many hindrances to happiness. From the hindrances below, I will pick one randomly to read, and speak, briefly, how it affects our happiness. The Hindrance I choose is number ____.

Hindrances

1) Self-pity "If only…"
2) Having an unthankful heart
3) Ostracized by community
4) Double-mindedness
5) Lack of purpose
6) Believing lies
7) Guilt (real or imagined)
8) Entitlement mentality
9) Sin, or sinful thinking
10) Unforgiveness
11) Debt
12) Shame
13) Anger
14) Isolation
15) Perfectionism
16) Lack of patience
17) Physical tiredness
18) Doubt and Unbelief
19) A Rebellious Heart
20) Mourning a loss
21) Pouting "I want it my way!"
22) Having an unthankful heart
23) Leaning on your own intellect
24) Being judgmental toward people.
25) Enabling abusive or poor behavior

44 - Hindrance Speaker: Let's live free of hindrances so we can brightly shine God's love in everything we do! Back to you, ____(Chairperson name)____.

45 - *Chairperson: Thank you, ____(Speaker name)____. We'll now work with one of the Happiness Tips. The place we left off last time was Page #____.* *[If the place isn't known, the Chairperson may choose any Tip, and when finished, bring the group back here.]*

(After working a Tip.)

46 - Gospel Speaker: We believe it is important to have a relationship with God, and that this relationship can help us find healing in our emotions. Let's take turns reading the following statements in the order we've been using. *[Chairperson prompts speakers in the existing order.]*

1) The main purpose of the Bible is to show mankind their need of Jesus Christ.

2) God wants to fellowship with mankind, but He can't until the issue of their sin has been dealt with.

3) Throughout the Bible there are prophecies about Jesus, and there are stories about Jesus.

4) All of these are there to show us the importance of Jesus.

5) Because of our tendency to sin, we need someone who would pay the penalty of our sin. And that was Jesus.

6) **John 3:16** says, "For God so loved the world, that He gave His]only begotten Son, that whoever believes in Him shall not perish, but have eternal life."

7) **Romans 1:16** says, "For I am not ashamed of the gospel, for it is the power of God for salvation to everyone who believes, to the Jew first and also to the Greek."

8) **Romans 6:23** says, "For the wages of sin is death, but the free gift of God is eternal life in Christ Jesus our Lord."

9) **Romans 5:8** says, "But God demonstrates His own love toward us, in that while we were yet sinners, Christ died for us."

10) Jesus, God's Son, came to earth to show us how to live, and to pay the penalty for our sin by dying on the cross.

11) Once we personally receive forgiveness for our sin, and ask Jesus to guide our lives, we find New Life! And we become part of God's family.

12) **John 3:3** says, "Truly, truly, I say to you, unless one is born again he cannot see the kingdom of God."

13) So, we must be born again. Is there anyone here who would like to become born again? And find New Life! And find forgiveness for their sins and become a part of God's family?

47 - *Chairperson: Please read along as I say the invitational prayer below.*

> **"Dear God, I see the sins that I have committed. I believe Jesus paid the penalty for my sin by His crucifixion. I receive your forgiveness for my sin. And I ask you to come into my life, and help me to live the rest of my life in a way that pleases you. Amen."**

48 - *Congratulations! If you've prayed this prayer sincerely, you are now born again! You are now a part of God's family! And we, as a group, will help you learn how to live a happy, fruitful life in Christ. Welcome to God's family!*

49 - *Chairperson: For those of us who are already born again, God asks us to tell the world that they can be born again. Here are some verses that bear this out. Let's take turns reading these verses out loud.*

14) **Mark 16:15** (Jesus tells us) "Go into all the world and preach the gospel to all creation."

15) **2 Corinthians 5:20**, "Therefore, we are ambassadors for Christ, as though God were making an appeal through us; we beg you on behalf of Christ, be reconciled to God."

16) **2 Corinthians 5:18**, "Now all these things are from God, who reconciled us to Himself through Christ and gave us the ministry of reconciliation,"

17) **2 Corinthians 5:14**, "For the love of Christ controls us, having concluded this, that one died for all, therefore all died;"

18) **2 Corinthians 3:6**, "who also made us adequate as servants of a new covenant, not of the letter but of the Spirit; for the letter kills, but the Spirit gives life."

50 - *So let's challenge ourselves to tell the Good News of Jesus wherever we go this week. May God help us!*

51 - *We would like to take time now to pray for each other's needs.* *[Chairperson asks each person individually if they have any prayer requests, writing each one down, then asks who would like to pray for each person. Then the Chairperson goes back through the list asking each person who offered to pray to do so.]*

52 - *Does anyone have any final words before we conclude our meeting?*

53 - *I will now offer a closing prayer...*

54 - *Our meetings are held* *[tell days/times].*

Meeting Options

Occasionally, Chairpersons may elect to have someone give their testimony of how God help them recover from a mental health condition. Another option is to add a segment in the meeting devoted to sharing The Lord's Supper with everyone.

Affirmation #1

"I DO NOT FEAR"

****

Throughout your day, try to recite out loud, the "I Do Not Fear" Affirmation.

Prayer of Dedication: "Father, I dedicate myself to live a life free of all fear. I now speak these Bible-based statements out loud to build in me a rock solid faith that keeps me at peace all day long."

The extra commas make the words more meditative and impactful. It also helps people read in unison during conference calls.

****

1) It is the Lord, who goes before me, He is with me, He will not leave me, nor fail me. I do not fear, nor am I dismayed. Based on Deuteronomy 31:8.

2) No one is able, to stand before me, all the days of my life. As God was with Moses, He is with me; He will never fail me, nor forsake me. Based on Joshua 1:5.

3) I am strong, and courageous, I am careful to obey, all the laws of God, I do not turn from it, to the right, or to the left, and I succeed, wherever I go. Based on Joshua 1:7.

4) I am strong, and courageous. I do not tremble, nor am I dismayed, for the Lord my God, is with me, wherever I go. Based on Joshua 1:9.

5) I listen to God, and I live securely, I am at ease, from the dread of evil. Based on Proverbs 1:33.

6) I walk in my way, securely, my foot does not stumble. Based on Proverbs 3:23.

7) When I lie down, I will not be afraid, when I lie down, my sleep is sweet. Based on Proverbs 3:24.

8) I am not afraid, of sudden fear, nor the onslaught, of the wicked, when they come, the Lord is my confidence, He keeps my foot, from being caught. Based on Proverbs 3:25-26.

9) The fear of man, brings a snare, but because I trust in the Lord, I am exalted. Based on Proverbs 29:25.

10) The Lord is a shield for me, He lifts up my head. Based on Psalm 3:3.

11) I lie down and sleep. I wake again, because the Lord sustains me. Based on Psalm 3:5.

12) I am not afraid, of tens of thousands of people, who have set themselves against me, all around. Based on Psalm 3:6.

13) When evil doers come up against me, they stumble and fall. Based on Psalm 27:2.

14) The LORD is my light, and my salvation, whom shall I fear? The Lord is the defense of my life, of whom shall I dread? Based on Psalm 27:1.

15) Though a host encamps against me, my heart will not fear; though war rises against me, I am confident. Based on Psalm 27:3.

16) For in my time of trouble, He conceals me in His tabernacle; In the secret place, of His tent, He hides me. He lifts me up, on a rock. Based on Psalm 27:5.

17) My head is lifted up, above the enemies, all around me; In His tent, I offer shouts of joy; I sing praises to the LORD. Based on Psalm 27:6.

18) Though my father and mother, forsake me, the LORD will take me up. Based on Psalm 27:10.

19) I wait for the LORD; I am strong, and my heart takes courage, I wait for the LORD. Based on Psalm 27:14.

20) I sought the Lord, and He answered me, and delivered me, from all my fears. Based on Psalm 34:4.

21) I stop myself, from being angry, I forsake my wrath, I do not fret, for any reason. Based on Psalm 37:8.

22) There is no reason for my soul to be in despair. My hope is in God, And I praise Him, He is the help, of my countenance. Based on Psalm 42:11.

23) I dwell in the shelter, of the Most High, and I abide, in the shadow of the Almighty. Based on Psalm 91:1.

24) I say of the Lord, "He is my refuge, and my fortress, my God, in him I trust." Based on Psalm 91:2.

25) Surely God delivers me, from the trappers snare, and from the deadly pestilence. Based on Psalm 91:3.

26) God covers me, with His pinions, under His wings, I seek refuge, His faithfulness, is my shield, and bulwark. Based on Psalm 91:4. (Bulwark is a defensive wall.)

27) I do not fear, the terror of night, nor the arrow, that flies by day, nor the pestilence, that stalks in the darkness, nor the destruction that destroys at noon. Based on Psalm 91:5-6. (Pestilence means deadly disease.)

28) A thousand fall at my side, ten thousand at my right hand, it does not approach me. Based on Psalm 91:7.

29) With my eyes, I see the recompense of the wicked, because I make the Lord, who is my refuge, my dwelling place. Based on Psalm 91:8,9. (Recompense means reward or payment)

30) No evil befalls me, neither any plague comes near my home. Based on Psalm 91:10.

31) God commands His angels charge over me, to guard me, in all my ways. They bear me up, in their hands, so I do not dash my foot, against a stone. Based on Psalm 91:11-12.

32) I tread upon the lion, and the cobra. The young lion, and the serpent, I trample under my feet. Based on Psalm 91:13.

33) Because God loves me, He delivers me, God sets me securely on high, because I know His name. Based on Psalm 91:14.

34) I call upon God, and He answers me. He is with me in trouble, and He rescues me, and honors me. Based on Psalm 91:15.

35) God is my salvation; I trust, and I am not afraid. The Lord God, is my strength, and my song. He is my salvation. Based on Isaiah 12:2.

36) I encourage myself when I'm exhausted, and I strengthen my knees, I say to my heart, "Take courage! Do not fear! My God, will come through, with vengeance. He comes! and saves me!" Based on Isaiah 35:3-4.

37) I do not fear, for God is with me. I do not anxiously look about me, for God is my God, He strengthens me, He helps me, He upholds me, with His righteous right hand. Based on Isaiah 41:10.

38) I do not fear, for the Lord my God, holds my right hand. It is He who says, "Do not fear, I will help you." Based on Isaiah 41:13.

39) I do not fear, for He says, "Fear not, for I have redeemed you; I have called you by name, you are mine." Based on Isaiah 43:1.

40) I do not fear, for He says, "When you pass through the waters, I will be with you; and through the rivers, they shall not overflow you; when you walk through the fire, you shall not be scorched, neither shall the flame burn you."   Based on Isaiah 43:2.

41) God has given me power, to trample on serpents, and scorpions, over all the power of the enemy. Nothing injures me! Based on Luke 10:19.

42) I am not afraid, for it is God my father's, good pleasure, to give me the kingdom. Based on Luke 12:32.

43) I have not received, the spirit of slavery, that leads to fear, but the spirit of adoption, as sons, so I cry "Abba Father!" Based on Romans 8:15.

44) Because God is for me, I do not fear, those against me. Based on Romans 8:31.

45) I stand fast, in one spirit, with one mind, striving together, for the faith of the gospel, without being alarmed, by my opponents. Based on Philippians 1:27-28.

46) I do not overly care, about anything, but in everything, by prayer and supplication, with thanksgiving, I make my requests to God. And the peace of God, which surpasses all comprehension, guards my heart, and my mind, in Christ Jesus. Based on Philippians 4:6-7. (Supplication means petition)

47) God has not given me, a spirit of timidity, but a spirit of power, of love, and of a discipline. Based on 2 Timothy 1:7.

48) God has said to me, "I will never desert you, nor forsake you." Based on Hebrews 13:5.

49) I confidently say, "The Lord is my helper, I am not afraid, what man can do to me? Based on Hebrews 13:6.

50) I do not fear, there is no fear in love. Perfect love, casts out all fear. God has made me perfect, in love. Based on 1 John 4:18.

51) I cast all my anxieties, onto God, because He cares for me. Based on 1 Peter 5:7.

Let's go back to the Affirmation Speaker role.

AFFIRMATION #2
"I AM STRONG"

****

Throughout your day, try to recite out loud, the "I Am Strong" Affirmation.

Prayer of Dedication: "Father, I dedicate myself to live this day with a 'strength conscious' mindset. I now speak these Bible-based statements out loud to build in me a strong spirit that carries me victoriously through each challenge in my day!"

The extra commas make the words more meditative and impactful. It also helps people read in unison during conference calls.

****

1) No man is able, to stand before me, all the days of my life, as God was with Moses, He is with me, my God will not leave me, nor forsake me, I am strong, I have good courage. Based on Joshua 1:5.

2) For by God, I can run upon a troop, and leap over a wall, Based on 2 Samuel 22:30.

3) God's Word is proven, He is a shield to me, because I trust Him. Based on 2 Samuel 22:31.

4) God is my rock, and my fortress, and my deliverer; my God my strength, in whom I take refuge; He is my shield, the horn of my salvation, my stronghold. Based on Psalm 18:2.

5) God arms me with strength, He makes my way blameless, He makes my feet, like hinds' feet, He sets me on high places, God trains my hands for battle, so that my arms, can bend a bow of bronze. Based on Psalm 18:32-34.

6) I pursue my enemies, I overtaken them, I do not turn back, until they are consumed, I shatter them, so they cannot rise, they fall under my feet. Based on Psalm 18:37,38.

7) God has armed me, with strength for battle, God subdues those under me, those who rise up against me. Based on Psalm 18:39.

8) I wait on the Lord; I am strong, and my heart takes courage, I wait on the Lord. Based on Psalm 27:14.

9) The Lord is my strength, and my shield, My heart trusts in Him. Based on Psalm 28:7.

10) Because of Your favor, upon my life, You have made my mountain, to stand strong. Based on Psalm 30:7.

11) I am strong, and my heart takes courage, I strengthen my heart, as I hope in the Lord. Based on Psalm 31:24.

12) There is no reason, for me to despair, or be disturbed. My hope is in God. And I praise Him, He helps my countenance shine, He is my God. Based on Psalm 42:11.

13) Through God, I push back my adversaries, Through God's name, I trample those, who rise up against me. Based on Psalm 44:5.

14) God is in the midst of me, I will not be moved: God helps me, when the morning dawns. Based on Psalm 46:5.

15) God is my salvation, and my glory, the rock of my strength, My refuge is in God. Based on Psalm 62:7.

16) I proclaim good news; Kings of armies flee. I remain, and I divide the spoil! Based on Psalms 68:11,12.

17) God is the strength, of my heart, forever. Based on Psalm 73:26.

18) I dwell in the shelter, of the Most High, and I abide in the shadow, of the Almighty. Based on Psalm 91:1.

19) I flourish like a palm tree, I grow like a cedar, in Lebanon, I am planted, in the house of the Lord, and I flourish, in the courts of my God. Based on Psalm 92:12 & 13.

20) God satisfies my mouth, with good things; so that my youth, is renewed like the eagles. Based on Psalm 103:5.

21) God causes me to be fruitful, and has made me stronger, than my enemies. Based on Psalm 105:24.

22) God rescues my soul from death, my eyes from tears, and my feet from stumbling. Based on Psalm 116:8.

23) God strengthens me, according to His Word. Based on Psalm 119:28.

24) Because I trust in the Lord, I am like Mount Zion, which cannot be moved, I abide forever. Based on Psalm 125:1.

25) In the day, that I cry out to God, He answers me, and emboldens me, with strengthen in my soul. Based on Psalm 138:3.

26) God is the Lord of my rock. He trains my hands for war, and my fingers for battle. Based on Psalm 144:1.

27) The Lord is my confidence, and He keeps my feet, from being caught. Based on Proverbs 3:26.

28) Because I fear the Lord, I have strong confidence, and my children, have a place of refuge. Based on Proverbs 14:26.

29) I gird myself with strength, I make my arms strong. Based on Proverbs 31:17.

30) Strength and dignity, are my clothing, I smile at the future. Based on Proverbs 31:25.

31) I am righteous through Christ, I hold to my way, I have clean hands, I grow stronger and stronger. Based on Job 17:9.

32) God gives me strength, when I'm weary. When I lack might, He increases my power. (My strength is increasing!) Based on Isaiah 40:29.

33) As I wait for the Lord, I gain new strength. I mount up, with wings like eagles; I run, and do not get tired, I walk, and do not become weary. Based on Isaiah 40:31.

34) No weapon, formed against me, prospers, every tongue, that accuses me, in judgment, God condemns. This is my heritage, God vindicates me! Based on Isaiah 54:17.

35) I know my God, I am strong, and I take action! Based on Daniel 11:32.

36) Jesus has given me power, and authority, over all demons, He has given me power, to cure diseases! Based on Luke 9:1, Mark 6:7,13 and Matthew 10:1,6, Matthew 28:18.

37) I go out, and preach everywhere, the Lord working with me, and He confirms His Word, with signs and wonders! Based on Mark 16:20.

38) Jesus has given me, authority, to tread on serpents, and scorpions, and over all power, of the enemy, nothing injures me. Based on Luke 10:19.

39) I receive power, when the Holy Spirit, comes upon me. (I invite, the Holy Spirit, to enter my life, I believe I have His power!) Based on Acts 1:8.

40) With great power, I give witness, to the resurrection, of the Lord Jesus, abundant grace is upon me! Based on Acts 4:33.

41) In all things, I overwhelmingly conqueror, through Christ, who loves me. Based on Romans 8:37.

42) I bear up under everything, I believe all things, I hope all things, I endure all things. Based on 1 Corinthians 13:7.

43) I am steadfast, immovable, always abounding, in the work of the Lord, and I know, that my toil, is not in vain, in the Lord. Based on 1 Corinthians. 15:58.

44) I am alert, I stand firm in the faith; I act like men, I am strong! Based on 1 Corinthians 16:13.

45) I may be afflicted, in every way, but I'm not crushed. I may be perplexed, but I'm not in despair, I may be persecuted, but I'm not forsaken; I may be struck down, but I'm not destroyed! Based on 2 Corinthians 4:8,9.

46) Christ's grace, is sufficient for me; His power is perfected, in my weakness. Based on 2 Corinthians 12:9.

47) Finally, I am strong in the Lord, and in the strength of his might. Based on Ephesians 6:10.

48) I can do all things, through Christ, who strengthens me. Based on Philippians 4:13.

49) The Lord makes me, to increase in love, toward others, so that He establishes my heart, without blame, in holiness, before God, at the coming, of my Lord Jesus, with all His saints. Based on 1 Thessalonians 3:13.

50) The God of all grace, who has called me, into His eternal glory, in Christ, will himself, perfect, confirm, strengthen, and establish me! Based on 1 Peter 5:10.

Let's go back to the Affirmation Speaker role.

AFFIRMATION #3
"I FLOW IN HARMONY AND LOVE"

****

Throughout your day, try to recite out loud, the "I Flow in Harmony and Love" Affirmation.

Prayer of Dedication: "Father, I dedicate myself to live this day with a love saturated mindset. I now speak these Bible-based statements out loud, to build in me a heart of love that is present in everything I think, say, and do."

The extra commas make the words more meditative and impactful. It also helps people read in unison during conference calls.

****

1) I am careful to remove the "log," out of my own eye, before trying to remove the speck, out of my brothers (or sisters) eye. Based on Matthew 7:5.

2) When Jesus saw the crowd, He had compassion on them. I too have compassion, on all who are in my life. Based on Matthew 9:36.

3) I work hard, to support the week, I remember the words, of the Lord Jesus, it is more blessed to give, than to receive. Jesus is making me, into a very compassionate, giving person. Based on Acts 20:35.

4) I do not think of myself, more highly than I ought, but to have sound judgment, allowing others to have importance too. Based on Romans 12:3.

5) I am devoted to others, with brotherly love; I give preference to others, I give them honor. Based on Romans 12:10.

6) I contribute, to the needs, of the saints, I practice hospitality. Based on Romans 12:13.

7) I do not repay evil for evil, I respect what is right, in the sight of all men. Based on Romans 12:17.

8) I am not overcome by evil, I overcome evil with good. Based on Romans 12:21.

9) I love my neighbor as myself. I never do wrong to my neighbor. When I love, I am fulfilling the law. Based on Romans 13:9,10.

10) I behave properly, as in the day, never carousing, and drunkenness, never in sexual promiscuity and sensuality, nor in strife, or jealousy. Based on Romans 13:13.

11) I pursue things, which make for peace, and the building up of others. Based on Romans 14:19.

12) I please my neighbor, for His good, for His edification. Based on Romans 15:2.

13) God who gives me perseverance and encouragement, helps me to be likeminded, with other people, according to Christ Jesus. Based on Romans 15:5.

14) Father, your love, has been shed abroad, in my heart, by the Holy Spirit, I therefore patient, I am kind, I am not jealous, I do not brag, and am not arrogant. Based on 1 Corinthians 13:4.

15) I do not act unbecomingly. I do not seek my own way. I am not provoked. I do not take into account a suffered wrong. Based on 1 Corinthians. 13:5.

16) I do not rejoice in unrighteousness, I rejoice in the truth. Based on 1 Corinthians 13:6.

17) I bear up under all things, I believe the best about people. I'm very hopeful, I endure all things. Thus, I am very patient with people. Based on 1 Corinthians 13:7.

18) My love never fails. Based on 1 Corinthians 13:8.

19) I pursue love. And I desire spiritual gifts. Based on 1 Corinthians 14:1.

20) When I see a brother or sister, caught in a trespass, I restore such a person, in a spirit of gentleness. Based on Galatians 6:1.

21) With all humility and gentleness, and with patience, I show tolerance toward others, in love. Based on Ephesians 4:2.

22) I am diligent, to preserve, the unity of the Spirit, with others, in the bond of peace. Based on Ephesians 4:3.

23) My conduct is worthy, of the gospel of Christ, I stand firm, in one spirit, with one mind, striving together, for the faith of the gospel. Based on Philippians 1:27.

24) I make Paul's joy complete, I have the same mind with others, I am united in spirit, I am intent on one purpose. Based on Philippians 2:2.

25) I do nothing from selfishness, or empty conceit, but with humility of mind, I regard others, more important than myself. Based on Philippians 2:3.

26) I don't merely look out, for my own interests, but also for the interests of others. Based on Philippians 2:4.

27) I do not neglect doing good, and sharing with others, for of such sacrifices, God is pleased. Based on Hebrews 13:16.

28) I have some of the world's goods, and when I see, my brother in need, I do not close my heart, against him, because God's love, abides in me. Based on1 John 3:17.

Let's go back to the Affirmation Speaker role.

AFFIRMATION #4
"I ONLY SPEAK RIGHT WORDS"

****

Throughout your day, try to recite out loud, the "I Only Speak Right Words" Affirmation.

Prayer of Dedication: "Father, I dedicate myself to live this day speaking only right words, words that are free of all negatives. I now speak these Bible-based statements out loud to remind me to keep all my words positive and faith-filled!"

The extra commas make the words more meditative and impactful. It also helps people read in unison during conference calls.

****

1) My words are as a honeycomb, sweet to the soul, and healing to the bones. Based on Psalm 16:24.

2) My words are like a wellspring of wisdom, and as a flowing brook. Based on Proverbs18:4.

3) Because I guard my mouth, and my tongue, I guard my soul from troubles. Based on Proverbs 21:23.

4) Because I am righteous, my mouth speaks wisdom, and my tongue speaks what is just. Based on Psalm 37:30.

5) My heart thinks of good things. I speak things that help others. My words are like those, of a ready writer, recording good things. Based on Psalm 45:1.

6) I put away from me, a deceitful mouth, and devious speech, I put far from me. Based on Proverbs 4:24.

7) I speak God's Words, because they are life to me, they are health, to all my body. Based on Proverbs 4:22.

8) All the words of my mouth, are in righteousness; there is nothing crooked, or perverted in them. Based on Proverbs 8:8.

9) I speak noble things, and the opening of my lips, reveal right things only. My mouth speaks truth, and wickedness, is an abomination to my words. Based on Proverbs 8:6,7.

10) I have the mouth, of a righteous man, my words are like a fountain of life. Based on Proverbs 10:11.

11) Because I am righteous, my words are like choice silver. Based on Proverbs 10:20.

12) Because I am righteous, my words feed many. Based on Proverbs 10:21.

13) Because I am righteous, the words of my mouth bring forth wisdom, continually. Based on Proverbs 10:31.

14) Because I am righteous, my lips know, what is acceptable. Based on Proverbs 10:32.

15) I am satisfied with good, by the fruit of my words. Based on Proverbs 12:14.

16) Because I have God's wisdom, my words bring healing. Based on Proverbs 12:18.

17) Because I guard my words, I preserve my life, He that talks too much invites ruin into his life. Therefore, I watch what I say. Based on Proverbs 13:3.

18) Because a harsh word stirs up anger, I answer people gently, and my gentle answers turn away wrath. Based on Proverbs 15:1.

19) Because I continually seek knowledge, my wisdom helps me speak what is acceptable. The mouth of fools spout foolishness. Based on Proverbs 15:2.

20) My soothing words produce a tree of life. Based on Proverbs 15:4.

21) I have joy, when I answer properly. My timely words produce delight! Based on Proverbs 15:23.

22) As I prepare my heart, each day with prayer, and the Word, I believe the answers, of my tongue, are from the Lord. Based on Proverbs 16:1.

23) Gold and jewels are valuable. My knowledgeable words are also valuable. Based on Proverbs 20:15.

24) My soft words, break a bone. (bone-like resistance, from others). Based on Proverbs 25:15.

25) Because I am wise, the words of my mouth, are gracious. Based on Ecclesiastes 10:12.

26) The Lord has given me, the words of a disciple. This helps me speak uplifting words to him who is weary. Based on Isaiah 50:4.

Let's go back to the Affirmation Speaker role.

AFFIRMATION #5

"I ONLY THINK RIGHT THOUGHTS"

****

Throughout your day, try to recite out loud, the "I Only Think Right Thoughts" Affirmation.

Prayer of Dedication: "Father, I dedicate myself to live this day thinking only right thoughts, thoughts that are free of all negatives. I now speak these Bible-based statements out loud to remind me to keep all my thoughts positive and faith-filled!"

The extra commas make the words more meditative and impactful. It also helps people read in unison during conference calls.

****

1) I trust in the Lord, with all my heart, and I do not lean, on my own understanding. In all my ways, I acknowledge Him, and He makes my paths straight. Based on Proverbs 3:5-6.

2) I meditate, on God's Word, day and night, I am like a tree, planted by streams, that yeilds forth its fruit, in season. And my leaves, do not wither, in whatever I do, I prosper. Based on Psalm 1:2-3.

3) I pray every day, for God's help, to keep the words of my mouth, and the meditation of my heart, acceptable, in His sight. Based on Psalm 19:14.

4) I thank God, that he leads me (and my thoughts), beside quiet waters, and he restores my soul, with good thoughts, and he leads me, in paths of righteousness, for His name's sake. Based on Psalm 23:2,3.

5) I am diligent, to treasure God's Word, in my heart, so that I, may not sin, against Him. Based on Psalm 119:11.

6) I ask God, to search me every day, to know my heart, and try my thoughts, to see if there is, any anxious thoughts in me, and if there is any hurtful way in me, And to lead me, in the everlasting way. Based on Psalm 139:23,24.

7) I watch over my heart, (my thoughts), with all diligence, for out of it, flow the springs of my life. Based on Proverbs 4:23.

8) I bring to God, the plans in my mind, and he helps me, to know which way to go. (This keeps my mind at rest.) Based on Proverbs 16:3.

9) My joyful heart, is good medicine. (So I keep myself happy, hopeful, and trusting in God.) Based on Proverbs 17:22.

10) Because I keep my mind, steadfast on God, He helps me have perfect peace. Based on Isaiah 26:3.

11) I forsake my old deeds and thoughts, and I return to the Lord, He has compassion on me, and He abundantly pardons me. Based on Isaiah 55:7.

12) I keep myself hopeful, because God has plans for my welfare, He has plans to give me, a future and a hope. Based on Jeremiah 29:11.

13) I am diligent, to love God, with all my heart, with all my soul, with all my mind. Based on Matthew 22:37.

14) Jesus left His peace with me, Jesus gave me His peace. I stop my heart, from being troubled, I never let it be fearful. Based on John 14:27.

15) Because I live after the Spirit, I mind the things of the Spirit, and not the flesh. Based on Romans 8:5.

16) I do not let myself, be conformed, to this world, but I allow myself, to be transformed, by the renewing of my mind. This way I am able to know the good, the acceptable, and the perfect will of God, for my life. Based on Romans 12:2.

17) The weapons that God has given me, are not fleshly, but divinely powered for the destruction of fortresses, in my mind. I destroy speculations, and every lofty thing, that rises up, against the knowledge of God, and I take, every thought captive, to the obedience of Christ. Based on 2 Corinthians 10:4,5.

18) As a person thinks, so are they. (And because I am a Christian, saved by the sacrifice of Jesus, I have been Born Again. I am a new creature in Christ Jesus. I have traded my sin nature, for God's nature, And now God's nature, is in my thoughts, as I give my mind to God, and His Word.) Based on Proverbs 23:7 & 2 Corinthians 5:17, Ephesians 4:22-24

19) This one thing I do, I forget those things which lie behind, so I can reach forward to what lies ahead. Based on Philippians 3:13.

20) I make sure, to not be anxious about anything, but in everything, by prayer, and supplication, with thanksgiving, I let my requests, be made known to God, And the peace of God, which surpasses all comprehension, will guard my heart, and my mind, through Christ Jesus. Based on Philippians 4:6,7.

21) (My mind, is an amazing gift from God, and I use it only as intended.) I use it to think on things that are honorable, right, pure, lovely, things that are of a good repute, things that have excellence, and worthy of praise. Based on Philippians 4:8.

22) I can do all things through Christ, (including keeping my mind, on right thoughts.) Based on Philippians 4:13.

23) I set my mind, on thoughts of God, Jesus, the Holy Spirit, and of heaven, not on the things that are on earth. Based on Colossians 3:2.

24) Because I keep my mind, on godly things, I am able to "Let the peace of Christ, rule in my heart." And I am thankful. Based on Colossians 3:15.

25) I thank God, that he has not given me a spirit of timidity, but a spirit that is powerful, and love-filled, and disciplined. (He has given me a mind, that is sound, in every regard, so all my thoughts, are faith-filled, and peace-filled.) Based on 2 Timothy 1:7.

26) Because I consider, what the Apostle Paul says, the Lord gives me understanding, in everything. Based on 2 Timothy 2:7

27) I am diligent, to present myself, approved of God, as a workman, who is never ashamed. This helps me to accurately handle, the word of truth. Based on 2 Timothy 2:15.

28) The Word of God in me, is living and active, and sharper than a two-edged sword, it helps me to discern, negative thoughts, and the intentions of my heart, (so I can quickly uproot them). Based on Hebrews 4:12.

29) I stay close to God, so I am never a double-minded person, a person who is unstable, in all their ways. Based on James 1:8.

30) Greater is He who is in me, than he who is in the world. Because God lives big in me, His Word lives big in my thinking, and triumphs over all my negative thoughts. Based on 1 John 4:4.

Let's go back to the Affirmation Speaker role.

AFFIRMATION #6

"I AM HAPPY BECAUSE..."

****

Throughout your day, try to recite out loud, the "I Am Happy Because..." Affirmation.

Prayer of Dedication: "Father, I dedicate myself to live this day rejoicing in the things you have given me. I now speak these Bible-based statements to remind me of all the good things I have because I am your child!"

The extra commas make the words more meditative and impactful. It also helps people read in unison during conference calls.

****

1) I am happy because, those who mourn, will be comforted! Based on Matthew 5:4.

2) I am happy because, I know how to glorify God, by letting my light shine, before men, by doing good works. Based on Matthew 5:16.

3) I am happy because, I don't have to have negative feelings, about my enemies, I love them, and I pray for them. Based on Matthew 5:44.

4) I am happy because, when I give, and pray, and fast, in secret, God rewards me openly. Based on Matthew 6:4,6.

5) I am happy because, all my needs are met, when I seek first God's kingdom, and His righteousness. Based on Matthew 6:33, Luke 12:31.

6) I am happy because, when I ask - I receive, when I seek - I find, when I knock - it is opened. Based on Matthew 7:7, Luke 11:10.

7) I am happy because, when I labor, and am heavy laden, Jesus bids me come, he gives me rest! Based on Matthew 11:28,29.

8) I am happy because, even a small amount of faith, can do so much. Based on Matthew 17:20.

9) I am happy because, when two people agree, in prayer, it will be done, by my Father in heaven. Based on Matthew 18:19.

10) I am happy because, where 2 or 3 believers are, Christ is in the midst. Based on Matthew 18:20.

11) I am happy because, all things are possible! Based on Matthew 19:26 & Mark 9:23.

12) I am happy because, when I give to the needy, I give to Christ! Based on Matthew 25:40.

13) I am happy because, Jesus can take, what little I have, and multiply it! Based on Mark 8:1-9.

14) I am happy because, Jesus lays out an easy way, to become great – become a servant of all! Based on Mark 9:35, 10:44

15) I am happy because, Jesus said, whatever I pray for, and believe I have received it, I shall have it! Based on Mark 11:24.

16) I am happy because, I don't have to worry, about saying the wrong things, Jesus said the Holy Ghost, will give me the words to say. Based on Mark 13:11.

17) I am happy because, Jesus doesn't care how little, my offering is, it's how much is left over that counts! Based on Mark 12:43,44.

18) I am happy because, God gives me purpose! Jesus tells me to "Go into all the world, and preach the gospel, to all creation." That's my purpose! Based on Mark 16:15.

19) I am happy because, whoever believes, and is baptized, will be saved! Based on Mark 16:16.

20) I am happy because, Jesus said we can heal people, in His name! Based on Mark 16:18.

21) I am happy because, Jesus said those who weep now, will one day laugh! Based on Luke 6:21.

22) I am happy because, I don't have to care, when people dislike me, Jesus said to rejoice, for my reward, in heaven, will be great! Based on Luke 6:22,23.

23) I am happy because, when Jesus is around, things happen, the blind see, lepers are cleansed! deaf people hear, the dead are raised, and the poor hear the gospel! Based on Luke 7:22.

24) I am happy because, I don't have to care! When people reject the gospel, I just shake it off! Based on Luke 9:5.

25) I am happy because, even devils are subject to us! through Jesus's name! Based on Luke 10:17.

26) I am happy because, Jesus give us power, to tread on serpents! And scorpions! And over all power, of the enemy! And nothing shall injure me! Based on Luke 10:19.

27) I am happy because, my name is written in heaven! Based on Luke 10:20.

28) I am happy because, God has numbered, the hairs on my head! Jesus said I have great value! Based on Luke 12:7.

29) I am happy because, if God feeds the ravens, He will certainly feed me, if God clothes the lilies, He will certainly clothe me. Based on Luke 12:24,28.

30) I am happy because, God says "whosoever"! God so loved the world, that He gave, His only beloved Son, that whosoever believes in Him, should not perish, but have eternal life! Based on John 3:16.

31) I am happy because, the water Jesus gives me, is a well of water, springing up, into eternal life. Based on John 4:14.

32) I am happy because, Jesus tells me what to work for, I do not labor for food that perishes, I labor for food that endures, to eternal life, which Jesus gives me. Based on John 6:27.

33) I am happy because, that Jesus is the bread of life, when I come to Jesus, I never hunger, and never get thirsty. Based on John 6:35.

34) I am happy because, Jesus is the light of my life, When I follow Him, I do not walk in darkness. I have the light of life! Based on John 8:12, 12:35,46.

35) I am happy because, it is truth, that sets me free! (So I keep searching for truth!) Based on John 8:32.

36) I am happy because, Jesus is my shepherd, I can learn His voice, Jesus lays down His life, for the sheep! Based on John 10:14-18,27.

37) I am happy because, Jesus give us an easy way, for people to know, we are His, when we love one another. Based on John 13:34,35.

38) I am happy because, I can keep my heart, from being troubled! Based on John 14:1,27.

39) I am happy because, Jesus is preparing, a place for me, in heaven! Based on John 14:2.

40) I am happy because, Jesus says who He is, "I am the way, the truth, and the life: no man comes to the father, but by me." Based on John 14:6.

41) I am happy because, Jesus tells us, the works that He does, we shall do also! And greater works! Based on John 14:12.

42) I am happy because, Jesus has given me, another Helper, the Holy Spirit. And He never leaves me! Based on John 14:16.

43) I am happy because, Jesus leaves me His peace. Based on John 14:27, 20:21.

44) I am happy because, I bear fruit! Jesus says, as I abide in Him, and He in me, I will bear much fruit! Based on John 15:2,4,5,16.

45) I am happy because, Jesus says, if I abide in Him, and His Word abides in me, I will ask, whatever I wish, and it'll be done for me! Based on John 15:7, 17:24.

46) I am happy because, Christ's joy remains in me, and my joy is FULL! Based on John 15:11. My joy is a joy, that no man, can take from me! Based on John 16:22.

47) I am happy because, Jesus calls me His Friend! not a servant, I am His friend, if I do whatsoever He commands. Based on John 15:14

48) I am happy because, Jesus says, I didn't choose Him, but He chose me! Based on John 15:16.

49) I am happy because, the Holy Spirit, teaches me all truth! Based on John 16:13.

50) I am happy because, I can rejoice, in my tribulations, because I know, my tribulation, brings about perseverance, and perseverance character, and character hope! Based on Romans 5:3,4.

51) I am happy because, God shows me His love! While I was still a sinner, Christ died for me! Based on Romans 5:8.

52) I am happy because, God gives me eternal life! The wages of my sin, is death, but the gift of God, is eternal life, in Christ Jesus. Based on Romans 6:23.

53) I am happy because, my present sufferings, are not worth comparing, with the glory, that will be revealed, in me! Based on Romans 8:18

54) I am happy because, God works all things, for my good, because I love Him. Based on Romans 8:28.

55) I am happy because, if God is for me, who can be against me? Based on Romans 8:31.

56) I am happy because, in all my trials, I am more than a conqueror, through Christ, who loves me! Based on Romans 8:37.

57) I am happy because, I don't have to conform to the world, I'm being transformed, by the renewing, of my mind. Based on Romans 12:2

58) I am happy because, I am joyful! I'm joyful in hope, I persevere in tribulation, and I'm faithful in prayer. Based on Romans 12:12.

59) I am happy because, I am enriched, by Christ, in all my speaking, and all my knowledge. Based on 1 Corinthians 1:5.

60) I am happy because, God uses my foolishness, to confound the wise, and He uses my weaknesses, to confound the mighty. Based on 1 Corinthians 1:27.

61) I am happy because, God has planned, amazing things, for me! in my after-life! Things human eyes can't see, human ears can't hear, nor things imagined. Based on 1 Corinthians 2:9.

62) I am happy because, I am important, even with my flaws! Based on 1 Corinthians 12:22,23.

63) I am happy because, God gives me victory! Though Christ! Based on 1 Corinthians 15:57.

64) I am happy because, God comforts me, in all my afflictions. Based on 2 Corinthians 1:4.

65) I am happy because, God causes me, to always triumph! In Christ! Based on 2 Corinthians 2:14.

66) I am happy because, I am a sweet smell of Christ, to those around me. Based on 2 Corinthians 2:15.

67) I am happy because, I'm an able minister, of the gospel! Based on 2 Corinthians 3:6.

68) I am happy because, I have strong hope, and great boldness in my speech! Based on 2 Corinthians 3:12.

69) I am happy because, I have freedom! Because the Spirit, of the Lord, is in me. Based on 2 Corinthians 3:17.

70) I am happy because, I am transforming, into God's image, from glory to glory! Based on 2 Corinthians 3:18.

71) I am happy because, my inner man, is being renewed, day by day! Based on 2 Corinthians 4:16.

72) I am happy because, I have glory! My light affliction, is producing in me, an eternal weight of glory! Based on 2 Corinthians 4:17.

73) I am happy because, I have a new home! My earthly "tent", is being torn down, but I have a new building, that God is making, eternal in the heavens! Based on 2 Corinthians 5:1.

74) I am happy because, I am righteous! God made Christ, to be sin for me, that I might have, Christ's righteousness! Based on 2 Corinthians 5:21.

75) I am happy because, I have great grace! God is able, to make all grace, abound to me, so that I, might abound in abundance, for every good deed! Based on 2 Corinthians 9:8.

76) I am happy because, God's grace is sufficient, When my life gets hard, Jesus tells me, His grace, will get me through! Based on 2 Corinthians 12:9a.

77) I am happy because, I can boast about my weaknesses, because that's when, Christ's power, comes in, and makes me strong! Based on 2 Corinthians 12:9b.

78) I am happy because, I know what's most important - Faith! And that it works by love. (I'm developing my faith!) Based on Galatians 5:6.

79) I am happy because, God calls me to freedom! I use my freedom, to serve others, in love. Based on Galatians 5:13.

80) I am happy because, God gives me, the fruit of the Spirit, I have Love and joy, peace and patience, kindness and goodness, faithfulness and gentleness, and self-control! Based on Galatians 5:22,23.

81) I am happy because, I can choose, to crucify my flesh, with its passions and desires. Based on Galatians 5:24.

82) I am happy because, I have help, in carrying my burdens, others are helping me, and I help them! Together, we fulfill, the law of Christ. Based on Galatians 6:2.

83) I am happy because, I never lose heart! I don't get weary, in well-doing, (I keep working, I keep helping, with God's help!) Based on Galatians 6:9.

84) I am happy because, God has chosen me, before the foundation, of the world, to be holy, and blameless, before Him. Based on Ephesians 1:4.

85) I am happy because, of God's rich mercy, and great love, toward me, even when I was dead, in my sins, He made me alive, with Christ! It is God's grace, that I've been saved. Based on Ephesians 2:4,5.

86) I am happy because, God has raised me up, with Christ, I am seated with Him, in heavenly places, in Christ Jesus. Based on Ephesians 2:6.

87) I am happy because, I am God's workmanship! created in Christ Jesus, to do good works, which He prepared, for me to walk, in them. Based on Ephesians 2:10.

88) I am happy because, I am a part of God's home! Together, we are a habitation, for God, by His of Spirit. Based on Ephesians 2:22.

89) I am happy because, I have access to God's wisdom! I have boldness, and confident access, through my faith, in God! Based on Ephesians 3:10,12.

90) I am happy because, God can do exceeding abundantly, above all I can ask, or think, according to His power, that's at works within me. Based on Ephesians 3:20.

91) I am happy because, I am a peace-maker! With God's help, I do my best, to preserve the unity, of the Spirit, in the bond of peace. Based on Ephesians 4:3.

92) I am happy because, God didn't leave me on my own! He's given me, apostles and prophets, evangelists, and pastors, and teachers, who help me grow, and serve, and be a blessing, to the Body of Christ. Based on Ephesians 4:11.

93) I am happy because, I have a new self! God tells me, to put on my new self, created in His likeness, in created in righteousness, and holiness, of the truth. Based on Ephesians 4:24.

94) I am happy because, I don't go to bed mad! I forgive everyone, before going to bed. Based on Ephesians 4:26.

95) I am happy because, I am tender-hearted, and quick to forgive! just like God, who forgave me through Christ. Based on Ephesians 4:32.

96) I am happy because, God made me a singer! I sing to myself, psalms and hymns, and spiritual songs, singing and making melody, in my heart, to the Lord. Based on Ephesians 5:19.

97) I am happy because, God made me a great worker! I serve my boss, as if I'm serving the Lord. I know, whatever good I do, I will receive a reward, from God! Based on Ephesians 6:5-9.

98) I am happy because, God wants me strong! Every day, I wear the armor of God, so I can stand, against,the schemes, of the devil. I put on, the belt of truth, the breastplate of righteousness, the shoes of the gospel, the shield of faith, the helmet of salvation, and the sword of the Spirit, which is the Word of God. Based on Ephesians 6:11-17.

99) I am happy because, I have confidence! I am confident that God, who began a good work, in me, will perfect it, until the day, of Christ Jesus. Based on Philippians 1:6.

100) I am happy because, I can stand firm! I stand firm, in one spirit, with one mind, striving together with others, for the faith of the gospel, and I'm never alarmed, by my opponents. Based on Philippians 1:27,28.

101) I am happy because of humility! I never do things, from selfishness or empty conceit, but with humility, I regard others, as more important, than myself. [7] Jesus made Himself nothing, taking the form of a bond-servant, and being made, in the likeness of men. (With God's help, I will do the same.) Based on Philippians 2:3,7.

102) I am happy because, I'm going to see every knee bow, and hear every tongue confess, that Jesus Christ is Lord! Based on Philippians 2:10,11.

103) I am happy because of purity, I do everything, without grumbling, or disputing, and I choose, to be blameless, and innocent, a child of God, above reproach, in the midst of a crooked, and perverse generation, in which I shine, like a light in the world, holding fast, the Word of Life! Based on Philippians 2:14-16.

104) I am happy because, I can forget my past! And reach forward, to what lies ahead, I press toward the goal, for the prize, of the upward call of God, in Christ Jesus. Based on Philippians 3:13,14.

105) I am happy because, God wants me joyful! in Him, Always!, So I rejoice! Based on Philippians 4:4.

106) I am happy because, I've learned to be gentle! to everyone! Based on Philippians 4:5.

107) I am happy because, God wants me carefree! He tells me, to not be careful about anything, I just pray about what I need, with thanksgiving, and the peace of God, which surpasses all comprehension, guards my heart, and my mind, in Christ Jesus. Based on Philippians 4:6,7.

108) I am happy because, God gives me guidance, on how to think, I only think on things, that are true, honorable and right, pure and lovely, things of good repute, things that have excellence, and are worthy of praise. Based on Philippians 4:8.

109) I am happy because I'm content, I have learned to be content, in whatsoever circumstances I'm in. Based on Philippians 4:11.

110) I am happy because, I can do all things through Christ, who strengthens me. Based on Philippians 4:13.

111) I am happy because, God promises to supply all of my needs! Based on Philippians 4:19.

112) I am happy because, I am being strengthened, with all power, according to God's glorious might, unto all steadfastness, and patience, and joyfulness! Based on Colossians 1:11.

113) I am happy because, God qualifies me, to share in the inheritance, of the saints in light! Based on Colossians 1:12.

114) I am happy because, when I was dead in my sins, and in the uncircumcision of my flesh, God made me alive with Christ, He forgave me, all my sins, and He canceled the certificate of debt, that was against me, He took it away, nailing it to the cross! Based on Colossians 2:13,14.

115) I am happy because, God has disarmed the rulers and authorities! And made a public display of them! By triumphing over them through Christ! Based on Colossians 2:15.

116) I am happy because, I have a new self! I have put off the old self, with its evil practices, and I've put on the new self, which is being renewed, in knowledge, in the image of my creator. Based on Colossians 3:9,10.

117) I am happy because of my peace! I can let, the peace of Christ, rule in my heart! Based on Colossians 3:15.

118) I am happy because, God makes me diligent, I obey my boss, not just when he's watching. I work, with a sincere heart, and Godly reverence. Based on Colossians 3:22.

119) I am happy because, God wants my life to win respect, so I lead a quiet life, attending my own business, working diligently. Based on 1 Thessalonians 4:11.

120) I am happy because, Jesus is returning! The day is coming, when the Lord Himself, shall descend from heaven, with a shout, and the voice of the archangel, and the trumpet of God, and the dead in Christ, shall arise! Then we who are alive, shall be caught up together, with them in the clouds, to meet the Lord, in the air, and so shall we be, forever with the Lord! Based on 1 Thessalonians 4:16,17.

121) I am happy because of God's help! He gives me people, who comfort me, and edify me. And I return the favor. Based on 1 Thessalonians 5:11.

122) I am happy because, God is a God of peace. He's sanctifying my spirit, soul and body, so that I'll be blameless, at the coming of my Lord. Based on 1 Thessalonians 5:23,24.

123) I am happy because, my faith and love are growing, larger and larger. Based on 2 Thessalonians 1:3.

124) I am happy because, I can persevere in my faith, in spite of my persecutions, and afflictions. Based on 2 Thessalonians 1:4.

125) I am happy because, God is counting me worthy of His calling, and is fulfilling, every desire, He has for me, so that my life, yields goodness and power. Based on 2 Thessalonians 1:11.

126) I am happy because, the name of Lord Jesus Christ, is being glorified in me, as I am in Him, according to the grace of God, and the Lord Jesus Christ. Based on 2 Thessalonians 1:12.

127) I am happy because, God chose me to be saved, through the sanctifying by the Spirit, and through faith in the truth. Based on 2 Thessalonians 2:13.

128) I am happy because, God loves me and gives me, eternal comfort, and good hope by grace. Based on 2 Thessalonians 2:16.

129) I am happy because, the Lord of peace Himself, continually gives me peace. Based on 2 Thessalonians 3:16.

130) I am happy because, the grace of our Lord to me, is more than abundant. Based on 1Timothy 1:14.

131) I am happy because, God wants all men saved, and to come to the knowledge, of the truth. Based on 1 Timothy 2:4.

132) I am happy because, my godliness profits me, in this life, and in the life to come. Based on 1Timothy 4:8.

133) I am happy because, nobody looks down on me, because I'm young, I am an example, to all believers, in my speech, in my conduct, in my love, in my faith, and in my purity. Based on 1Timothy 4:12.

134) I am happy because, I have great gain, because I have godliness, and contentment! Based on 1Timothy 6:6.

135) I am happy because, God did not give me a spirit of timidity, but of power, of love, and of discipline! Based on 2 Timothy 1:7.

136) I am happy because, Christ Jesus destroyed death! and has brought me life, and immortality! Through the gospel! Based on 2 Timothy 1:10.

137) I am happy because, I have no shame! I know in whom I believe, and I am convinced, that Christ is able to guard, what I've entrusted to Him, until that day. Based on 2 Timothy 1:12.

138) I am happy because, I am fully convinced, in the marvelous grace, that is given to me, in Christ Jesus. Based on 2 Timothy 2:1.

139) I am happy because, I've learned how to endure hardship, like a good soldier, of Christ Jesus. Based on 2 Timothy 2:3.

140) I am happy because, God tells me not to get entangled, in my life's affairs, so that I may please Christ, who has enlisted me, as a soldier. Based on 2 Timothy 2:4.

141) I am happy because, God tells me not to quarrel, which leads to stress, but to be kind to everyone, able to teach, patient when wronged. Based on 2 Timothy 2:24.

142) I am happy because, all scripture is God-inspired, and is profitable in teaching, reproof and correction, and training in righteousness. Based on 2 Timothy 3:16.

143) I am happy because, there is stored for me, a crown of righteousness, which Jesus will award me, on that day. Based on 2 Timothy 4:8.

144) I am happy because, the Lord stands beside me, and gives me strength, so that through me, the gospel is preached, and Gentiles are being rescued, from the lion's mouth. Based on 2 Timothy 4:17.

145) I am happy because, God rescues me, from every evil deed, He will bring me safely, to His heavenly kingdom. Based on 2 Timothy 4:18.

146) I am happy because, Christ gave Himself for me, to redeem me, from every lawless deed, to purify me, for Himself, a person for His possession, zealous, to do good deeds. Based on Titus 2:14.

147) I am happy because, the Word of God is living and active, sharper than any two-edged sword, revealing the difference, between my soul and spirit, and joints and marrow, it helps me judge my thoughts, and the intentions of my heart. Based on Hebrews 4:12.

148) I am happy because of faith, I picture in my mind what I want, and I have a conviction that I will get it. Based on Hebrews 11:1.

149) I am happy because, I know what pleases God - faith! When I come to God, I believe He exists, and that He rewards me, because I seek Him. Based on Hebrews 11:6.

150) I am happy because, I'm not alone! there's a heavenly crowd, watching me "run my race", so I lay aside, every encumbrance, and sin which seeks to entangle me, and I run with endurance, the race that is set before me, fixing my eyes on Jesus, the author and perfecter, of my faith. Jesus endured the cross, I can certainly endure my trial. Based on Hebrews 12:1,2.

151) I am happy because, I count it all joy, when I encounter various trials, because I know, the testing of my faith, develops endurance, I let my endurance, have its perfect result, so that I am perfect, and complete, lacking nothing! Based on James 1:2-4.

152) I am happy because of humility! When I humble myself, in the presence of the Lord, He exalts me! Based on James 4:10.

153) I am happy because of humility again! When I humble myself, under the mighty hand of God, He exalts me, at the proper time! Based on 1 Peter 5:6.

154) I am happy because, I can cast all my anxieties, onto Christ, because He cares or me! Based on 1 Peter 5:7.

155) I am happy because, the God of all grace, who has called me, into His eternal glory, in Christ, will Himself perfect me and confirm me, and strengthen me and establish me! Based on 1 Peter 5:10.

156) I am happy because, when I confess my sins, God is faithful and righteous, to forgive my sins, and cleanse me, from all unrighteousness. Based on 1 John 1:9.

157) I am happy because, there is no fear in love, rather perfect love, casts out fear! Based on 1 John 4:18.

158) I am happy because, he who has the Son has life! Based on 1 John 5:12.

Let's go back to the Affirmation Speaker role.

Core Beliefs

****

<u>Choose Your Core Beliefs</u>

Our thoughts are influenced by our beliefs. Positive beliefs help keep our thinking and our responses to life's problems positive.

The goal is to make these core beliefs the final word in our lives. No matter what our feelings say or what the circumstances try to tell us, these foundational beliefs are what we are going to use when thinking about ourselves, when making decisions in our lives, and when we are praying about our needs and wants.

If we come across a belief that we would like to adopt but seems untrue to us, read out loud the scripture verses associated with the belief. The truth of these verses will slowly sink into our minds and over time will become real in our hearts.

CORE BELIEF #1

****

"Based on the following scriptures, I believe God loves me, and that I am valuable."

****

Below are some scriptures that talk about God's love for humanity. The most notable way God showed His love for us is in the offering of His only Son, Jesus, to die on the cross for our sins. Indeed, His love for us is great.

Remember that this is a <u>Core Belief</u>. Unless we believe this to be true, our lives can seem meaningless and hopeless. So let's renew our minds to the truth that God loves us, and that He has an amazing plan for our lives!

1) **Nehemiah 9:17** "But You are a God of forgiveness, Gracious and compassionate, Slow to anger and abounding in lovingkindness; And You did not forsake them."

2) **Psalm 17:7** "Wondrously show Your lovingkindness, O Savior of those who take refuge at Your right hand From those who rise up against them."

3) **Psalm 25:7** "Do not remember the sins of my youth or my transgressions; According to Your lovingkindness remember me, For Your goodness' sake, O Lord."

4) **Psalm 36:7** "How precious is Your lovingkindness, O God! And the children of men take refuge in the shadow of Your wings."

5) **Psalm 48:9** "We have thought on Your lovingkindness, O God, In the midst of Your temple."

6) **Psalm 52:8** "But as for me, I am like a green olive tree in the house of God; I trust in the lovingkindness of God forever and ever."

7) **Psalm 63:3** "Because Your lovingkindness is better than life, My lips will praise You."

8) **Psalm 86:15** "But You, O Lord, are a God merciful and gracious, Slow to anger and abundant in lovingkindness and truth."

9) **Psalm 103:8** "The Lord is compassionate and gracious, Slow to anger and abounding in lovingkindness."

10) **Psalm 103:11** "For as high as the heavens are above the earth, So great is His lovingkindness toward those who fear Him."

11) **Psalm 109:26** "Help me, O Lord my God; Save me according to Your lovingkindness."

12) **Psalm 136:26** "Give thanks to the God of heaven, For His lovingkindness is everlasting"

13) **Exodus 34:6** "Then the Lord passed by in front of him and proclaimed, "The Lord, the Lord God, compassionate and gracious, slow to anger, and abounding in lovingkindness and truth;"

14) **Isaiah 41:10** "Do not fear, for I am with you; Do not anxiously look about you, for I am your God. I will strengthen you, surely I will help you, Surely I will uphold you with My righteous right hand.'"

15) **Isaiah 41:13** "For I am the Lord your God, who upholds your right hand, Who says to you, 'Do not fear, I will help you.'

16) **Isaiah 49:16** "Behold, I have inscribed you on the palms of My hands; Your walls are continually before Me."

17) **Isaiah 54:10** "For the mountains may be removed and the hills may shake, But My lovingkindness will not be removed from you, And My covenant of peace will not be shaken," Says the Lord who has compassion on you."

18) **Jeremiah 29:11** "For I know the plans that I have for you,' declares the Lord, 'plans for welfare and not for calamity to give you a future and a hope."

19) **Jeremiah 31:3** "The Lord appeared to him from afar, saying, "I have loved you with an everlasting love; Therefore I have drawn you with lovingkindness."

20) **Zephaniah 3:17** "The Lord your God is in your midst, A victorious warrior. He will exult over you with joy, He will be quiet in His love, He will rejoice over you with shouts of joy."

21) **Mark 10:21** "Looking at him, Jesus felt a love for him and said to him, "One thing you lack: go and sell all you possess and give to the poor, and you will have treasure in heaven; and come, follow Me."

22) **John 3:16** "For God so loved the world, that He gave His only begotten Son, that whoever believes in Him shall not perish, but have eternal life."

23) **John 14:21** "He who has My commandments and keeps them is the one who loves Me; and he who loves Me will be loved by My Father, and I will love him and will disclose Myself to him."

24) **John 15:9** "Just as the Father has loved Me, I have also loved you; abide in My love."

25) **John 16:27** "for the Father Himself loves you, because you have loved Me and have believed that I came forth from the Father."

26) **Romans 5:5** "and hope does not disappoint, because the love of God has been poured out within our hearts through the Holy Spirit who was given to us."

27) **Romans 5:8** "But God demonstrates His own love toward us, in that while we were yet sinners, Christ died for us."

28) **Romans 8:35** "Who will separate us from the love of Christ? Will tribulation, or distress, or persecution, or famine, or nakedness, or peril, or sword?"

29) **Romans 8:37** "But in all these things we overwhelmingly conquer through Him who loved us."

30) **Romans 8:38,39** "For I am convinced that neither death, nor life, nor angels, nor principalities, nor things present, nor things to come, nor powers, nor height, nor depth, nor any other created thing, will be able to separate us from the love of God, which is in Christ Jesus our Lord."

31) **Romans 15:30** "Now I urge you, brethren, by our Lord Jesus Christ and by the love of the Spirit, to strive together with me in your prayers to God for me,"

32) **2 Corinthians 5:14** "For the love of Christ controls us, having concluded this, that one died for all, therefore all died;"

33) **2 Corinthians 13:11** "Finally, brethren, rejoice, be made complete, be comforted, be like-minded, live in peace; and the God of love and peace will be with you."

34) **2 Corinthians 13:14** "The grace of the Lord Jesus Christ, and the love of God, and the fellowship of the Holy Spirit, be with you all."

35) **Galatians 2:20** "I have been crucified with Christ; and it is no longer I who live, but Christ lives in me; and the life which I now live in the flesh I live by faith in the Son of God, who loved me and gave Himself up for me."

36) **Ephesians 2:4** "But God, being rich in mercy, because of His great love with which He loved us,"

37) **Ephesians 3:17-19** "so that Christ may dwell in your hearts through faith; and that you, being rooted and grounded in love, may be able to comprehend with all the saints what is the breadth and length and height and depth, and to know the love of Christ which surpasses knowledge, that you may be filled up to all the fullness of God."

38) **Ephesians 5:1,2** "Therefore be imitators of God, as beloved children; and walk in love, just as Christ also loved you and gave Himself up for us, an offering and a sacrifice to God as a fragrant aroma."

39) **Ephesians 5:25** "Husbands, love your wives, just as Christ also loved the church and gave Himself up for her,"

40) **2 Thessalonians 2:16** "Now may our Lord Jesus Christ Himself and God our Father, who has loved us and given us eternal comfort and good hope by grace,"

41) **2 Thessalonians 3:5** "May the Lord direct your hearts into the love of God and into the steadfastness of Christ."

42) **Titus 3:4** "But when the kindness of God our Savior and His love for mankind appeared,"

43) **1 Peter 5:6,7** "Therefore humble yourselves under the mighty hand of God, that He may exalt you at the proper time, casting all your anxiety on Him, because He cares for you."

44) **1 John 3:1** "See how great a love the Father has bestowed on us, that we would be called children of God; and such we are. For this reason the world does not know us, because it did not know Him."

45) **1 John 3:16** "We know love by this, that He laid down His life for us; and we ought to lay down our lives for the brethren."

46) **1 John 4:7,8** "Beloved, let us love one another, for love is from God; and everyone who loves is born of God and knows God. [8] The one who does not love does not know God, for God is love."

47) **1 John 4:9** "By this the love of God was manifested in us, that God has sent His only begotten Son into the world so that we might live through Him."

48) **1 John 4:10** "In this is love, not that we loved God, but that He loved us and sent His Son to be the propitiation for our sins."

49) **1 John 4:11** "Beloved, if God so loved us, we also ought to love one another."

50) **1 John 4:16** "We have come to know and have believed the love which God has for us. God is love, and the one who abides in love abides in God, and God abides in him."

51) **1 John 4:19** "We love, because he first loved us."

52) **Jude 1:21** "keep yourselves in the love of God, waiting anxiously for the mercy of our Lord Jesus Christ to eternal life"

53) **Revelation 1:5** "keep yourselves in the love of God, waiting anxiously for the mercy of our Lord Jesus Christ to eternal life."

The goal of speaking these verses out loud is to fully believe the truth that God loves us and that we have immense value. We need to become so convinced of this that nothing could convince us otherwise. Reading these scriptures over and over will help us make this truth more a reality in our hearts.

Let's turn back to the Beliefs Speaker role.

CORE BELIEF #2

****

"Based on the following scriptures, I believe Christ's crucifixion on the cross has paid the penalty for my sin, and that I am destined to live eternally with Christ."

****

Unless we are convinced that our sins are forgiven, we'll never reach full happiness. If need be, we can read out loud the following scriptures to renew our minds to adopt this vital Core Belief.

1) **John 3:16** "For God so loved the world, that He gave His only begotten Son, that whoever believes in Him shall not perish, but have eternal life."

2) **John 3:17** "For God did not send the Son into the world to judge the world, but that the world might be saved through Him."

3) **Acts 13:38** "Therefore let it be known to you, brethren, that through Him forgiveness of sins is proclaimed to you,"

4) **Acts 13:39** "and through Him everyone who believes is freed from all things, from which you could not be freed through the Law of Moses."

5) **Acts 15:11** "1 But we believe that we are saved through the grace of the Lord Jesus, in the same way as they also are."

6) **Acts 16:30,31** "and after he brought them out, he said, "Sirs, what must I do to be saved?" They said, "Believe in the Lord Jesus, and you will be saved, you and your household.""

7) **Romans 1:16** "For I am not ashamed of the gospel, for it is the power of God for salvation to everyone who believes, to the Jew first and also to the Greek."

8) **Romans 3:22-24** "even the righteousness of God through faith in Jesus Christ for all those who believe; for there is no distinction; for all have sinned and fall short of the glory of God, being justified as a gift by His grace through the redemption which is in Christ Jesus;"

9) **Romans 3:25** "whom God displayed publicly as a propitiation in His blood through faith. This was to demonstrate His righteousness, because in the forbearance of God He passed over the sins previously committed;"

10) **Romans 5:1** "Therefore, having been justified by faith, have peace with God through our Lord Jesus Christ,"

11) **Romans 10:4**." For Christ is the end of the law for righteousness to everyone who believes."

12) **Romans 10:9** "that if you confess with your mouth Jesus as Lord, and believe in your heart that God raised Him from the dead, you will be saved;"

13) **Romans 10:12,13** "For there is no distinction between Jew and Greek; for the same Lord is Lord of all, abounding in riches for all who call on Him; for "Whoever will call on the name of the Lord will be saved.""

14) **1 Corinthians 6:11** "Such were some of you; but you were washed, but you were sanctified, but you were justified in the name of the Lord Jesus Christ and in the Spirit of our God."

15) **1 Corinthians 15:3** "For I delivered to you as of first importance what I also received, that Christ died for our sins according to the Scriptures,"

16) **2 Corinthians 5:18** "Now all these things are from God, who reconciled us to Himself through Christ and gave us the ministry of reconciliation,"

17) **2 Corinthians 5:19** "namely, that God was in Christ reconciling the world to Himself, not counting their trespasses against them, and He has committed to us the word of reconciliation."

18) **2 Corinthians 5:20** "Therefore, we are ambassadors for Christ, as though God were making an appeal through us; we beg you on behalf of Christ, be reconciled to God."

19) **Galatians 1:4** "who gave Himself for our sins so that He might rescue us from this present evil age, according to the will of our God and Father,"

20) **Galatians 2:16** "nevertheless knowing that a man is not justified by the works of the Law but through faith in Christ Jesus, even we have believed in Christ Jesus, so that we may be justified by faith in Christ and not by the works of the Law; since by the works of the Law no flesh will be justified."

21) **Galatians 3:14** "in order that in Christ Jesus the blessing of Abraham might come to the Gentiles, so that we would receive the promise of the Spirit through faith."

22) **Galatians 3:26** "For you are all sons of God through faith in Christ Jesus."

23) **Ephesians 1:7** "In Him we have redemption through His blood, the forgiveness of our trespasses, according to the riches of His grace."

24) **Ephesians 1:13** "In Him, you also, after listening to the message of truth, the gospel of your salvation—having also believed, you were sealed in Him with the Holy Spirit of promise,"

25) **Ephesians 2:4,5** "But God, being rich in mercy, because of His great love with which He loved us, even when we were dead in our transgressions, made us alive together with Christ (by grace you have been saved),"

26) **Ephesians 2:8** "For by grace you have been saved through faith; and that not of yourselves, it is the gift of God;"

27) **Ephesians 2:13** "But now in Christ Jesus you who formerly were far off have been brought near by the blood of Christ."

28) **Ephesians 3:9** "and to bring to light what is the administration of the mystery which for ages has been hidden in God who created all things;"

29) **Ephesians 4:32** "Be kind to one another, tender-hearted, forgiving each other, just as God in Christ also has forgiven you."

30) **Colossians 1:14** "in whom we have redemption, the forgiveness of sins."

31) **Colossians 1:20-22** "and through Him to reconcile all things to Himself, having made peace through the blood of His cross; through Him, I say, whether things on earth or things in heaven. And although you were formerly alienated and hostile in mind, engaged in evil deeds, yet He has now reconciled you in His fleshly body through death, in order to present you before Him holy and blameless and beyond reproach."

32) **Colossians 1:27** "to whom God willed to make known what is the riches of the glory of this mystery among the Gentiles, which is Christ in you, the hope of glory."

33) **Colossians 2:13** "When you were dead in your transgressions and the uncircumcision of your flesh, He made you alive together with Him, having forgiven us all our transgressions,"

34) **1 Thessalonians 1:10** "and to wait for His Son from heaven, whom He raised from the dead, that is Jesus, who rescues us from the wrath to come."

35) **1 Thessalonians 5:9,10** "For God has not destined us for wrath, but for obtaining salvation through our Lord Jesus Christ, who died for us, so that whether we are awake or asleep, we will live together with Him."

36) **2 Thessalonians 2:13** "But we should always give thanks to God for you, brethren beloved by the Lord, because God has chosen you from the beginning for salvation through sanctification by the Spirit and faith in the truth."

37) **1 Timothy 1:15** "It is a trustworthy statement, deserving full acceptance, that Christ Jesus came into the world to save sinners, among whom I am foremost of all."

38) **1 Timothy 1:16** "Yet for this reason I found mercy, so that in me as the foremost, Jesus Christ might demonstrate His perfect patience as an example for those who would believe in Him for eternal life."

39) **1 Timothy 2:5,6** "For there is one God, and one mediator also between God and men, the man Christ Jesus, 6 who gave Himself as a ransom for all, the testimony given at the proper time."

40) **2 Timothy 1:9** "who has saved us and called us with a holy calling, not according to our works, but according to His own purpose and grace which was granted us in Christ Jesus from all eternity,"

41) **2 Timothy 1:10** "but now has been revealed by the appearing of our Savior Christ Jesus, who abolished death and brought life and immortality to light through the gospel,"

42) **2 Timothy 2:10** "For this reason I endure all things for the sake of those who are chosen, so that they also may obtain the salvation which is in Christ Jesus and with it eternal glory."

43) **2 Timothy 3:15** "and that from childhood you have known the sacred writings which are able to give you the wisdom that leads to salvation through faith which is in Christ Jesus."

44) **Titus 2:14** "who gave Himself for us to redeem us from every lawless deed, and to purify for Himself a people for His own possession, zealous for good deeds."

45) **Titus 3:3-7** "For we also once were foolish ourselves, disobedient, deceived, enslaved to various lusts and pleasures, spending our life in malice and envy, hateful, hating one another. 4 But when the kindness of God our Savior and His love for mankind appeared, 5 He saved us, not on the basis of deeds which we have done in righteousness, but according to His mercy, by the washing of regeneration and renewing by the Holy Spirit, 6 whom He poured out upon us richly through Jesus Christ our Savior, 7 so that being justified by His grace we would be made heirs according to the hope of eternal life."

46) **Hebrews 7:25** "Therefore He is able also to save forever those who draw near to God through Him, since He always lives to make intercession for them."

47) **Hebrews 9:12-15** "and not through the blood of goats and calves, but through His own blood, He entered the holy place once for all, having obtained eternal redemption. [13] For if the blood of goats and bulls and the ashes of a heifer sprinkling those who have been defiled sanctify for the cleansing of the flesh, [14] how much more will the blood of Christ, who through the eternal Spirit offered Himself without blemish to God, cleanse your conscience from dead works to serve the living God? [15] For this reason He is the mediator of a new covenant, so that, since a death has taken place for the redemption of the transgressions that were *committed* under the first covenant, those who have been called may receive the promise of the eternal inheritance."

48) **Hebrews 9:28** "so Christ also, having been offered once to bear the sins of many, will appear a second time for salvation without reference to sin, to those who eagerly await Him."

49) **Hebrews 10:10** "By this will we have been sanctified through the offering of the body of Jesus Christ once for all."

50) **Hebrews 10:12** "but He, having offered one sacrifice for sins for all time, sat down at the right hand of God,"

51) **1 Peter 1:18-19** "knowing that you were not redeemed with perishable things like silver or gold from your futile way of life inherited from your forefathers, but with precious blood, as of a lamb unblemished and spotless, the blood of Christ."

52) **1 John 1:7** "but if we walk in the Light as He Himself is in the Light, we have fellowship with one another, and the blood of Jesus His Son cleanses us from all sin."

53) **1 John 1:9** "If we confess our sins, He is faithful and righteous to forgive us our sins and to cleanse us from all unrighteousness."

54) **1 John 2:2** "and He Himself is the propitiation for our sins; and not for ours only, but also for those of the whole world."

55) **1 John 2:12** "I am writing to you, little children, because your sins have been forgiven you for His name's sake."

56) **1 John 2:25** "This is the promise which He Himself made to us: eternal life."

57) **1 John 4:9** "By this the love of God was manifested in us, that God has sent His only begotten Son into the world so that we might live through Him."

58) **1 John 4:10** "In this is love, not that we loved God, but that He loved us and sent His Son to be the propitiation for our sins."

59) **1 John 2:1** "My little children, I am writing these things to you so that you may not sin. And if anyone sins, we have an Advocate with the Father, Jesus Christ the righteous;"

60) **1 John 5:11** "And the testimony is this, that God has given us eternal life, and this life is in His Son."

61) **Revelation 1:5** "and from Jesus Christ, the faithful witness, the firstborn of the dead, and the ruler of the kings of the earth. To Him who loves us and released us from our sins by His blood."

62) **Revelation 5:9** "And they *sang a new song, saying, "Worthy are You to take the book and to break its seals; for You were slain, and purchased for God with Your blood men from every tribe and tongue and people and nation;""

The goal of speaking these verses out loud is to fully believe the truth that Christ's death on the cross paid the penalty of our sin. Our salvation happens when we ask God/Jesus to forgive our sins, and ask Him to guide us the rest of our lives.

We need to become so convinced of God's faithfulness to forgive us, that nothing could convince us otherwise. Reading these scriptures over and over will help us make this truth more a reality in our hearts.

Note

This Core Belief is about believing that the sacrifice that Jesus made on the cross has paid for our sin. Have you ever taken the step to ask God to forgive you for all your sins? Have you invited Him to come into your life? If not, and you'd like to, there is a prayer below you can pray to invite Him into your life:

Invitation Prayer

"Dear God, I see the sins that I have committed. I believe Jesus paid the penalty for my sin by his crucifixion. I receive your forgiveness for my sin. And I ask you to come into my life and guide me. Help me live out the destiny you have for me. In Jesus's name I pray. Amen."

If you've prayed this prayer, call us. We'd love to hear from you, and to help you get a great start in your new found faith!

USA: 213-426-8223   Canada: 289-723-2420   Email: victorytipsprogram@gmail.com

Let's turn back to the Beliefs Speaker role.

CORE BELIEF #3

****

"Based on the following scriptures, I believe God wants me to enjoy perfect peace at all times."

****

If we don't believe this Core Belief, we'll always wonder when it is OK to be nervous. It's best to believe that peace is always available. And we overcome anything that tries to rob us of God's peace. The peace God gives us passes all understanding (Philippians 4:7) and should never be given up.

1) **Numbers 6:26** "The Lord lift up His countenance on you, And give you peace.'"

2) **Psalm 4:8** "In peace I will both lie down and sleep, For You alone, O Lord, make me to dwell in safety."

3) **Psalm 16:8** "I have set the Lord continually before me; Because He is at my right hand, I will not be shaken."

4) **Psalm 23:1-3** "The Lord is my shepherd, I shall not want. He makes me lie down in green pastures; He leads me beside quiet waters. He restores my soul; He guides me in the paths of righteousness For His name's sake."

5) **Psalm 27:1** "The Lord is my light and my salvation; Whom shall I fear? The Lord is the defense of my life; Whom shall I dread?"

6) **Psalm 29:11** "The Lord will give strength to His people; The Lord will bless His people with peace."

7) **Psalm 37:11** "But the humble will inherit the land And will delight themselves in abundant prosperity."

8) **Psalm 37:37** "Mark the blameless man, and behold the upright; For the man of peace will have a posterity."

9) **Psalm 85:8** "I will hear what God the Lord will say; For He will speak peace to His people, to His godly ones; But let them not turn back to folly."

10) **Psalm 91:1** "He who dwells in the shelter of the Most High, Will abide in the shadow of the Almighty."

11) **Psalm 94:13** "That You may grant him relief from the days of adversity, Until a pit is dug for the wicked."

12) **Psalm 125:1** "Those who trust in the Lord Are as Mount Zion, which cannot be moved but abides forever."

13) **Proverbs 1:33** "But he who listens to me shall live securely And will be at ease from the dread of evil."

14) **Proverbs 3:17** "Her ways are pleasant ways And all her paths are peace."

15) **Proverbs 3:23-24** "Then you will walk in your way securely And your foot will not stumble. When you lie down, you will not be afraid; When you lie down, your sleep will be sweet."

16) **Isaiah 26:3** "The steadfast of mind You will keep in perfect peace, Because he trusts in You."

17) **Isaiah 32:17** "And the work of righteousness will be peace, And the service of righteousness, quietness and confidence forever."

18) **Isaiah 32:18** "Then my people will live in a peaceful habitation, And in secure dwellings and in undisturbed resting places;"

19) **Isaiah 48:18** "If only you had paid attention to My commandments! Then your well-being would have been like a river, And your righteousness like the waves of the sea."

20) **Isaiah 54:10** "For the mountains may be removed and the hills may shake, But My lovingkindness will not be removed from you, And My covenant of peace will not be shaken," Says the Lord who has compassion on you."

21) **Isaiah 54:13** "All your sons will be taught of the Lord; And the well-being of your sons will be great."

22) **Isaiah 55:12** "For you will go out with joy And be led forth with peace; The mountains and the hills will break forth into shouts of joy before you, And all the trees of the field will clap their hands."

23) **Isaiah 57:2** "He enters into peace; They rest in their beds, Each one who walked in his upright way."

24) **Isaiah 57:19** "Creating the praise of the lips. Peace, peace to him who is far and to him who is near," Says the Lord, "and I will heal him."

25) **Jeremiah 33:6** "Behold, I will bring to it health and healing, and I will heal them; and I will reveal to them an abundance of peace and truth."

26) **Haggai 2:9** "The latter glory of this house will be greater than the former,' says the Lord of hosts, 'and in this place I will give peace,' declares the Lord of hosts."

27) **Malachi 2:5** "My covenant with him was one of life and peace, and I gave them to him as an object of reverence; so he revered Me and stood in awe of My name."

28) **Mark 9:50** "Salt is good; but if the salt becomes unsalty, with what will you make it salty again? Have salt in yourselves, and be at peace with one another."

29) **Luke 1:79** "To shine upon those who sit in darkness and the shadow of death, To guide our feet into the way of peace."

30) **Luke 2:14** "Glory to God in the highest, And on earth peace among men with whom He is pleased."

31) **Luke 21:19** "By your endurance you will gain your lives."

32) **John 14:27** "Peace I leave with you; My peace I give to you; not as the world gives do I give to you. Do not let your heart be troubled, nor let it be fearful."

33) **John 16:33** "These things I have spoken to you, so that in Me you may have peace. In the world you have tribulation, but take courage; I have overcome the world."

34) **John 20:19** "So when it was evening on that day, the first day of the week, and when the doors were shut where the disciples were, for fear of the Jews, Jesus came and stood in their midst and *said to them, "Peace be with you.""

35) **Acts 10:36** "The word which He sent to the sons of Israel, preaching peace through Jesus Christ (He is Lord of all) "

36) **Romans 2:10** "but glory and honor and peace to everyone who does good, to the Jew first and also to the Greek."

37) **Romans 5:1** "Therefore, having been justified by faith, we have peace with God through our Lord Jesus Christ,"

38) **Romans 8:6** "For the mind set on the flesh is death, but the mind set on the Spirit is life and peace,"

39) **Romans 14:17** "for the kingdom of God is not eating and drinking, but righteousness and peace and joy in the Holy Spirit."

40) **Romans 15:13** "Now may the God of hope fill you with all joy and peace in believing, so that you will abound in hope by the power of the Holy Spirit."

41) **1 Corinthians 1:3** "Grace to you and peace from God our Father and the Lord Jesus Christ."

42) **1 Corinthians 14:33** "for God is not a God of confusion but of peace, as in all the churches of the saints."

43) **2 Corinthians 1:2** "Grace to you and peace from God our Father and the Lord Jesus Christ."

44) **2 Corinthians 7:4** "Great is my confidence in you; great is my boasting on your behalf. I am filled with comfort; I am overflowing with joy in all our affliction."

45) **2 Corinthians 13:11** "Finally, brethren, rejoice, be made complete, be comforted, be like-minded, live in peace; and the God of love and peace will be with you."

46) **Galatians 1:3** "Grace to you and peace from [a]God our Father and the Lord Jesus Christ,"

47) **Galatians 5:22** "But the fruit of the Spirit is love, joy, peace, patience, kindness, goodness, faithfulness,"

48) **Ephesians 2:14,15** "For He Himself is our peace, who made both groups into one and broke down the barrier of the dividing wall, by abolishing in His flesh the enmity, which is the Law of commandments contained in ordinances, so that in Himself He might make the two into one new man, thus establishing peace,"

49) **Ephesians 2:16,17** "and might reconcile them both in one body to God through the cross, by it having put to death the enmity. And He came and preached peace to you who were far away, and peace to those who were near;"

50) **Ephesians 4:3** "being diligent to preserve the unity of the Spirit in the bond of peace."

51) **Philippians 1:2** "Grace to you and peace from God our Father and the Lord Jesus Christ."

52) **Philippians 4:11,12** "Not that I speak from want, for I have learned to be content in whatever circumstances I am. I know how to get along with humble means, and I also know how to live in prosperity; in any and every circumstance I have learned the secret of being filled and going hungry, both of having abundance and suffering need."

53) **Philippians 4:6,7** "Be anxious for nothing, but in everything by prayer and supplication with thanksgiving let your requests be made known to God. And the peace of God, which surpasses all comprehension, will guard your hearts and your minds in Christ Jesus."

54) **Philippians 4:9** "The things you have learned and received and heard and seen in me, practice these things, and the God of peace will be with you."

55) **Colossians 1:2** "To the saints and faithful brethren in Christ who are at Colossae: Grace to you and peace from God our Father."

56) **Colossians 1:20** "and through Him to reconcile all things to Himself, having made peace through the blood of His cross; through Him, I say, whether things on earth or things in heaven."

57) **Colossians 3:15** "Let the peace of Christ rule in your hearts, to which indeed you were called in one body; and be thankful."

58) **1 Thessalonians 1:1** "Paul and Silvanus and Timothy, To the church of the Thessalonians in God the Father and the Lord Jesus Christ: Grace to you and peace."

59) **1 Thessalonians 3:13** "so that He may establish your hearts without blame in holiness before our God and Father at the coming of our Lord Jesus with all His saints."

60) **1 Thessalonians 5:13** "and that you esteem them very highly in love because of their work. Live in peace with one another."

61) **2 Thessalonians 2:2** "that you not be quickly shaken from your composure or be disturbed either by a spirit or a message or a letter as if from us, to the effect that the day of the Lord has come."

62) **2 Thessalonians 2:17** "comfort and strengthen your hearts in every good work and word."

63) **2 Thessalonians 3:16** "Now may the Lord of peace Himself continually grant you peace in every [a]circumstance. The Lord be with you all!"

64) **2 Timothy 1:2** "To Timothy, my beloved son: Grace, mercy and peace from God the Father and Christ Jesus our Lord."

65) **Titus 1:4** "To Titus, my true child in a common faith: Grace and peace from God the Father and Christ Jesus our Savior."

66) **James 5:8** "You too be patient; strengthen your hearts, for the coming of the Lord is near."

67) **2 Peter 1:2** "Grace and peace be multiplied to you in the knowledge of God and of Jesus our Lord,"

The goal of speaking these verses out loud is to fully believe the truth that God wants us peaceful at all times. We need to become so convinced of this that nothing could convince us otherwise. Reading these scriptures over and over will help us make this truth more a reality in our hearts.

Let's turn back to Beliefs Speaker

CORE BELIEF #4

****

"Based on the following scriptures, I believe I have an enemy - Satan."

****

In 1 Timothy 6:12, we read, "Fight the good fight of faith..." Here we see the Christian life is a battle, a continuous fight for our faith. If we keep our faith intact, then our minds are kept at rest. If we succumb to the plots of our enemy, Satan, who seeks to undermine our faith, then we lose the peace and happiness God has for us, and life becomes difficult. You may not have faith in God at this time; in that case, the enemy will try to steal your faith in yourself. He knows if he can take your self-confidence, he can pull you down in every other aspect of your life. So beware of your enemy! Here are some other scriptures that support this belief that we have an enemy - Satan.

1) **Genesis 3:1** "Now the serpent was more crafty than any beast of the field which the Lord God had made. And he said to the woman, "Indeed, has God said, 'You shall not eat from any tree of the garden'?"

2) **Genesis. 3:4,5** "The serpent said to the woman, "You surely will not die! For God knows that in the day you eat from it your eyes will be opened, and you will be like God, knowing good and evil."

3) **Genesis 3:14** "The Lord God said to the serpent, "Because you have done this, Cursed are you more than all cattle, And more than every beast of the field; On your belly you will go, And dust you will eat All the days of your life;"

4) **Deuteronomy. 32:17** "They sacrificed to demons who were not God, To gods whom they have not known, New gods who came lately, Whom your fathers did not dread."

5) **Job 1:6** "Now there was a day when the sons of God came to present themselves before the Lord, and Satan also came among them."

6) **Job 2:3-7** "The LORD said to Satan, "Have you considered My servant Job? For there is no one like him on the earth, a blameless and upright man fearing God and turning away from evil. And he still holds fast his integrity, although you incited Me against him to ruin him without cause." [4] Satan answered the LORD and said, "Skin for skin! Yes, all that a man has he will give for his life. [5] However, put forth Your hand now, and touch his bone and his flesh; he will curse You to Your face." [6] So the LORD said to Satan, "Behold, he is in your power, only spare his life."

7) **1 Chronicles 21:1** "Then Satan stood up against Israel and moved David to number Israel."

8) **Matthew 4:1-11** "Then Jesus was led up by the Spirit into the wilderness to be tempted by the devil. ² And after He had fasted forty days and forty nights, He then became hungry. ³ And the tempter came and said to Him, "If You are the Son of God, command that these stones become bread." ⁴ But He answered and said, "It is written, 'MAN SHALL NOT LIVE ON BREAD ALONE, BUT ON EVERY WORD THAT PROCEEDS OUT OF THE MOUTH OF GOD.'" ⁵ Then the devil took Him into the holy city and had Him stand on the pinnacle of the temple, ⁶ and *said to Him, "If You are the Son of God, throw Yourself down; for it is written, 'HE WILL COMMAND HIS ANGELS CONCERNING YOU'; and 'ON *their* HANDS THEY WILL BEAR YOU UP, SO THAT YOU WILL NOT STRIKE YOUR FOOT AGAINST A STONE.'" ⁷ Jesus said to him, "On the other hand, it is written, 'YOU SHALL NOT PUT THE LORD YOUR GOD TO THE TEST.'" ⁸ Again, the devil took Him to a very high mountain and showed Him all the kingdoms of the world and their glory; ⁹ and he said to Him, "All these things I will give You, if You fall down and worship me." ¹⁰ Then Jesus *said to him, "Go, Satan! For it is written, 'YOU SHALL WORSHIP THE LORD YOUR GOD, AND SERVE HIM ONLY.'" ¹¹ Then the devil *left Him; and behold, angels came and *began* to minister to Him."

9) **Matthew 4:24** "The news about Him spread throughout all Syria; and they brought to Him all who were ill, those suffering with various diseases and pains, demoniacs, epileptics, paralytics; and He healed them."

10) **Matthew 8:28-33** "When He came to the other side into the country of the Gadarenes, two men who were demon-possessed met Him as they were coming out of the tombs. *They were* so extremely violent that no one could pass by that way. ²⁹ And they cried out, saying, "What business do we have with each other, Son of God? Have You come here to torment us before the time?" ³⁰ Now there was a herd of many swine feeding at a distance from them. ³¹ The demons *began* to entreat Him, saying, "If You *are going to* cast us out, send us into the herd of swine." ³² And He said to them, "Go!" And they came out and went into the swine, and the whole herd rushed down the steep bank into the sea and perished in the waters. ³³ The herdsmen ran away, and went to the city and reported everything, including what had happened to the demoniacs." (See Mark 5:2-20 for same story)

11) **Matthew 10:1** "Jesus summoned His twelve disciples and gave them authority over unclean spirits, to cast them out, and to heal every kind of disease and every kind of sickness."

12) **Matthew 12:22** "Then a demon-possessed man who was blind and mute was brought to Jesus, and He healed him, so that the mute man spoke and saw."

13) **Matthew 12:24** "But when the Pharisees heard this, they said, "This man casts out demons only by Beelzebul the ruler of the demons."

14) **Matthew 12:43-45** "Now when the unclean spirit goes out of a man, it passes through waterless places seeking rest, and does not find *it*. ⁴⁴ Then it says, 'I will return to my house from which I came'; and when it comes, it finds *it* unoccupied, swept, and put in order. ⁴⁵ Then it goes and takes along with it seven other spirits more wicked than itself, and they go in and live there; and the last state of that man becomes worse than the first. That is the way it will also be with this evil generation."

15) **Matthew 13:19** "When anyone hears the word of the kingdom and does not understand it, the evil one comes and snatches away what has been sown in his heart. This is the one on whom seed was sown beside the road."

16) **Matthew 13:38,39** "and the field is the world; and as for the good seed, these are the sons of the kingdom; and the tares are the sons of the evil one; and the enemy who sowed them is the devil, and the harvest is the end of the age; and the reapers are angels."

17) **Matthew 17:14-18** "When they came to the crowd, a man came up to Jesus, falling on his knees before Him and saying, [15] "Lord, have mercy on my son, for he is a lunatic and is very ill; for he often falls into the fire and often into the water. [16] I brought him to Your disciples, and they could not cure him." [17] And Jesus answered and said, "You unbelieving and perverted generation, how long shall I be with you? How long shall I put up with you? Bring him here to Me." [18] And Jesus rebuked him, and the demon came out of him, and the boy was cured at once." (Same story in Mark 9:17-29, Luke 9:37-42)

18) **Matthew 25:41** "Then He will also say to those on His left, 'Depart from Me, accursed ones, into the eternal fire which has been prepared for the devil and his angels:'"

19) **Mark 1:23-26** "Just then there was a man in their synagogue with an unclean spirit; and he cried out, saying, "What business do we have with each other, Jesus of Nazareth? Have You come to destroy us? I know who You are—the Holy One of God!" And Jesus rebuked him, saying, "Be quiet, and come out of him!" Throwing him into convulsions, the unclean spirit cried out with a loud voice and came out of him."

20) **Mark 3:11** "Whenever the unclean spirits saw Him, they would fall down before Him and shout, "You are the Son of God!"

21) **Mark 3:22-26** "The scribes who came down from Jerusalem were saying, "He is possessed by Beelzebul," and "He casts out the demons by the ruler of the demons." And He called them to Himself and began speaking to them in parables, "How can Satan cast out Satan? If a kingdom is divided against itself, that kingdom cannot stand. If a house is divided against itself, that house will not be able to stand. If Satan has risen up against himself and is divided, he cannot stand, but he is finished!"

22) **Mark 6:7** "And He *summoned the twelve and began to send them out in pairs, and gave them authority over the unclean spirits;"

23) **Mark 7:25-30** "But after hearing of Him, a woman whose little daughter had an unclean spirit immediately came and fell at His feet. [26] Now the woman was a Gentile, of the Syrophoenician race. And she kept asking Him to cast the demon out of her daughter. [27] And He was saying to her, "Let the children be satisfied first, for it is not good to take the children's bread and throw it to the dogs." [28] But she answered and *said to Him, "Yes, Lord, *but* even the dogs under the table feed on the children's crumbs." [29] And He said to her, "Because of this answer go; the demon has gone out of your daughter." [30] And going back to her home, she found the child lying on the bed, the demon having left."

24) **Mark 9:38** "John said to Him, "Teacher, we saw someone casting out demons in Your name, and we tried to prevent him because he was not following us."

25) **Mark 16:9** "Now after He had risen early on the first day of the week, He first appeared to Mary Magdalene, from whom He had cast out seven demons."

26) **Mark 16:17** "These signs will accompany those who have believed: in My name they will cast out demons, they will speak with new tongues;"

27) **Luke 4:2,6** "for forty days, being tempted by the devil. And He ate nothing during those days, and when they had ended, He became hungry. V6. And the devil said to Him, "I will give You all this domain and its glory; for it has been handed over to me, and I give it to whomever I wish.""

28) **Luke 10:18** "And He said to them, "I was watching Satan fall from heaven like lightning.""

29) **Luke 4:33-35** "In the synagogue there was a man possessed by the spirit of an unclean demon, and he cried out with a loud voice, ³⁴"Let us alone! What business do we have with each other, Jesus of Nazareth? Have You come to destroy us? I know who You are—the Holy One of God!" ³⁵ But Jesus rebuked him, saying, "Be quiet and come out of him!" And when the demon had thrown him down in the midst *of the people*, he came out of him without doing him any harm.""

30) **Luke 4:41** "Demons also were coming out of many, shouting, "You are the Son of God!" But rebuking them, He would not allow them to speak, because they knew Him to be the Christ."

31) **Luke 8:27,28** "And when He came out onto the land, He was met by a man from the city who was possessed with demons; and who had not put on any clothing for a long time, and was not living in a house, but in the tombs. 28 Seeing Jesus, he cried out and fell before Him, and said in a loud voice, "What business do we have with each other, Jesus, Son of the Most High God? I beg You, do not torment me.""

32) **Luke 10:17** "The seventy returned with joy, saying, "Lord, even the demons are subject to us in Your name.""

33) **Luke 11:14,15** "And He was casting out a demon, and it was mute; when the demon had gone out, the mute man spoke; and the crowds were amazed. ¹⁵ But some of them said, "He casts out demons by Beelzebul, the ruler of the demons.""

34) **Luke 13:16** "And this woman, a daughter of Abraham as she is, whom Satan has bound for eighteen long years, should she not have been released from this bond on the Sabbath day?""

35) **Luke 22:31** "Simon, Simon, behold, Satan has demanded permission to sift you like wheat;"

36) **John 8:44** "You are of your father the devil, and you want to do the desires of your father. He was a murderer from the beginning, and does not stand in the truth because there is no truth in him. Whenever he speaks a lie, he speaks from his own nature, for he is a liar and the father of lies."

37) **John 10:20** "Many of them were saying, "He has a demon and is insane. Why do you listen to Him?""

38) **John 13:2** "During supper, the devil having already put into the heart of Judas Iscariot, the son of Simon, to betray Him,"

39) **Acts 5:3** "But Peter said, "Ananias, why has Satan filled your heart to lie to the Holy Spirit and to keep back some of the price of the land?""

40) **Acts 5:16** "Also the people from the cities in the vicinity of Jerusalem were coming together, bringing people who were sick or afflicted with unclean spirits, and they were all being healed."

41) **Acts 8:7** "For in the case of many who had unclean spirits, they were coming out of them shouting with a loud voice; and many who had been paralyzed and lame were healed."

42) **Acts 13:10** "and said, "You who are full of all deceit and fraud, you son of the devil, you enemy of all righteousness, will you not cease to make crooked the straight ways of the Lord?""

43) **Acts 16:16-18** " It happened that as we were going to the place of prayer, a slave-girl having a spirit of divination met us, who was bringing her masters much profit by fortune-telling. [17] Following after Paul and us, she kept crying out, saying, "These men are bond-servants of the Most High God, who are proclaiming to you the way of salvation." [18] She continued doing this for many days. But Paul was greatly annoyed, and turned and said to the spirit, "I command you in the name of Jesus Christ to come out of her!" And it came out at that very moment."

44) **Acts 19:12-16** "so that handkerchiefs or aprons were even carried from his body to the sick, and the diseases left them and the evil spirits went out. [13] But also some of the Jewish exorcists, who went from place to place, attempted to name over those who had the evil spirits the name of the Lord Jesus, saying, "I adjure you by Jesus whom Paul preaches." [14] Seven sons of one Sceva, a Jewish chief priest, were doing this. [15] And the evil spirit answered and said to them, "I recognize Jesus, and I know about Paul, but who are you?" [16] And the man, in whom was the evil spirit, leaped on them and subdued all of them and overpowered them, so that they fled out of that house naked and wounded."

45) **Acts 26:18** "to open their eyes so that they may turn from darkness to light and from the dominion of Satan to God, that they may receive forgiveness of sins and an inheritance among those who have been sanctified by faith in Me.'"

46) **Romans 16:20** "The God of peace will soon crush Satan under your feet. The grace of our Lord Jesus be with you."

47) **1 Corinthians 7:5** "Stop depriving one another, except by agreement for a time, so that you may devote yourselves to prayer, and come together again so that Satan will not tempt you because of your lack of self-control."

48) **1 Corinthians 10:20,21** "No, but I say that the things which the Gentiles sacrifice, they sacrifice to demons and not to God; and I do not want you to become sharers in demons. You cannot drink the cup of the Lord and the cup of demons; you cannot partake of the table of the Lord and the table of demons."

49) **2Corinthians 2:11** "so that no advantage would be taken of us by Satan, for we are not ignorant of his schemes"

50) **2 Corinthians 11:3** "But I am afraid that, as the serpent deceived Eve by his craftiness, your minds will be led astray from the simplicity and purity of devotion to Christ."

51) **2 Corinthians 11:14,15** "No wonder, for even Satan disguises himself as an angel of light Therefore it is not surprising if his servants also disguise themselves as servants of righteousness, whose end will be according to their deeds."

52) **2 Corinthians 12:7** "Because of the surpassing greatness of the revelations, for this reason, to keep me from exalting myself, there was given me a thorn in the flesh, a messenger of Satan to torment me—to keep me from exalting myself!"

53) **Ephesians 2:2** "in which you formerly walked according to the course of this world, according to the prince of the power of the air, of the spirit that is now working in the sons of disobedience."

54) **Ephesians 4:27** "and do not give the devil an opportunity."

55) **1 Thessalonians 2:18** "For we wanted to come to you—I, Paul, more than once—and yet Satan hindered us."

56) **Ephesians 6:11-16** "Put on the full armor of God, so that you will be able to stand firm against the schemes of the devil. [12] For our struggle is not against flesh and blood, but against the rulers, against the powers, against the world forces of this darkness, against the spiritual *forces* of wickedness in the heavenly *places*. [13] Therefore, take up the full armor of God, so that you will be able to resist in the evil day, and having done everything, to stand firm. [14] Stand firm therefore, HAVING GIRDED YOUR LOINS WITH TRUTH, and HAVING PUT ON THE BREASTPLATE OF RIGHTEOUSNESS, [15] and having shod YOUR FEET WITH THE PREPARATION OF THE GOSPEL OF PEACE; [16] in addition to all, taking up the shield of faith with which you will be able to extinguish all the flaming arrows of the evil *one*."

57) **1 Thessalonians 3:5** "For this reason, when I could endure it no longer, I also sent to find out about your faith, for fear that the tempter might have tempted you, and our labor would be in vain."

58) **2 Thessalonians 2:9** "that is, the one whose coming is in accord with the activity of Satan, with all power and signs and false wonders,"

59) **1 Timothy 1:20** "Among these are Hymenaeus and Alexander, whom I have handed over to Satan, so that they will be taught not to blaspheme."

60) **1 Timothy 3:6, 7** "and not a new convert, so that he will not become conceited and fall into the condemnation incurred by the devil. [7] And he must have a good reputation with those outside the church, so that he will not fall into reproach and the snare of the devil."

61) **1 Timothy 4:1** "But the Spirit explicitly says that in later times some will fall away from the faith, paying attention to deceitful spirits and doctrines of demons,"

62) **1 Timothy 5:15** "for some have already turned aside to follow Satan."

63) **2 Timothy 2:26** "and they may come to their senses and escape from the snare of the devil, having been held captive by him to do his will."

64) **Hebrews 2:14** "Therefore, since the children share in flesh and blood, He Himself likewise also partook of the same, that through death He might render powerless him who had the power of death, that is, the devil,"

65) **James 2:19** "You believe that God is one. You do well; the demons also believe, and shudder."

66) **James 4:7** "Submit therefore to God. Resist the devil and he will flee from you."

67) **1 Peter 5:8,9** "Be of sober spirit, be on the alert. Your adversary, the devil, prowls around like a roaring lion, seeking someone to devour. But resist him, firm in your faith, knowing that the same experiences of suffering are being accomplished by your brethren who are in the world."

68) **1 John 2:13** "I am writing to you, fathers, because you know Him who has been from the beginning. I am writing to you, young men, because you have overcome the evil one. I have written to you, children, because you know the Father."

69) **1 John 3:8** "the one who practices sin is of the devil; for the devil has sinned from the beginning. The Son of God appeared for this purpose, to destroy the works of the devil."

70) **1 John 3:10** "By this the children of God and the children of the devil are obvious: anyone who does not practice righteousness is not of God, nor the one who does not love his brother."

71) **1 John 3:12** "not as Cain, who was of the evil one and slew his brother. And for what reason did he slay him? Because his deeds were evil, and his brother's were righteous."

72) **1 John 5:18** "We know that no one who is born of God sins; but He who was born of God keeps him, and the evil one does not touch him."

73) **Jude 1:9** "But Michael the archangel, when he disputed with the devil and argued about the body of Moses, did not dare pronounce against him a railing judgment, but said, "The Lord rebuke you!"

74) **Revelation 2:9-13** "'I know your tribulation and your poverty (but you are rich), and the blasphemy by those who say they are Jews and are not, but are a synagogue of Satan. [10] Do not fear what you are about to suffer. Behold, the devil is about to cast some of you into prison, so that you will be tested, and you will have tribulation for ten days. Be faithful until death, and I will give you the crown of life. [11] He who has an ear, let him hear what the Spirit says to the churches. He who overcomes will not be hurt by the second death.' [12] "And to the angel of the church in Pergamum write: The One who has the sharp two-edged sword says this: [13] 'I know where you dwell, where Satan's throne is; and you hold fast My name, and did not deny My faith even in the days of Antipas, My witness, My faithful one, who was killed among you, where Satan dwells.'"

75) **Revelation 2:24** "But I say to you, the rest who are in Thyatira, who do not hold this teaching, who have not known the deep things of Satan, as they call them—I place no other burden on you."

76) **Revelation 3:9** "Behold, I will cause those of the synagogue of Satan, who say that they are Jews and are not, but lie—I will make them come and bow down at your feet, and make them know that I have loved you."

77) **Revelation 9:20** "The rest of mankind, who were not killed by these plagues, did not repent of the works of their hands, so as not to worship demons, and the idols of gold and of silver and of brass and of stone and of wood, which can neither see nor hear nor walk;"

78) **Revelation 12:9-12** "And the great dragon was thrown down, the serpent of old who is called the devil and Satan, who deceives the whole world; he was thrown down to the earth, and his angels were thrown down with him. [10] Then I heard a loud voice in heaven, saying, "Now the salvation, and the power, and the kingdom of our God and the authority of His Christ have come, for the accuser of our brethren has been thrown down, he who accuses them before our God day and night. [11] And they overcame him because of the blood of the Lamb and because of the word of their testimony, and they did not love their life even when faced with death. [12] For this reason, rejoice, O heavens and you who dwell in them. Woe to the earth and the sea, because the devil has come down to you, having great wrath, knowing that he has *only* a short time."

79) **Revelation 20:1-10** "Then I saw an angel coming down from heaven, holding the key of the abyss and a great chain in his hand. [2] And he laid hold of the dragon, the serpent of old, who is the devil and Satan, and bound him for a thousand years; [3] and he threw him into the abyss, and shut *it* and sealed *it* over him, so that he would not deceive the nations any longer, until the thousand years were completed; after these things he must be released for a short time. [4] Then I saw thrones, and they sat on them, and judgment was given to them. And I *saw* the souls of those who had been beheaded because of their testimony of Jesus and because of the word of God, and those who had not worshiped the beast or his image, and had not received the mark on their forehead and on their hand; and they came to life and

reigned with Christ for a thousand years. [5] The rest of the dead did not come to life until the thousand years were completed. This is the first resurrection. [6] Blessed and holy is the one who has a part in the first resurrection; over these the second death has no power, but they will be priests of God and of Christ and will reign with Him for a thousand years. [7] When the thousand years are completed, Satan will be released from his prison, [8] and will come out to deceive the nations which are in the four corners of the earth, Gog and Magog, to gather them together for the war; the number of them is like the sand of the seashore. [9] And they came up on the broad plain of the earth and surrounded the camp of the saints and the beloved city, and fire came down from heaven and devoured them. [10] And the devil who deceived them was thrown into the lake of fire and brimstone, where the beast and the false prophet are also; and they will be tormented day and night forever and ever."

The above scriptures show us that Satan is a real entity.

Let's turn back to the Beliefs Speaker role.

CORE BELIEF #5

****

"Based on the following scriptures, I believe I have another enemy - my fleshly appetites."

****

In 1 Timothy 6:12, we read, "Fight the good fight of faith...". Here we see that the Christian life is a battle, a continuous fight for our faith. If we keep our faith intact, our minds are kept at rest. If we succumb to the plots of our enemy, Satan, to undermine our faith, then we lose the peace and happiness God has for us, and life becomes difficult. Another enemy of the Christian can be the fleshly appetites of the physical body. They can crave things that are not good and can be a distraction taking our focus off of Christ and His plan for our lives. Allowing our fleshly appetites to have their way negatively in our lives will lead us toward anxiety and defeat.

1) **Romans 6:13** "and do not go on presenting the members of your body to sin as instruments of unrighteousness; but present yourselves to God as those alive from the dead, and your members as instruments of righteousness to God."

2) **Romans 7:5** "For while we were in the flesh, the sinful passions, which were aroused by the Law, were at work in the members of our body to bear fruit for death."

3) **Romans 7:18** "For I know that nothing good dwells in me, that is, in my flesh; for the willing is present in me, but the doing of the good is not."

4) **Romans 8:1,2** "Therefore there is now no condemnation for those who are in Christ Jesus. For the law of the Spirit of life in Christ Jesus has set you free from the law of sin and of death."

5) **Romans 8:3** "For what the Law could not do, weak as it was through the flesh, God did: sending His own Son in the likeness of sinful flesh and as an offering for sin, He condemned sin in the flesh,"

6) **Romans 8:4** "so that the requirement of the Law might be fulfilled in us, who do not walk according to the flesh but according to the Spirit"

7) **Romans 8:5** "For those who are according to the flesh set their minds on the things of the flesh, but those who are according to the Spirit, the things of the Spirit."

8) **Romans 8:8** "and those who are in the flesh cannot please God."

9) **Romans 8:9** "However, you are not in the flesh but in the Spirit, if indeed the Spirit of God dwells in you. But if anyone does not have the Spirit of Christ, he does not belong to Him."

10) **Romans 8:10,11** "If Christ is in you, though the body is dead because of sin, yet the spirit is alive because of righteousness. But if the Spirit of Him who raised Jesus from the dead dwells in you, He who raised Christ Jesus from the dead will also give life to your mortal bodies [e]through His Spirit who dwells in you."

11) **Romans 8:12** "So then, brethren, we are under obligation, not to the flesh, to live according to the flesh."

12) **Romans 8:13,14** "for if you are living according to the flesh, you must die; but if by the Spirit you are putting to death the deeds of the body, you will live. [14] For all who are being led by the Spirit of God, these are sons of God."

13) **Galatians 5:16** "But I say, walk by the Spirit, and you will not carry out the desire of the flesh."

14) **Galatians 5:17-18** "For the flesh sets its desire against the Spirit, and the Spirit against the flesh; for these are in opposition to one another, so that you may not do the things that you please. [18] But if you are led by the Spirit, you are not under the Law."

15) **Galatians 5:19-21** "Now the works of the flesh are manifest, which are these; Adultery, fornication, uncleanness, lasciviousness, [20] Idolatry, witchcraft, hatred, variance, emulations, wrath, strife, seditions, heresies, [21] Envyings, murders, drunkenness, revellings, and such like: of the which I tell you before, as I have also told you in time past, that they which do such things shall not inherit the kingdom of God."

16) **Galatians 5:22-25** "But the fruit of the Spirit is love, joy, peace, patience, kindness, goodness, faithfulness, [23] gentleness, self-control; against such things there is no law. [24] Now those who belong to Christ Jesus have crucified the flesh with its passions and desires. [25] If we live by the Spirit, let us also walk by the Spirit."

17) **Ephesians 4:22-24** "that, in reference to your former manner of life, you lay aside the old [p]self, which is being corrupted in accordance with the lusts of deceit, [23] and that you be renewed in the spirit of your mind, [24] and put on the new self, which in the likeness of God has been created in righteousness and holiness of the truth."

18) **Colossians 3:5** "Therefore consider the members of your earthly body as dead to immorality, impurity, passion, evil desire, and greed, which amounts to idolatry:"

19) **1 Peter 1:14-16** "As obedient children, do not be conformed to the former lusts which were yours in your ignorance, [15] but like the Holy One who called you, be holy yourselves also in all your behavior; [16] because it is written, "You shall be holy, for I am holy.""

20) **1 Peter 2:11** "Beloved, I urge you as aliens and strangers to abstain from fleshly lusts which wage war against the soul."

21) **1 John 3:5-7** "You know that He appeared in order to take away sins; and in Him there is no sin. [6] No one who abides in Him sins; no one who sins has seen Him or knows Him. [7] Little children, make sure no one deceives you; the one who practices righteousness is righteous, just as He is righteous;"

The goal of speaking these verses out loud is to fully believe the truth that our fleshly appetites are at war with us. We need to become so convinced of this that nothing could convince us otherwise. Reading these scriptures over and over will help us make this truth more a reality in our hearts.

Let's turn back to the Beliefs Speaker role.

CORE BELIEF #6

****

"Based on the following scriptures, I believe God wants me to enjoy good physical health."

****

This belief can be difficult to adopt because so many people who pray for healing don't get healed. This is a mystery. However, we know that God responds to faith. Whenever Jesus healed someone, the scriptures say or imply that Jesus marveled at the person's faith. That is what we want Jesus to observe in us; we want Him to marvel at our faith. Thus, the purpose of saying these verses is to help keep our faith strong while we wait for God to move in our situation. As a side-benefit, we will enjoy peace of mind while we wait.

1) **Exodus 15:26** "And He said, "If you will give earnest heed to the voice of the Lord your God, and do what is right in His sight, and give ear to His commandments, and keep all His statutes, I will put none of the diseases on you which I have put on the Egyptians; for I, the Lord, am your healer."

2) **Psalm 30:2** "O Lord my God, I cried to You for help, and You healed me."

3) **Psalm 103:3** "Who pardons all your iniquities, Who heals all your diseases;"

4) **Psalm 107:20** "He sent His word and healed them, And delivered them from their destructions."

5) **Proverbs 3:8** "It will be healing to your body And refreshment to your bones."

6) **Proverbs 4:20-22** "My son, give attention to my words; Incline your ear to my sayings. [21] Do not let them depart from your sight; Keep them in the midst of your heart. [22] For they are life to those who find them And health to all their body."

7) **Proverbs 10:27** "The fear of the Lord prolongs life, But the years of the wicked will be shortened."

8) **Isaiah 53:4-5** "Surely our griefs He Himself bore, And our sorrows He carried; Yet we ourselves esteemed Him stricken, Smitten of God, and afflicted. But He was pierced through for our transgressions, He was crushed for our iniquities; The chastening for our well-being fell upon Him, And by His scourging we are healed."

9) **Jeremiah 17:14** "Heal me, O Lord, and I will be healed; Save me and I will be saved, For You are my praise."

10) **Jeremiah 30:17** "'For I will restore you to health And I will heal you of your wounds,' declares the Lord, 'Because they have called you an outcast, saying: "It is Zion; no one cares for her."

11) **Jeremiah 33:6** "Behold, I will bring to it health and healing, and I will heal them; and I will reveal to them an abundance of peace and truth."

12) **Hosea 6:1** "Come, let us return to the Lord. For He has torn us, but He will heal us; He has wounded us, but He will bandage us."

13) **Malachi 4:2** "But for you who fear My name, the sun of righteousness will rise with healing in its wings; and you will go forth and skip about like calves from the stall."

14) **Matthew 4:23-24** "Jesus was going throughout all Galilee, teaching in their synagogues and proclaiming the gospel of the kingdom, and healing every kind of disease and every kind of sickness among the people. The news about Him spread throughout all Syria; and they brought to Him all who were ill, those suffering with various diseases and pains, demoniacs, epileptics, paralytics; and He healed them."

15) **Matthew 8:7** "Jesus said to him, "I will come and heal him.""

16) **Matthew 8:13** "And Jesus said to the centurion, "Go; it shall be done for you as you have believed." And the servant was healed that very moment."

17) **Matthew 8:15-17** "He touched her hand, and the fever left her; and she got up and waited on Him. When evening came, they brought to Him many who were demon-possessed; and He cast out the spirits with a word, and healed all who were ill. This was to fulfill what was spoken through Isaiah the prophet: "He Himself took our infirmities and carried away our diseases.""

18) **Matthew 9:35** "Jesus was going through all the cities and villages, teaching in their synagogues and proclaiming the gospel of the kingdom, and healing every kind of disease and every kind of sickness."

19) **Matthew 12:10** "And a man was there whose hand was withered. And they questioned Jesus, asking, "Is it lawful to heal on the Sabbath?"—so that they might accuse Him."

20) **Matthew 12:13** "Then He said to the man, "Stretch out your hand!" He stretched it out, and it was restored to normal, like the other."

21) **Matthew 12:15** "But Jesus, aware of this, withdrew from there. Many followed Him, and He healed them all,"

22) **Matthew 12:22** "Then a demon-possessed man who was blind and mute was brought to Jesus, and He healed him, so that the mute man spoke and saw."

23) **Matthew 14:14** "When He went ashore, He saw a large crowd, and felt compassion for them and healed their sick."

24) **Matthew 15:28** "Then Jesus said to her, "O woman, your faith is great; it shall be done for you as you wish." And her daughter was healed at once."

25) **Matthew 15:30** "And large crowds came to Him, bringing with them those who were lame, crippled, blind, mute, and many others, and they laid them down at His feet; and He healed them."

26) **Matthew 19:2** "and large crowds followed Him, and He healed them there."

27) **Matthew 21:22** "And all things you ask in prayer, believing, you will receive."

28) **Mark 1:34** "And He healed many who were ill with various diseases, and cast out many demons; and He was not permitting the demons to speak, because they knew who He was."

29) **Mark 3:10** "for He had healed many, with the result that all those who had afflictions pressed around Him in order to touch Him."

30) **Mark 6:5-6** "And He could do no miracle there except that He laid His hands on a few sick people and healed them. And He wondered at their unbelief. And He was going around the villages teaching."

31) **Mark 16:18** "they will pick up serpents, and if they drink any deadly poison, it will not hurt them; they will lay hands on the sick, and they will recover."

32) **Luke 4:18** "The Spirit of the Lord is upon Me, Because He anointed Me to preach the gospel to the poor. He has sent Me to proclaim release to the captives, And recovery of sight to the blind, To set free those who are oppressed,"

33) **Luke 4:40** "While the sun was setting, all those who had any who were sick with various diseases brought them to Him; and laying His hands on each one of them, He was healing them."

34) **Luke 5:15** "But the news about Him was spreading even farther, and large crowds were gathering to hear Him and to be healed of their sicknesses."

35) **Luke 6:17-19** "Jesus came down with them and stood on a level place; and there was a large crowd of His disciples, and a great throng of people from all Judea and Jerusalem and the coastal region of Tyre and Sidon, [18] who had come to hear Him and to be healed of their diseases; and those who were troubled with unclean spirits were being cured. [19] And all the people were trying to touch Him, for power was coming from Him and healing them all."

36) **Luke 8:43,44,47,48** "And a woman who had a hemorrhage for twelve years, and could not be healed by anyone, [44] came up behind Him and touched the fringe of His cloak, and immediately her hemorrhage stopped… [47] When the woman saw that she had not escaped notice, she came trembling and fell down before Him, and declared in the presence of all the people the reason why she had touched Him, and how she had been immediately healed. [48] And He said to her, "Daughter, your faith has made you well; go in peace.""

37) **Luke 9:11** "But the crowds were aware of this and followed Him; and welcoming them, He began speaking to them about the kingdom of God and curing those who had need of healing."

38) **Luke 9:42** "While he was still approaching, the demon slammed him to the ground and threw him into a convulsion. But Jesus rebuked the unclean spirit, and healed the boy and gave him back to his father."

39) **Luke 13:11-16** "And there was a woman who for eighteen years had had a sickness caused by a spirit; and she was bent double, and could not straighten up at all. [12] When Jesus saw her, He called her over and said to her, "Woman, you are freed from your sickness." [13] And He laid His hands on her; and immediately she was made erect again and *began* glorifying God. [14] But the synagogue official, indignant because Jesus had healed on the Sabbath, *began* saying to the crowd in response, "There are six days in which work should be done; so come during them and get healed, and not on the Sabbath day." [15] But the Lord answered him and said, "You hypocrites, does not each of you on the Sabbath untie his ox or his donkey from the stall and lead him away to water *him*? [16] And this woman, a daughter of Abraham as she is, whom Satan has bound for eighteen long years, should she not have been released from this bond on the Sabbath day?""

40) **Luke 14:3-4** "And Jesus answered and spoke to the lawyers and Pharisees, saying, "Is it lawful to heal on the Sabbath, or not?" But they kept silent. And He took hold of him and healed him, and sent him away.""

41) **Luke 17:12-15** "As He entered a village, ten leprous men who stood at a distance met Him; [13] and they raised their voices, saying, "Jesus, Master, have mercy on us!" [14] When He saw them, He said to them, "Go and show yourselves to the priests." And as they were going, they were cleansed. [15] Now one of them, when he saw that he had been healed, turned back, glorifying God with a loud voice,"

42) **Luke 22:50-51** "And one of them struck the slave of the high priest and cut off his right ear. But Jesus answered and said, "Stop! No more of this." And He touched his ear and healed him.""

43) **Acts 3:12** "But when Peter saw this, he replied to the people, "Men of Israel, why are you amazed at this, or why do you gaze at us, as if by our own power or piety we had made him walk?""

44) **Acts 4:29-31** "And now, Lord, take note of their threats, and grant that Your bond-servants may speak Your word with all confidence, [30] while You extend Your hand to heal, and signs and wonders take place through the name of Your holy servant Jesus." [31] And when they had prayed, the place where they had gathered together was shaken, and they were all filled with the Holy Spirit and *began* to speak the word of God with boldness."

45) **Acts 10:38** "You know of Jesus of Nazareth, how God anointed Him with the Holy Spirit and with power, and how He went about doing good and healing all who were oppressed by the devil, for God was with Him.""

46) **1 Cor**inthians **12:7-10** "But to each one is given the manifestation of the Spirit for the common good. [8] For to one is given the word of wisdom through the Spirit, and to another the word of knowledge according to the same Spirit; [9] to another faith by the same Spirit, and to another gifts of healing by the one Spirit, [10] and to another the effecting of miracles, and to another prophecy, and to another the distinguishing of spirits, to another *various* kinds of tongues, and to another the interpretation of tongues.""

47) **James 5:14-16** "Is anyone among you sick? *Then* he must call for the elders of the church and they are to pray over him, anointing him with oil in the name of the Lord; [15] and the prayer offered in faith will restore the one who is sick, and the Lord will raise him up, and if he has committed sins, they will be forgiven him. [16] Therefore, confess your sins to one another, and pray for one another so that you may be healed. The effective prayer of a righteous man can accomplish much.""

48) **1Peter 2:24** "and He Himself bore our sins in His body on the cross, so that we might die to sin and live to righteousness; for by His wounds you were healed.""

49) **3 John 1:2** "Beloved, I pray that in all respects you may prosper and be in good health, just as your soul prospers.""

The goal of speaking these verses out loud is to fully believe the truth that God wants us to enjoy good health. We need to become so convinced of this that nothing could convince us otherwise. Reading these scriptures over and over will help us make this truth more a reality in our hearts.

Let's turn back to the Beliefs Speaker role.

TYPES OF ABUSE

****

When most people hear the word "abuse" they usually think of something very extreme, such as punching or kicking. However, abuse can take non-physical forms too. The following is a list of 6 types of abuse.

Physical

- Any unwanted physical contact
- Kicking, punching
- Pulling, pushing
- Slapping, hitting
- Pulling hair
- Arm twisting
- Holding against wall
- Squeezing hand, arm
- Choking
- Shooting
- Locking in a room
- Standing too close
- Stopping from leaving
- Restraining in any way
- Picking them up
- Holding or hugging when unwanted
- Pointing finger, poking
- Murder
- Hitting with objects
- Tickling
- Spitting

Sexual

- Forcing sex (rape)
- Total lack of intimacy
- Forcing certain positions
- Total lack of intimacy
- Sleeping around
- Hounding for sex
- Intimidation by knowledge or reputation
- Retaliating by refusing sex
- Put downs
- Being rough
- Using sex as basis for argument
- Treating someone as a sex object
- Pornography
- Forcing people to have sex with others

Emotional/Verbal/Psychological

- Forcing people to have sex with others
- Refusing to do things with them
- Getting your own way
- Pressuring them
- Not coming home
- Real or suggested involvement with another person
- Manipulation
- Annoying mannerisms, e.g. snapping fingers
- Saying "Do you remember what happened last time"
- Making threats to them about you, e.g. killing yourself

Financial

- Withholding money
- Spending money foolishly or beyond means
- Not spending money on special occasions, e.g. their birthday
- Making the decisions in terms of how money is spent

Environmental

- Locking them in
- Taking the phones with you to work
- Slamming doors
- Breaking things
- Throwing objects
- Turning the stereo/TV up loud
- Harming pets
- Throwing their clothes out
- Ripping their clothes

Social

- Not taking responsibility for children
- Embarrassment in front of children
- Putting down or ignoring in public
- Accusing them of sleeping
- Not saying what is on your mind
- Never really forgiving
- Lying
- Accusing them of sleeping around
- Treating them as a child
- Putting them on a pedestal
- False accusations
- Raising your voice with them
- Agreeing with them even though you don't
- Making them fearful
- Putting them or their family down
- Starting arguments
- Not letting them see their friends
- Using a continual joke or putdown about them with others
- Choosing friends or family over them
- Using kids as a weapon
- Abusing children physically or sexually
- Not taking them out
- Keeping them busy in the kitchen, e.g. during a party
- Change of personality with others
- Not being nice to their friends
- Making a "scene"

Emotional/Verbal/Psychological

- Insulting
- Yelling
- Name calling
- Verbal threats
- Intimidation
- Playing "mind games"
- Overpowering their emotions
- Brainwashing
- Bringing up old issues and arguing with them
- Putting them down for things they have done in the past
- Inappropriate expression of jealousy
- Turning around a situation against them
- Laughing in their face
- Silence
- Walking away from them in a discussion
- Finding and verbalizing their faults
- Comparing them to others to conform to a role
- Overtly sarcastic or critical
- Lack of consideration for their opinion
- Trying to get last word in
- Pre-violence cues
- Isolation, e.g. not telling them what you are doing

<u>Author's Message</u>

Dear friend,

I hope this manual helps you realize that with effort you can achieve a life free of nagging anxiety and depression. I wish this manual existed 40 years ago when I needed it. It wasn't, so I had to stumble along in life - hurting, wasting time thinking about life, trying to figure out how to psyche myself up to face life every day, wasting time reading unhelpful books, wasting time and money seeing various counselors who didn't help me. I would like to think this will be the last self-help book you'll ever need, but I would never endorse that. It's important to stay hungry for truth. So buy as many books as you like, keep learning. Trust God to deliver you from anything that is hindering you, so you can become everything He wants you to be. Life is short, so live it to the full. Get well, not just for you, but for your family and friends. Most of all, get well so God can use you to help others who struggle.

"One life 'twill soon be past, only what's done for Christ will last." One way to really make an impact for Christ is by getting involved in helping people with their mental health challenges. This program is one way to do that. We offer you the opportunity to learn how to be a chairperson for a Victory Tips group. In the beginning it can be a conference call group. Then, as your confidence grows, you may want to lead a community group in a public venue where you live. It is exhilarating watching people transform into happy, healthy individuals. You will feel great knowing that you played a part in seeing these people get healed.

For the next 60 seconds, I am taking my focus off of this book, and I'm thinking about you. I am envisioning the potential that resides in you… and I'm thinking back in history at all the world-shakers that the church of Jesus Christ has ever produced, and I'm thinking, "I could be looking at another world-shaker, right here, right now –You!" It is sobering. Thus, my goal is to be there for you, and inspire you to seek God with everything you have. Make Him a priority in your life. I will run alongside you until you reach your goal of peace and happiness. And I will do whatever I can to help you become a world-shaker Christian. That is my commitment to you. I invite you to contact me and we will see where this leads. I'm hoping it leads to tens…, hundreds…, and even thousands more people being helped out of anxiety and depression. Wouldn't that be awesome? Let's see.

To your happiness and success,

Vince
289-723-2420 (Canada)
213-426-8223 (United States)
victorytipsvince@gmail.com

Message To The Strong

The problem of poor mental health in society is so staggering that it is going to require everyone pitching-in to help those who struggle emotionally. The Bible teaches that we who are strong ought to help those who are weak, and this includes those with mental health challenges.

a) **Romans 15:1** "Now we who are strong ought to bear the weaknesses of those without strength and not *just* please ourselves."

b) **1 Thessalonians 5:14** "We urge you, brethren, admonish the unruly, encourage the fainthearted, help the weak, be patient with everyone."

c) **Hebrews 12:12** "Therefore, strengthen the hands that are weak and the knees that are feeble,"

d) **Psalm 41:1** "How blessed is he who considers the helpless; The LORD will deliver him in a day of trouble."

e) **Isaiah 35:3** "Encourage the exhausted, and strengthen the feeble."

Even if we are strong, and those in our family, and circle of friends are strong, our lives can be severely affected by a stranger who has a random outburst. Please consider what you can do to help those who struggle emotionally.

The Victory Tips Program makes it easy to lead a weekly support group. By using this program, or parts of it, you will be doing your part to reach out to those who struggle. Don't wait until a co-worker, or a classmate of one your children reacts out of deep anxiety or depression. Reach out today. Make a difference where you are. With everyone doing their bit, we can help eradicate desperate feelings and actions in our communities. You are stronger and more helpful than you think!

Occasionally, we meet someone who is head and shoulders above everyone else, spiritually. We may not realize it at the time. But years later, we will remember them and say what the two travelers who were on the road to Emmaus said, *"Did not our heart burn within us, while he talked with us by the way, and while he opened to us the scriptures?"* This unique person is 'gripped' with the gospel, sharing it, teaching it, praying for more of God in their life, and the lives of others. It permeates everything about them. They are marked <u>*by*</u> God, and *for* God. Almost like John the Baptist. It's just on them. They have a narrow focus, so they are unencumbered by life's problems. This makes them jovial and fun to be with. And it attracts others who want to be like them. When a person like that comes into our lives, we'll want to make room on our agenda and spend some time with them. Perhaps, some of the Spirit that is on them will rub off on us. And if nothing else, we'll get to watch a fire burn, and be warmed by it. It is these kinds of people who make the most impact for God, for their family, for their church, and for the world.

Made in the
USA
Columbia, SC

81073717R00124